MW01630473

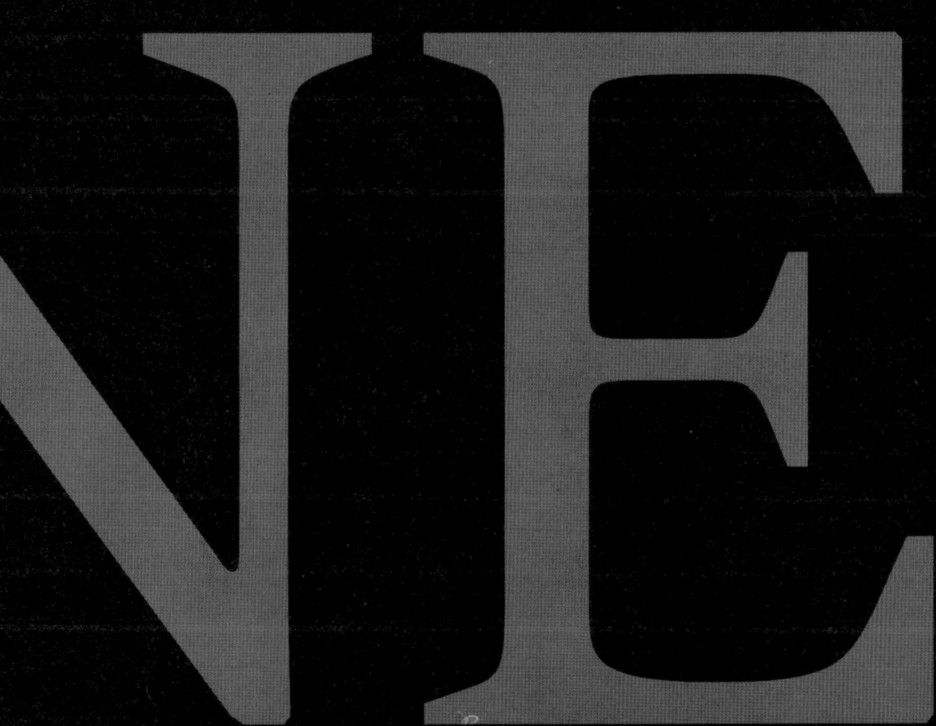
NE

LINE

CREATIVE PAINTING

English-language edition for the United States, its territories and dependencies, and Canada published 2007 by Barron's Educational Series, Inc.

Original title of the book in Spanish: *Trazo*

Published by Parramón Ediciones, S.A., Barcelona, Spain

All inquiries should be addressed to:
Barron's Educational Series, Inc.
250 Wireless Boulevard
Hauppauge, NY 11788
www.barronseduc.com

ISBN-13: 978-0-7641-6007-3
ISBN-10: 0-7641-6007-9

Library of Congress Control Number 2006920213

Editor: María Fernanda Canal
Editorial Assistant/Illustration Archivist: Carmen Ramos
Text: Josep Asunción, Gemma Guasch
Exercises: Josep Asunción, Gemma Guasch, Vicenç Ballestar, Josep María Ametlla
Graphic Design: Toni Inglès
Photography: Estudio Nos & Soto
Layout: Toni Inglès
Production: Rafael Marfil

Translation: Michael Brunelle and Beatriz Cortabarria

Printed in Spain
9 8 7 6 5 4 3 2 1

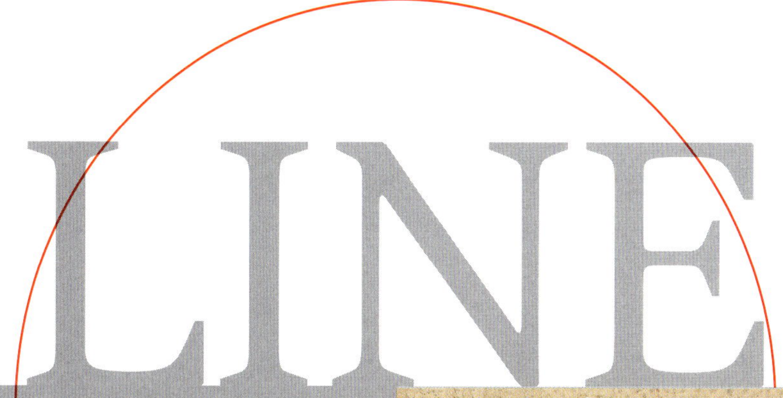

LINE

CREATIVE PAINTING

Gemma Guasch
Josep Asunción

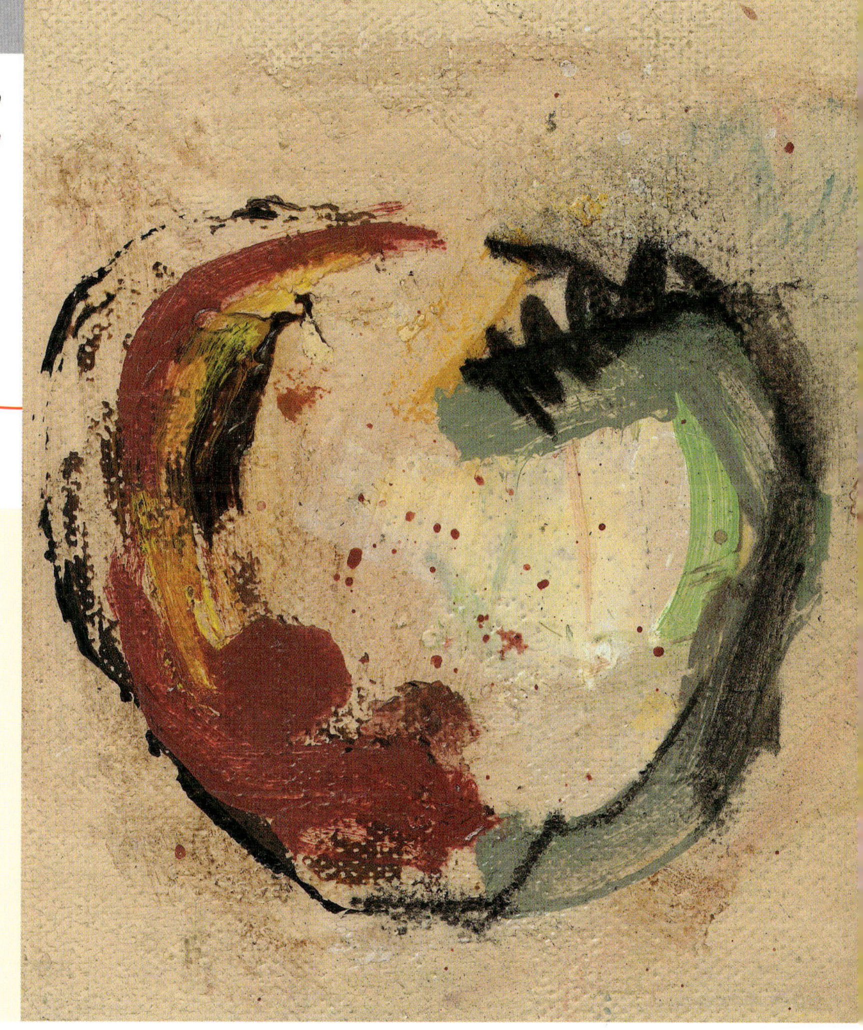

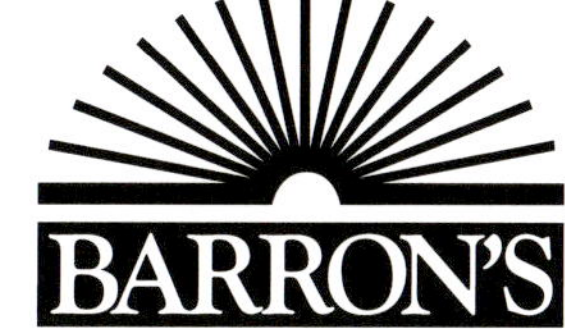

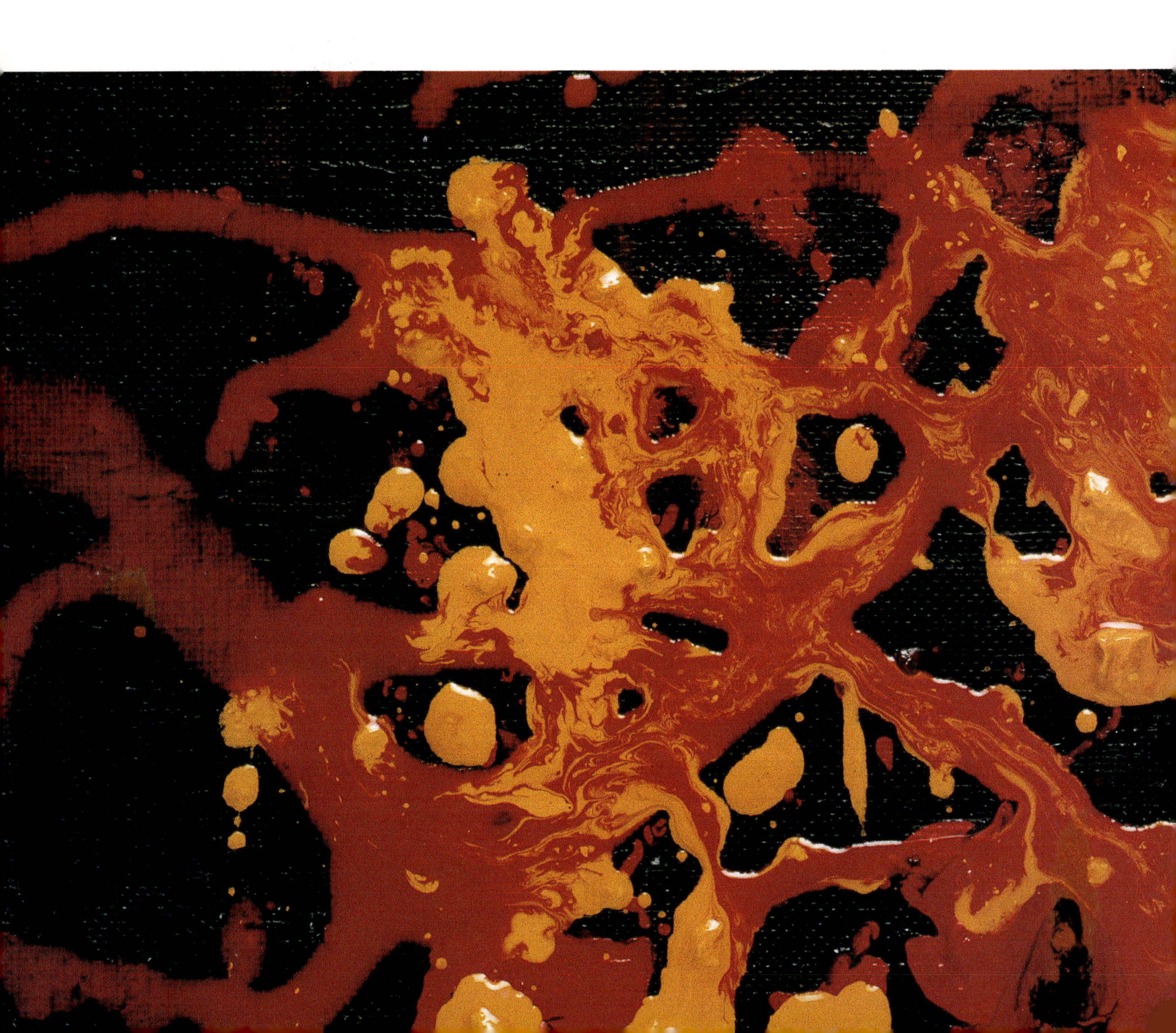

Contents

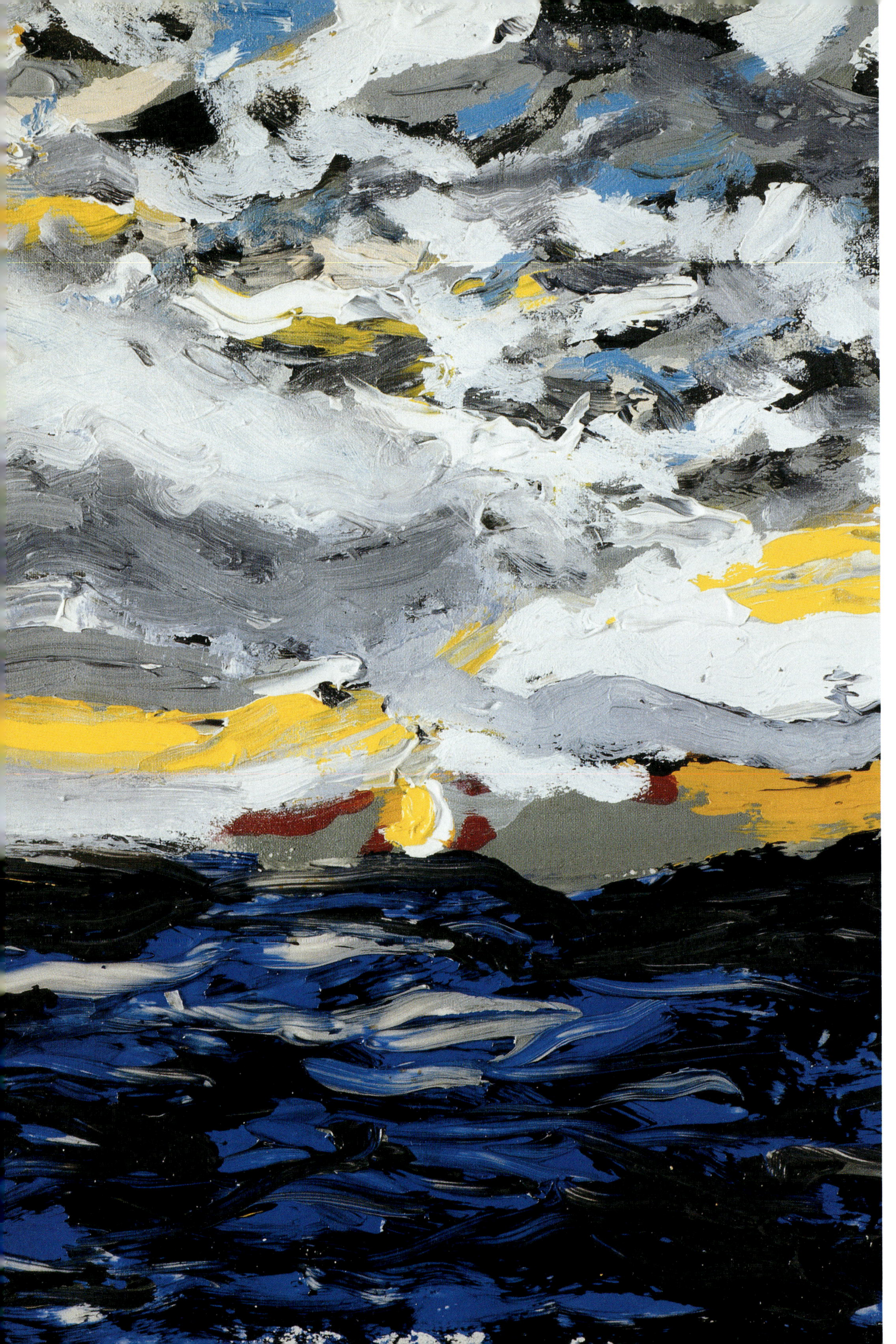

Introduction

There is no art without creation, and in painting creativity is an indispensable ingredient that every painter must develop. Creativity implies risk taking and courage; creativity is to engage in adventure, pursuing individuality and innovation and the search for a personal answer. But there is no use for jumping into the water without knowing how to swim: the experience will not last very long. Learning to paint is learning how to move within the visual language of painting, the same way that learning to swim is learning how to move in the water. This book encourages you to jump into the water but equipped with help that on the one hand promotes the development of creativity and on the other goes deep into understanding the medium, the pictorial language.

Verbal language is made of alphabet and syntax; words and silent spaces have a meaning in each sentence, just as each sentence does in the overall text. The same thing happens with a painting: the pictorial language consists of elements that acquire meaning in the composition, as in spoken language. The painting alphabet is made of color, form, space, and line. The first three (color, form, and space) are closely related to the image and the last one (line) to the physical appearance of the painting. If we compare it again with spoken language, color, form, and space would be the words, the pauses, the expressions or the sentences, and the line would be the tone, the speed, and the emotional charge of the speaker.

It would be absurd to study each one of these four elements in complete isolation from the other, since all four are as interrelated as are the words, the pauses, and the intonation of discourse. However, it is possible to focus on each one of them to learn in depth how visual language works and how to produce a creative solution by using that language. In this book we will focus our attention on the line. Following an introduction that explains the theory of line in relation to painting, we present fifteen creative approaches, grouped by pictorial genre, that help the reader experiment with line in an inventive way, looking for his or her own personal language.

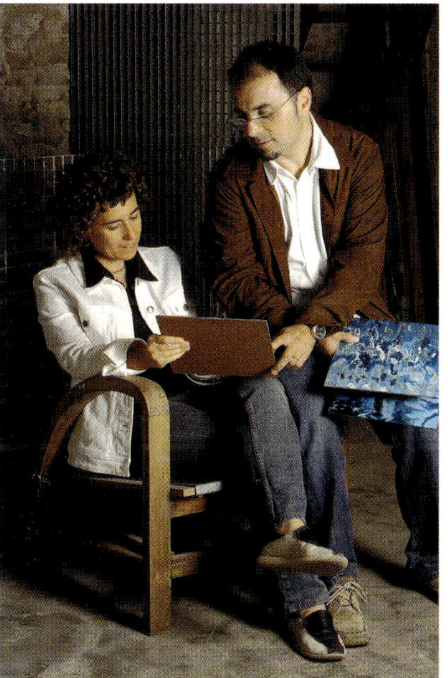

Gemma Guasch and Josep Asunción

Gemma Guasch and Josep Asunción are two visual artists who combine their artistic work with the teaching of painting. They both have degrees in fine arts from the University of Barcelona, and both have had many shows in Spain, Italy, and Germany. Since 1995 they have worked jointly on projects under the name of CREART, a cultural association that experiments with collective artistic creations. Their extensive experience as professors of painting at the Escuela de Artes y Oficios of the Diputación de Barcelona (School of Arts and Crafts of the City of Barcelona) supports each of the approaches of this book.

"Painting is done with the brain and not with the hands."
Michelangelo,
Letter to Monsignor Aliotti,
1542

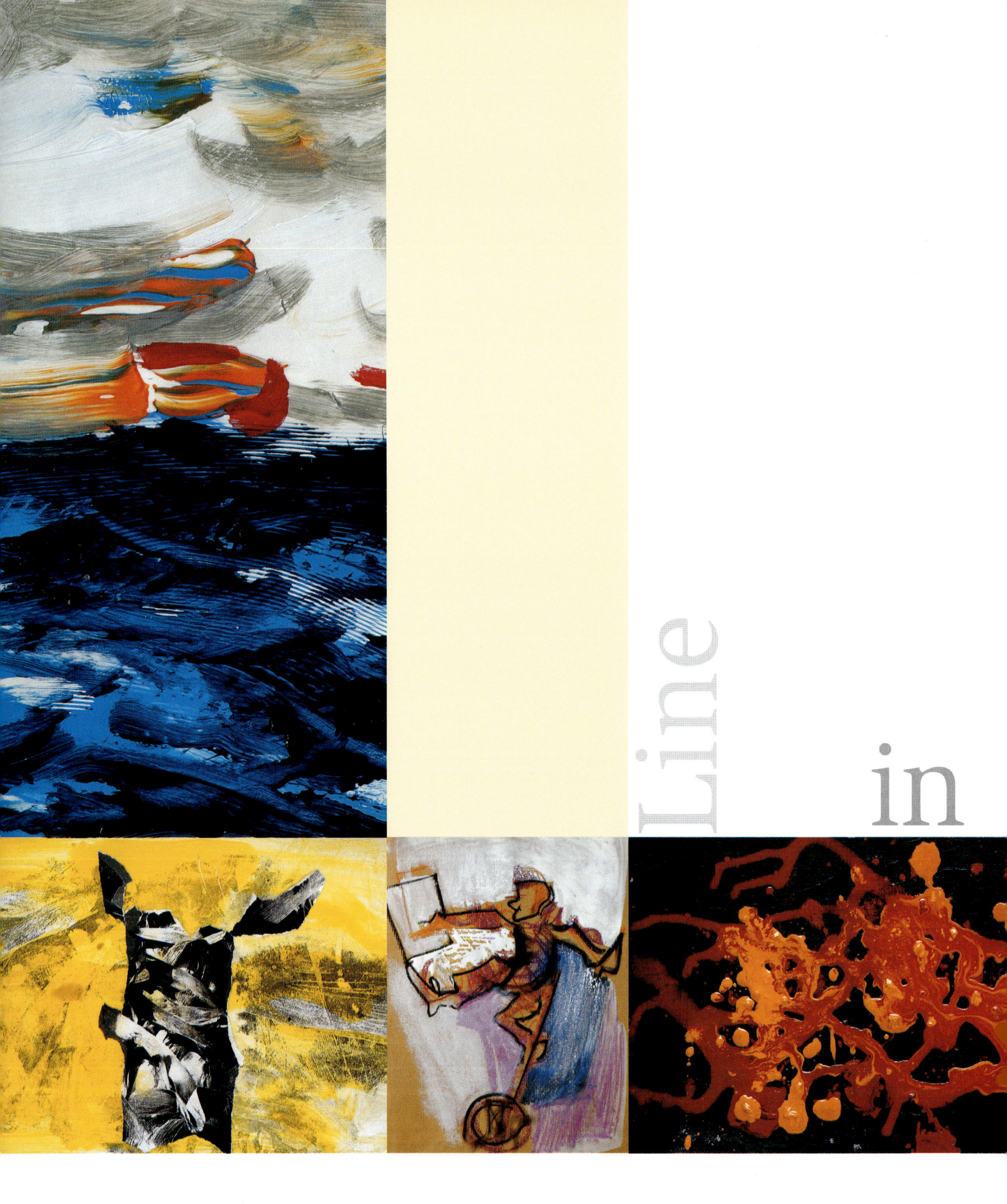

Line in

visual language

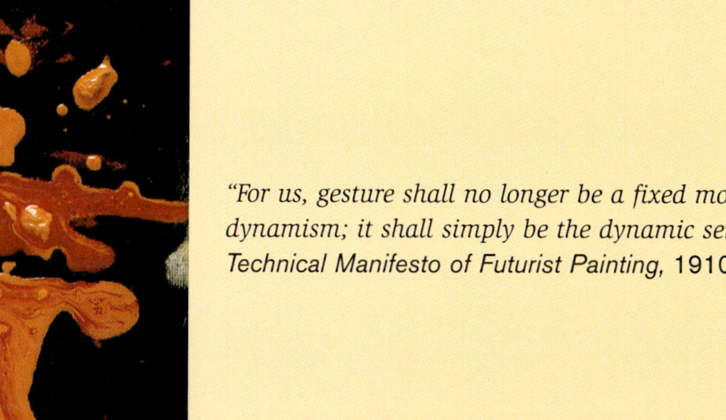

"For us, gesture shall no longer be a fixed moment in universal dynamism; it shall simply be the dynamic sensation itself."
Technical Manifesto of Futurist Painting, 1910.

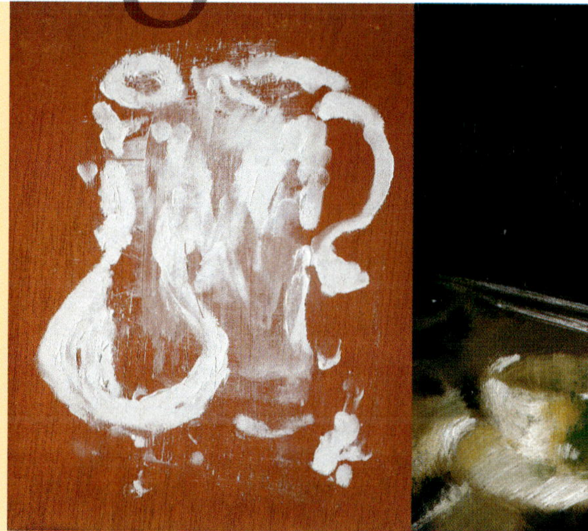

Line and visual perception

In Western cultures, the painting process has been disguised for many years by eliminating the artist's personal touch. In Eastern cultures, on the other hand, that mark has been valued as the personal human expression, conveying feelings such as fear, weakness, energy, security, and so on. These are the ideas that are perceived through a medium generally known as line. When we speak of process, or line, we do not mean so much *what* is contained in that image (colors used, composition, forms) but *how* it has been made physically, with what materials, tools, and the intention behind each gesture and each texture.

The main characteristic of the visual perception of line is that it leads us to a second level of perception: touch, going from an optical to a tactile approach. Although in many paintings the image relegates the materials with which it was made to a secondary level, in others the artist seems to appeal directly to the sense of touch, captivating viewers through the use of materials, inviting us to touch them. At this level, the psychic impact is superior to the visual impact because touch is the primary sense in humans, tied to the earliest perceptive experiences. As Tàpies eloquently wrote in his essay *Reality As Art*: "I remember having thought of—and made—works of art in which I wanted to allude to the presence of, for example, a reptile, and I did it without drawing it, but by simply creating the texture that depicted a surface that looked like scales."

"A pen drawing by Rembrandt, seen upside down, could be easily mistaken for a completely abstract calligraphy piece . . . one can see in Rembrandt drawings the pleasure that he felt from using only pen and ink. He could give a head and a hand an intense sense and expression, but if we covered the head and the hand, the other parts of the drawing would look like calligraphy motifs. So, in 'pen exercises' I found expressive pleasure in the liberal use of pen and ink. The drawings began that way and later some became figures, landscapes, and one of them a horse."
Henry Moore

D

Henry Moore,
Pen exercise number 9: Horseback Riders Crossing a Canyon, 1970.
Henry Moore Foundation
(Yorkshire, United Kingdom).

The main difference between gesture and texture is that the former conveys an isolated form or an exact action and the latter refers to an extension formed by myriad similar elements; one leaf and the foliage are not the same. Gesture helps identify the forms that constitute the images; on the other hand, texture defines the skin of those forms or the space that contains them **(A)**.

When we read a visual image we always follow an order, and line is a fundamental tool for establishing a hierarchy of importance. So, for example, impastos, precision, and radical gestures are noticed first, while out-of-focus elements, imprecision, and diluted soft lines are relegated to a second level **(B)**.

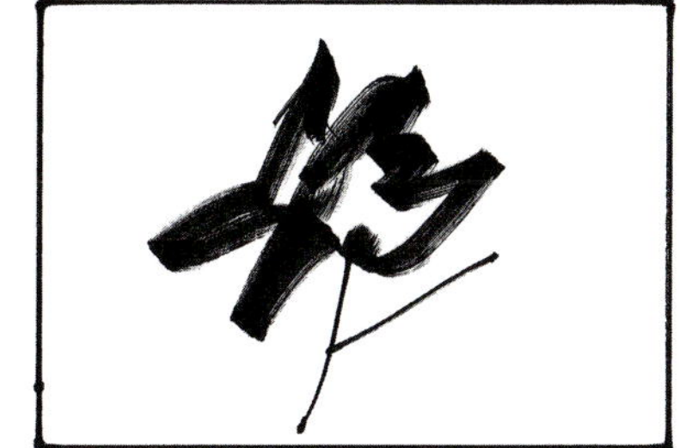

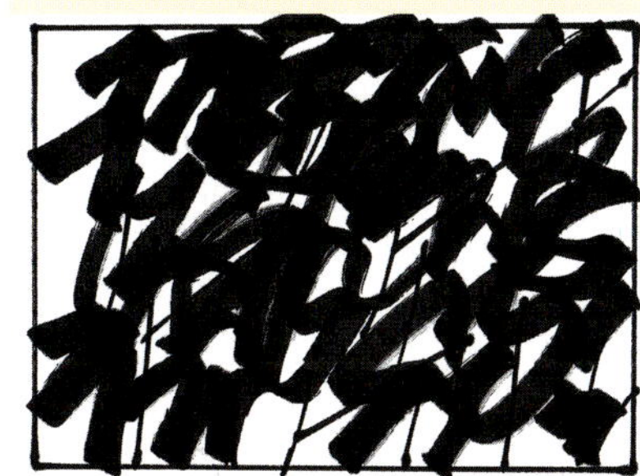

A

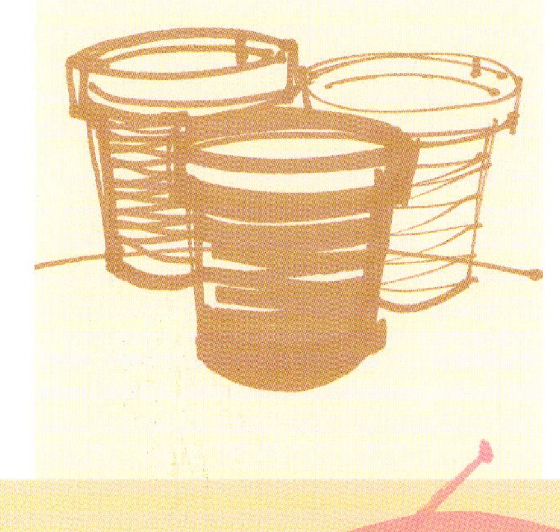

B

Through the laws of perception developed by Gestalt psychologists, we know that the mind tends to complete the information that is received by correcting the deficiencies and grouping similar visual stimuli. Therefore, it becomes possible for a line that has been drawn quickly or clumsily to continue representing an object (C), and for the mind, as in Rorschach tests or the pen drawings of Henry Moore (1898–1986) (D), to imagine forms in very imprecise lines.

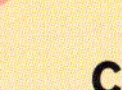

C

Factors that affect line

The common element of all the variables of line is the selection of materials and their intervention. When we talk about materials we are basically referring to the support and the medium, and intervention is the way in which that medium has been applied to the support.

Supports

Each support has its own expressive language that helps us convey specific effects through the use of lines. A linen canvas expresses elegance and sobriety, burlap coarseness and durability, and a cotton canvas freshness and natural feeling. Recycled paper and wrapping paper express humbleness, whereas the uneven surface of a sheet of handmade paper conveys craftsmanship. We can also experiment with nontraditional supports such as sheet metal, Formica, and vinyl, among others.

Media

The materials that constitute each medium provide different effects. Watercolors make fluid, transparent, and sensual lines; oils convey silkiness, density, and gloss. Acrylic paint is a versatile medium that can behave like watercolor, oil, and other types of paint and can be combined easily with other media. Today, artists are experimenting with the combination of other materials and the introduction of new nontraditional substances, such as varnish, enamel, and metallic industrial paints.

Applicators

These are the tools that are used to apply the pictorial material to the support. In addition to the traditional applicators (brushes, spatulas, ink pens, and so forth), which come in a variety of materials and thicknesses, there are other, less conventional implements such as reeds, brushes, sprays, or your own fingers.

Speed

The body, through the hand, transmits energy to each line that is drawn; by altering its speed, we can convey different emotions through our work. A line made slowly and steadily transmits a reflective mood, but also weakness; as the speed of the line increases it becomes less precise but gains in energy and dynamism, enriching the result with spontaneous effects, such as spattering.

Intensity

The term "wet technique" refers to the amount of paint with which the applicator is charged, and "dry technique" refers to the pressure exerted on the applicator. There is a close cause-effect relationship: little intensity produces soft, poetic, and light results; great intensity produces expressionistic, dense, and heavy results.

Modulation

This is the shape formed by the line, which is determined by the hand's movements. There are as many styles of line as there are painters, since this can be considered the artist's "pictorial calligraphy." Here, we find lines that can be sinuous, tremulous, angular, smooth, striking, casual, twisted, and so on.

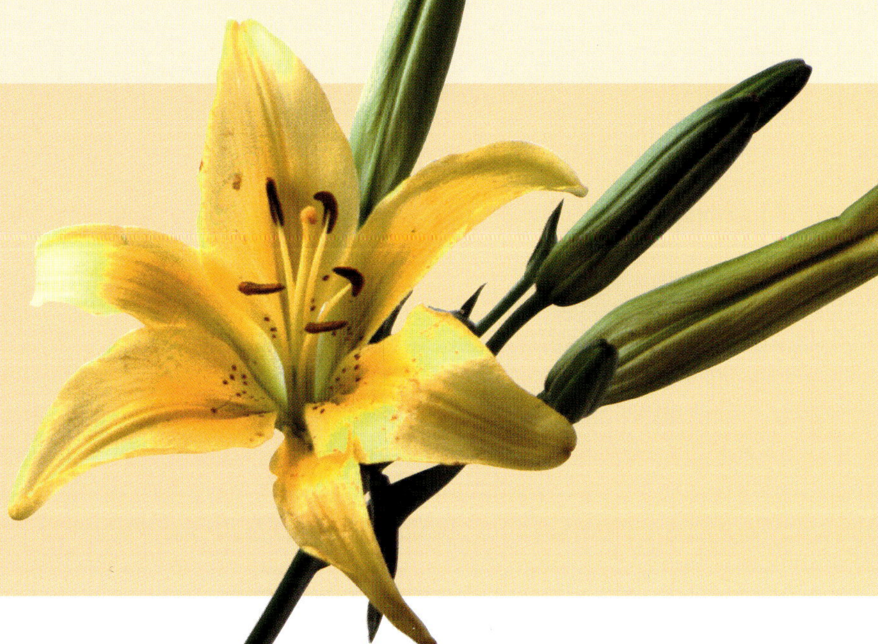

We can create very different plastic effects from a single model by modifying the lines.

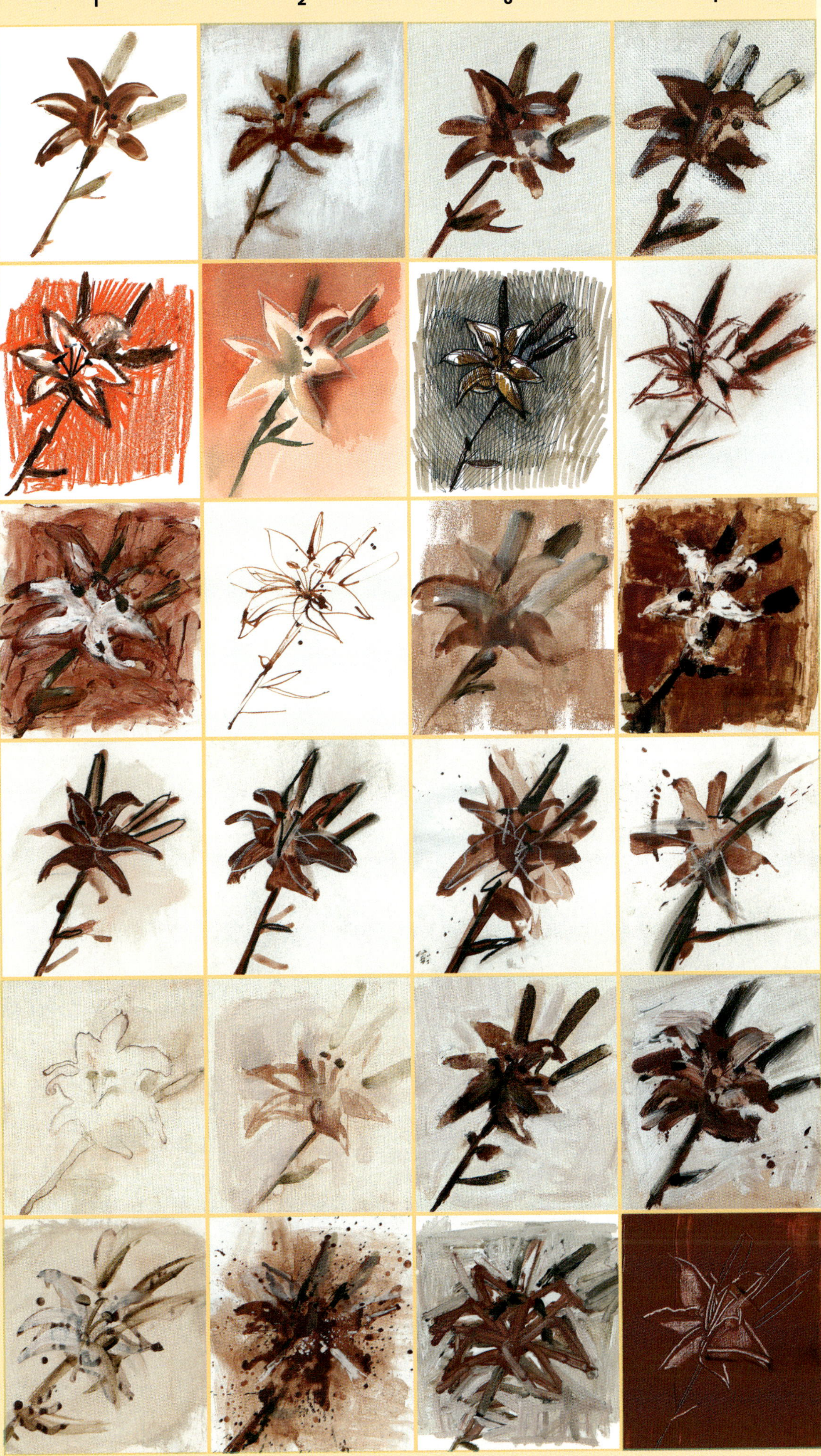

Different supports
1. paper
2. wood
3. canvas
4. burlap

Different media
1. crayon
2. watercolor
3. marker
4. chalk

Different applicators
1. fingers
2. reed
3. sponge
4. spatula

Different speed
from slow **(1)**
to very fast **(4)**

Different intensities
from very diluted **(1)**
to heavily charged **(4)**

Different modulation
1. sinuous
2. spattered
3. short brushstrokes
4. scraping

Types and characteristics of line

The same sentence said with different intonations can have completely opposite meanings. For example, the expression "I am tired" can mean fatigue if we say it slowly and in a soft voice, or anger when it is said loudly and in a forceful way. The same is true in painting, and that verbal tone has its equivalent in the visual language.

Lines are divided into two large groups: gestures and textures. In each group we find variations according to the elements that were involved in the creation process (support, medium, application, speed, intensity, and modulation).

Gestures

Gestural lines define forms or concentrate their energy around specific points or areas (figurative or abstract). At this level, gestural movements can be descriptive, precise, and direct, capable of defining the objects fluently; or soft, blended, and airy, able to convey a faint atmosphere. In terms of density, lines can be delicate, broken, and soft, which can convey vulnerability and tenuousness; or energetic, dynamic, and passionate, an invitation to living intensely.

It is possible to recognize primitive, sketchy, and basic gestures in compositions that are fresh and devoid of the sloppiness of graffiti; or gestural lines that let energy flow freely, as in the minimalist, essentialist, and reflexive approaches of Zen painting; or the liquid, fluid, and casual lines of action painting.

Textures

When we perceive texture visually we are reminded of a tactile feeling, which is why, to define them, we use words that refer to those tactile experiences: heavy-light, coarse-smooth, soft-hard, rigid-flexible, flat-rugged (broken, folded, cut, porous, wrinkled, pierced, sharp, striated, crackled), cool-warm, dry-wet, even-uneven, consistent-inconsistent, liquid-viscous, solid-misty.

The appeal of most textures is found in the procedure used to create them, such as transferred textures made with the imprints of objects, or *frottage;* or scratched, faded, and striated textures, which indicate a physical intervention on the material while still wet. In this sense, we also find the classic textures of drawing and painting: crosshatching, graphic, and reticulated textures that are more visual than tactile, and diffused, atmospheric, and airy textures that are reminiscent of warm and welcoming feelings.

Other textures are truly inviting to the touch. By incorporating materials and paint we can achieve realistic relief effects, such as the earthy coarse, and volumetric, very appropriate for landscapes; as well as the impasto,

Crosshatching, graphic, reticular textures

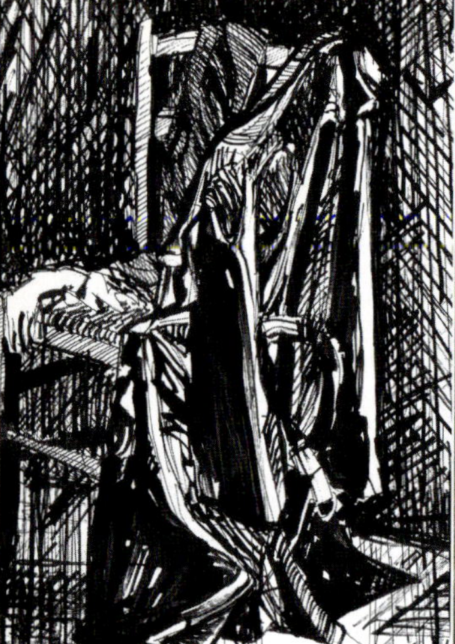

Atmospheric, diffused, blurry textures

Earthy, coarse, volumetric textures

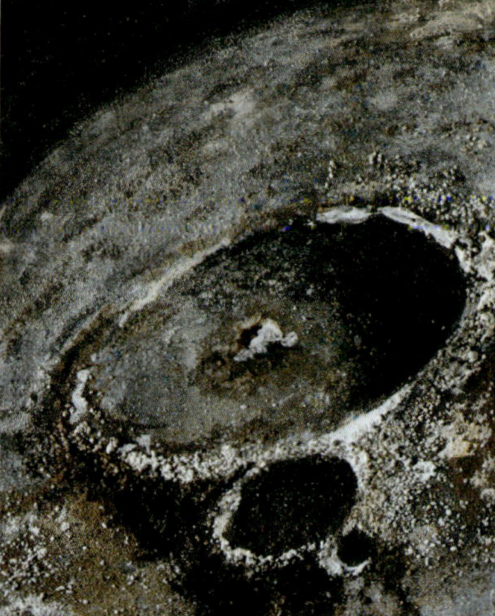

Transferred, printed, marked textures

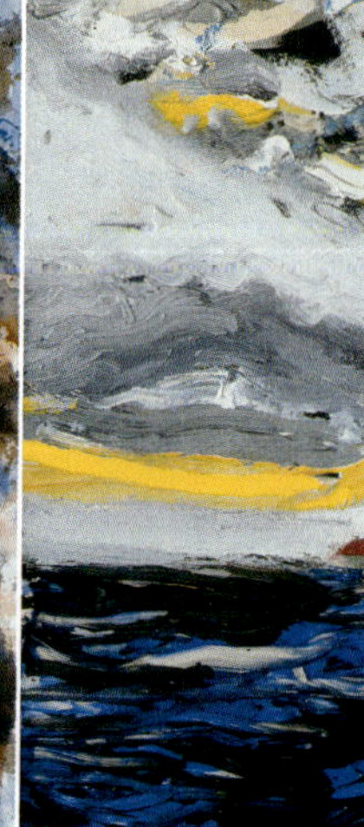

Textures

gel-like, and creamy textures of skies and seascapes.

Following this same volume criteria, we find such opposing extremes as the flat, even, and smooth textures typical of collage or the real, material, and volumetric ones of material painting and object painting, which incorporate objects and materials directly, without working them too much.

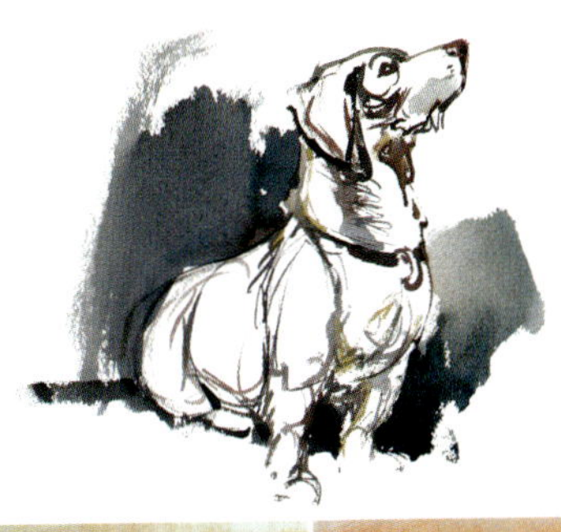

Descriptive, precise, direct gestures

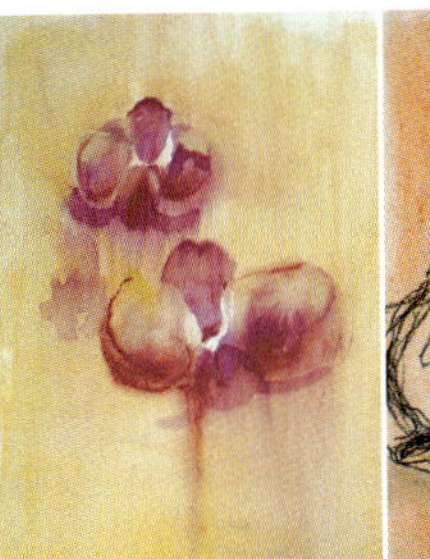

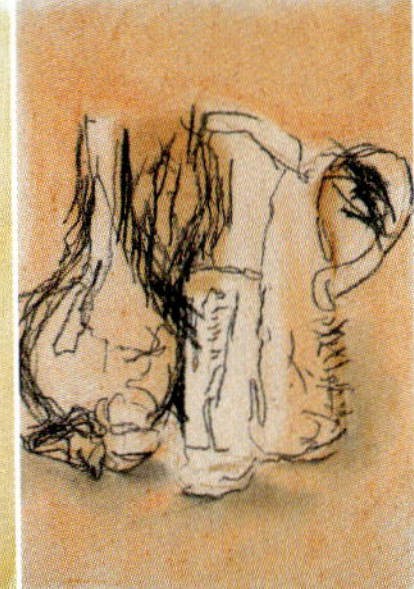

Smooth, blended, airy gestures

Fragile, broken, weak gestures

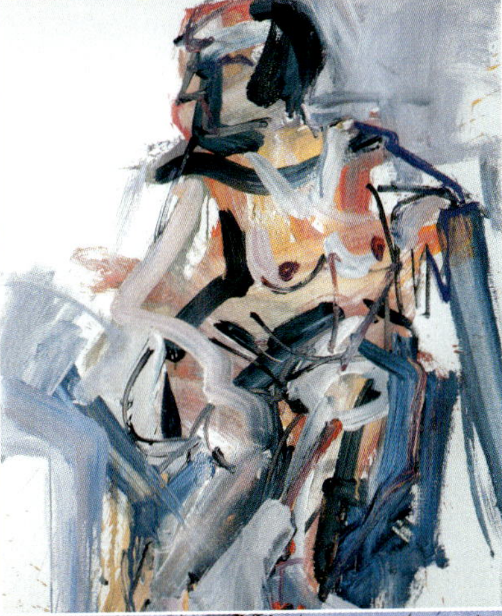

Energetic, dynamic, passionate gestures

Gestures

Scratched, faded, scraped textures

Minimalist, essentialist, reflexive gestures

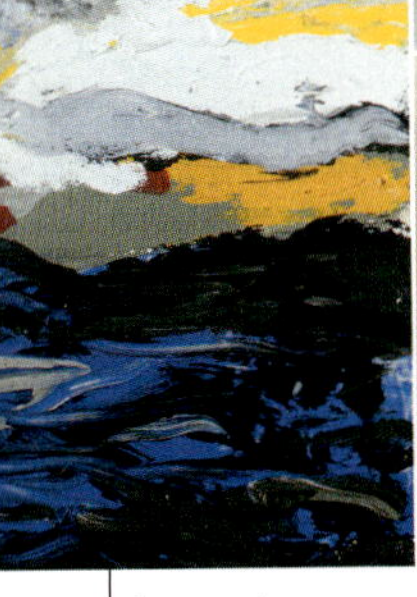

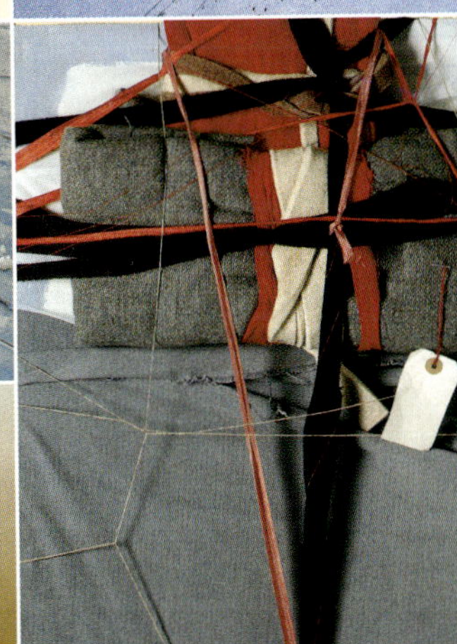

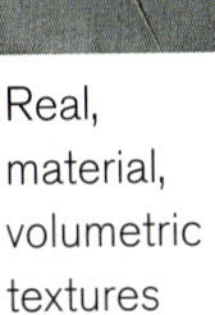

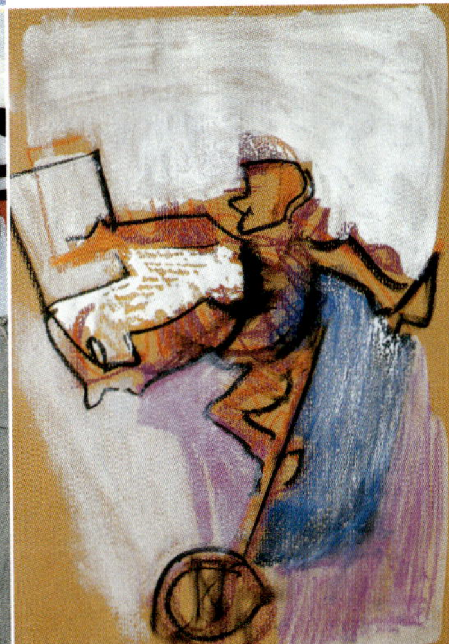

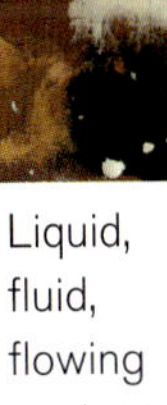

Impasto, gel-like, creamy textures

Flat, uniform, smooth textures

Real, material, volumetric textures

Primitive, sketchy, elemental gestures

Liquid, fluid, flowing gestures

Line in painting

Antoni Tàpies (born in 1923) is one of the greatest exponents of European Informalism, which appeared around the middle of the twentieth century. As its name indicates, this tendency, which was very aggressive in the beginning, pronounced itself against all that was formal, against academicism, whether figurative or abstract. At this historical moment, art began to pursue the materiality of the artwork itself; the work by Tàpies manifests that tendency through the perception of matter in a constant state of transformation, which has its foundation in Asian thought and spirituality. His work, commonly known as "material painting," creates its own universe where the physical action on the materials is shown through a very rich range of media: painting, drawing, collage, assemblage, scraping, *frottage,* and many other less traditional applications, like burning, piercing, wrinkling, tearing, sewing, and folding. *Tierra y azul* (*Earth and Blue*) is a mixed-media painting on a 58 × 45 inch (146 × 114 cm) board; its geometric structure depicts the symbol of the cross, a recurring element in this artist's work, and it reminds us of the game of hopscotch. The painting is a metaphor of the spiritual path in life; although the square representing heaven appears as the logical end to the journey, Tàpies proposes the desert and solitude as the final destination, a place to find oneself and personal evolution.

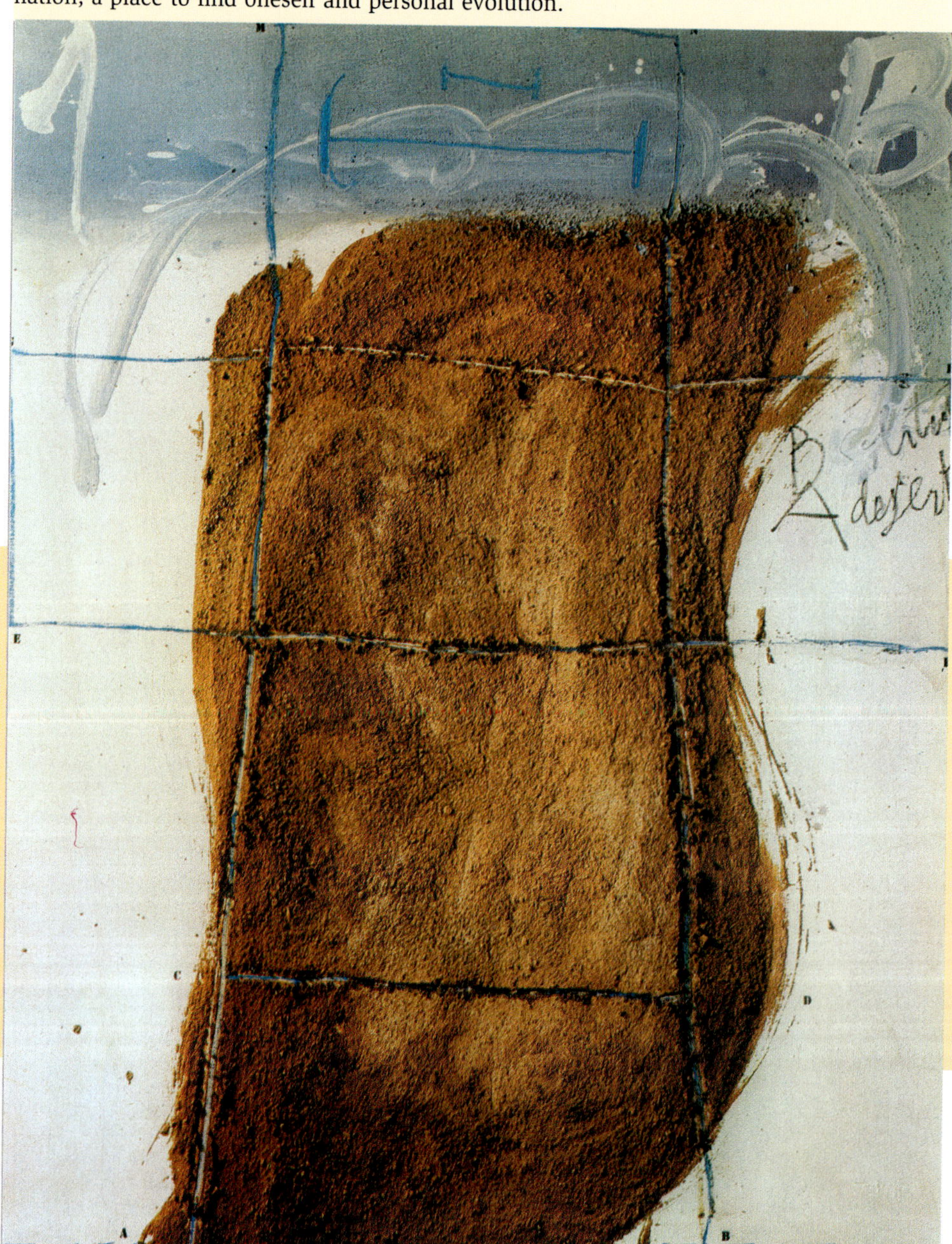

"When you look you should never think that painting—or any other thing in the world—'must be' limited to what many think it should be. Painting must be everything. It can be the solar clarity in the middle of a wind gust. It can be a cloud in the storm. It can be the footprint of a person on the journey of life, or a foot that stomps on the ground—why not?—to say 'Enough already.' It can be the sweet aroma of the dawn, full of hope, or the sour smell of a prison. It can be the bloodstains of a wound, or the song in a clear blue or yellow sky of an entire village. It can be what we are, today, now, always. I invite all of you to play, to observe carefully . . . I invite you to think."

Antoni Tàpies

The approach of Tàpies in this piece represents a perfect overview of his work because it shows the balance between two worlds: order—or a mental state—(symbols, geometry, alphabet), and chaos—or an emotional state—(child's play, randomness, impulsive gestures).

A. Application of sand: soil with vinyl glue placed on a board in an irregular shape to reinforce its changing character, like the common ground where hopscotch is played.

B. Pictorial lines: on the one hand, the blue square for the sky and, on the other, the description of the motion of a virtual jump (a double fatal jump) with quick, organic, vigorous brushstrokes. The number one indicates the beginning of the jump, and several grouped numbers (number of attempts) its end.

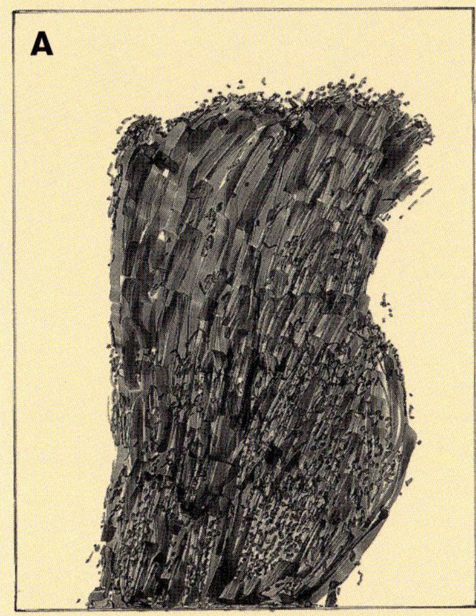

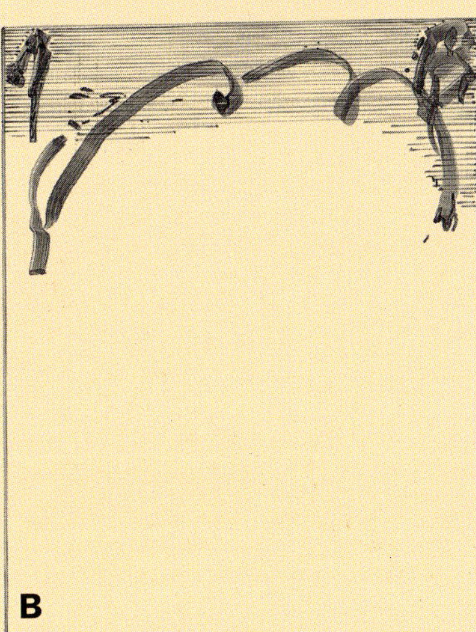

C. Drawing: lines drawn with a crayon and letters written with charcoal depict the square shapes of the game, as well as written words ("B solitude, A desert" in the F–H box), which are reminiscent of primitive graffiti. Several segments in the box for the sky express the idea of getting smaller in the space.

D. Scratching (*Grattage*): as in the game, the grid has been depicted by drawing it on the earth. Scratching the surface of the material reinforces its volume.

E. Stencils: small letters painted with the help of stencils signal the borders of the territory in a scrupulous ascending order. The letters I, J, K, and L, not visible, match the edges of the intersecting squares, the space of fusion between horizontal and vertical, heaven and earth, matter and spirit.

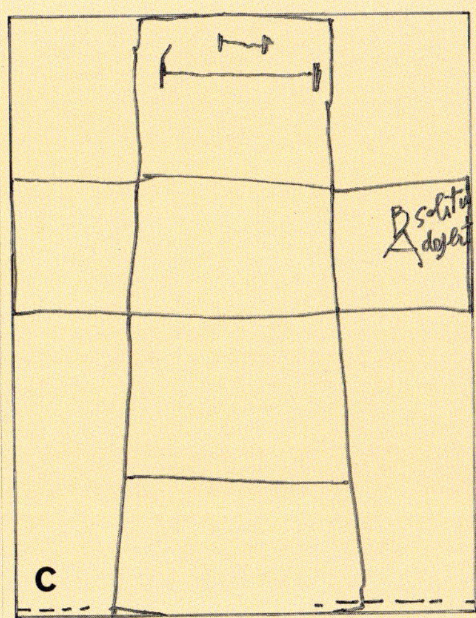

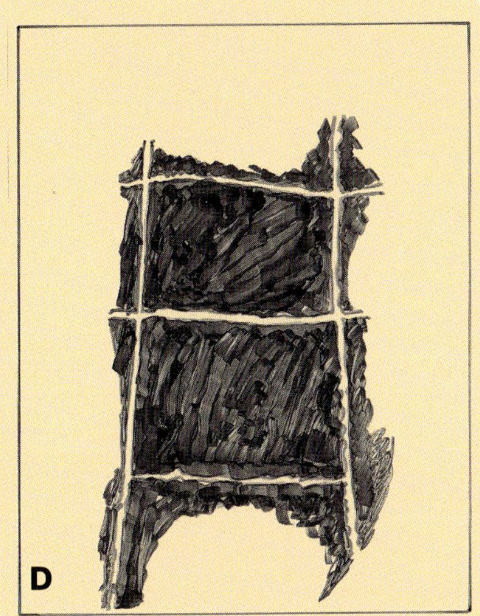

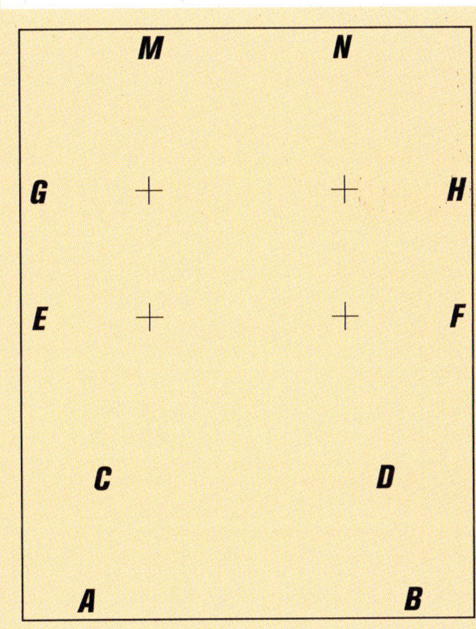

Antoni Tàpies,
Tierra y azul, 1973.
Private collection.

Line and personal expression

In each period of the history of painting, we find clear differences between its painters; that is what we call "style." Style is the painter's personal calligraphy, which often says more about him or her and the artist's vision of the world than of the subjects depicted. Painting helps express contents that would be difficult to explain otherwise; as Arman would say: "If my intention were to show, I think I would have used the pen rather than the brush." As we saw in previous pages, as with intonation in an oral discourse, or calligraphy in a manuscript, line directly affects the expressive sense of the image contained in a painting. In painting, "how" is ultimately more eloquent than "what."

The discovery of photography in the nineteenth century marked a change in painting. Impressionism was the first movement that broke away from the rules of the academy, which were based on the faithful representation of reality according to certain canons. There are two elements that are explored during this period: color and line. The loose brushstroke of Mary Cassatt (1844–1926) is a clear example of personal Impressionist expression, the lyrical and tender approach to a subject that she depicted throughout her artistic career: motherhood.

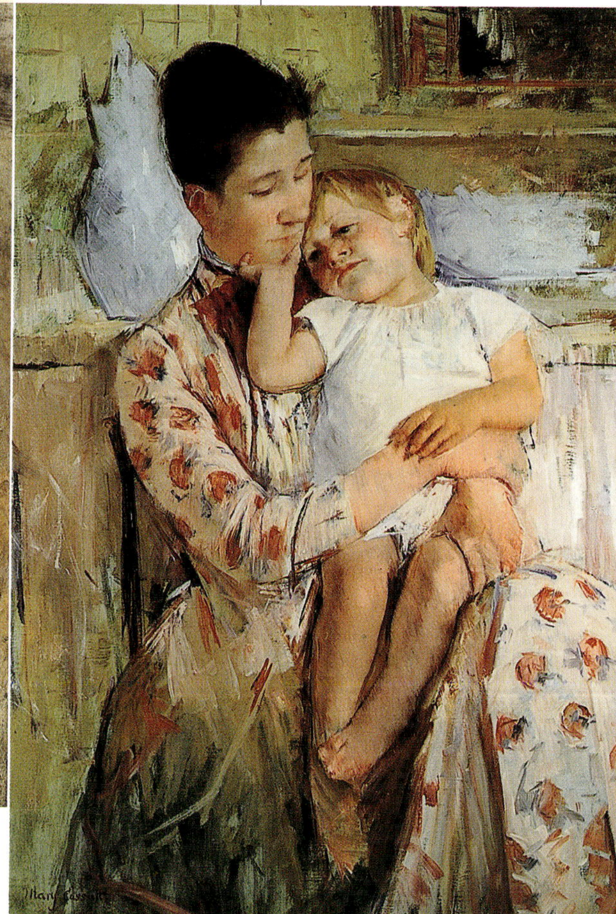

Mary Cassatt, *Emmie and Her Child*, 1889. Wichita Art Museum (Kansas, United States).

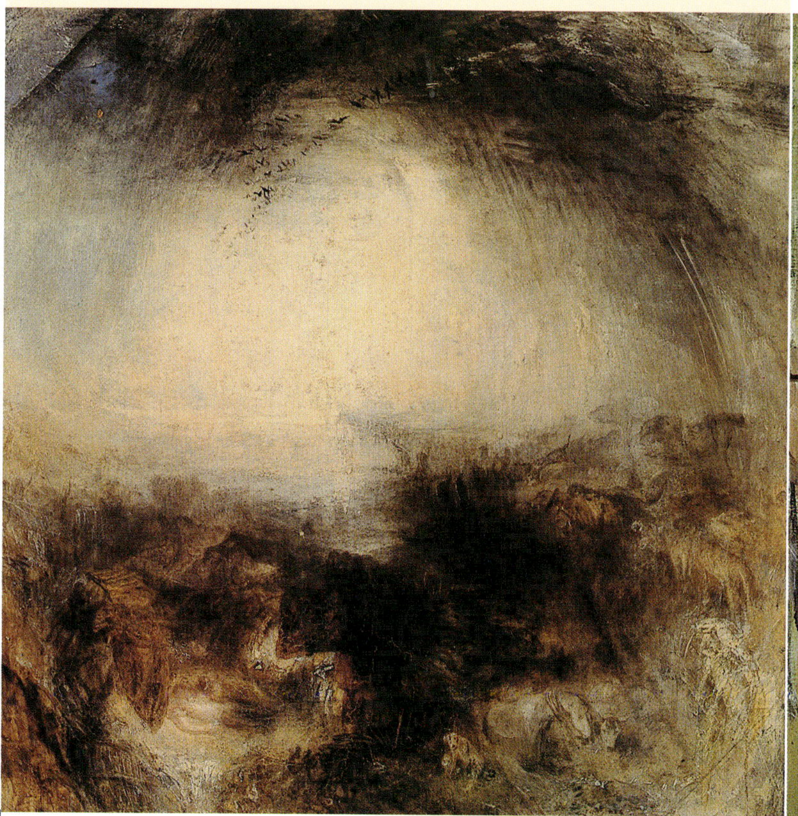

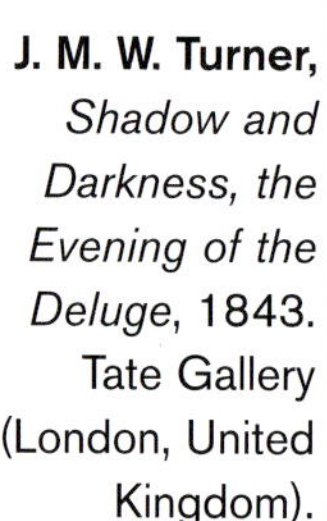

J. M. W. Turner, *Shadow and Darkness, the Evening of the Deluge*, 1843. Tate Gallery (London, United Kingdom).

The dense, airy, and atmospheric lines of Joseph Mallord William Turner (1775–1851) are a paradigm of Romanticism. A well-known tale expresses this connection between line and lively approach. Legend says that, on a certain occasion, a lady and an unknown older gentleman were traveling by coach on a mountain road through an intense storm. Suddenly, the gentleman opened the window and traveled for quite some time with his body hanging halfway out. When he got back inside, completely soaked, he repeated these words: "It is extraordinary, sublime, fantastic . . . ." He invited the lady to experience the same feeling, and, disregarding etiquette she complied. Years later, the lady visited an exhibit in London by the great J. M. W. Turner, and she recognized the experience of that bizarre trip in his paintings. She was introduced to the painter and when she shook his hand, she remembered him: it was the gentleman in the coach.

> *"I am making a vigorous primitive work, more vigorous than that of black artists and Picasso's. Why? Because I belong to the twentieth century, I come from Picasso . . . I have crossed over the wall of abstraction, of surrealism, etc. My work has it all. You should not feel trapped inside a compartment."*
>
> **Karel Appel,** Letter to Corneille, Christmas of 1947–1948.

Karel Appel (1921–2006) is perhaps the best-known painter of the Cobra group. The cobra, at once a very dangerous and sacred snake, was chosen as the symbol of this feisty movement born after World War II in the Netherlands and northern countries. Its members understood creative expression as a universal right and the reconstructive tool for a better world. They drank from the primitive fountain of human creativity that was not yet contaminated by Western rules and conventions: totems and magic signs of primitive cultures, Eastern calligraphy, prehistoric and medieval art, popular art, naïf art, and the creations of children and people with psychological disabilities. They searched for a conscious regression of those archetypical images that the Swiss psychiatrist Carl Gustav Jung detected in the deepest layers of the subconscious.

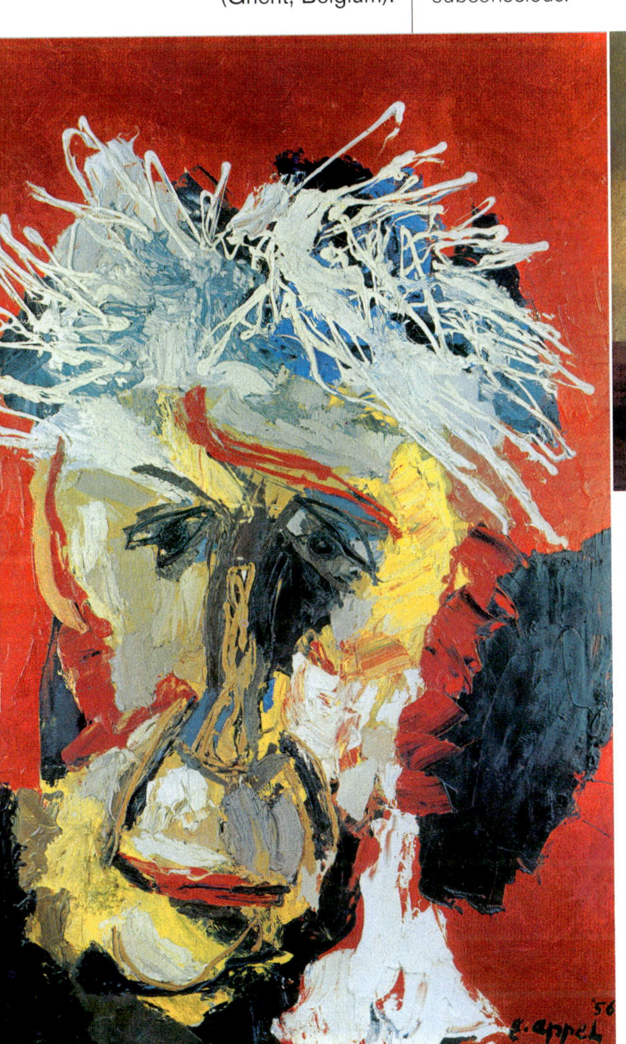

Karel Appel,
Barbaric Nude, 1957.
Museum van Hedendaagse Kunst
(Ghent, Belgium).

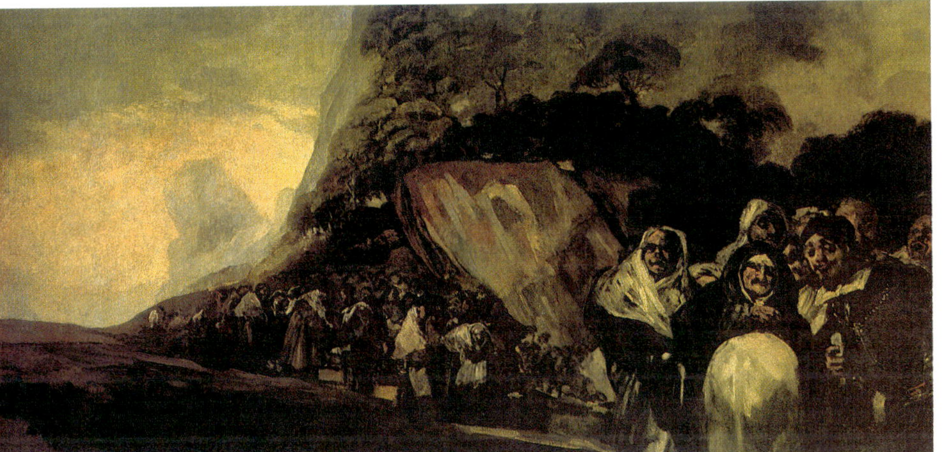

Francisco de Goya,
Pilgrimage to San Isidro (detail),
1820–1823.
Prado Museum
(Madrid, Spain).

The expressionistic and tragic line of Goya (1746–1828) in his well-known "black paintings" is the personal note of a painter who experienced a double drama in this period: deafness and political persecution. In these series of mural paintings executed at the Quinta del Sordo, his refuge-residence, can be detected a sense of freedom of expression that is ahead of his time. It is no surprise that the painters of the German Expressionist movement Die Brücke (The Bridge, initiated in 1905) considered him the true father of Expressionism.

Experimenting with line

The painter, when he or she decides to experiment with line, goes deeply into a work of personal self-acknowledgment. This is done first through gesture, by which the artist liberates his or her own energy and with it his or her passions, desires, and fears; gesture is the hallmark that reveals the artist's personality, the personal view of the world. Second, through the dialog with matter, the artist integrates the message contained in the gesture.

In this searching mode, we find common ground in many painters: the desire to attain a truly free, wild, fresh line without any rational adornments or restrictions. To do this, in terms of gesture, they resort to methods that promote lack of control, such as randomness, automatic painting, or action painting; and as far as texture goes, they are in tune with the message of the materials, the feelings awakened by them, how they act on the canvas . . . what they are capable of expressing in the hands of the artist.

Like the North American Abstract Expressionist painters, Cy Twombly (born in 1928) manifests an exuberant gestural style, although it is closer to the automatic writing of psychic improvisation typical of Surrealism. In his work process, his hand is guided by prerational impulses until a powerful metawriting of lines, symbols, and scribbling is achieved. The observer, in the presence of his work, is forced to make a tremendous reading effort to ultimately abandon that objective opening the channel for communication at a more formal and sensible level. As Twombly says, "Each line is the actual recognition of itself, its inner history. It does not explain anything, it is the fruit of an individual incarnation."

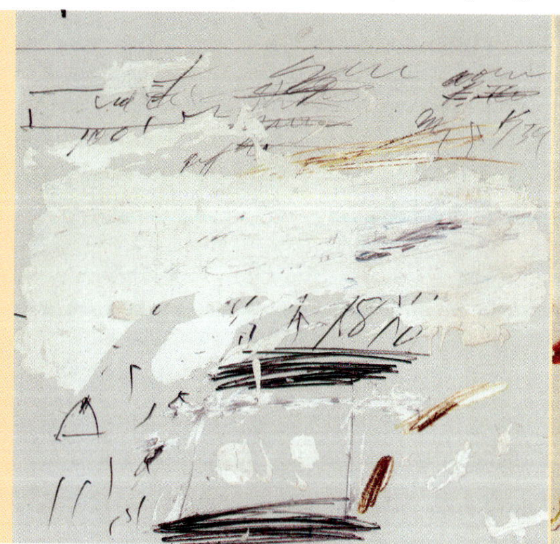

Cy Twombly,
Sheet no. 15 of the series *Poems of the Sea*, 1959. The Dia Art Foundation (Beacon, New York, United States).

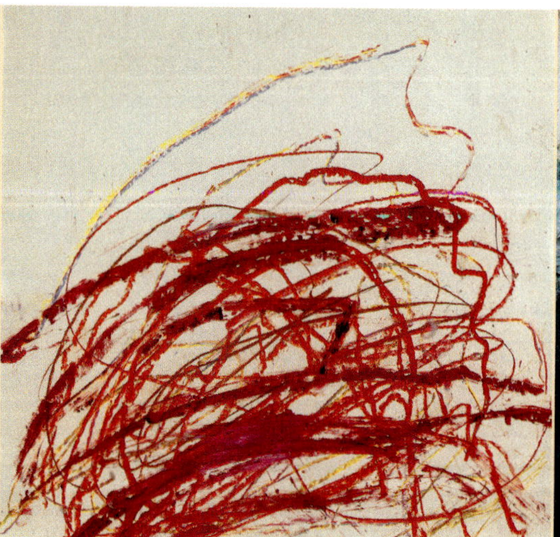

Cy Twombly,
Sheet no. 2 of the series *Gaeta (For the Love of Fire and Water)*, 1981. Private collection.

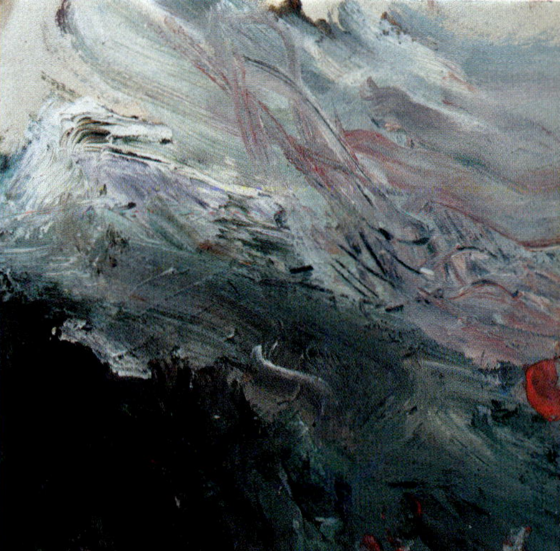

Cy Twombly,
Sheet no. 2 of the series *Gaeta VIII*, 1986. Private collection.

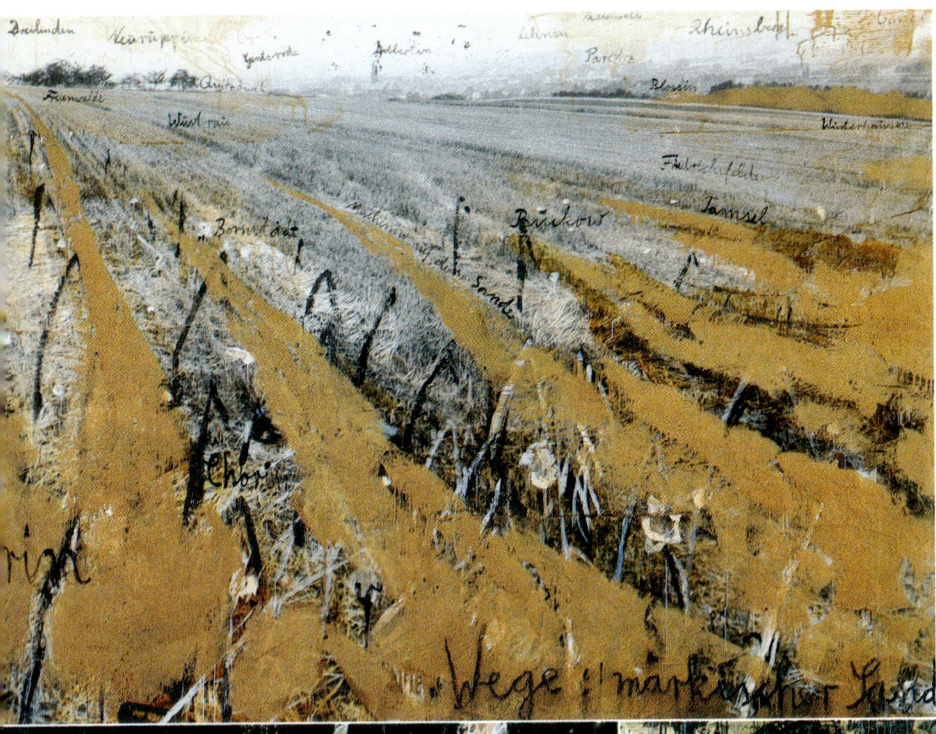

In his paintings, Anselm Kiefer (born in 1945) uses texture with a high philosophical and spiritual content, and he does it from the symbolism of the materials chosen and their energy. In *Your Golden Hair, Margarite–Johannis-Nacht,* there is a double meaning in the use of the straw: on the one hand, beauty as the metaphor of the feminine and luminous dimension of Germany, and on the other, as the horror for the danger that it contains as a highly flammable material.

In *Emanation*, a huge 164 × 112 inch (410 × 280 cm) canvas, he speaks of an encounter between the celestial and terrestrial through the use of molten lead. With the lead, he reminds us of the cycle of rain, and expresses the concept of God's existence in all things, flowing in all the elements from Him and through Him. In *Marching in Sand*, he combines photographs over the entire surface of a large 62 × 144 inch (155 × 360 cm) canvas with text and real sand to create a perfect fusion between image and body, gesture and texture.

Anselm Kiefer,
Marching in Sand, 1980. Saatchi Gallery (London, United Kingdom).

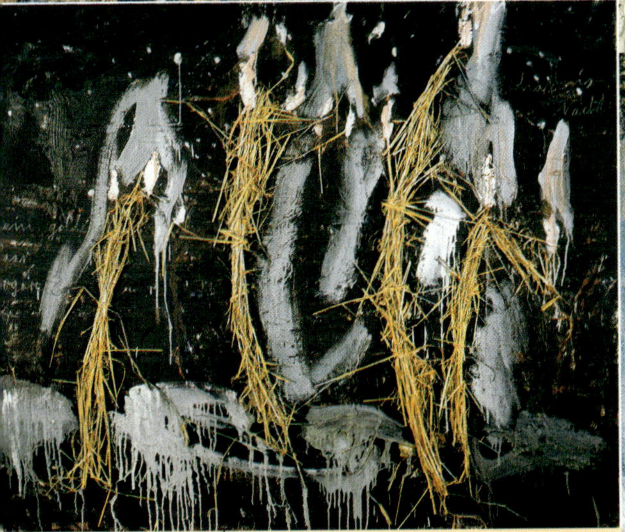

Anselm Kiefer,
Your Golden Hair, Margarite–Johannis-Nacht, 1981. Private collection.

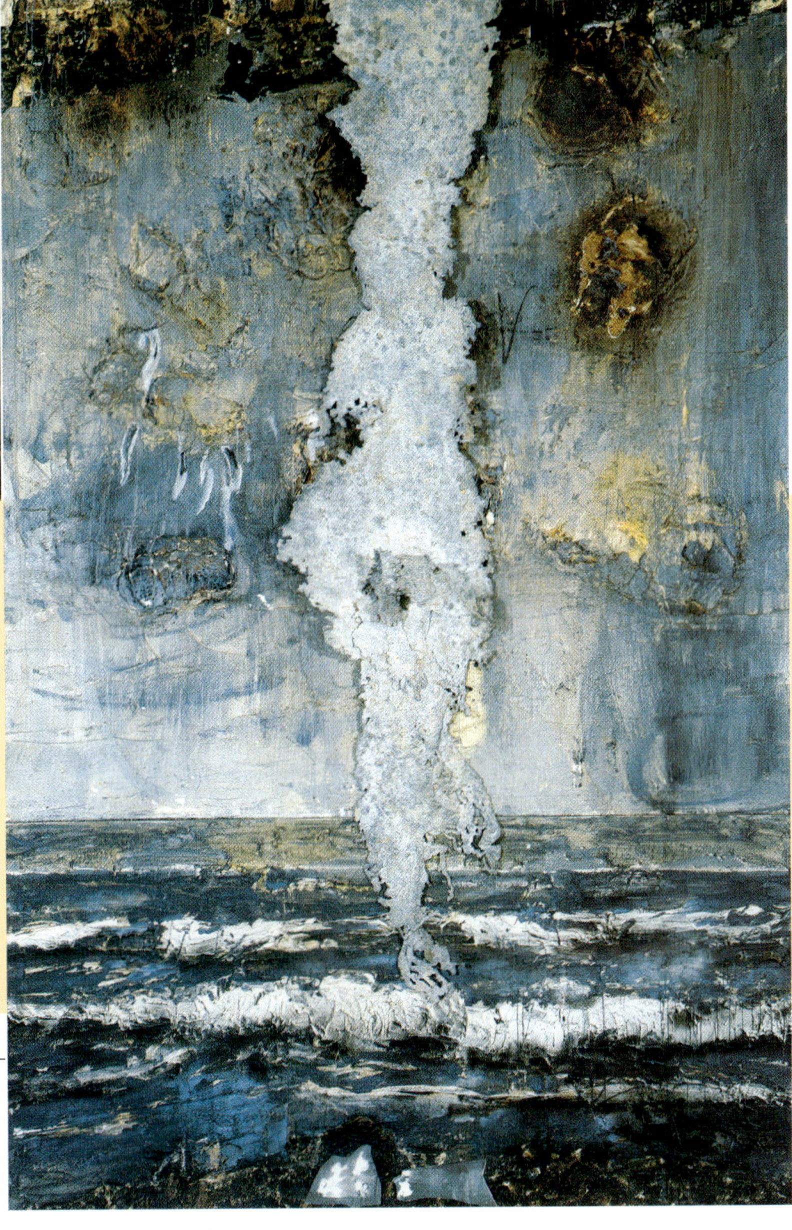

Anselm Kiefer,
Emanation, 1984–1986. Private collection.

The encounter with nature awakens in the painter a need to capture and to transmit the energy contained in each element before him. In the following creative projects we see some of the approaches based on the way lines and areas of colors are applied. The first one is a descriptive line exercise that conveys with realism the way a moving animal acts. The second one is based on a footprint: when nature is directly imprinted on the canvas through transfer, or *frottage.* The third revisits the gestural line, this time in an interpretive manner.

Line in

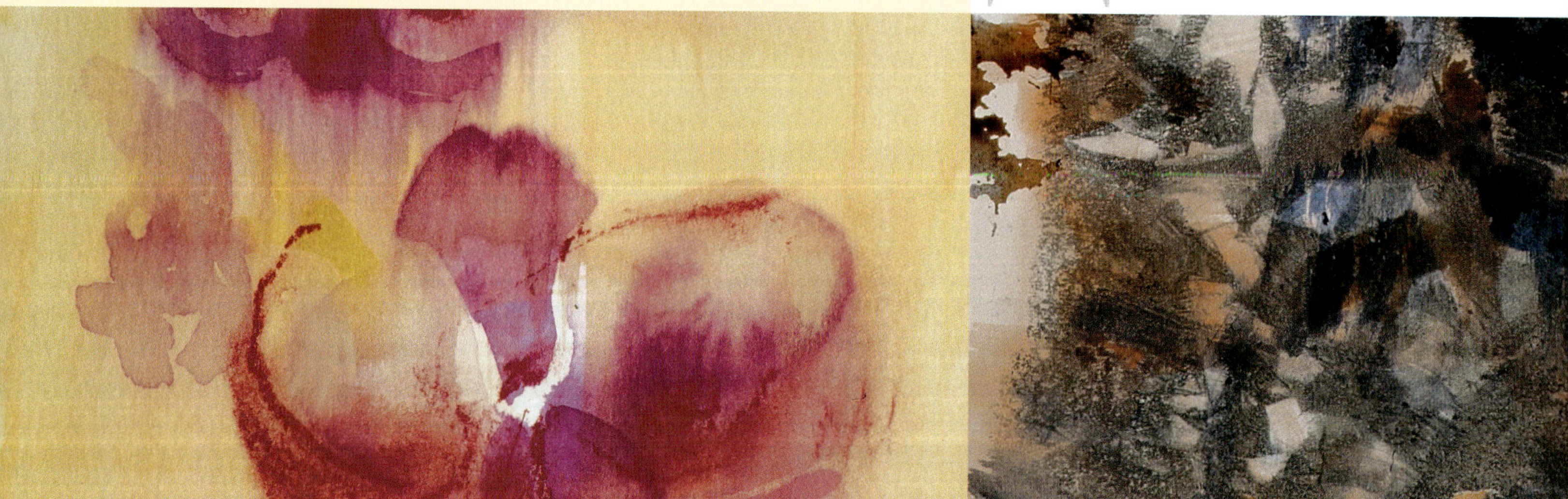

living nature

"One thing is sure, and it is that a painting interests me as long as I can shed on it a light that can be called (and here comes the problem of understanding with regard to words) life, presence, existence, or reality."
Jean Dubuffet

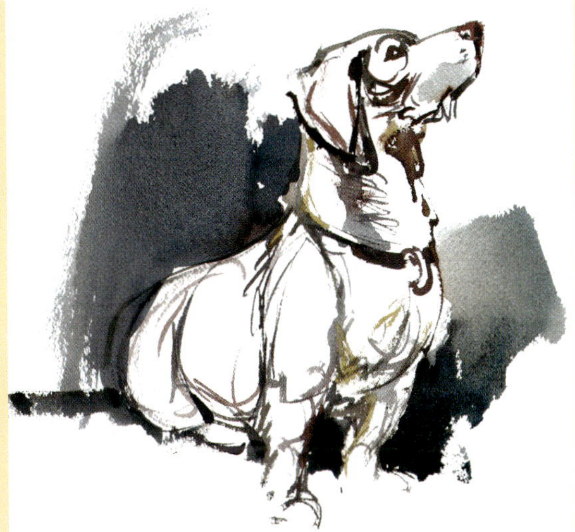

Descriptive, precise, and direct gestures

Henri de Toulouse-Lautrec (1864–1901) was one of the most important painters of French Impressionism. He was famous especially for his ability to create descriptive lines directly and quickly. When we look at one of his pieces, especially his sketches, we have the feeling that each line has been drawn naturally, almost effortlessly; this is a sign of natural virtuosity that is found in only a few painters. It consists of an ability that comes from the painter's sharp sense of observation: he lived with his models, especially with those from the world of performing arts and show business, and he was impregnated by their personal energy to the point that he could depict their character and personal drama with four quick lines. The speed and intensity of each line of his bulldog sketch expresses the ferocity of the animal while describing its anatomy at the same time. Here, the artist's intention is to introduce to us the sense of reality, not just appearances.

Henri de Toulouse-Lautrec, *Mademoiselle Palmyre's Bulldog*, 1897. Musée d'Albi (France).

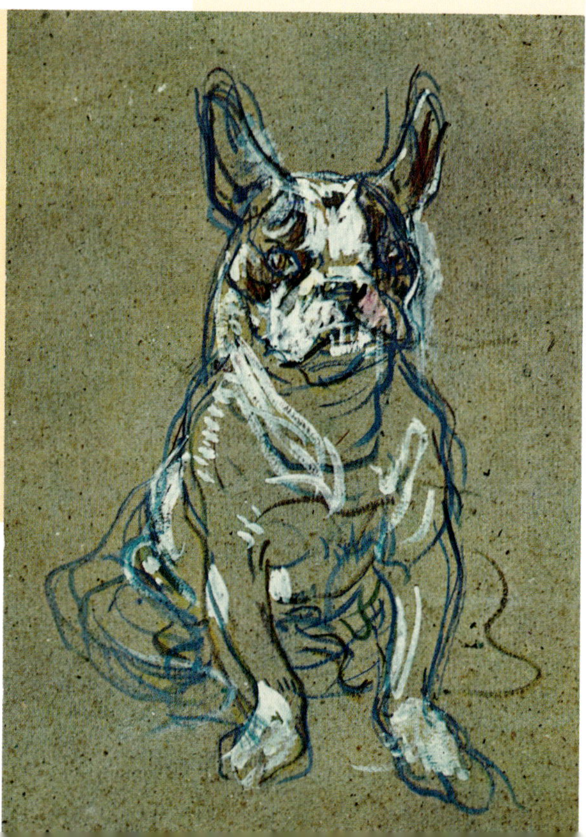

Representing animals in motion with descriptive lines

This first example has been executed by Vicenç Ballestar, a painter with ample experience in the representation of animals. A photo session was conducted with a Dachshund as the model, moving naturally through the yard. The artist, who is used to observing at length each movement and pose of his model, makes a series of watercolor sketches from those photographs. He quickly captures the main gestures and translates them into precise and well-formed brushstrokes.

"A distinctive characteristic of Japanese painting is the strength of the brushstroke (. . .). When representing an object that suggests power, for example an abrupt cliff, the beak or the claws of a bird, the claws of a tiger, or the trunk or the branches of a tree, at the moment the brush is applied the feeling of strength must be invoked and felt through the artist's entire nervous system and conveyed by his arm and hand to the brush, so it can be transmitted to the painted object."
Henry P. Bowie,
On the Laws of Japanese Painting, 1911.

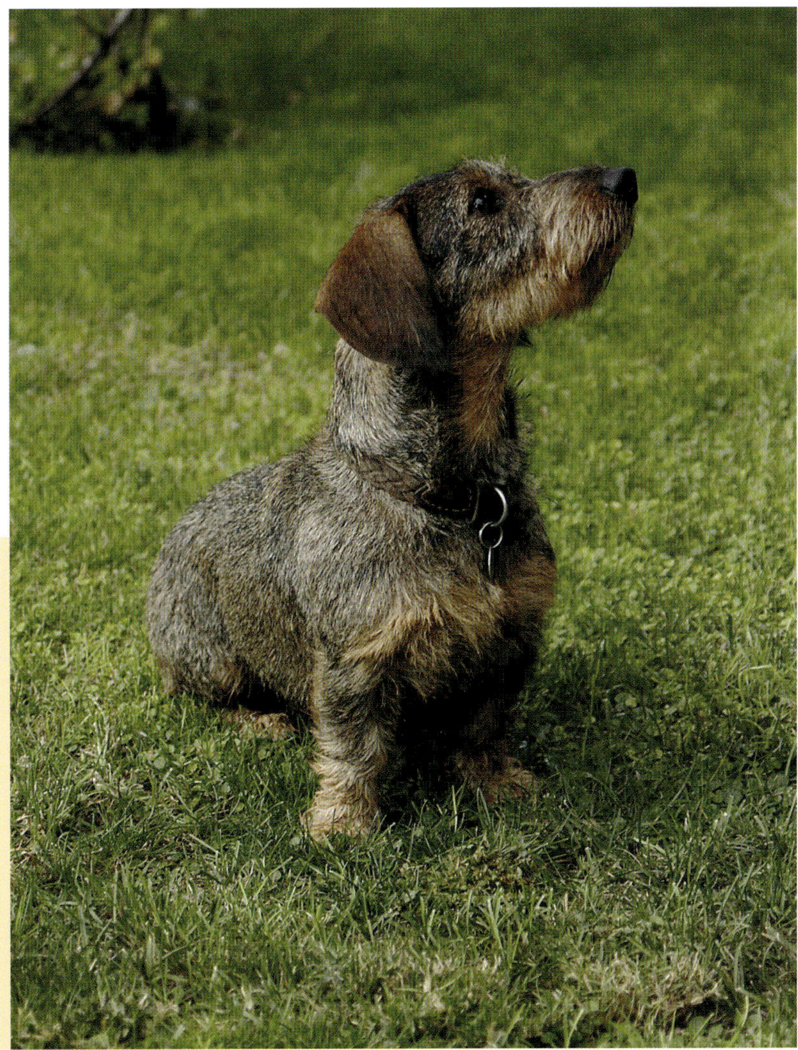

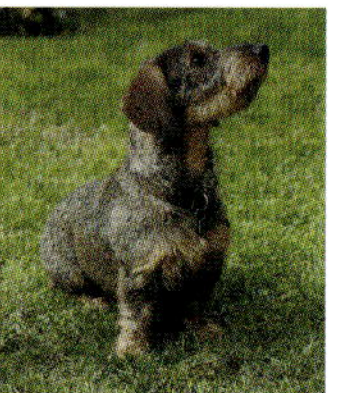

3 We finish defining the entire body by working the extremities and part of the hair. To suggest the texture of the hair, we use the thinnest brush and a very quick and loose stroke.

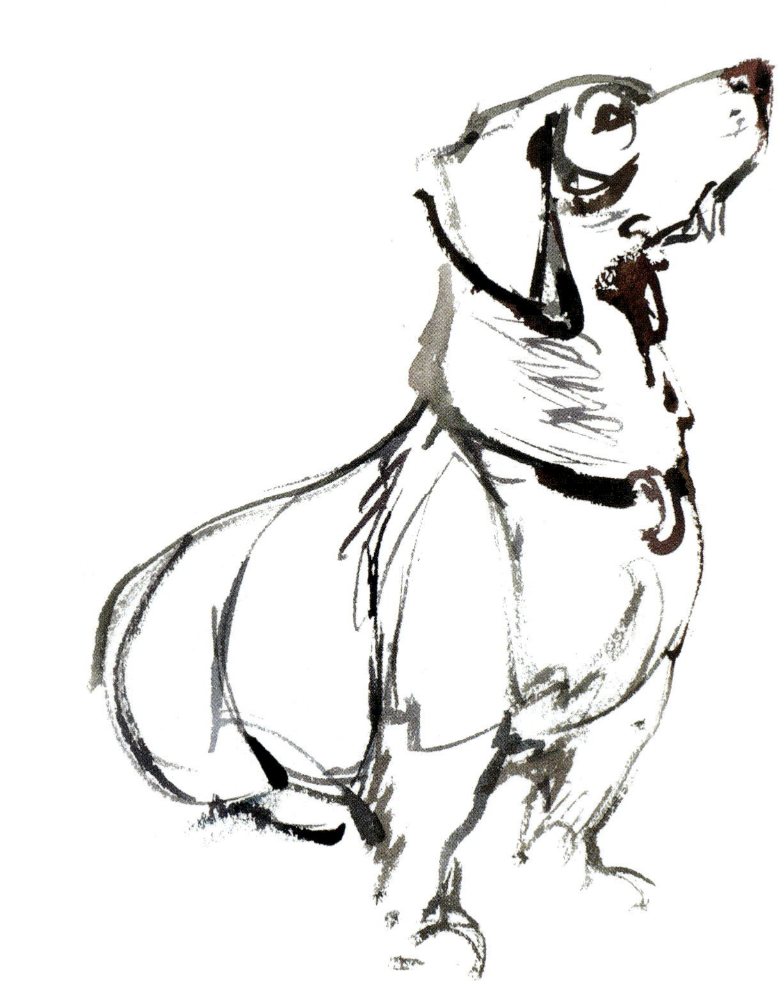

1 First, we plan the watercolor by drawing the outlines of the dog's main volume with the tip of a medium-size brush: the thorax and from here its extension to the tail and the head. The posture of the animal is defined with sinuous and rounded lines that emphasize its muscular anatomy.

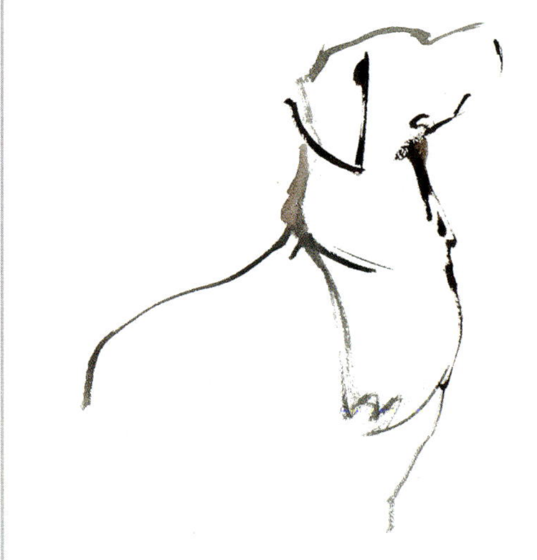

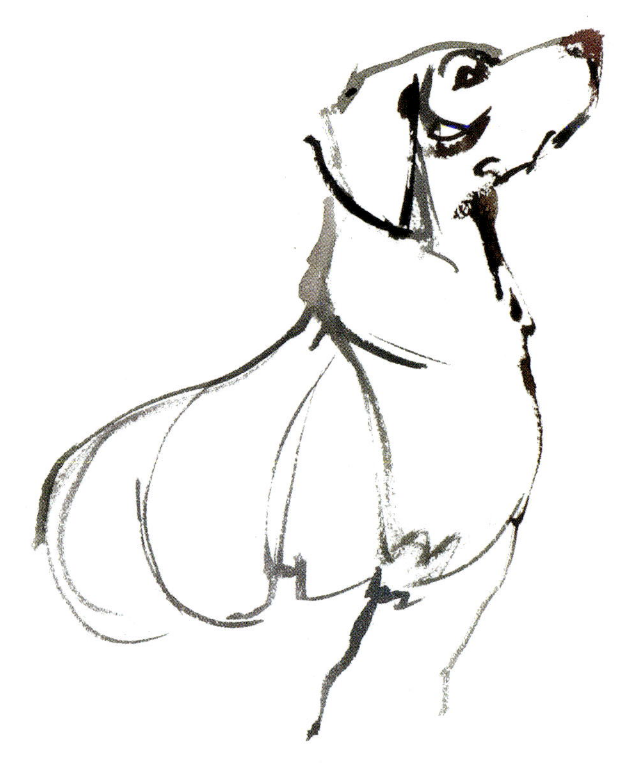

2 Next, we introduce some essential features such as the eye and the snout. These details give presence and expression to the animal. We continue by defining the volumes of the body without paying attention to light and shadow values, since we are working at all times with the linear gestural line, like Toulouse-Lautrec.

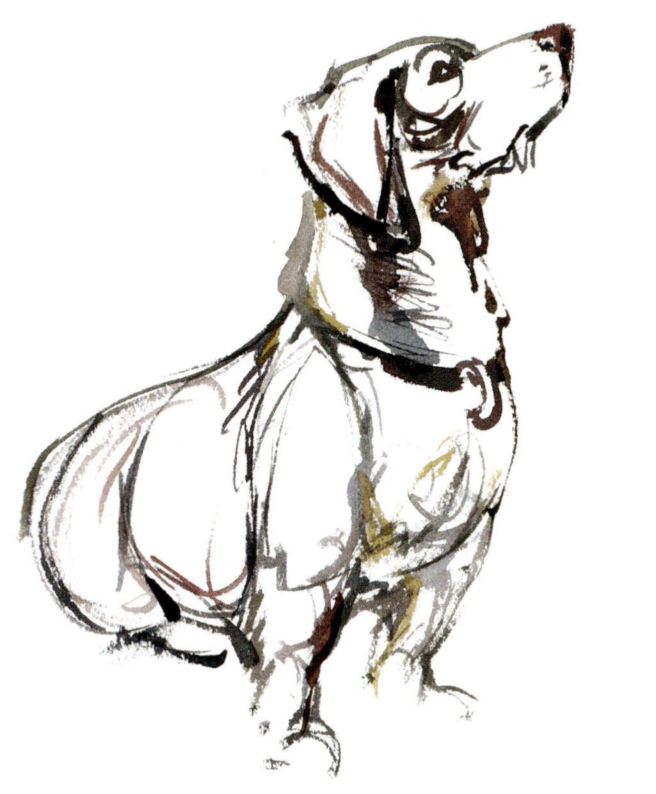

4 We finish with some touches of color that reinforce the various areas of the dog's anatomy and the quality of its fur. The crisscrossed color lines create dynamism and tension and the more diluted brushstrokes take away the harshness of the line and provide a soft feeling.

5 We finish the work by detaching the figure from the background with blotches of color applied with a very thick brush charged with a dark gray-blue tone. The gradation of each color of the background has been created by working wet on wet very fast and without trying too much to preserve the natural characteristic of a sketch.

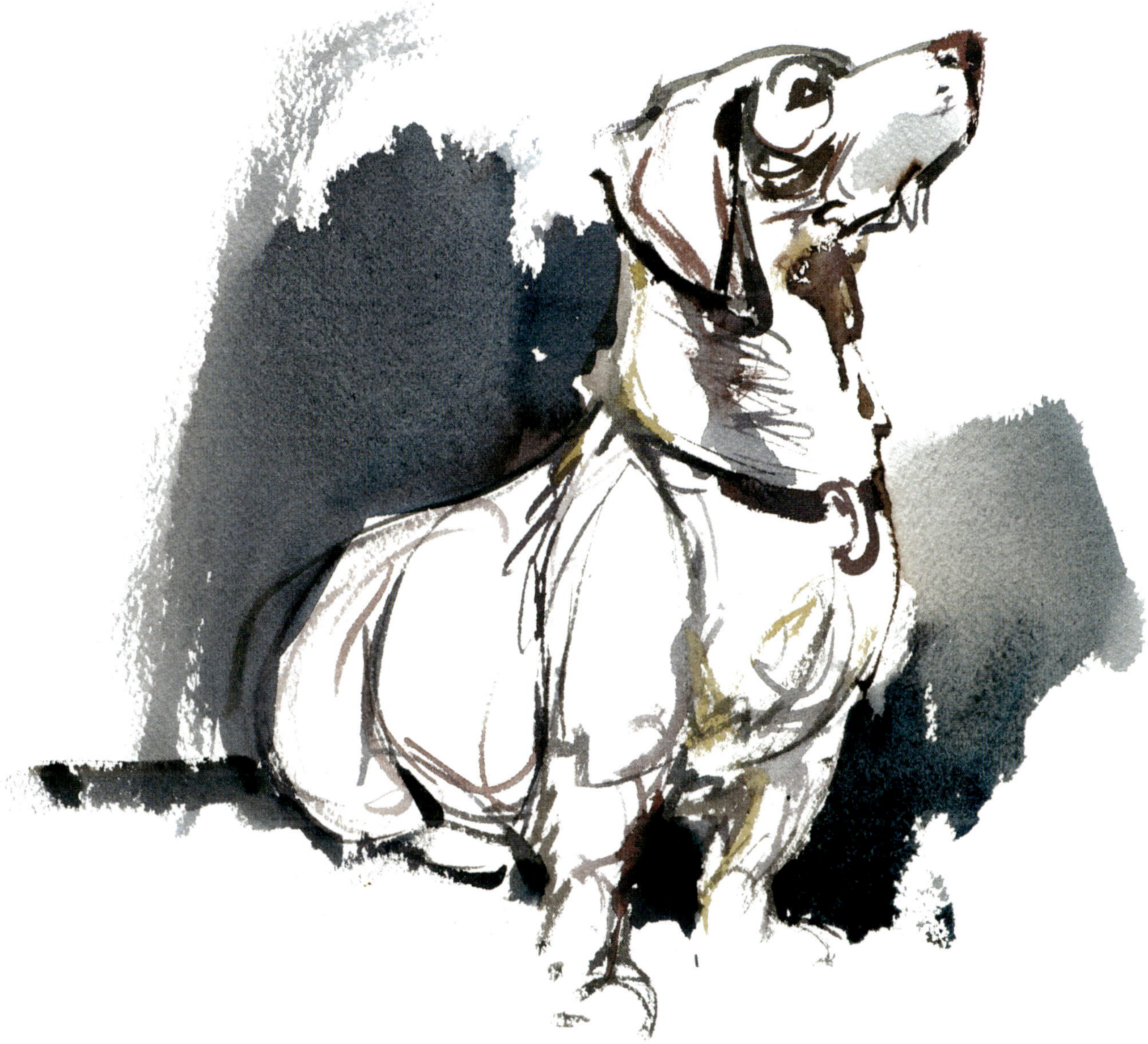

Other versions

Following the same steps, the artist has made several sketches of the little dog in different poses: running, jumping, looking, resting . . . emphasizing in each case the most expressive detail of this animal.

This piece is the most elaborate and detailed of the gallery. When the animals chosen are in resting positions, the sketches can be very detailed and very natural. It is worth observing carefully the position of each brushstroke, which form the grass and the little dog in some very visually pleasing undulations.

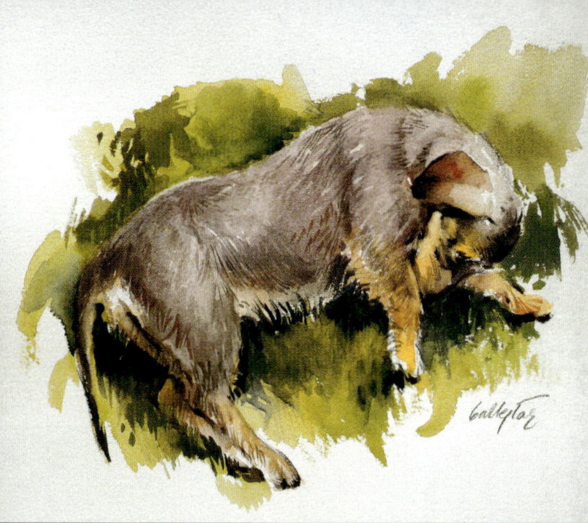

The silhouette of the dog has been executed without a preliminary drawing, painting the background and leaving the area for the mass of the animal unpainted. Then, the basic anatomy of the animal has been defined with a few, well-positioned lines. This watercolor wash maintains its realism and poetic feeling despite the absence of color.

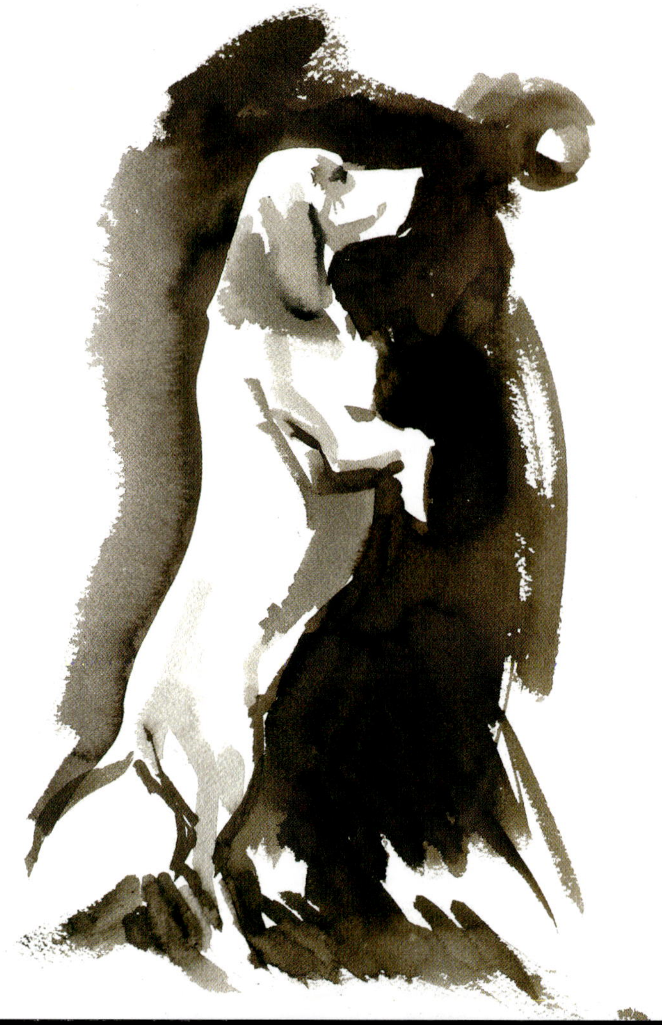

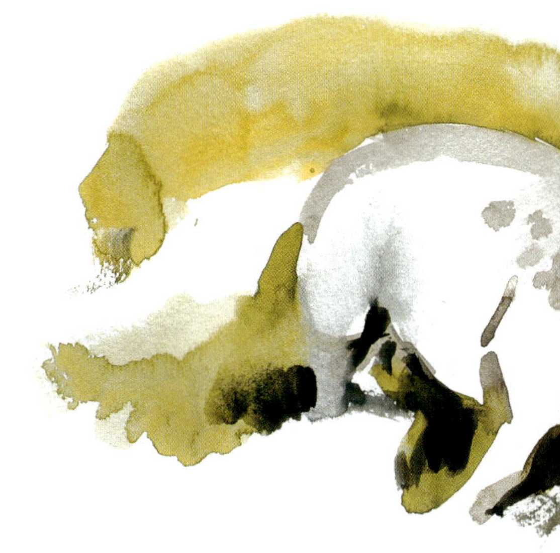

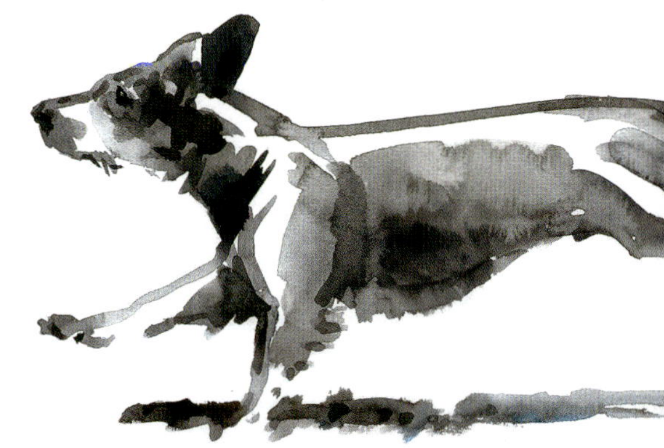

To provide a greater sense of movement to this watercolor, the lines have been applied with quick and decisive brushstrokes without too much thought; the artist is carried away impulsively by the view of the dog as it runs in front of the camera. The back is drawn first, because it is what sets up the subsequent work. A sketch like this would be difficult to execute from life due to the great speed at which the action develops.

In this watercolor the artist has resorted to color instead of line to define the anatomy of the animal in the same pose as on previous pages. Working with areas of color makes it possible to create gradations easily and thus achieve a greater feeling of volume. The color also blends naturally in the wet medium that is created on the paper in such a way that greater textural realism is achieved.

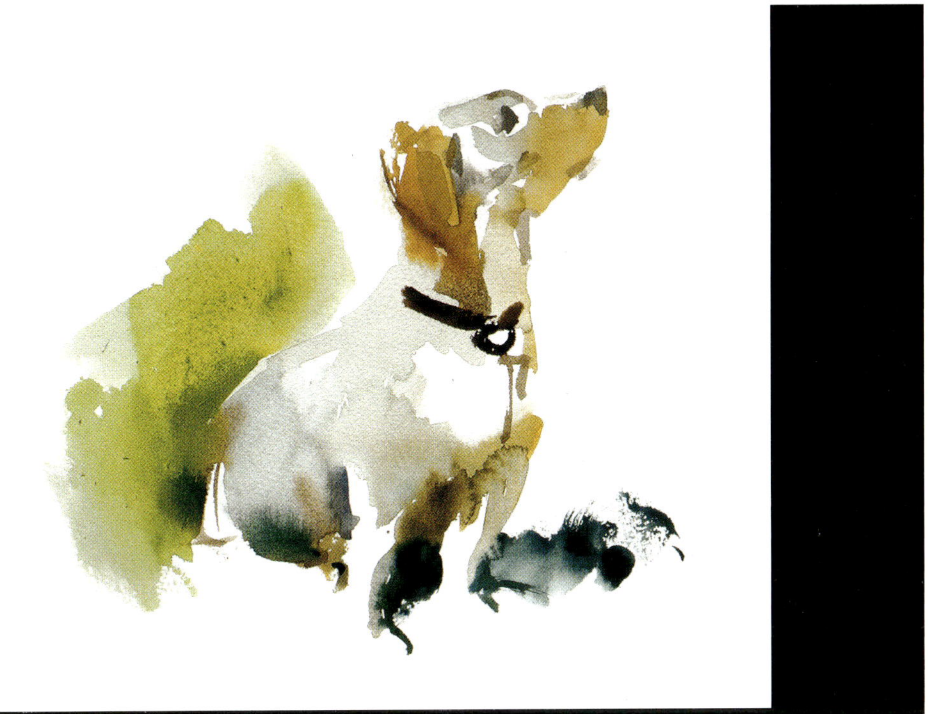

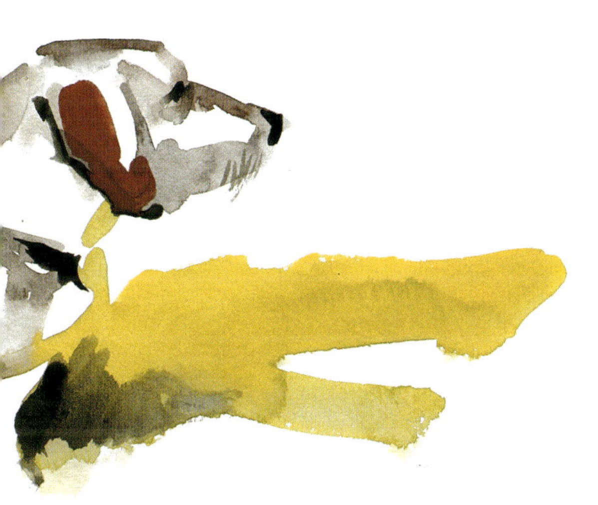

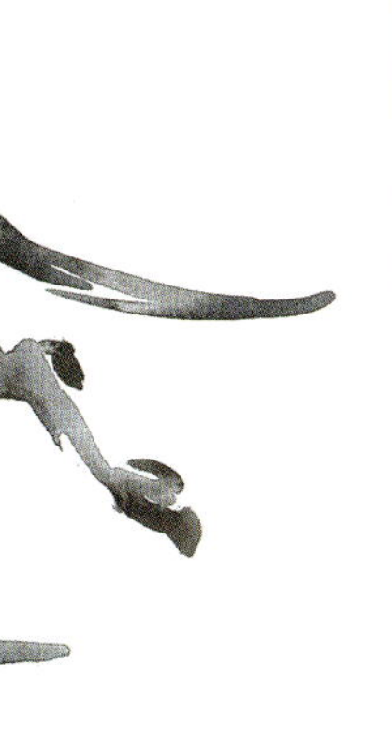

This magnificent watercolor has been executed with a slow brushstroke combining lines and areas of color. It is commendable the way the artist has controlled the intensity of each brushstroke; depending on the charge of color of each line, a different chiaroscuro effect is achieved and some accents are added, like the ear, the collar, and the legs.

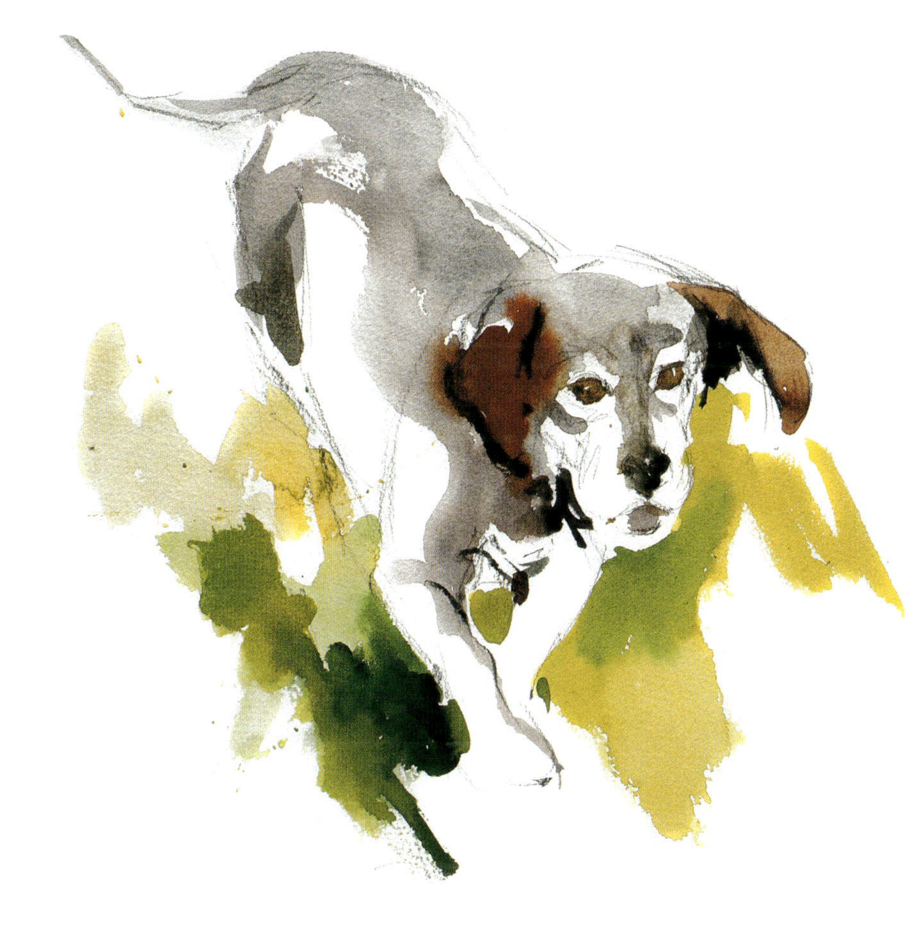

Here, the artist has resorted to the previous pencil drawing to block in and to properly proportion the difficult foreshortening of this pose. Then, each area has been defined in relation to the hair with strokes of gradated color; certain parts of the animal are left unpainted and defined in contrast against the background. The general direction of the brushstroke is diagonal, which provides dynamism to the scene.

New approaches

Other models

To offer a different animal theme, we have chosen a feathered creature. The representation of this stork is not so different from the little dog, since it consists only of applying each brushstroke in the proper direction. On a mammal it is fur, on a bird it is feathers. One of the two washes has been executed according to the anatomy of the bird, the other to the mass that occupies the space.

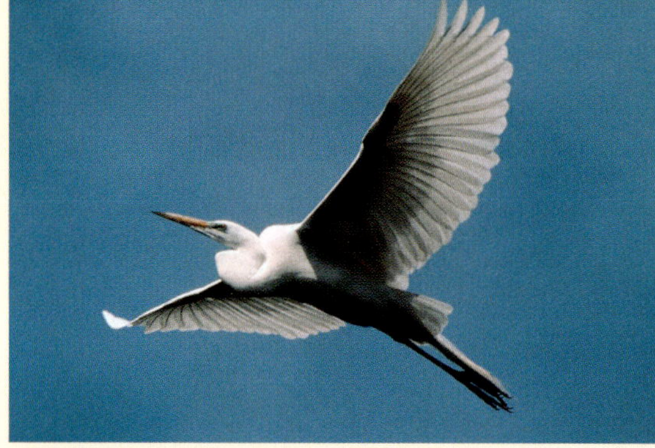

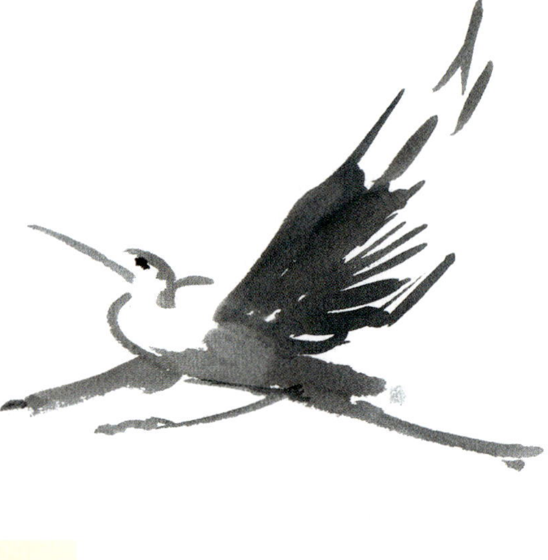

Other media

This time Ballestar has executed the same theme with oils, emphasizing the plasticity of this medium through impastos and blending. The brushstrokes continue to be well defined, as with watercolors, although because there is not as much variety in the brushstroke, the fine lines of the fur are lost. On the other hand, the animal has greater presence due to the volume created with the color mass.

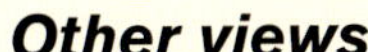

Other views

The painter who devoted the most attention to the representation of the animal world was Franz Marc (1880–1916). For this German painter, who, together with Wassily Kandinsky was a member of the group Der Blaue Reiter (The Blue Rider), animals were more than just a subject for painting; they were the spiritual connection to nature. Although Marc was not interested in the exact description of his models, but rather in the representation of their strength and vitality, his pieces are not lacking in formal accuracy, because his lines were directed by a deep knowledge of the models, fruit of the admiration that he professed for them.

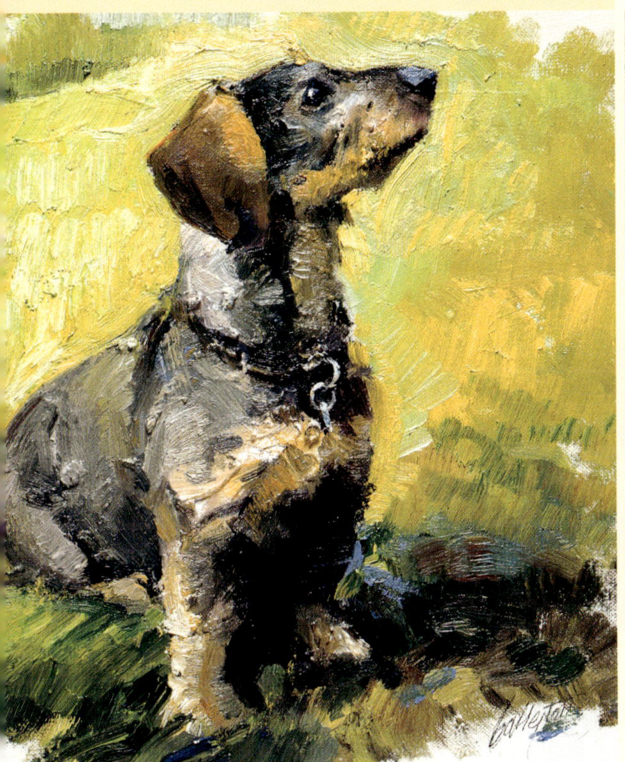

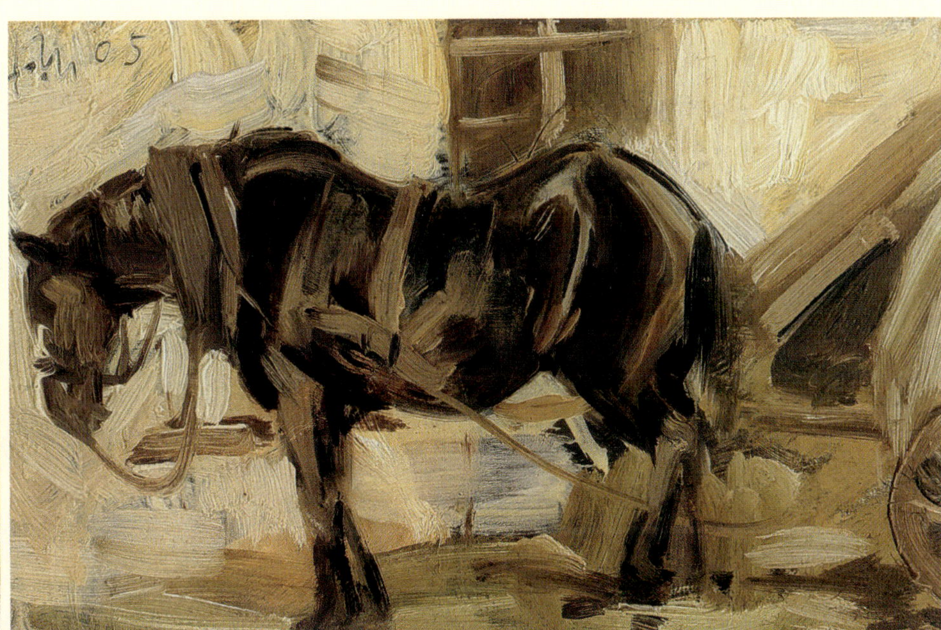

Franz Marc,
Small Study of a Horse II, 1905.
Franz-Marc Museum
(Kochel am See, Germany).

Creative approach 02

Transferred, printed, and marked textures

Robert Rauschenberg (born in 1925) is one of the greatest exponents of twentieth century American painting. An approach that he used very often and that he called "combines" consisted of the transfer of images onto canvas or paper through various printing methods: serigraphy, photosensitive emulsion, photoengraving, cyanotype, even radiography. In this sense, photography is a vital medium in his aesthetic search.

An insatiable curiosity helps him turn technical errors into opportunities for excellent results: inverted and distorted images found by accident when handling inks, printmaking solvents, and water colorants during the transfer and application of effects. During the 1980s, the decade to which *Tanya's Veil* belongs, he transferred photographs of his world travels using solvents and a large serigraphy press. Since 1992, he has been making transfers by scanning, enlarging, and manipulating digitzed images and printing them with an Iris printer (a fine-art inkjet process that uses water-based vegetable colorants).

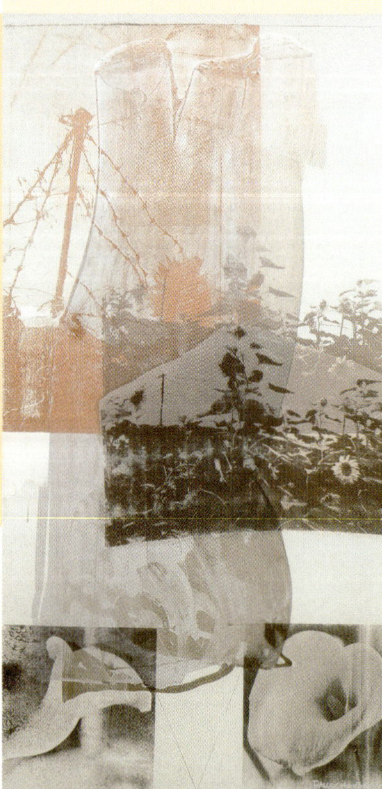

Robert Rauschenberg,
Tanya's Veil (Whale) (Rescue), 1984.
Private collection.

Experimenting with transfers, prints, and frottage *based on plants*

An excellent way of representing natural elements with great realism is to transfer their image through photographs or texture using the technique of *frottage.* In this creative approach, Josep Asunción has worked with the lines that a palm tree leaves on paper if its image is transferred or if we make an impression of its texture.

The techniques used are photocopy transfer and the imprints of textures soaked in colored ink. The result is a suggestive and artistic image that is very realistic, but also enormously creative.

"I was impressed by the obsession that caused my exalted eyes to look at the wood floors, whose cracks had been made deeper by a thousand and one scrubbings. So I decided to investigate the symbolism of that obsession, and with the idea of helping my meditation and hallucination faculties I made a series of drawings of the wood planks, placing over them at random sheets of paper that I rubbed with charcoal. Upon carefully observing the drawings resulting from this … it surprised me to notice the intensification of my visionary capacity and the hallucinatory succession of contradictory images, ones on top of the others."
Max Ernst
Beyond Painting, 1948.

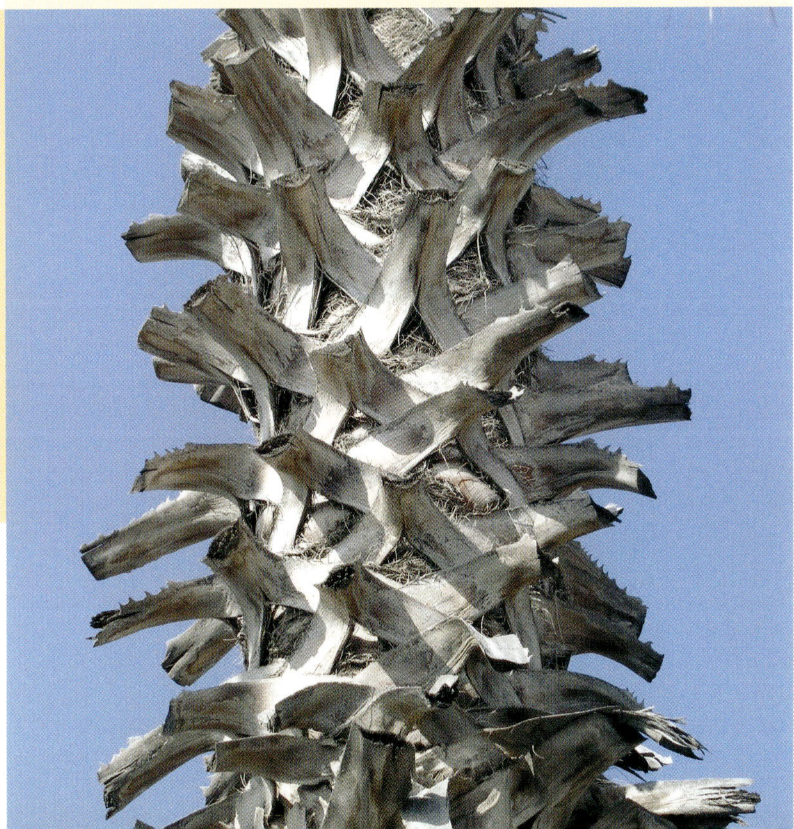

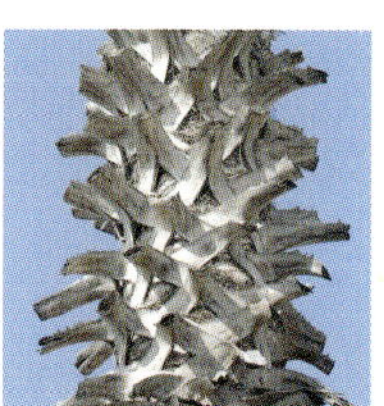

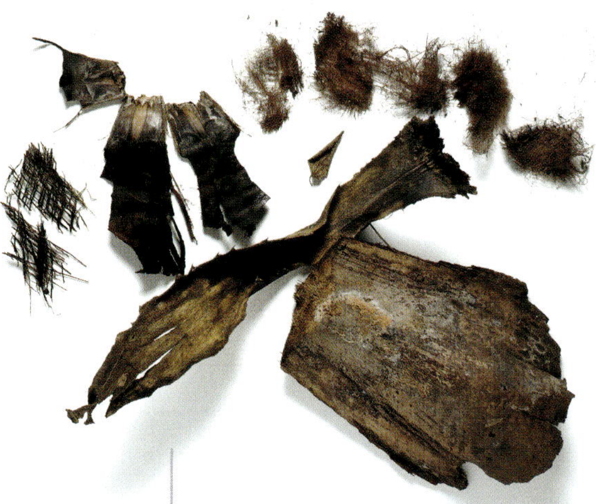

1 We are going to work with two elements from the trunk of the palm tree: pieces of its bark and photographs. The pieces of bark can be used directly as applicators to stamp their prints on the paper. They will also be used later on to experiment with *frottage* as an alternative approach.

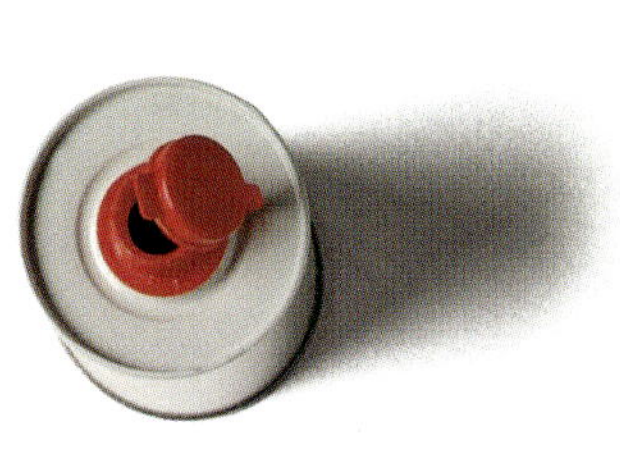

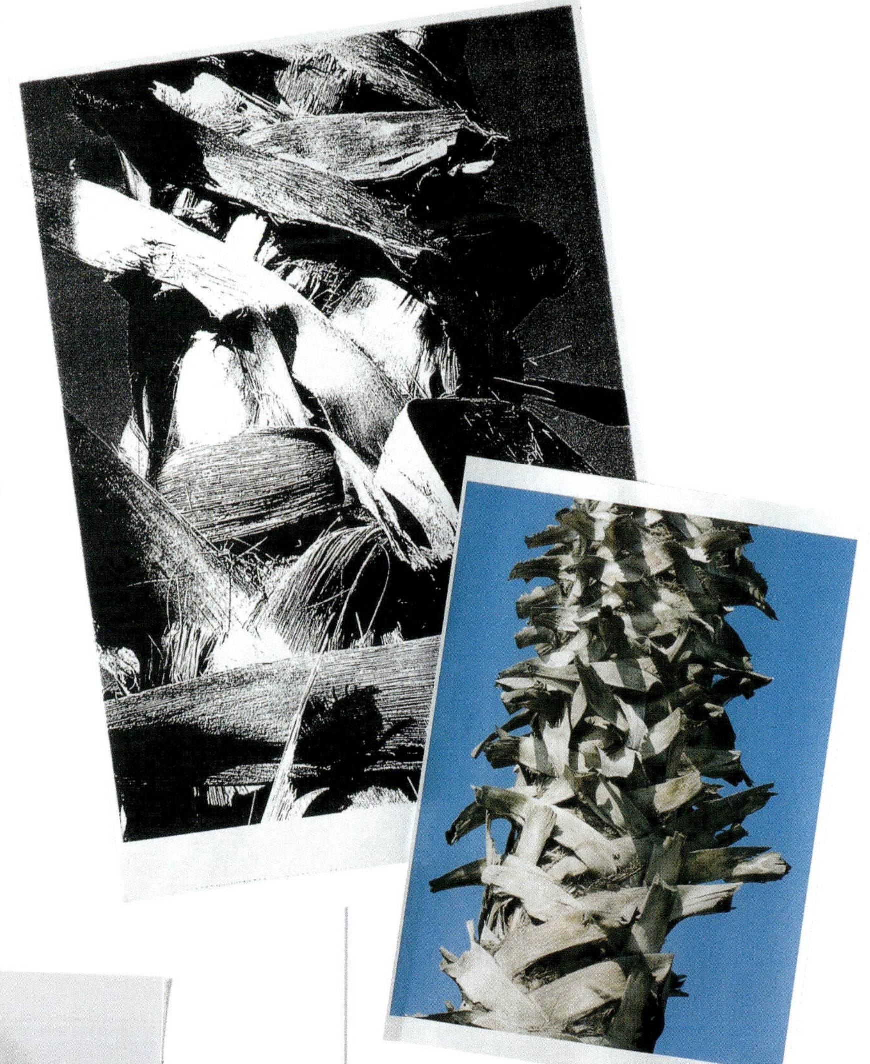

2 There are several techniques for transferring a photograph onto a support. We are going to do a very easy one consisting of transferring a photocopy of it with universal solvent, a substance that dislodges the ink of the photocopy when applied to the reverse of the paper. The first step is to photocopy the photograph and to experiment with its size.

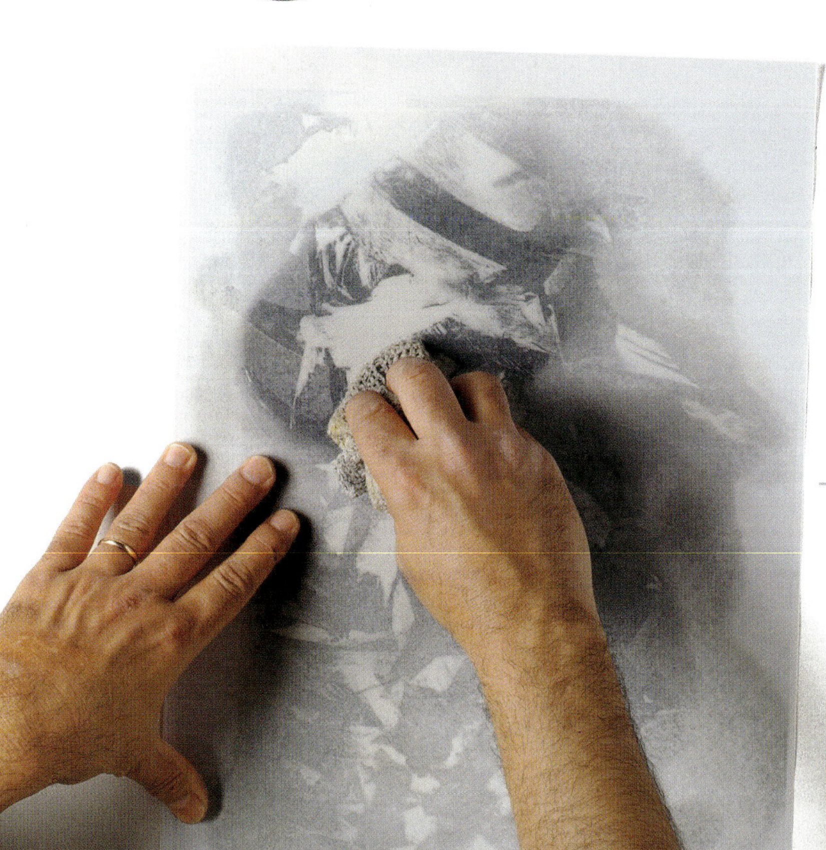

3 To make the transfer, it is recommended that the paper support be glossy, even coated paper. Holding the photocopy firmly in place we rub the reverse with a rag dipped in solvent, although the rag should not be completely wet, since excess solvent could smear the image. This technique should be carried out in a well-ventilated room, and using a mask to avoid inhaling the solvent's vapors.

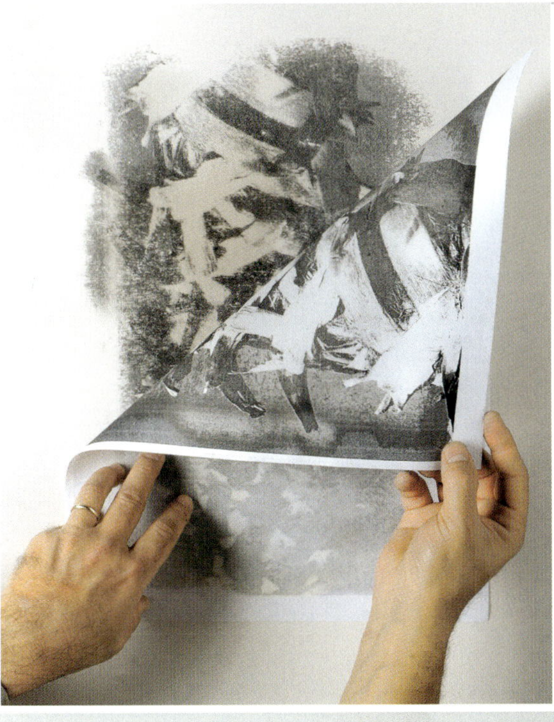

4 We lift the photocopy carefully to avoid disturbing the transferred image if the ink is still very wet. The success of this transfer method depends on the brand of the photocopier (due to the inks that are used) and the paper.

5 Over the transferred image we apply ink with a sponge, and then we create the transfer of the imprints of texture. We soak the pieces of bark with blue ultramarine ink and apply them slowly in a creative way.

6 The final piece has numerous blue and brown marks that combine with the transferred photographic image in a suggestive manner. This way, we achieve a perfect combination of line and real image, the same way that Rauschenberg did.

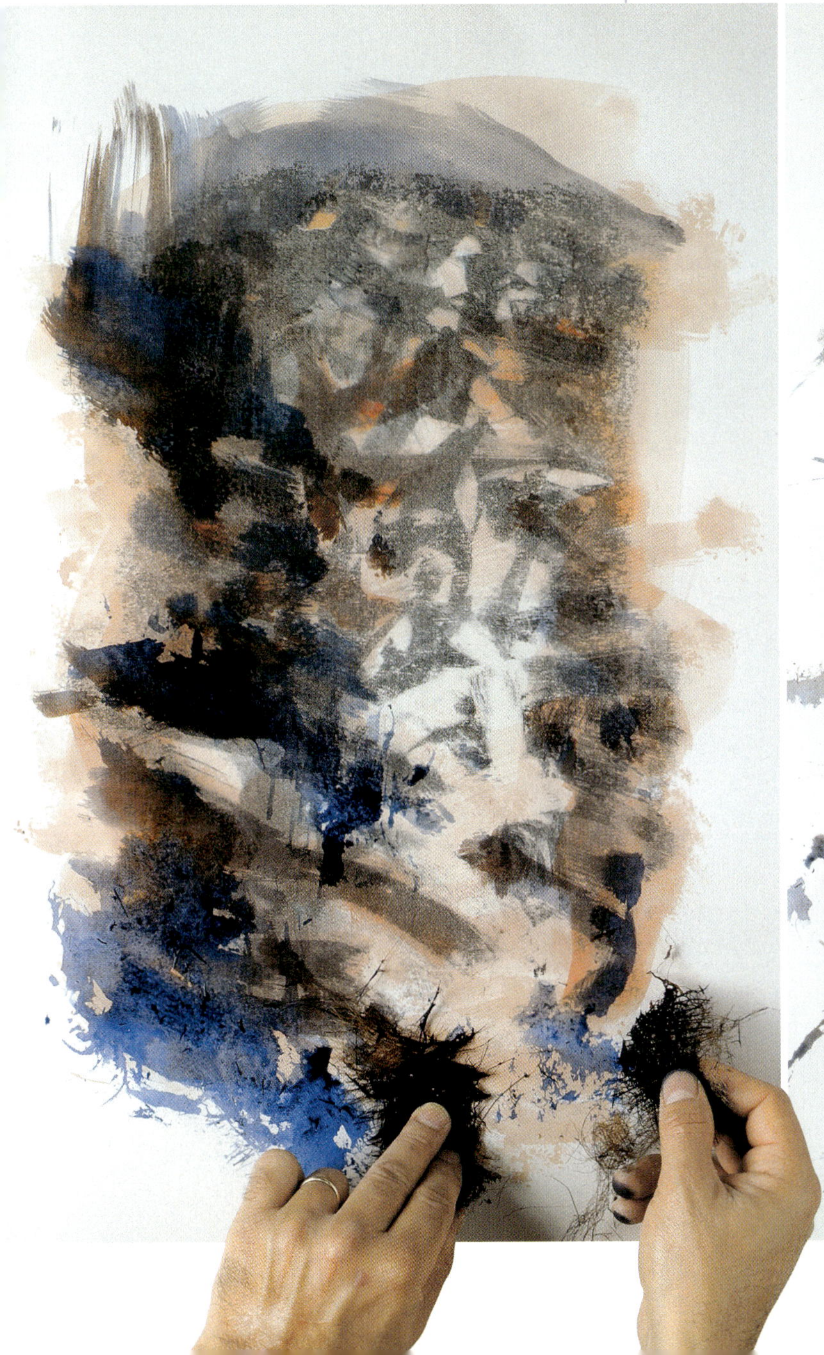

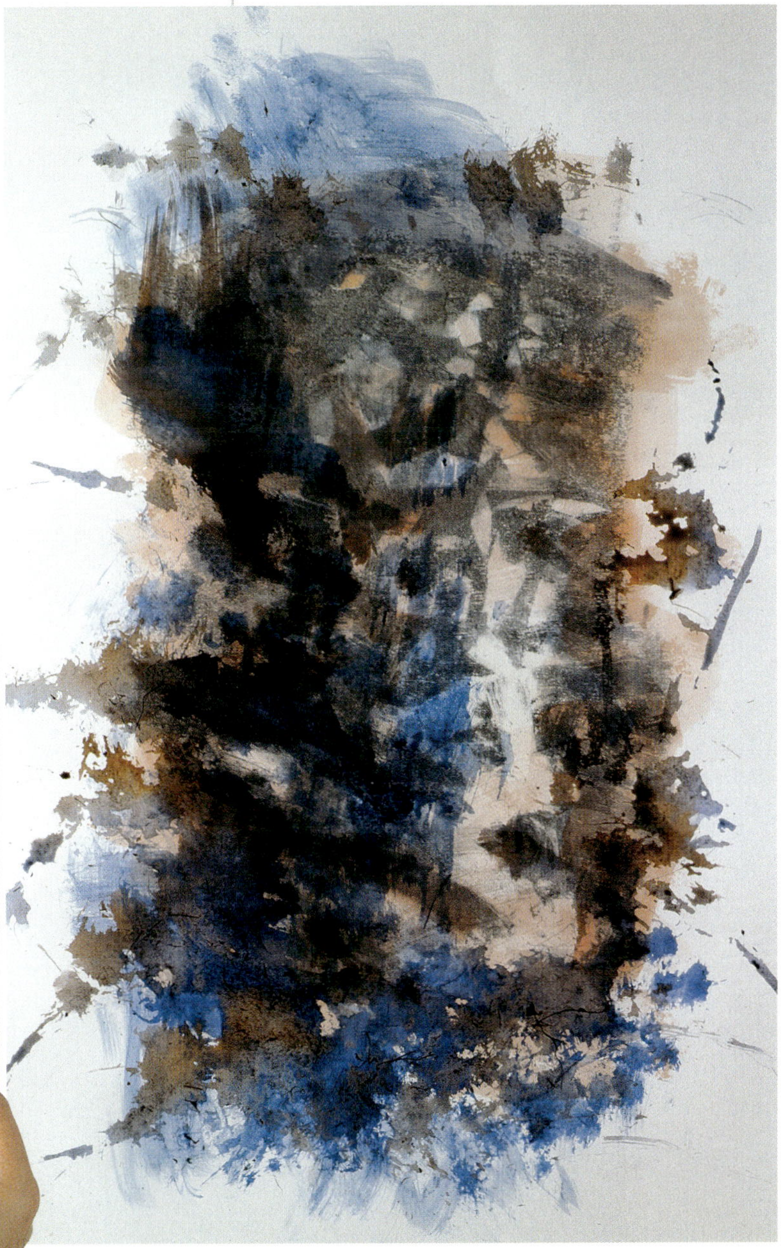

Other versions

By combining the transfer, inks, the print, and papers, the artist has created a rich gallery of different, suggestive approaches that are very appealing visually.

This transfer has undergone two subsequent interventions. First, the image's background was painted with black ink and then gently washed under running water while the ink was still wet. Next, once dry, the second layer of yellow color was applied on the trunk to create a strong chromatic and formal contrast.

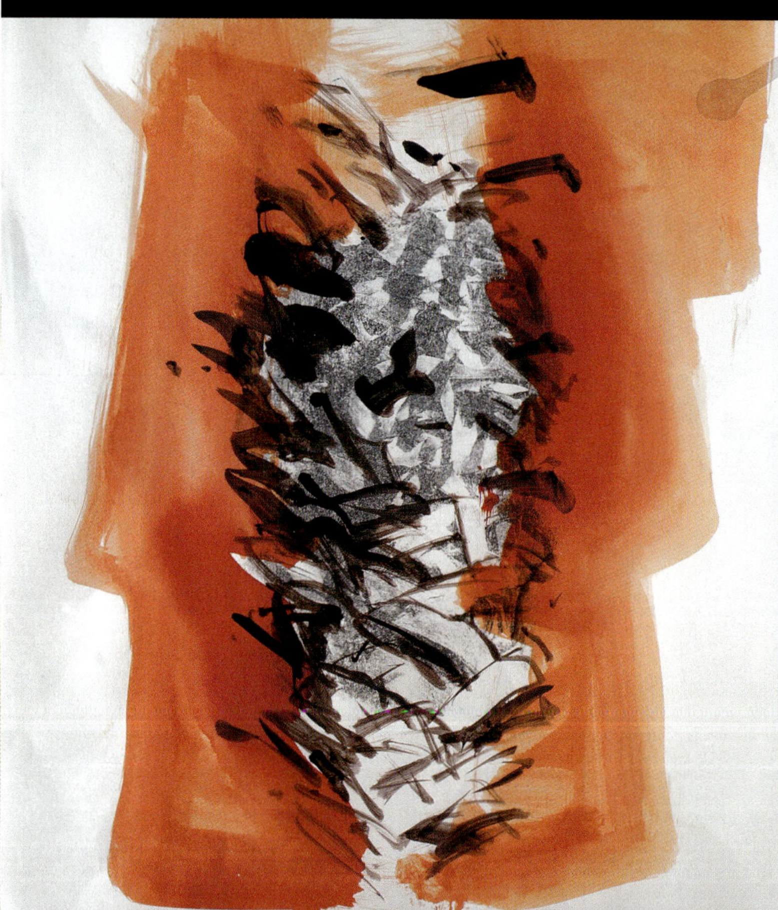

This image contains transfer techniques, but also incorporates a traditional treatment, in that the brushstrokes applied over the transferred image follow the guidelines of a pictorial representation of the palm tree's rhythm.

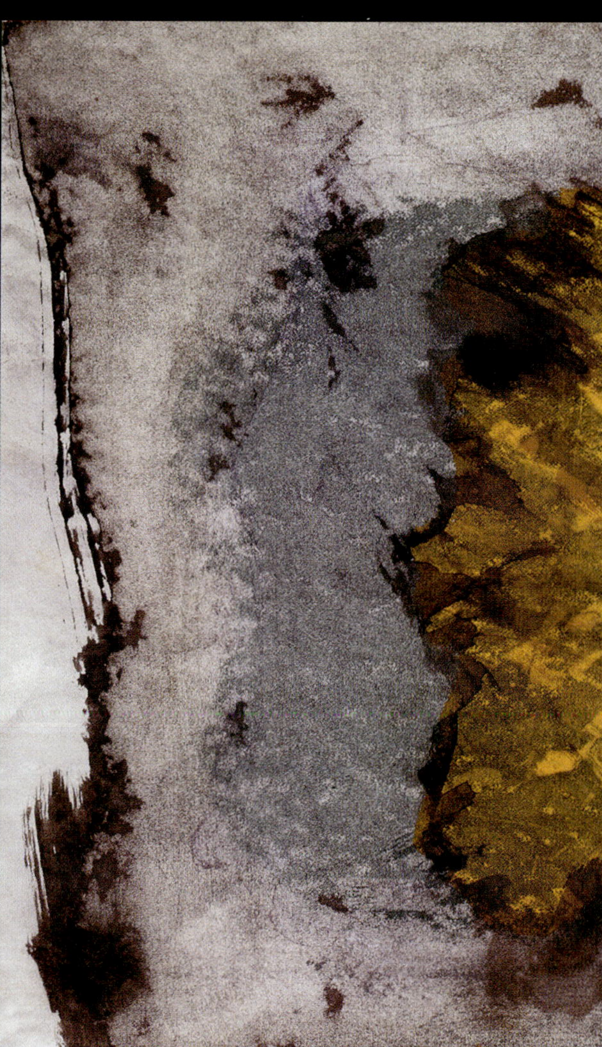

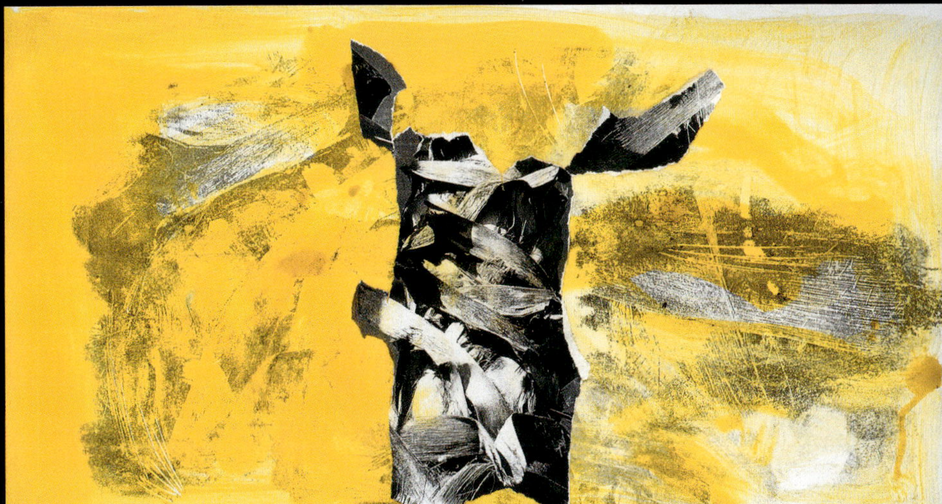

Several photocopies of the photographic image have been transferred onto glossy coated paper, an approach that has created an abstract texture. Next, another transfer made on regular paper has been added, followed by an overall glazing of yellow ink. The result is this unique representation of the theme.

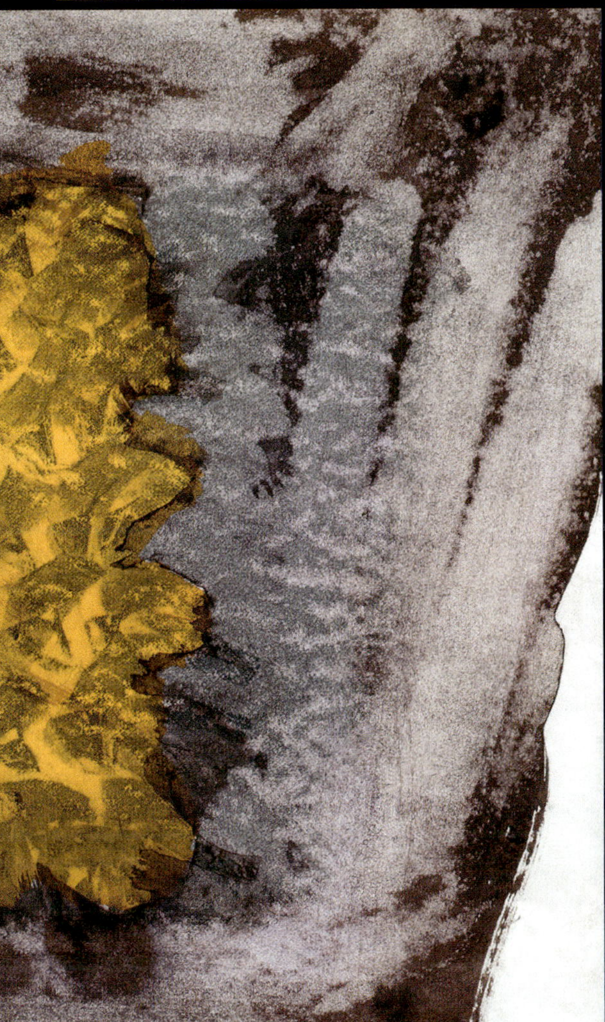

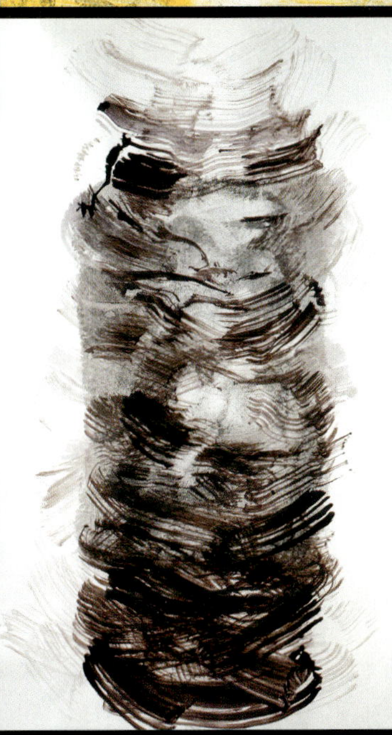

This time, the creative lines that are combined with the transferred image have been applied by dragging a piece of bark soaked in brown ink. The striated effect of the arched bands provides texture.

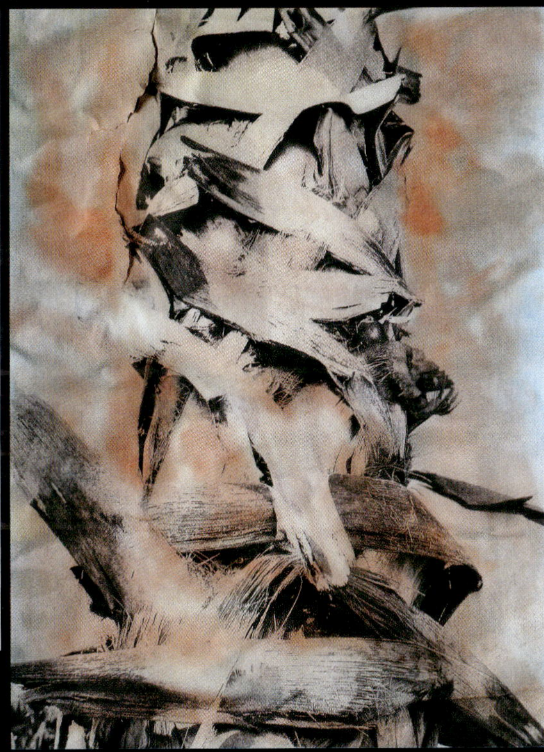

Here, we show how a transfer of a color photocopy is made. The transfer has been placed under running water for a vigorous wash that dilutes the colors and fades the image.

New approaches

Other models

This time, we begin with the image of a water lily; a color photocopy of it is transferred onto a piece of colored construction paper. To emphasize the aquatic nature of the subject, the paint is splattered over the transferred image and heavier brushstrokes of acrylic paint are added in such a way that the transparent areas are alternated with opaque areas.

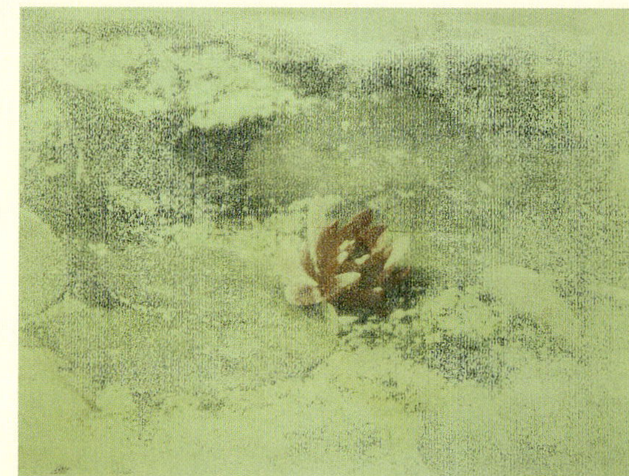

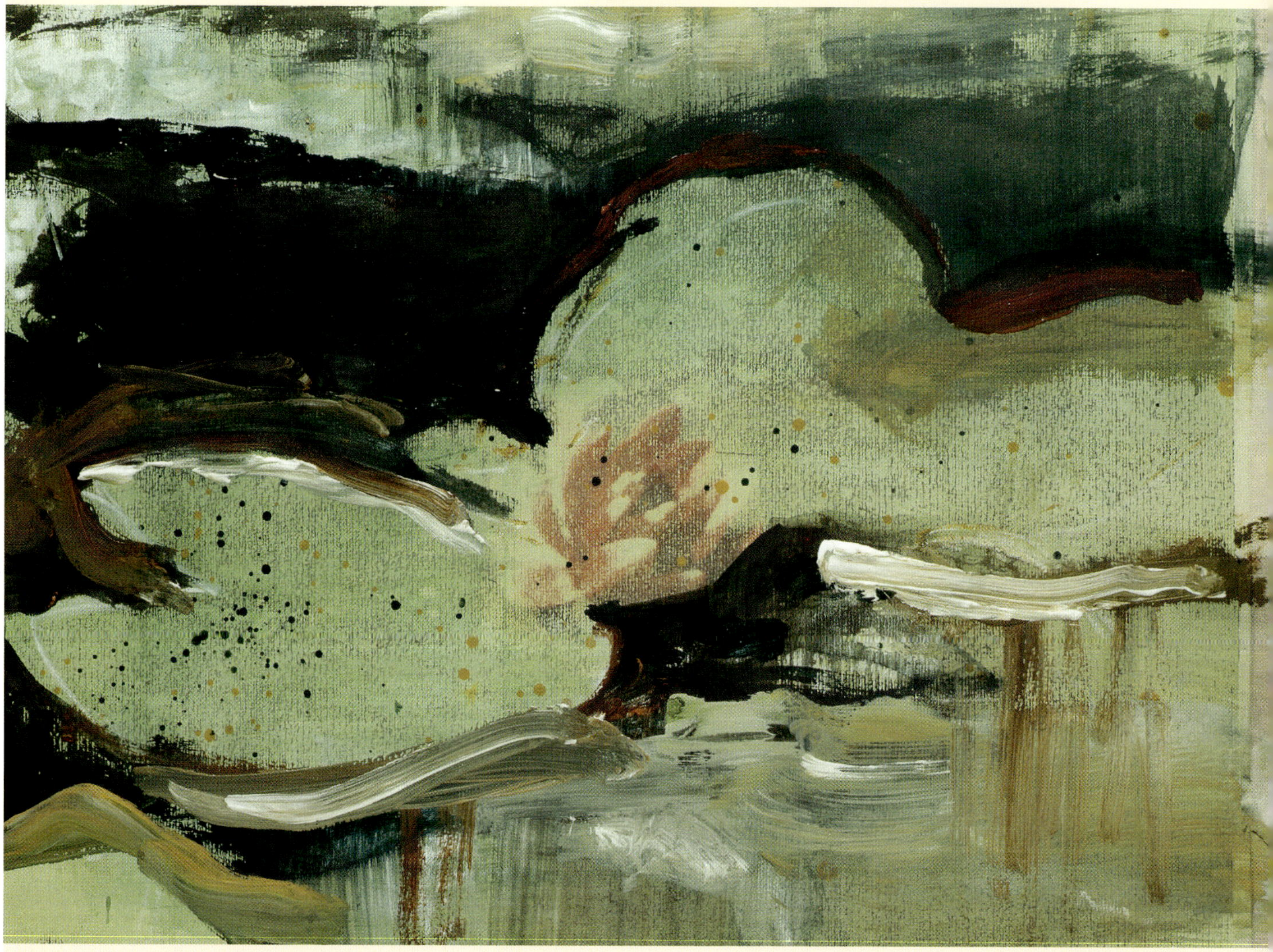

Other media

The alternative medium to photo transfers is *frottage.* The most prominent artist who experimented with this technique was Max Ernst (1891–1976), whose discovery of the method can be read in the quote that opens this section. The *frottage* of the palm tree has been done on lightweight paper using crayons combined with charcoal. The technique is very simple; it consists of placing a piece of paper over some textured object and rubbing it with a pencil, charcoal, pastel, or crayons until the image of its outline comes through.

Other views

Fascinated by the mysteries of nature, Max Ernst was considered the most curious and imaginative painter of the natural world of the twentieth century. His paintings are difficult to categorize, although their surrealist features are the easiest to recognize due to the role of unconsciousness and spirituality in his iconography. His curiosity led him to explore techniques that were little known during his time, making him a pioneer of *frottage,* collage, and dripping. He applied these techniques because he wanted to give his paintings textured effects that were truly fascinating. The painting *Porte Saint-Denis* is a clear example of *frottage,* a technique that produces a faithful imprint of the real object, but that lets you be creative as well due to the texture that is added.

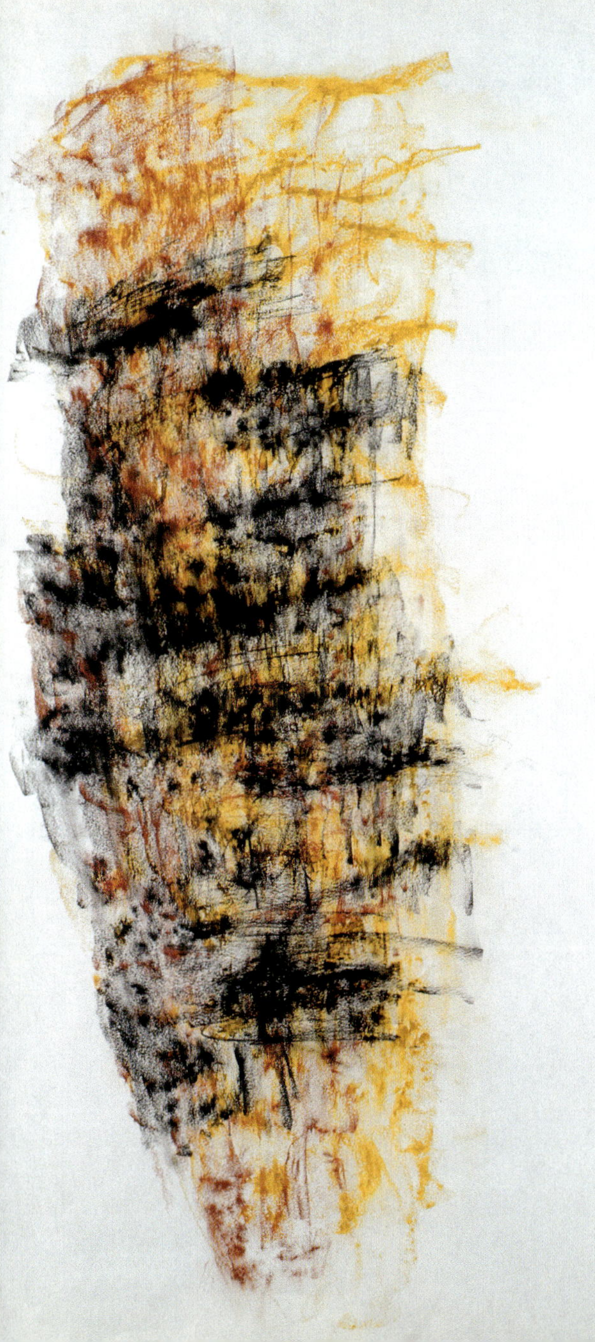

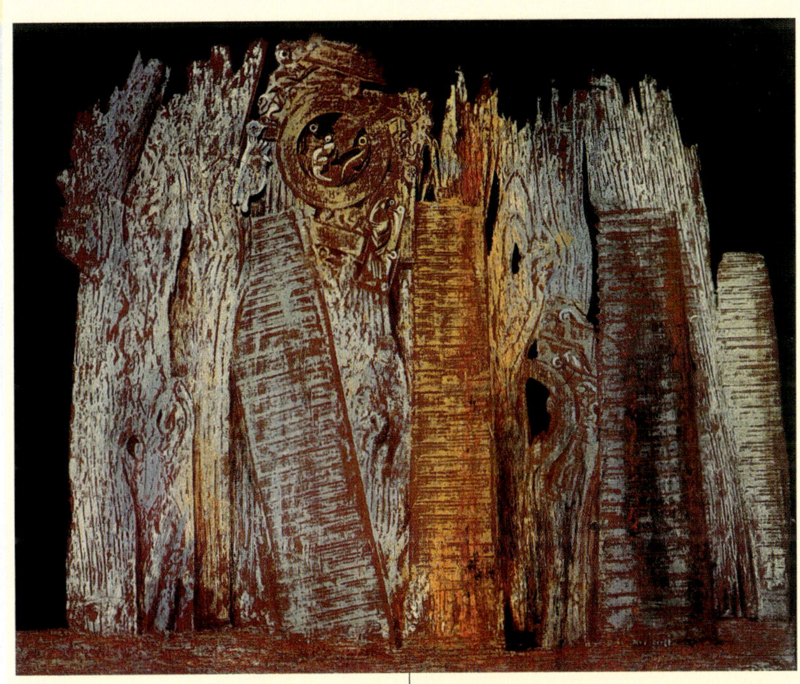

Max Ernst,
Vision Provoked by the Night: Scene of Porte Saint-Denis, 1927.
Private collection.

Light, blended, and airy lines

Creative approach 03

The fascination with undefined edges and diffused spaces without the presence of any lines is a common feature in work by Georgia O'Keeffe (1887–1986). All ninety-eight years of the life of this painter were a declaration of her affinity for aesthetic pleasure. She spent half of her life in the New Mexico desert, fascinated by its light and nature, painting until she started to lose her eyesight, around 1972. A good portion of her work deals with forms of nature in the feminine body, which she often identified with an open flower; her floral paintings have been interpreted as the first fruit of the physical existence of women. Her work is borderline between abstract and figurative, inspired by Kandinsky and by the work of her husband, the photographer and gallery exhibitor Alfred Stieglitz, who was instrumental in acknowledging and spreading her work, a true challenge for a woman of her time. The rounded lines and rhythmic vortexes of paintings like *Two Calla Lilies on Pink*, with soft gradations extending over the entire surface, inspire a musical quality to which she herself referred when she said: "Since I don't know how to sing, I paint."

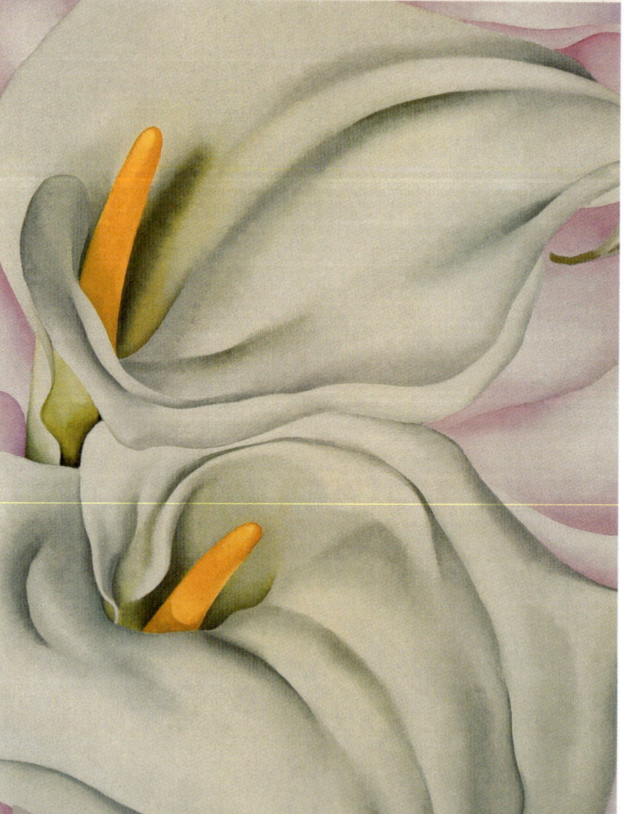

Georgia O'Keeffe, *Two Calla Lilies on Pink*, 1928. Philadelphia Museum of Art (Pennsylvania, United States).

Representing flowers with rubbed and blended lines

In this work, executed by Josep Asunción, the theme of the flower is approached as an element to be experimented with using airy, blended, and diffused lines, especially in the modeling of the petals, which are very soft. Watercolors have been selected as the medium of choice for their plastic effects, which provide a fluid feeling through diluted colors, washes, glazing, juxtaposition of colors, rich contours, and transparency. The support is paper and the applicators are soft ox-hair brushes and sponges.

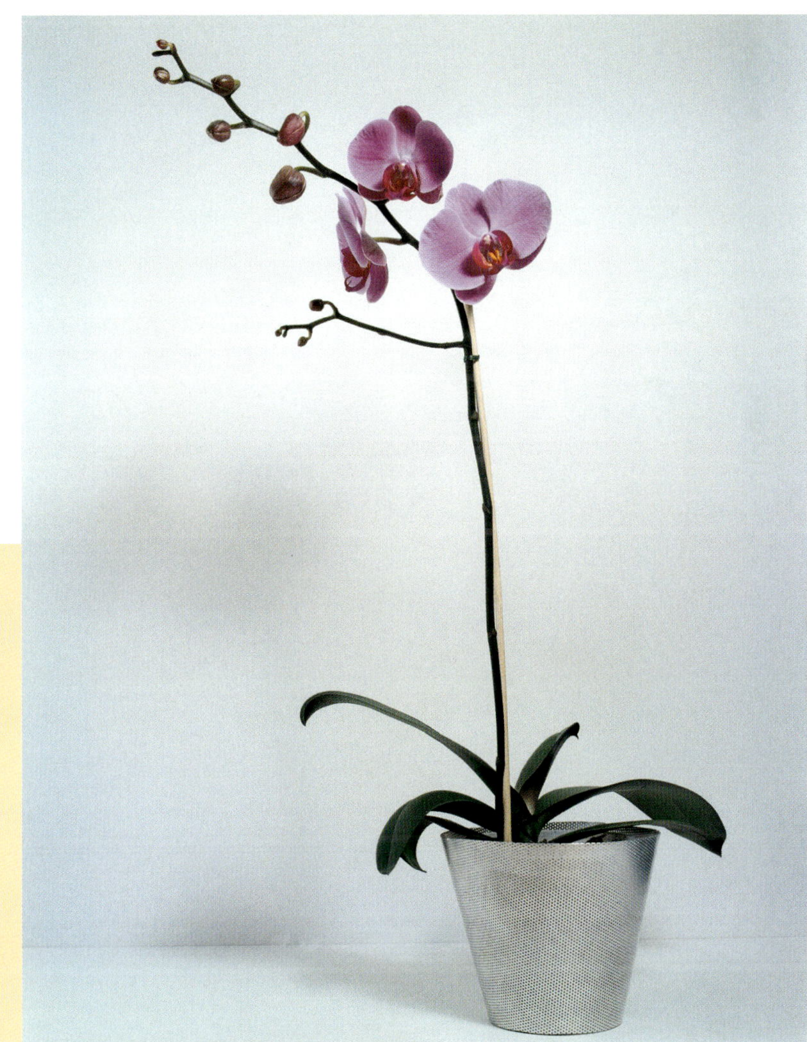

"Most people in cities go hurriedly here and there, they do not have time to look at a flower. I want them to see it, whether they want to or not."
Georgia O'Keeffe

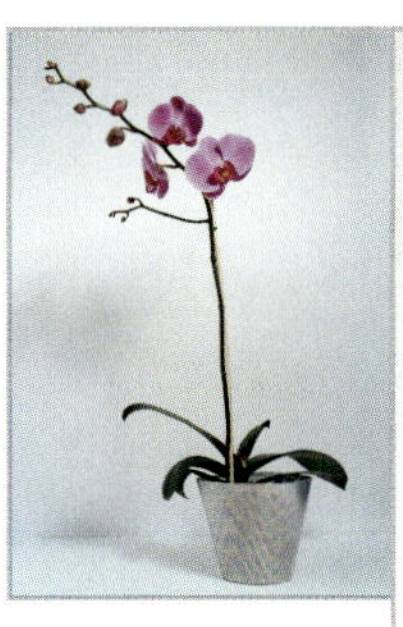

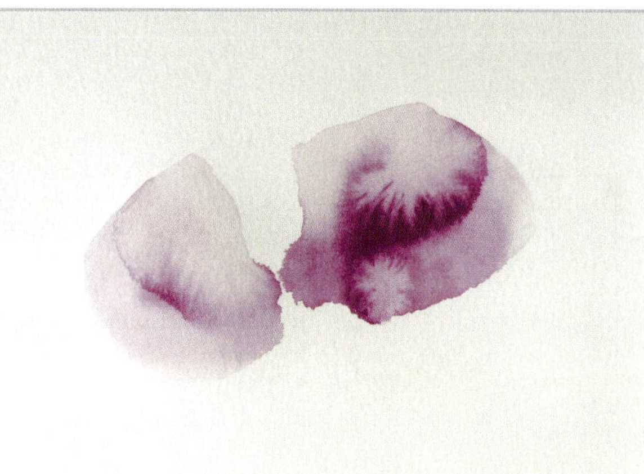

1 With the brush soaked in clean water we define the silhouette of the first petals and then gently apply the color with the brush over those wet areas. This procedure creates soft and suggestive gradations, as long as we do not overdo the color or spread it with the brush over the entire initial area.

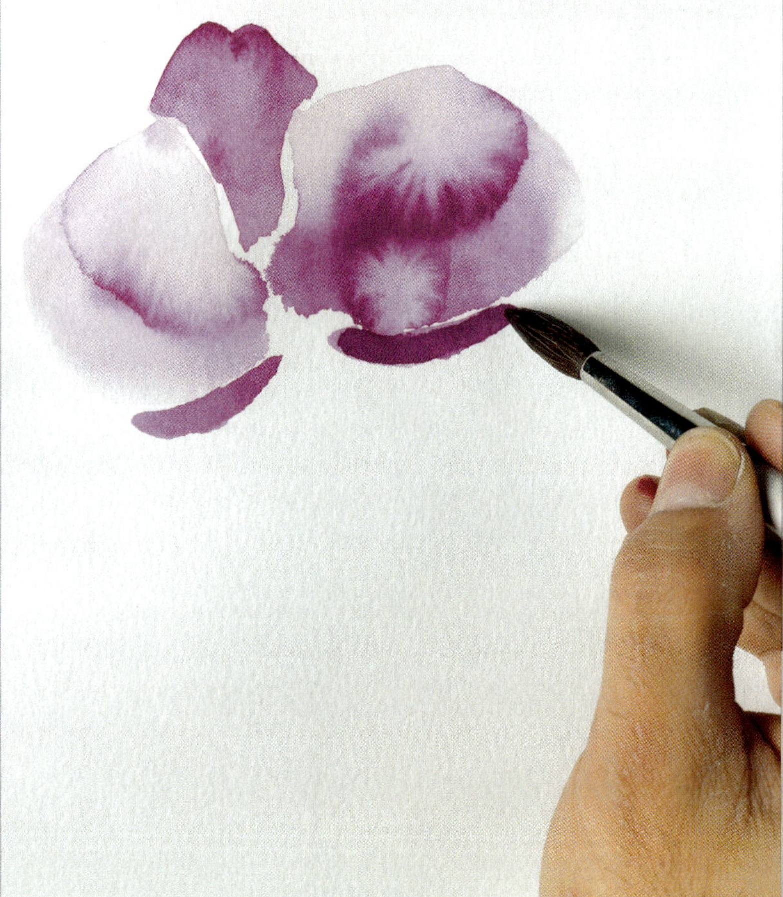

2 We construct the other petals of the flower, trying not to overdo this approach, to create a variety of effects.

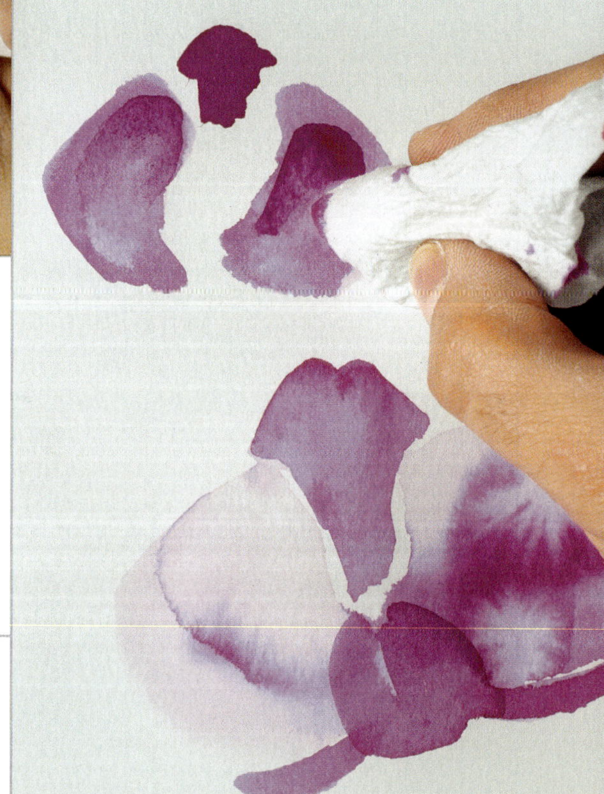

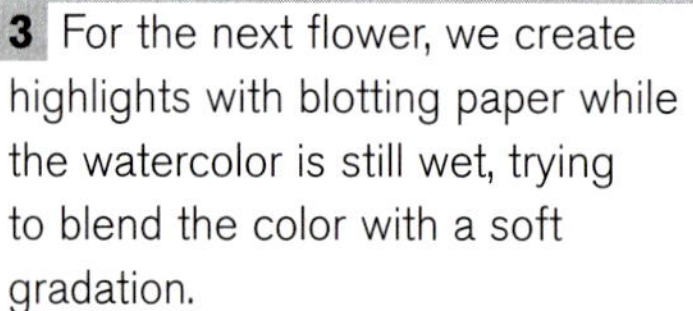

3 For the next flower, we create highlights with blotting paper while the watercolor is still wet, trying to blend the color with a soft gradation.

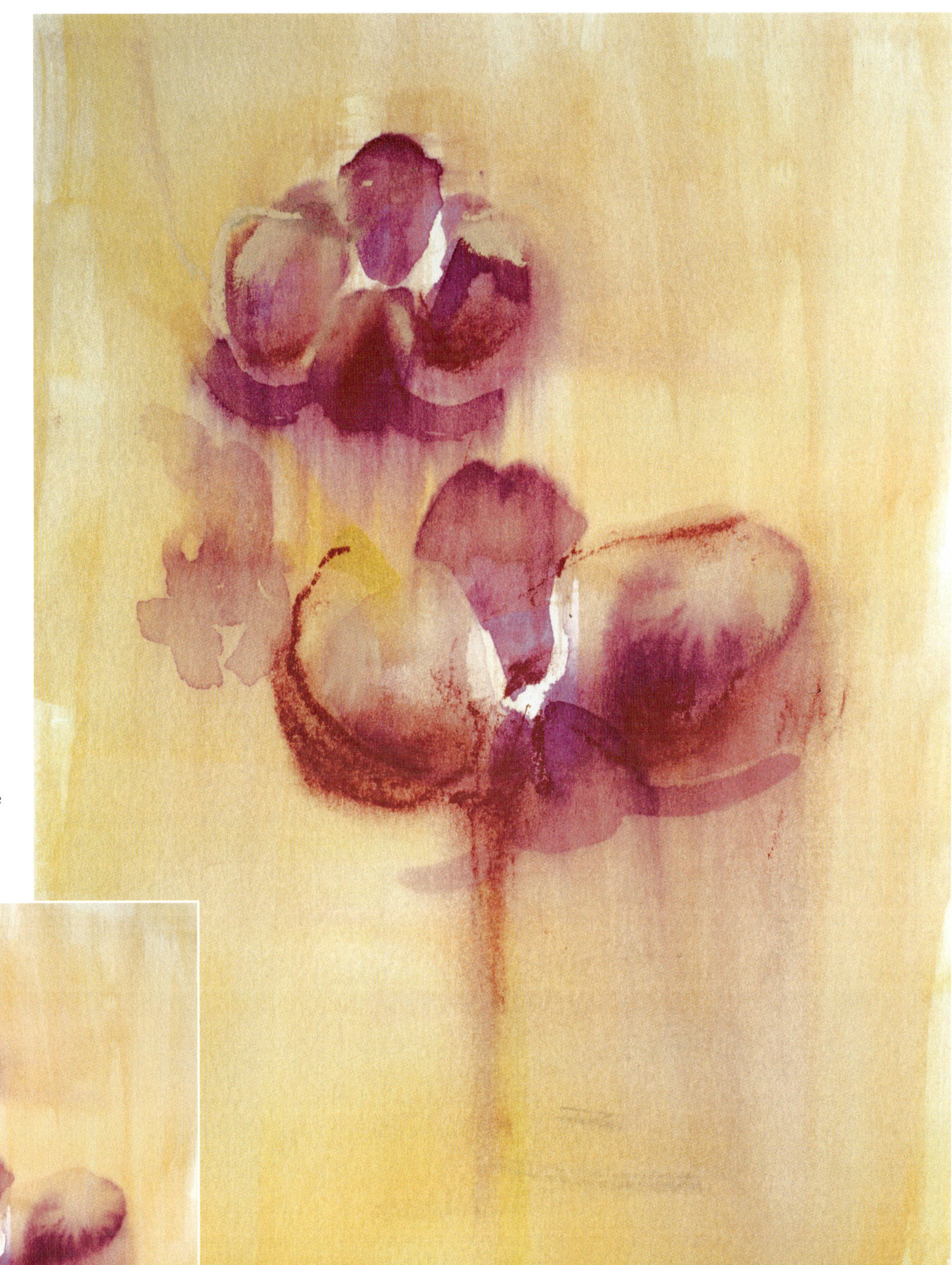

4 A very diluted third flower serves to create different planes on the watercolor. A different-color glaze applied over the entire piece with a sponge gives the painting an atmospheric feeling of warm, soft light. We leave the centers of the flowers that are located in the foreground and middle ground unpainted to represent highlights.

5 We finish the work with lines of carmine color, carefully applying them over the areas whose color we want to emphasize. These lines are drawn with watercolor pencils, a medium similar to crayon and oil sticks.

Other versions

In this gallery we experiment with watercolor in search of airy, diffused, and soft effects to emphasize the sensuality and delicate feeling of the orchid's petals. In some cases, graphite is also used to create elements of tension and to make the work vibrate.

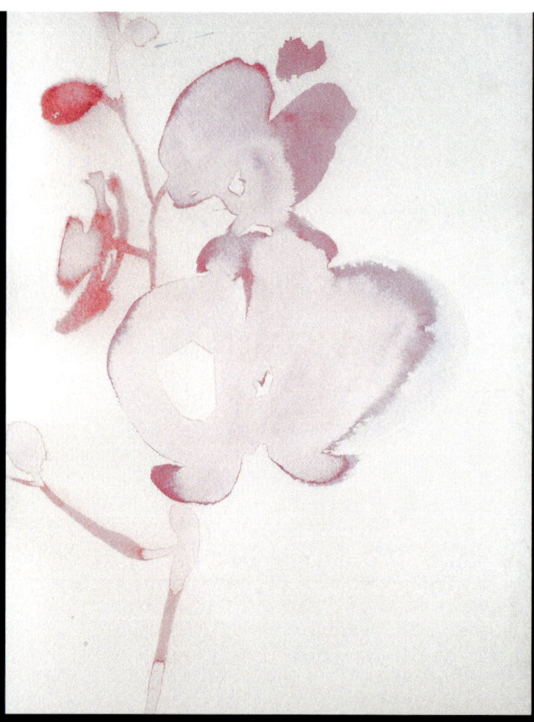

This is the image resulting from a wash applied over a watercolor that is still wet. The piece was placed under running water until a certain amount of color, depending on the airiness desired, was washed off.

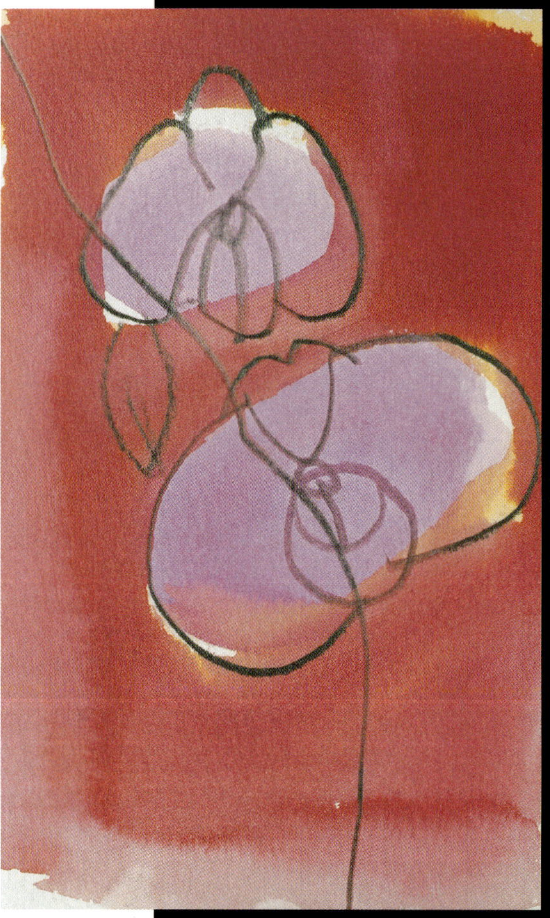

In this watercolor, a flat and transparent stroke is combined with the radical and hard line of graphite in stick form. The line, drawn decisively, contrasts with the flowing nature of watercolors, emphasizing their liquid, immaterial appearance.

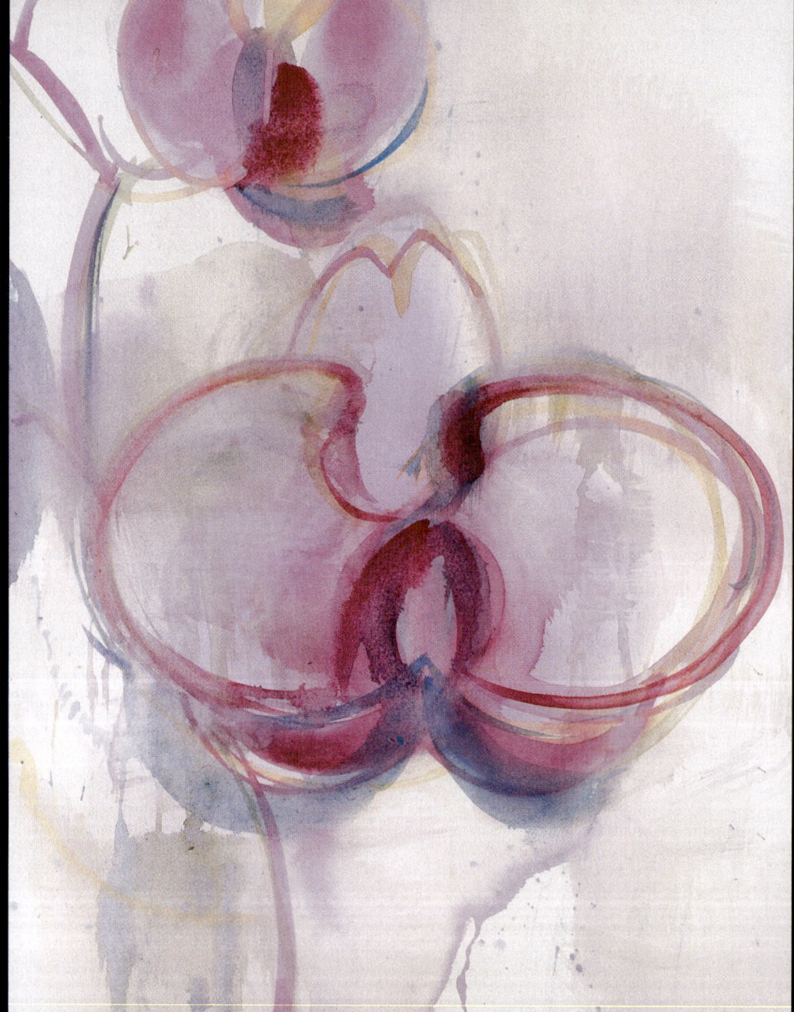

By using sinuous and quick brushstrokes over areas of very diluted color, we have achieved a fluid feeling and very clear transparency. The color of the background was achieved by moving the sheet of paper, which created interesting forms produced by the paint running off in different directions.

This is the most atmospheric watercolor of the gallery. It has been worked entirely with a sponge, observing the drying times. To avoid a completely dissolved look and to preserve areas of blended, although not uniform, color, most of the work has been executed on wet—however, not soaking wet—paper.

In this watercolor the effect of softness has been achieved by applying different amounts of pressure on the sponge. While the preliminary brushstroke was still wet, we changed its appearance by manipulating it with a sponge, removing or redistributing the color. Finally, using a cotton rag we created some highlights by redrawing the petals using hand motions.

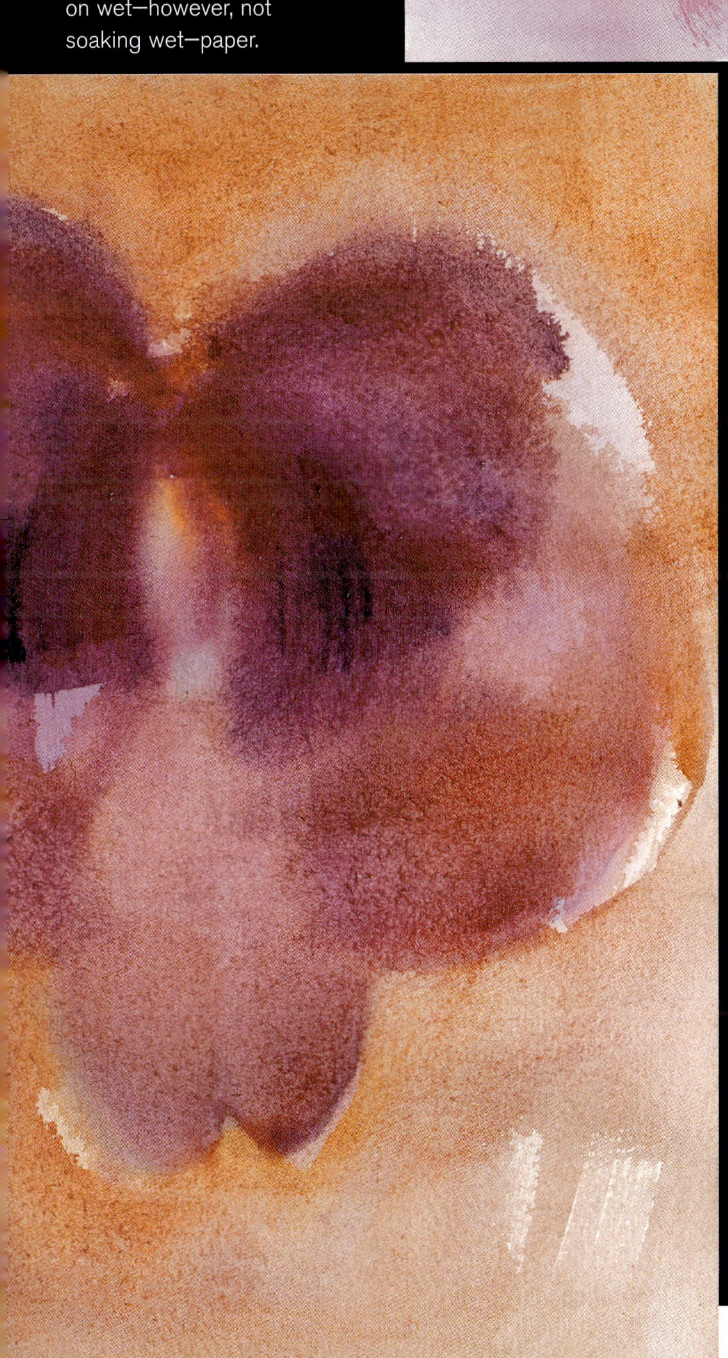

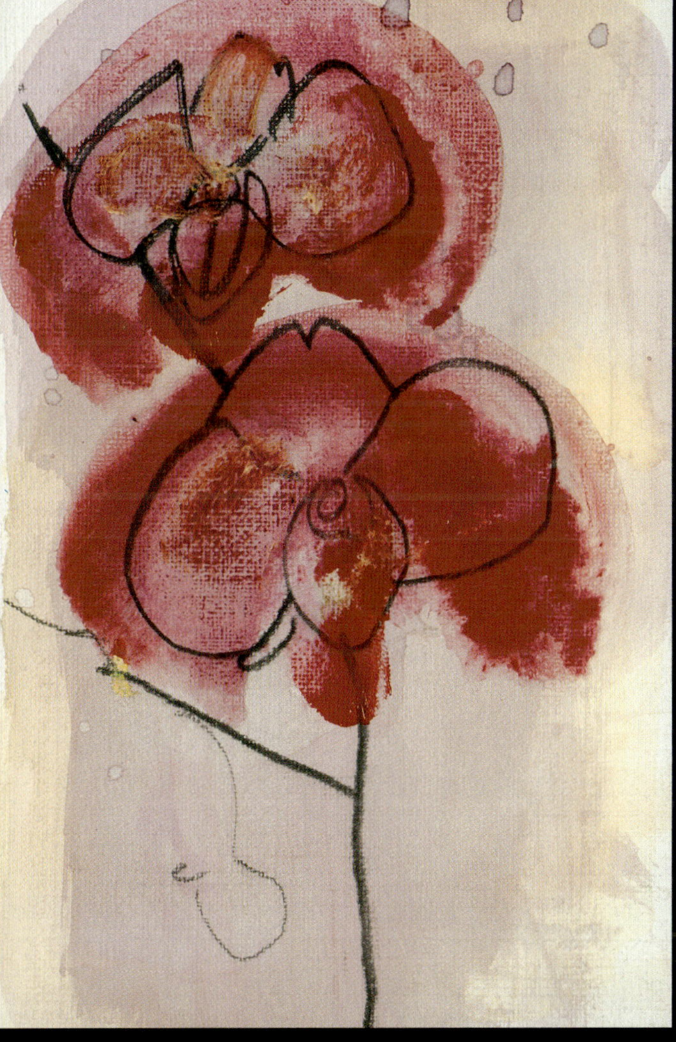

This representation results from the combination of various techniques: gradation, wash, paint, and lines with graphite. The final effect is rich in contrasts due to the combination of densities and transparencies.

New approaches

Other models

As an alternative to the project, the artist has chosen another flower with more volume than the orchid. This time, several different watercolors have been made. In one of them, a transparent effect has been emphasized by applying color in such a way that the different layers do not overlap, thus showing the intermediate areas; the layers have been allowed to dry to prevent them from mixing. In the other, the background has been painted by reserving an area to describe the flower in a very immaterial way with thin lines of liquid watercolor drawn with a reed pen and traces of gently applied watercolor pencil.

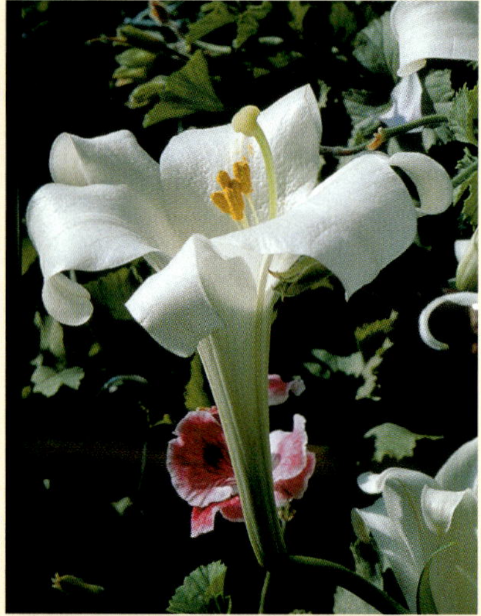

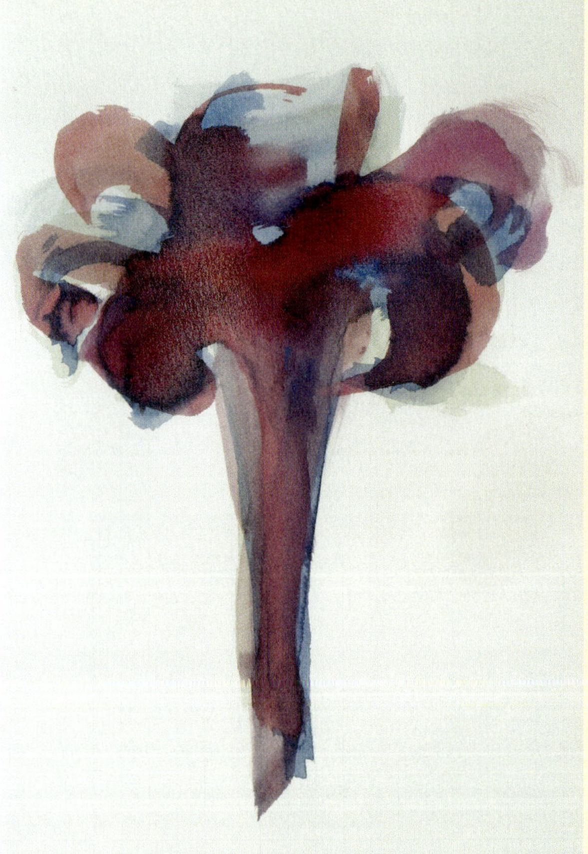

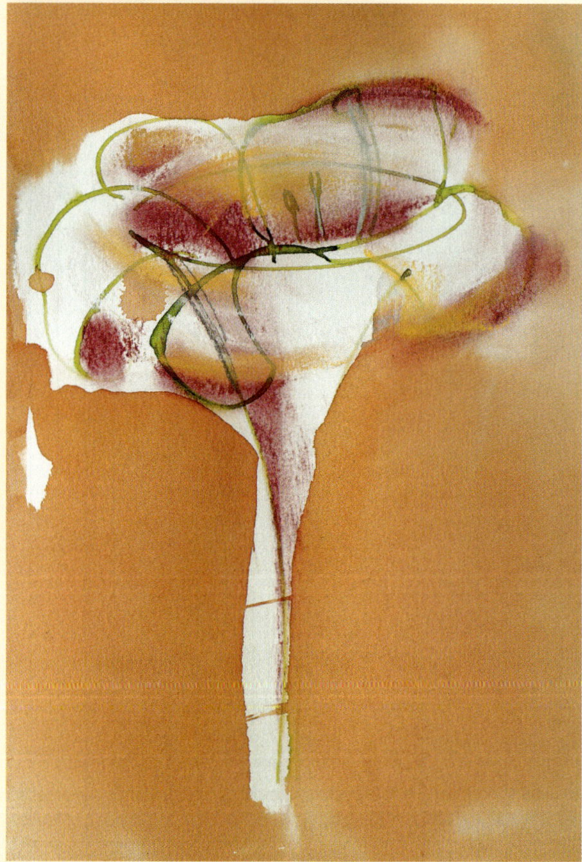

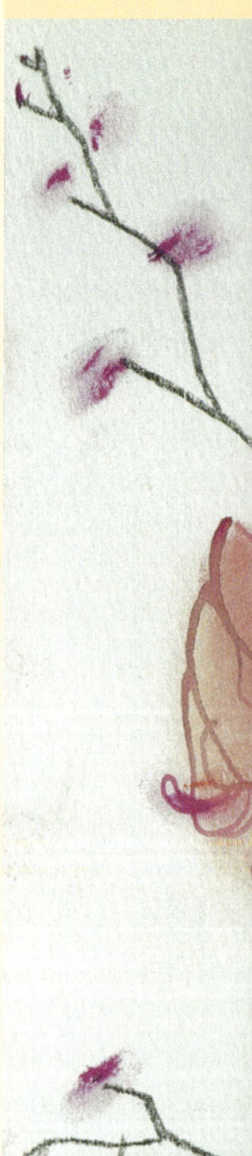

Other media

Pastels are the most suitable dry medium to create airy and soft effects due to their fine pigments, which produce very soft colors when blended with a cotton ball. To create tension in that softness, the painter made thin lines over it with graphite and liquid watercolor applied with a reed pen.

Other views

Let us look at a work by Maria Vladimorovna Ender (1897–1942), a Russian artist who actively participated in the Russian avant-garde movement of the beginning of the twenieth century, just before the Soviet Revolution. She taught art in the old city of Leningrad, where she specialized in the visual perception of form and color applied to architecture. Her work is extremely delicate and of great beauty. She was part of a group of Leningrad artists who explored the possibilities of nonobjective art. The watercolor that we see here shows an organic theme, but in reality it is borderline between abstract and figurative.

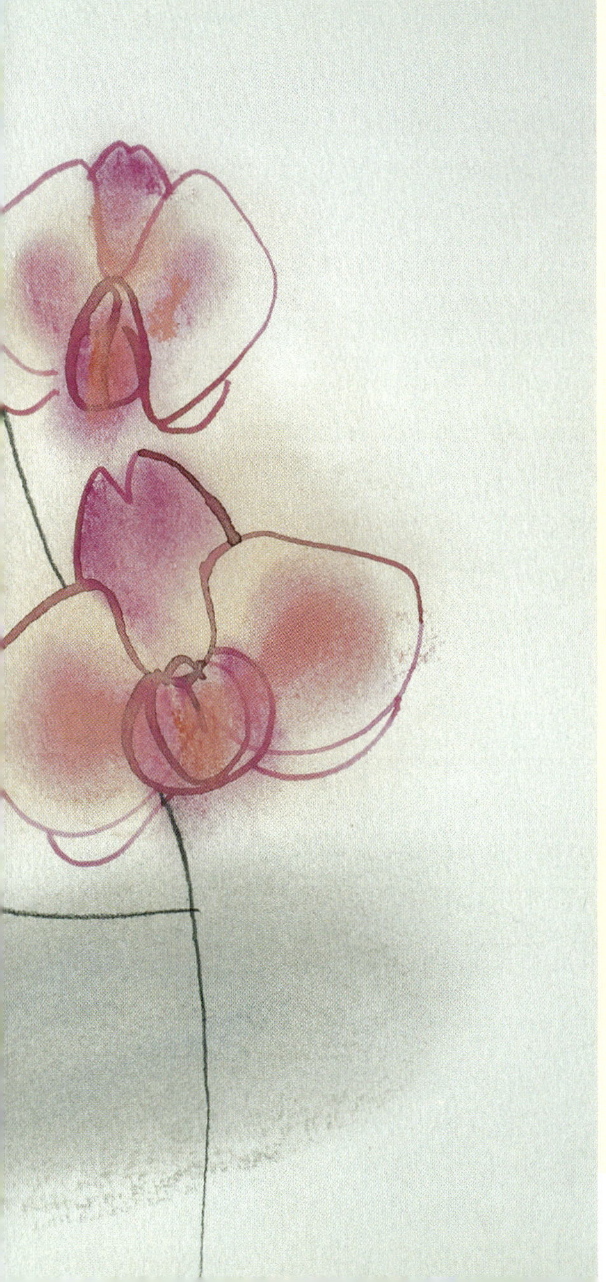

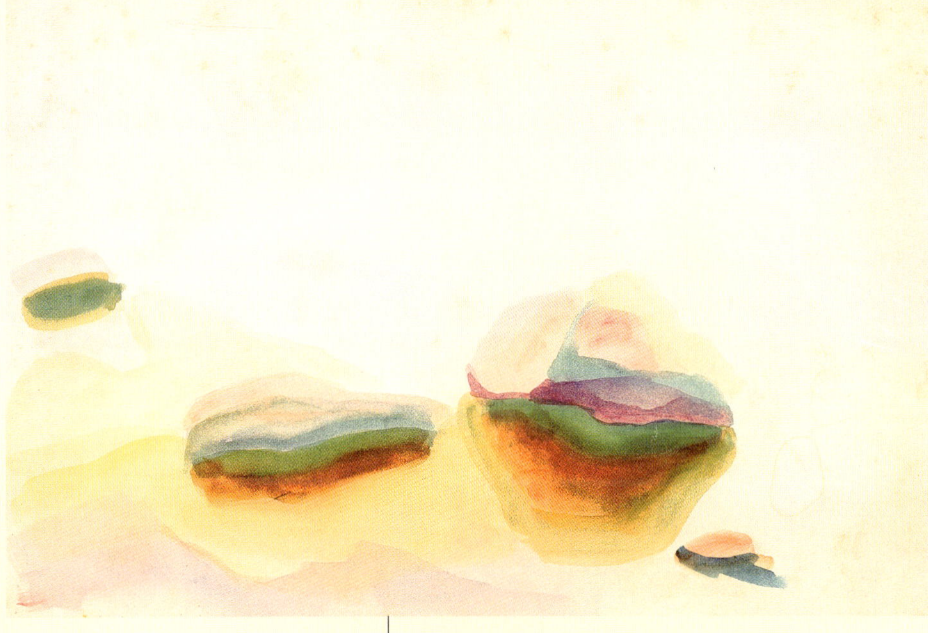

Maria Vladimorovna Ender,
Untitled, undated.
Private collection.

Still life, from its origins as a genre, has been used by the painter to experiment with his or her own language, without any intention of communicating important messages. It is often taken as an excuse to try out lines, strokes, contrasts, compositions, color palettes . . . to search for a personal hallmark, the same way a person looks at himself in a mirror for identity. Three line projects are presented in this chapter, related to resources that define objects and atmospheres: graphic lines, crosshatching (between line and stroke), and areas of color without edges, in *sfumato*.

Line in

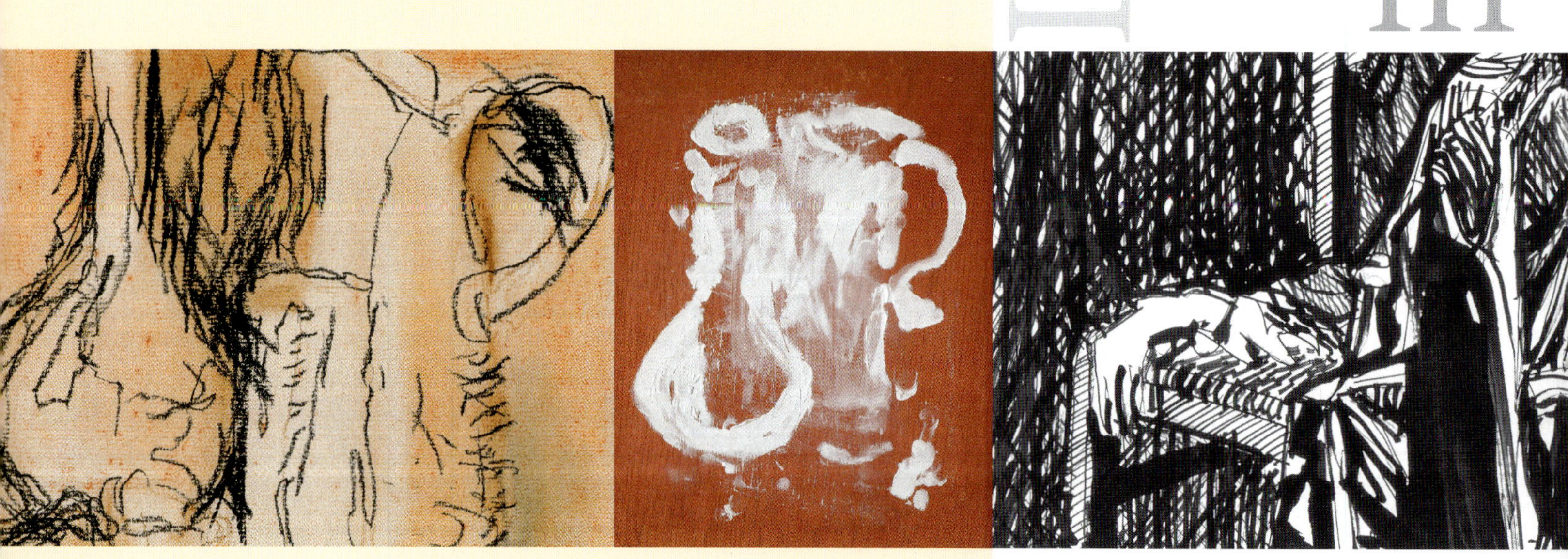

still life

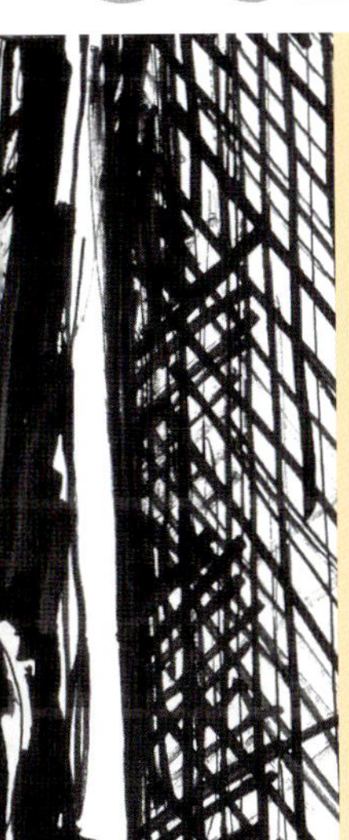

"One must work the technique consciously for so long that he ends up mastering it unconsciously; it is then that a sense of spontaneity emerges."
Henri Matisse,
Farbe und Gleichnis, Gesammelte Schriften, 1955.

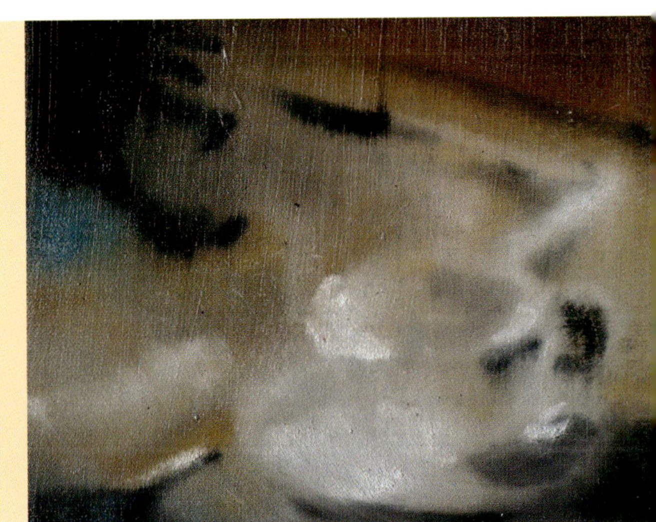

Fragile, broken, and weak lines

For many, the paintings of Giorgio Morandi (1890–1964) are more visual poetry than painting, pure lyricism. This Italian painter lived secluded in his inner world, far from public life despite being a well-known artist; he remained faithful to his intimate view of art as an opportunity for aesthetic display. His work, present in every important museum, is recognized for the characteristic of his strokes, whether lines or areas of color. Morandi's stroke is always fragile, delicate, as if it were to vanish. His work is never imposing; it is a vehicle for contemplation and for aesthetic pleasure that leads us to the experience of human vulnerability as a place to find mystery and oneself. Although he also painted landscapes, still life is the genre that is present through most of his body of work (paintings, drawings, and prints): groups of simple bottles that convey intimacy, pain, and loneliness.

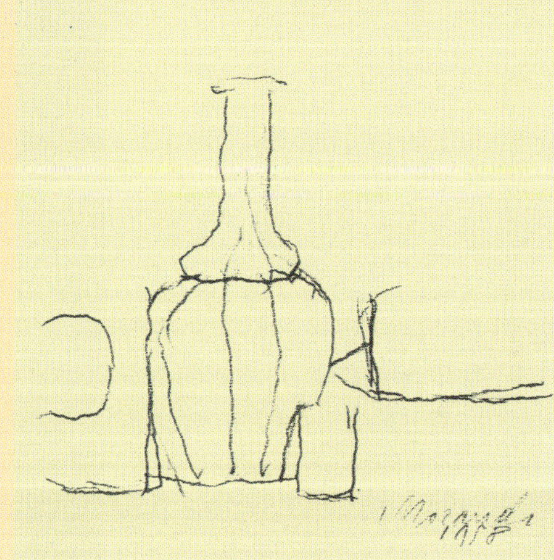

Giorgio Morandi,
Still Life, 1958.
La Casa dell'Arte
Sasso Marconi (Italy).

Light lines in a still life with objects

This creative approach developed by Gemma Guasch explores the expressive possibilities of lines that are applied very gently, without much strength or contained force. This is part of a still life with glass where lines disappear or are interrupted, since there are no solid volumes, but transparent ones, reflections, and approximations. The project has been executed with sanguine and black crayon on Ingres paper.

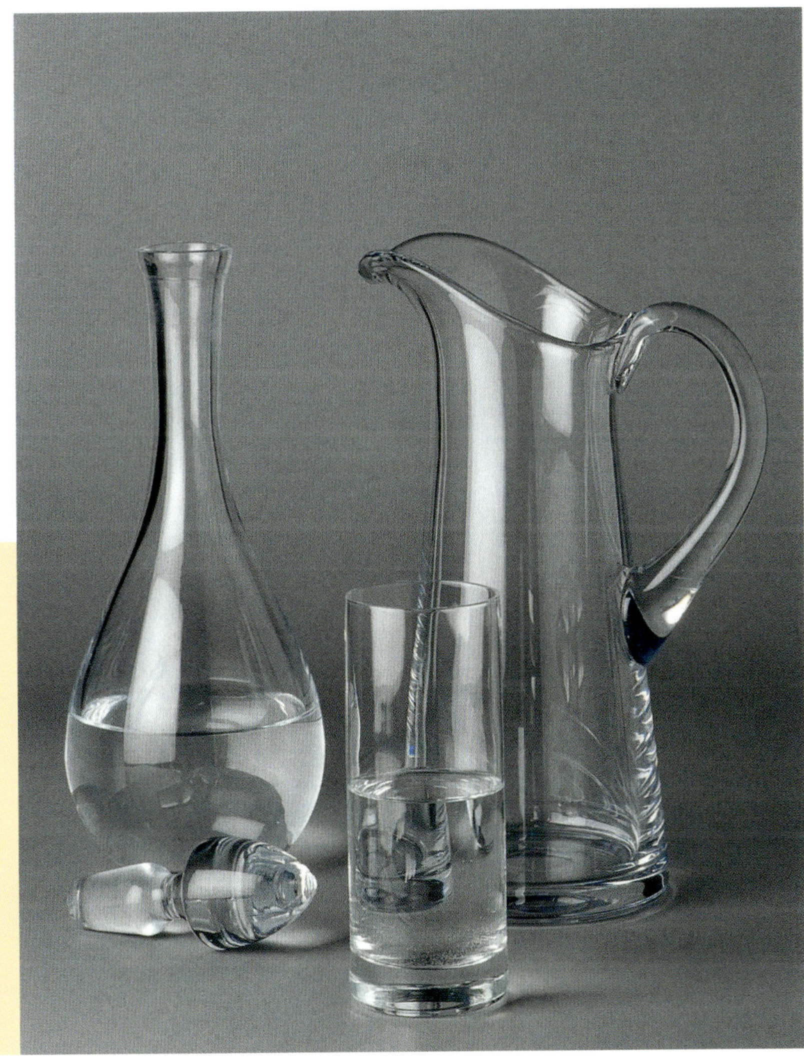

"In painting, and I suspect that in almost anything, what is superfluous gets in the way . . . I would like to arrive at a complex expressivity but without any obstacles . . . to the mystery of things that are transparent."
Fernando Zóbel
Reflections by Zóbel for *El misterio de lo transparente,* 1972.

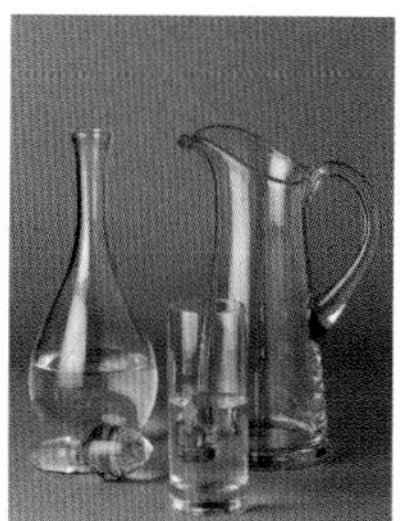

1 To create a base that conveys a fragile feeling, we cover one area of the paper with sanguine crayon, without applying too much pressure, blending it with the fingers without evening it out very much. This way, we make a cold surface more appealing by adding a human touch with the fingerprints.

3 Next, we intensify some areas and erase others to create light and shadow variations on the paper. This chiaroscuro must be soft to avoid making the scene too dramatic; it will establish the position of the elements in a three-dimensional space.

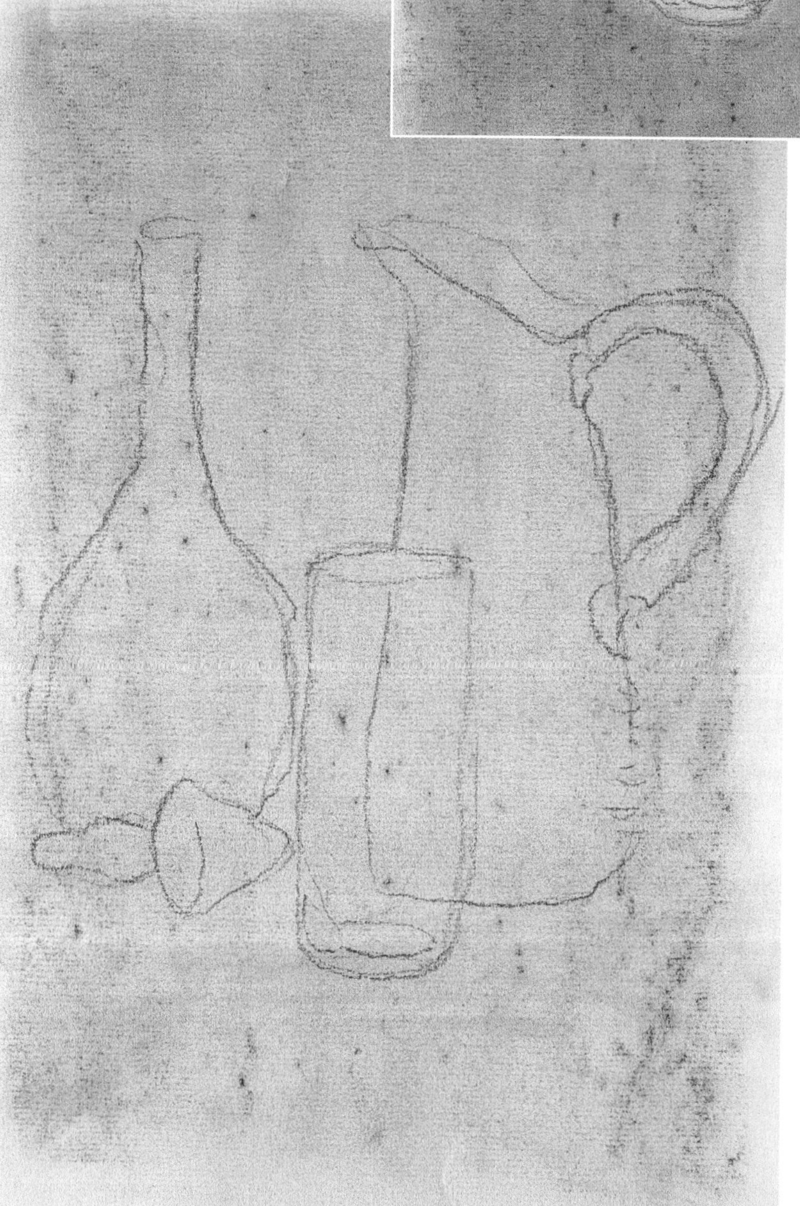

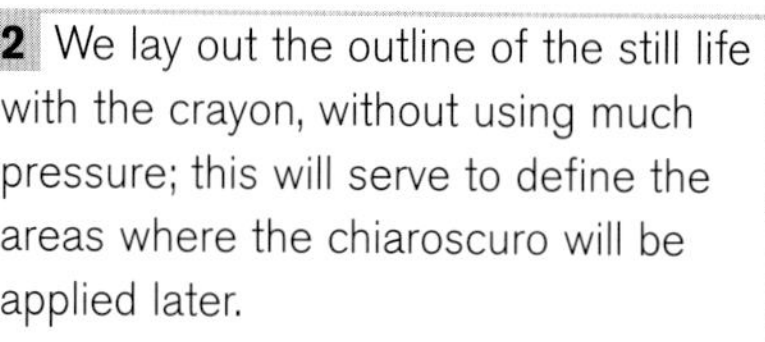

2 We lay out the outline of the still life with the crayon, without using much pressure; this will serve to define the areas where the chiaroscuro will be applied later.

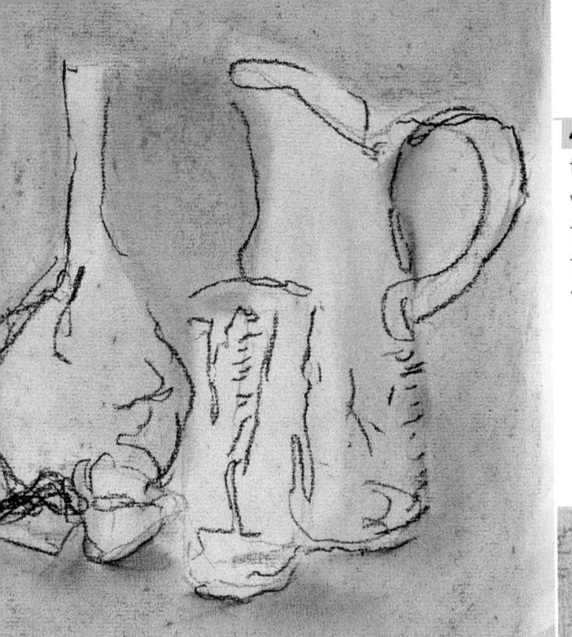

4 The gestural lines drawn from the luminous atmosphere that we have created must be soft, tentative, and broken. This way the work will appear unfinished, with ambiguous lines.

5 To finish, we draw several quick lines that are aimed at defining the theme, but that are not confined to the limits of the objects, as if they were very difficult to capture and represent, or as if it would only be possible to draw them with a trial-and-error approach, without definite lines.

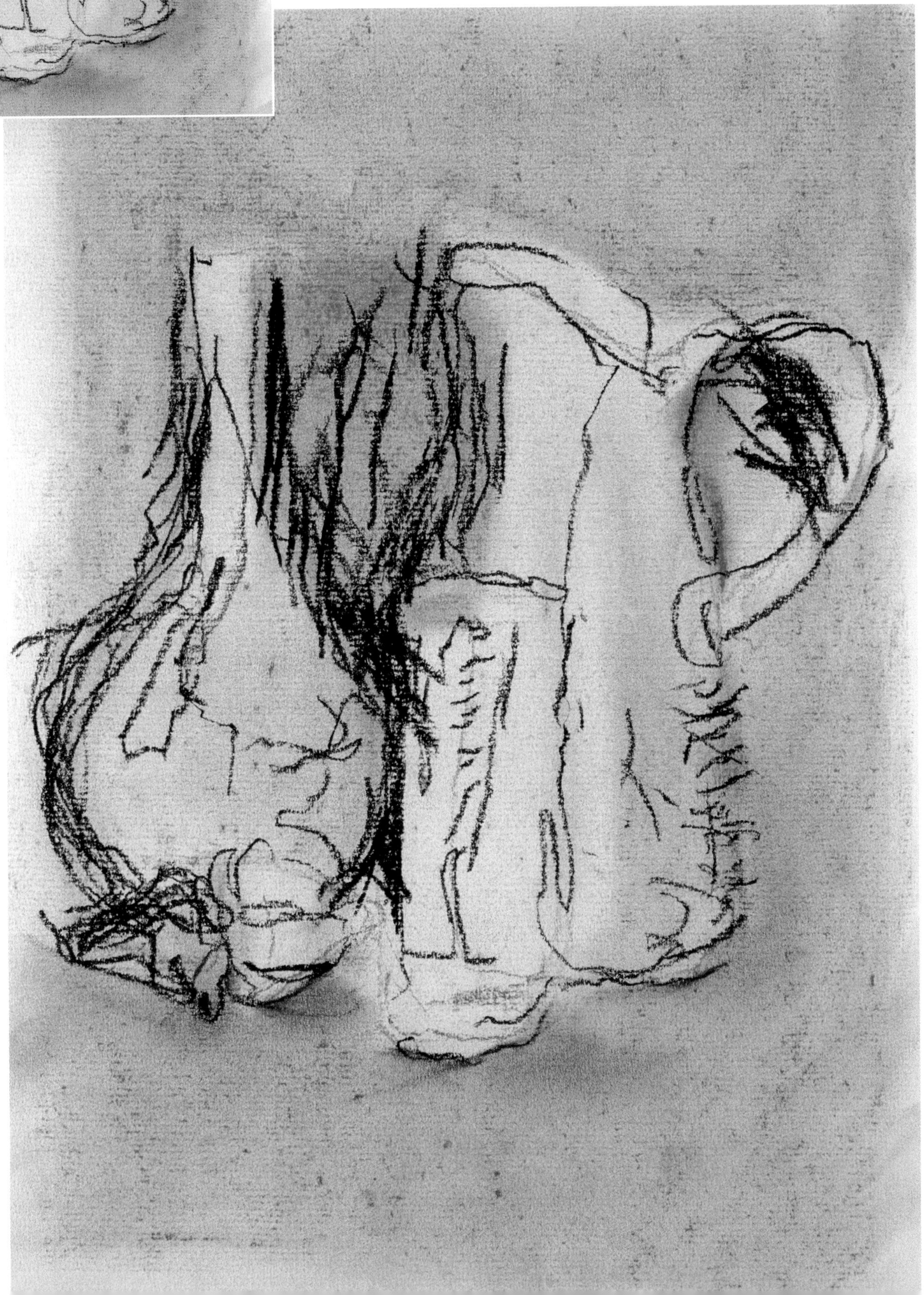

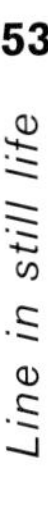

Other versions

With the same gestural approach, the artist has continued to play with the formal elements of the composition: the silhouette, the masses, the contours, the interstitial spaces, and the chiaroscuro. The results of this experimentation are always soft and lyrical.

The presence of this drawing is determined by its background, as if the air that surrounds the objects turned dense and solid, leaving only their negative image exposed. This approach produces the effect of dematerializing the objects.

With very soft and tentative lines the artist has outlined the figures in an incomplete manner, placing the exterior and interior contours of reflections and transparencies at the same level. The outline appears as the last mark of the object before it vanishes completely.

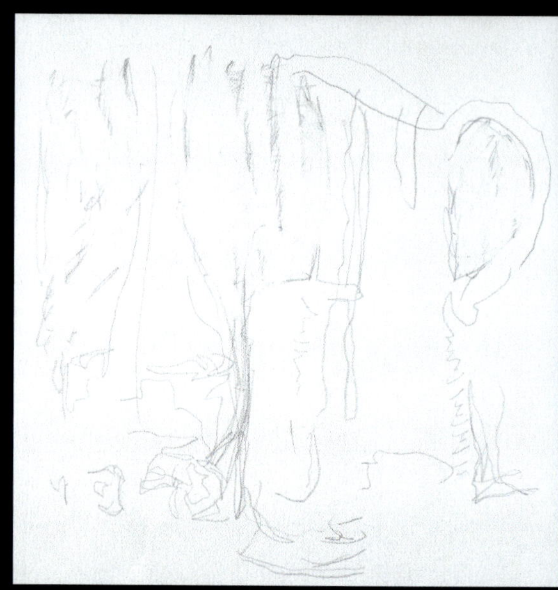

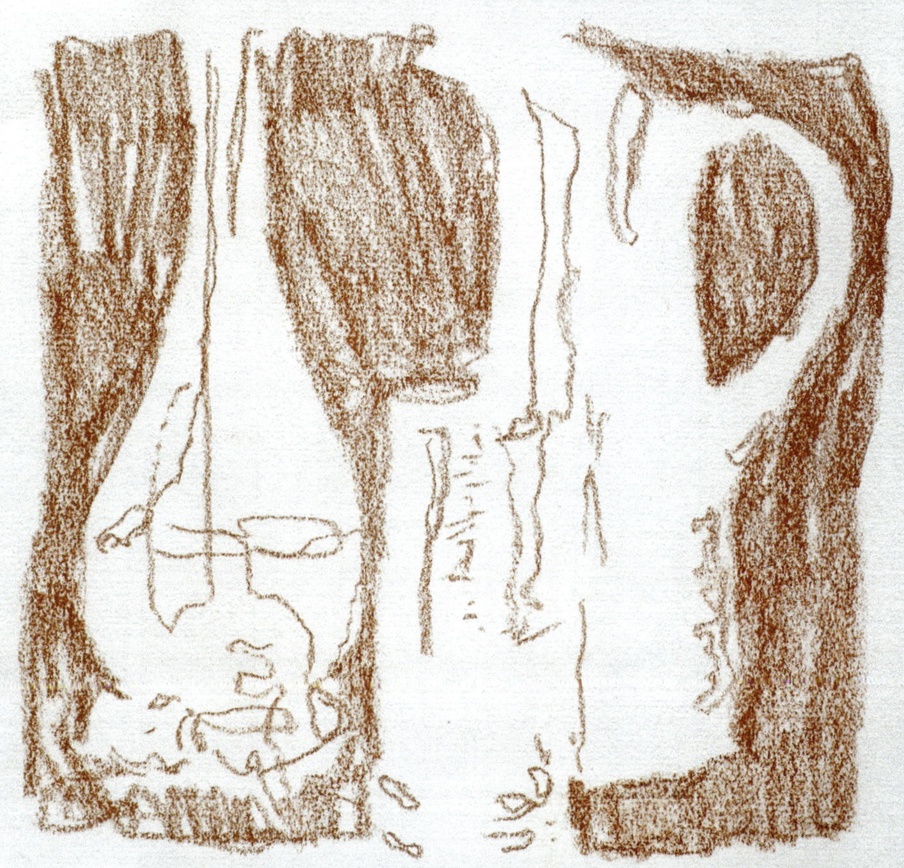

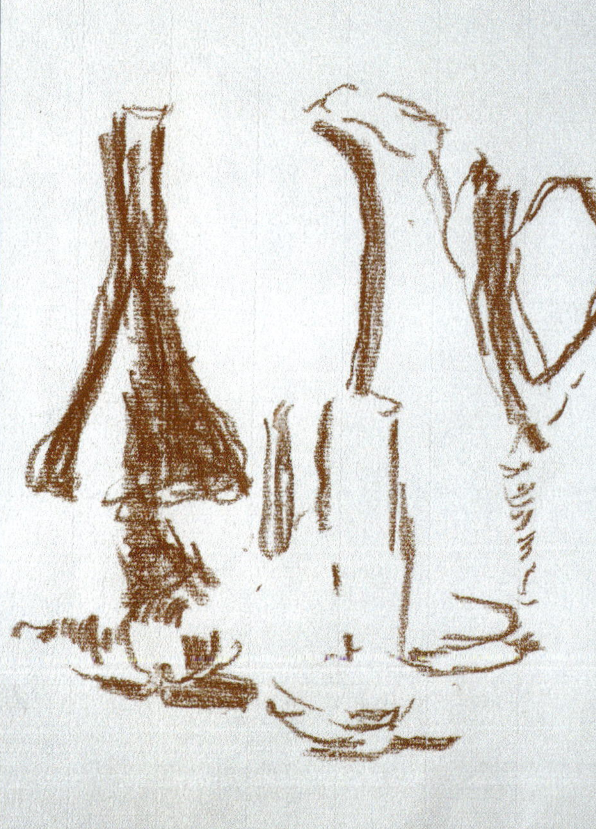

Here, the principle that rules the composition is maximum contrast, as if the objects were under a very intense blinding light that does not let us see their features. The strategic placement of the few strokes and lines gives us a hint of the subject.

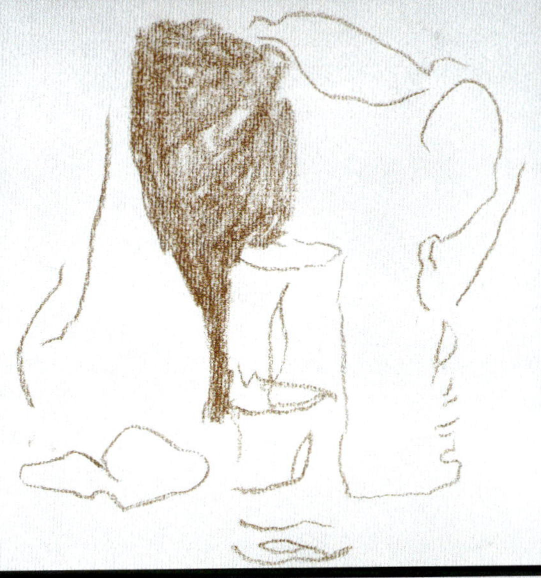

This crayon drawing focuses on the interstitial spaces, specifically between the two tall pitchers, reminiscent of many Morandi still lifes. This creates a surreal element that has great presence, one that appears as a third, inverted object.

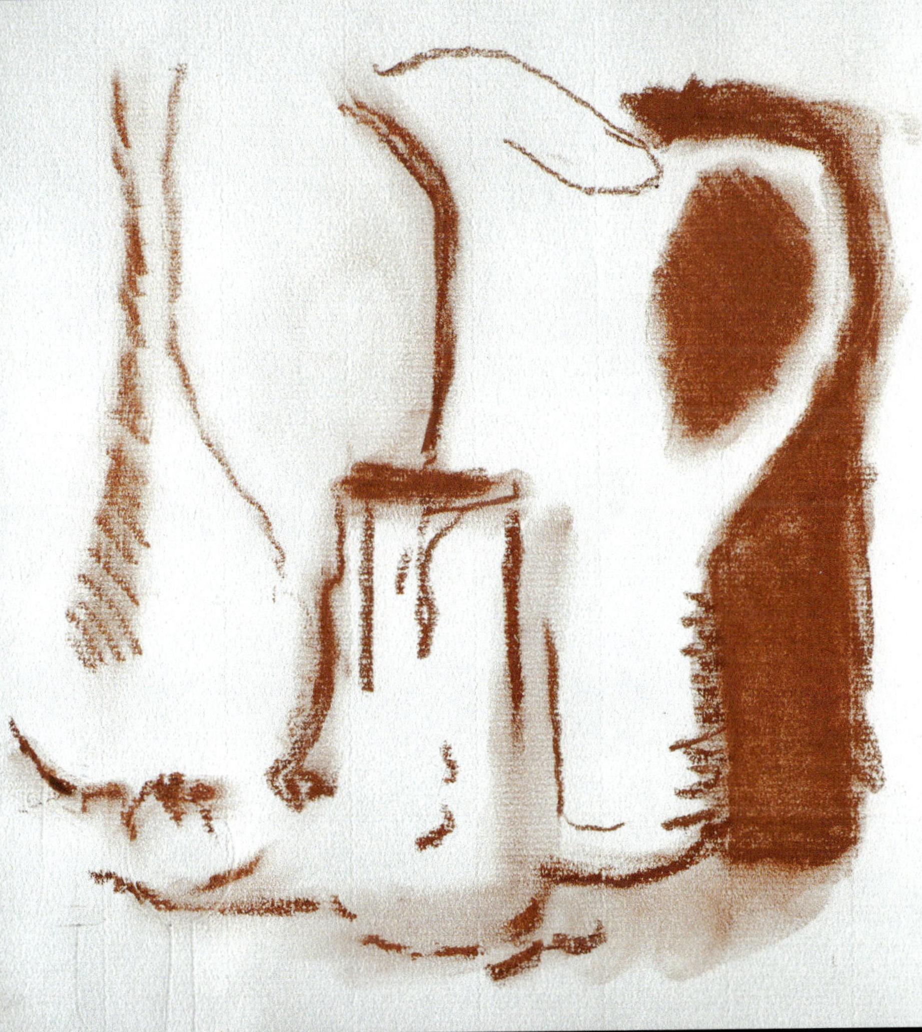

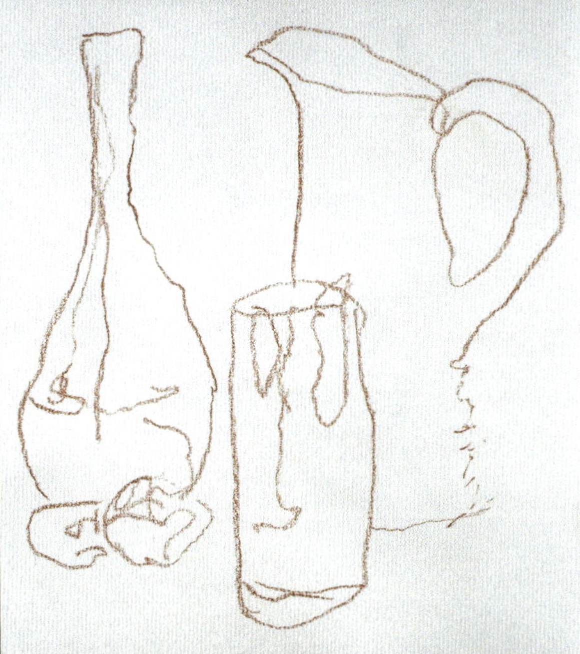

The silhouette and some contour lines are the linear features that define this still life. When the object is described with a single line, it becomes more mental and symbolic, less corporeal. If, in addition, this line is ambiguous or varies, the image vanishes to become a memory or an illusion, not a reality.

In this drawing the lines and the areas of color have been blended into a visual blur, which makes the objects less defined. This approach is often used to create mystery, fragility, and ambiguity.

New approaches

Other models

Continuing with the idea of fragile and delicate themes, the painter has chosen a still life with spectacles. This subject matter lends itself to a delicate approach; since it does not have a massive structure, it is transparent, and its thin frame conveys visual suppleness. The result is a combination of diffused and tentative lines that downplays the background and makes the object look fragile.

Other media

This time, Gemma Guasch has chosen acrylics, a medium that is completely different from crayons. The two still lifes seen here have been executed on a wood board treated with a layer of primer mixed with red acrylic. One of them shows heavy and imperfect white lines applied with the fingers, and the other is the negative, created by scratching the fresh paint with a thin spatula.

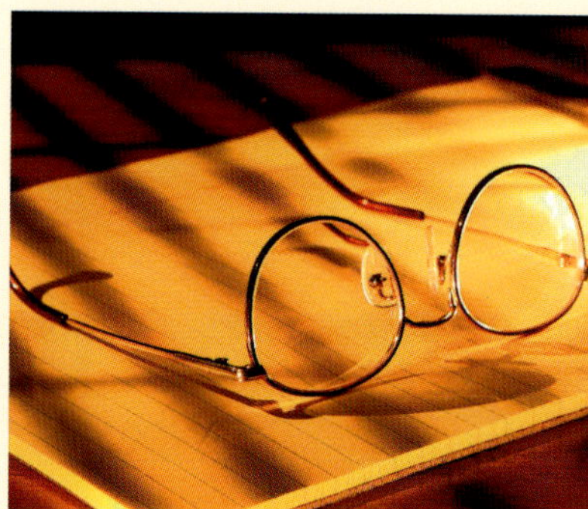

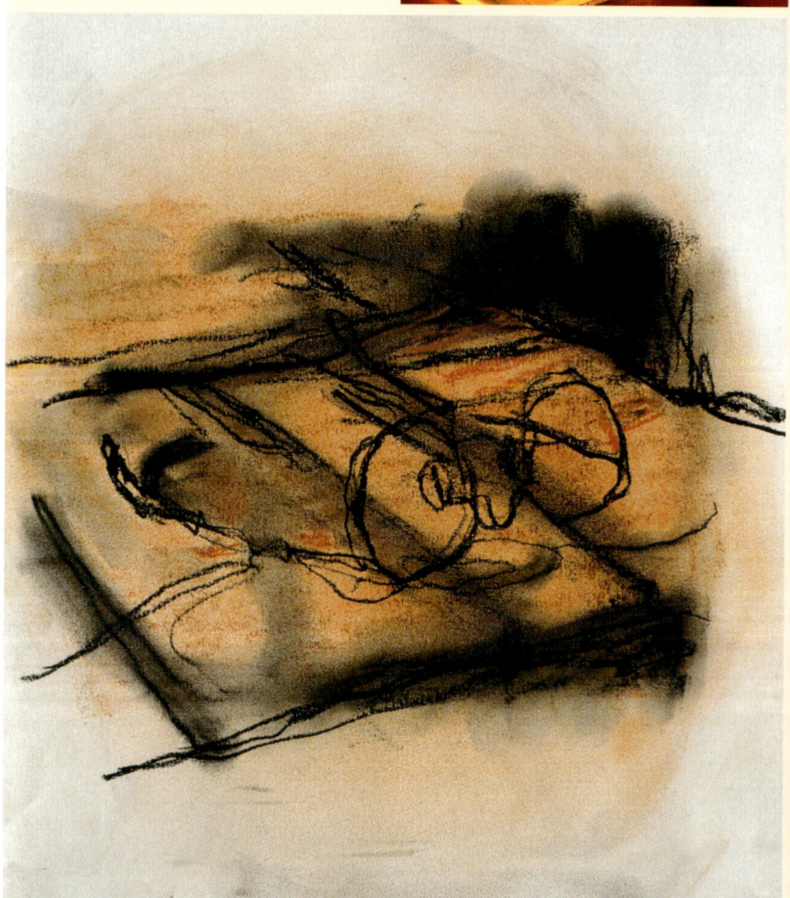

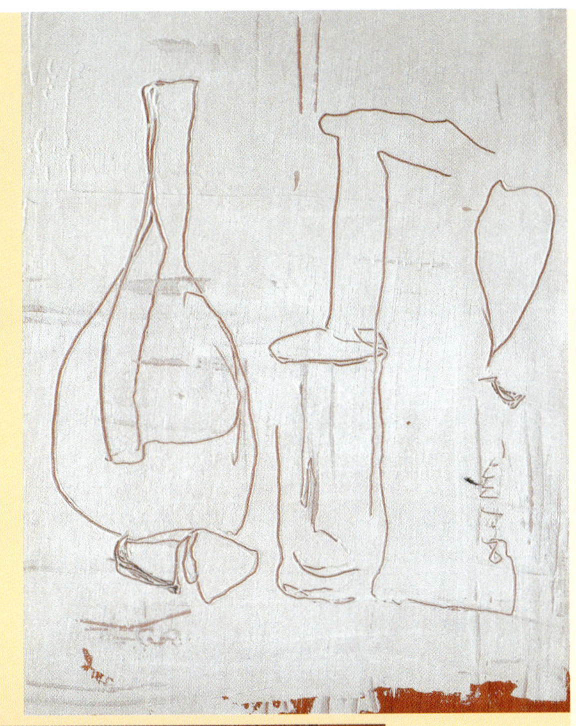

Other views

Luc Tuymans (born in 1958) is one of the most important representatives of contemporary painting. His work deals with subjects related to pain, solitude, danger, and failure, according to his views on art: "All art is failure. How one fails is a different matter." His paintings are classified as "endless anguish" provoked by the surreal effect with which real things are shown, using quiet colors and faint lines, images that are discolored like old photographs. He very accurately refers to his work as "immaterial paintings."

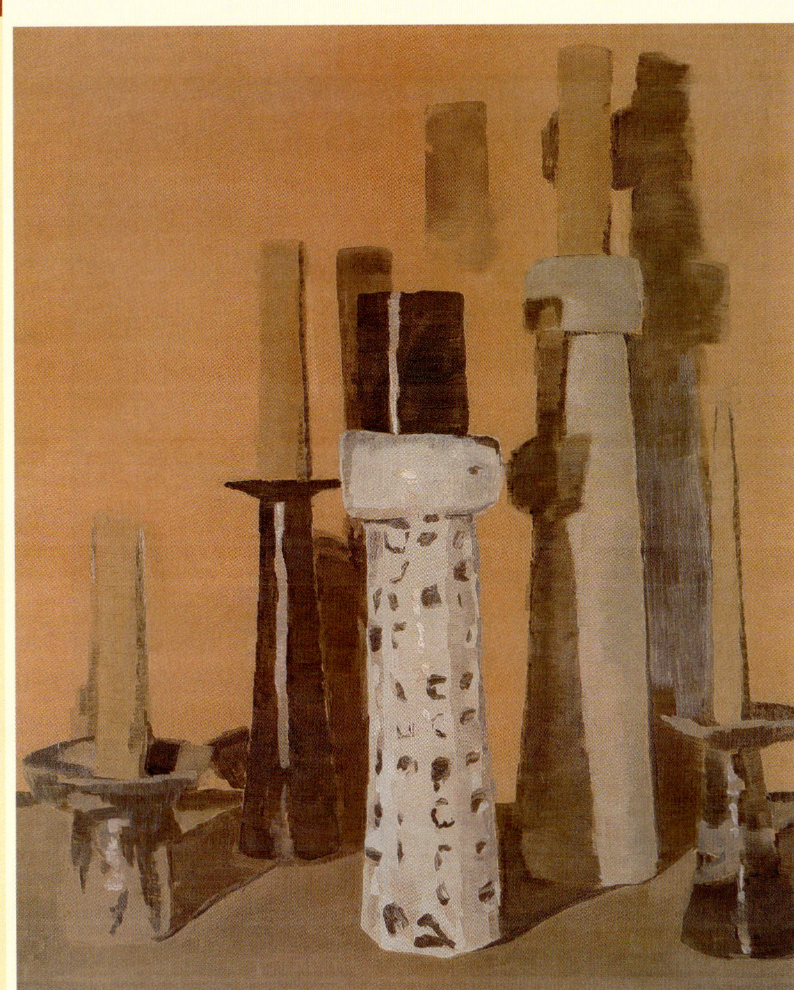

Luc Tuymans,
Intolerance, 1994.
Private collection.

Hatched, graphic, and reticular textures

The use of crosshatching as a drawing technique dates back to the origins of printmaking and pen-and-ink work, although the practice became popular during the second half of the twentieth century with the Pop Art movement, when crosshatching was often incorporated into commercial and design work. David Hockney (born in 1937), one of the most important artists of Pop Art, executes his work with a very pure approach to the image through the use of flat inks and clean outlines, often resorting to photography. His style is clearly influenced by Matisse and Picasso, and it contains a strong erotic and humorous charge. His themes are based on popular culture and are treated in a naturalistic—although not realistic—manner. One of the most interesting aspects of Hockney is his expertise in drawing and printmaking. These works are very clean, the lines of his drawings are very meticulous, and he uses crosshatching as a way to explain areas of color or chiaroscuro, as can be seen in this print with chair and hat from 1972.

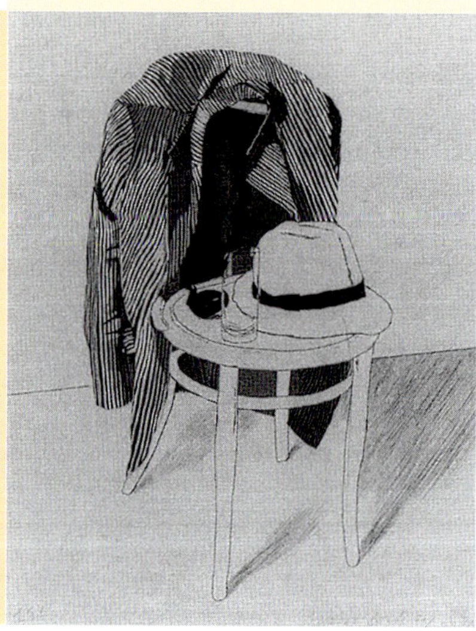

David Hockney, *Panama Hat*, 1972. Etching and aquatint, edition of 125.

Experimenting with hatching in an interior with chair and clothing

In the following exercise, Josep Asunción begins a traditional still life with clothing hanging on a chair, as in Hockney's print. The medium used is ink, applied with an ink pen and a reed pen of different sizes and widths to achieve various kinds of crosshatching. The support is a type of paper that, although smooth, can adapt to different wet techniques. The artist experiments with different crosshatching methods, changing the applicator and the direction of the lines to achieve a range of effects.

"(. . .) On certain occasions, during a conversation about Cubism, somebody told me that that type of painting had to do with an internal vision. I explained to him that that was the only vision that we have, the only one that exists. For the time being, there is no other."
David Hockney,
The Way I See It, 1994.

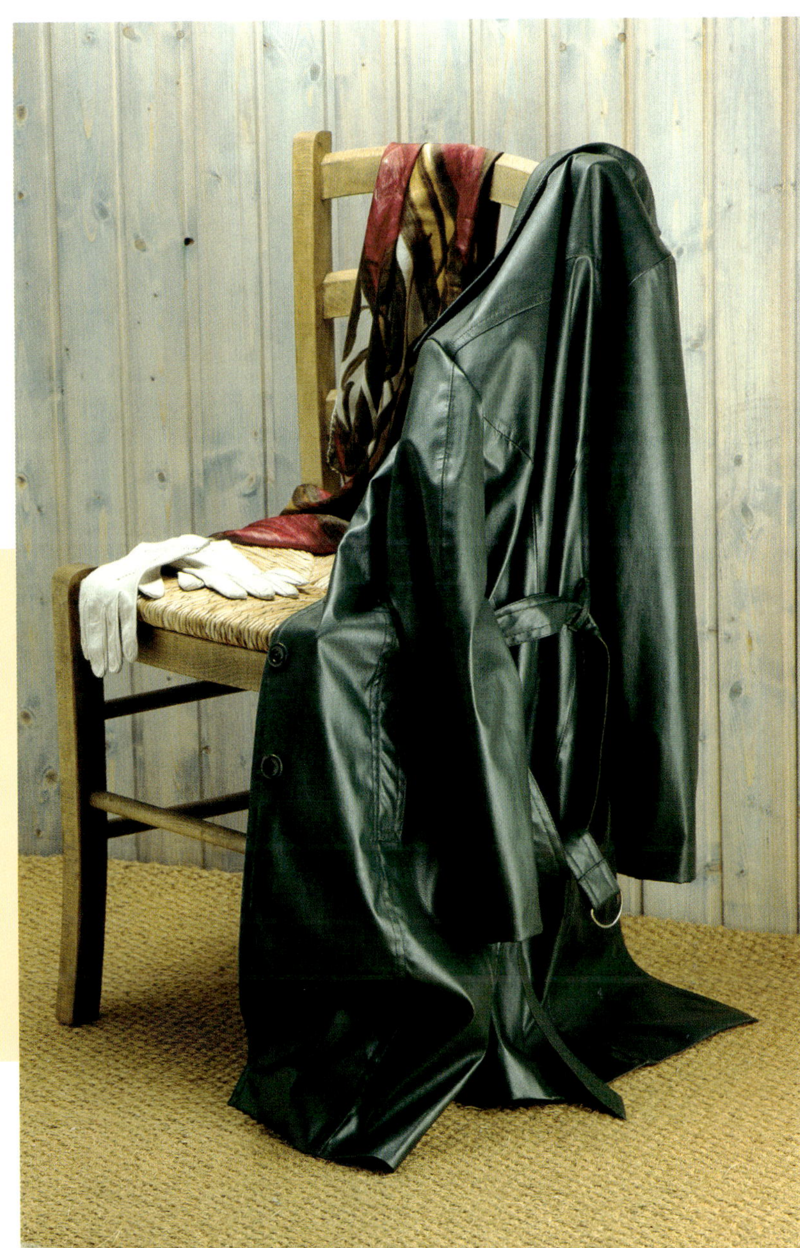

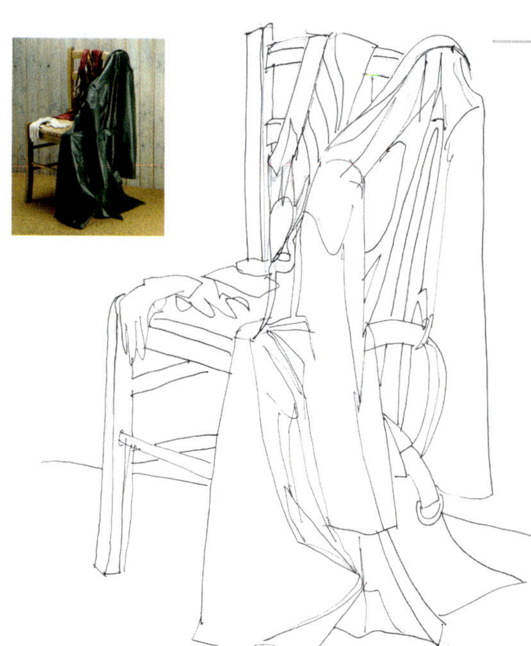

1 We draw the still life with a medium-hard pencil and without applying too much pressure, trying to establish the main outlines properly. We go over the final drawing lines with a thin ink pen. When the ink is dry we erase the preliminary pencil lines.

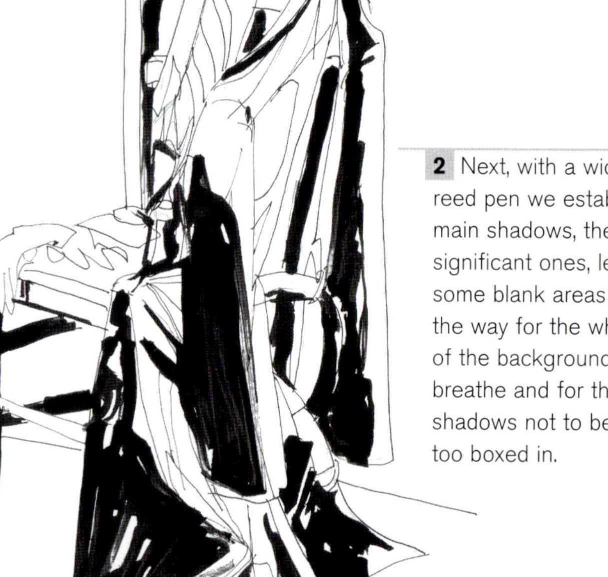

2 Next, with a wide-cut reed pen we establish the main shadows, the most significant ones, leaving some blank areas along the way for the white of the background to breathe and for the shadows not to be too boxed in.

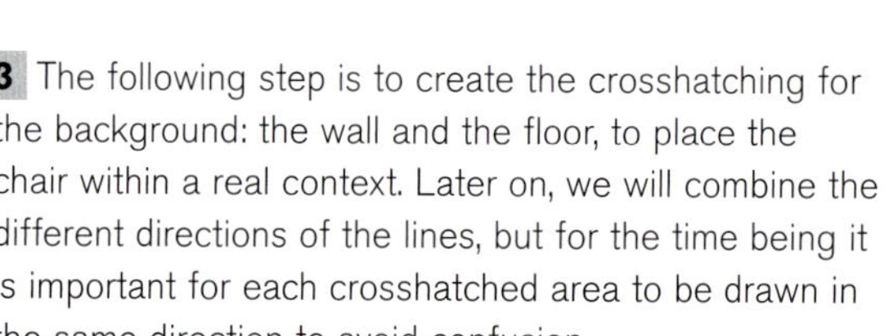

3 The following step is to create the crosshatching for the background: the wall and the floor, to place the chair within a real context. Later on, we will combine the different directions of the lines, but for the time being it is important for each crosshatched area to be drawn in the same direction to avoid confusion.

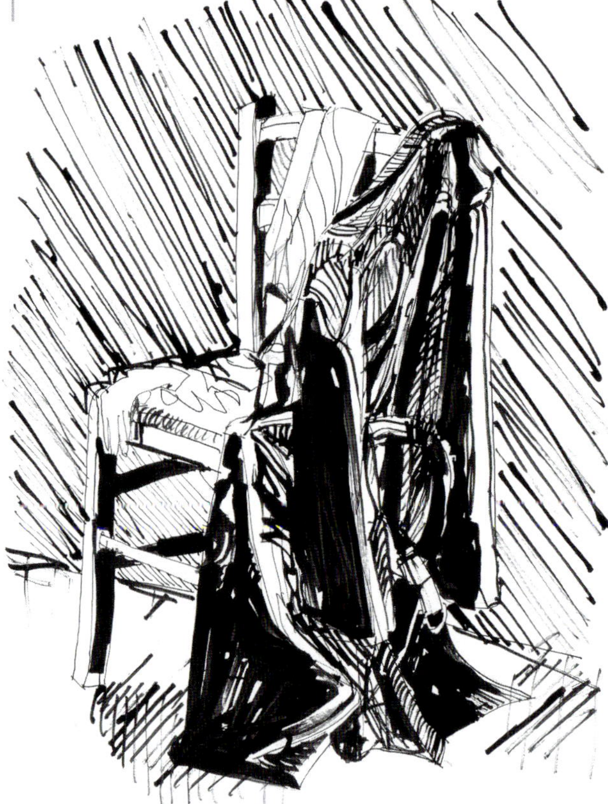

4 The drawing is completed with the addition of crosshatching that combines a variety of directions and densities. Density creates a relationship between the lines and their thickness. For the muted grays we use very thin lines, without overlapping too much; for the dark grays we use heavier lines and more overlapping.

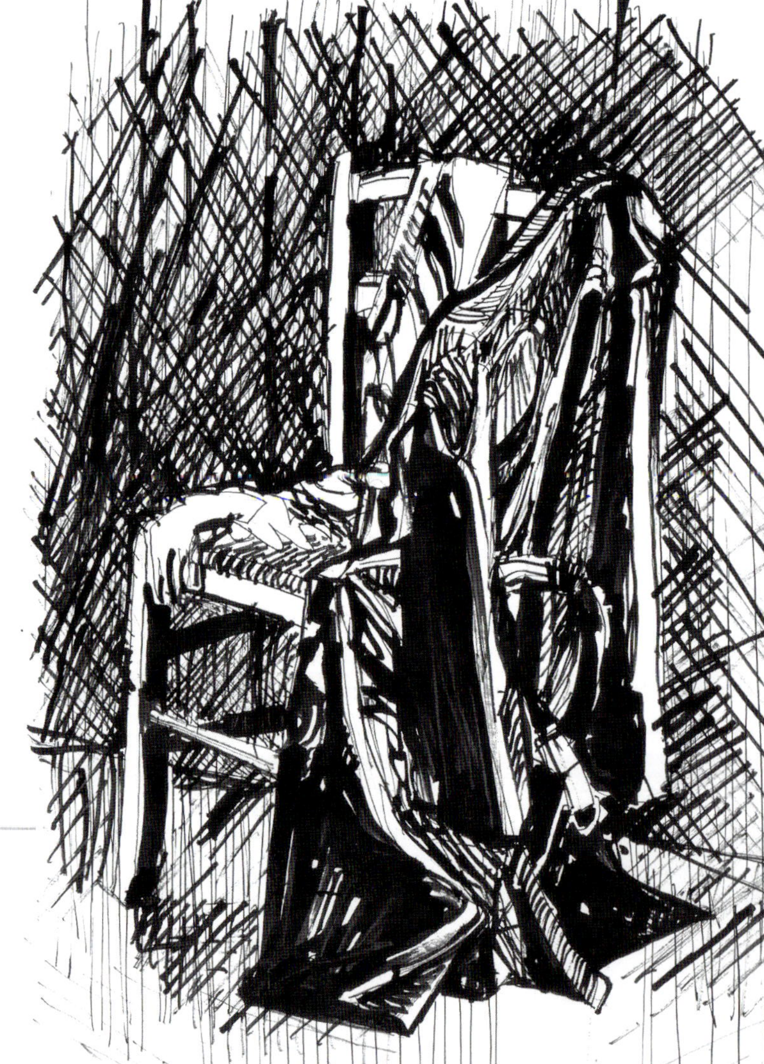

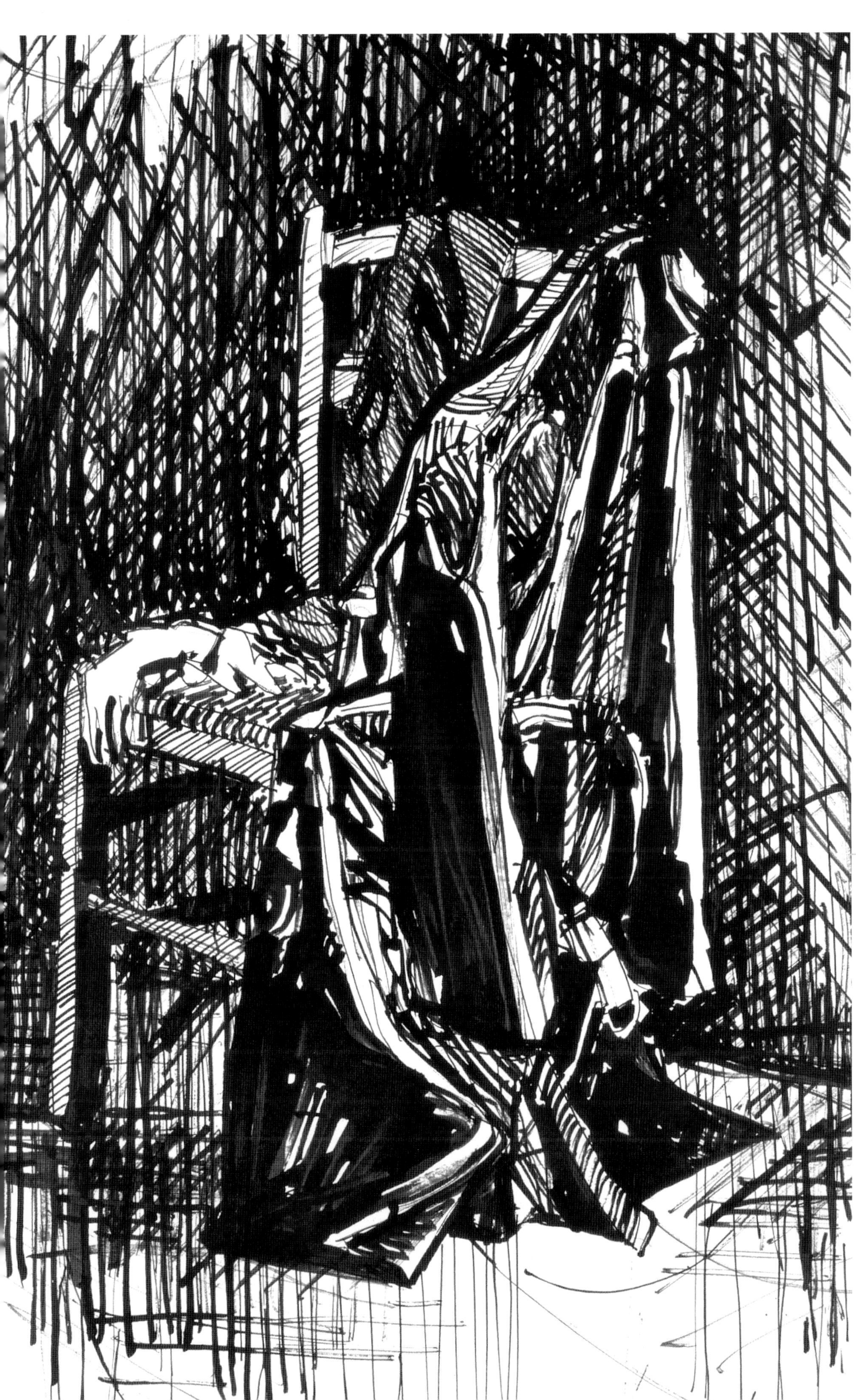

5 To finish, we adjust the light and shadow values throughout the drawing. The white that represents the brightest light has been left in reserve from the beginning; otherwise the piece may have looked too dark.

Other versions

By varying the applicator and the intensity of the lines, expressed by their thickness and proximity, the artist has experimented with different ways to create the chiaroscuro of the same still life.

For this drawing a wide-tip reed pen was used to create an area of crosshatching by superimposing the two perpendicular layers. A single-direction line was used to draw the jacket because the reed pen is wide, so we need to control the number of lines.

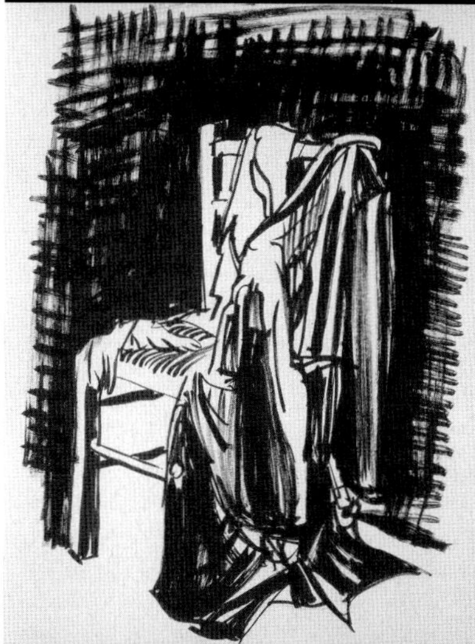

This is the most involved drawing of this gallery, executed with dots, which, depending on their number and proximity, can produce different grays.

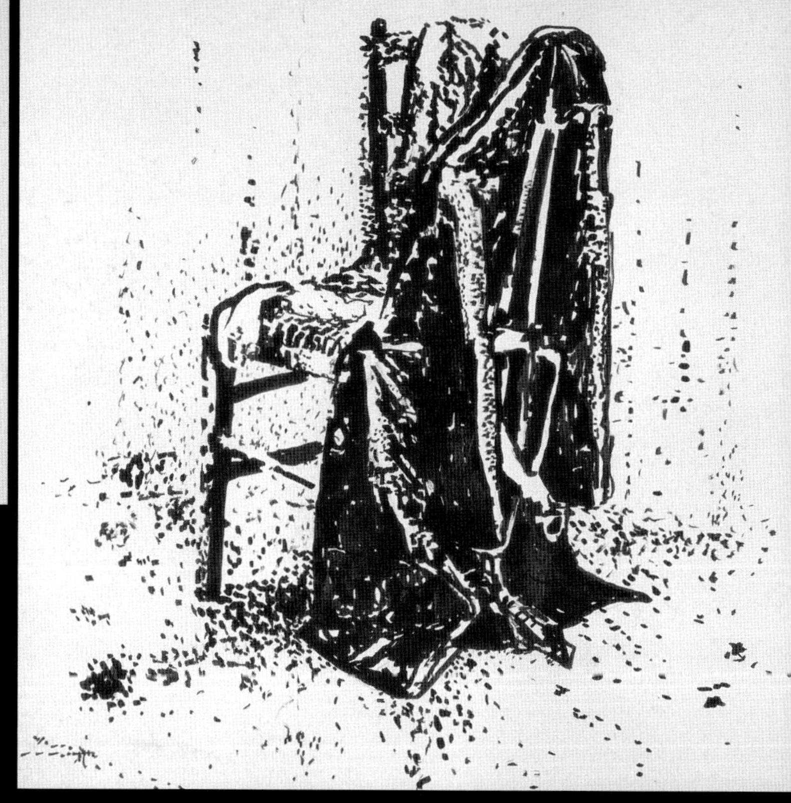

The tenebrism of the large black areas in this work is the result of applying ink directly with a brush, leaving some horizontal bands of the floor unpainted to set them apart from the wall and the areas of light on the object.

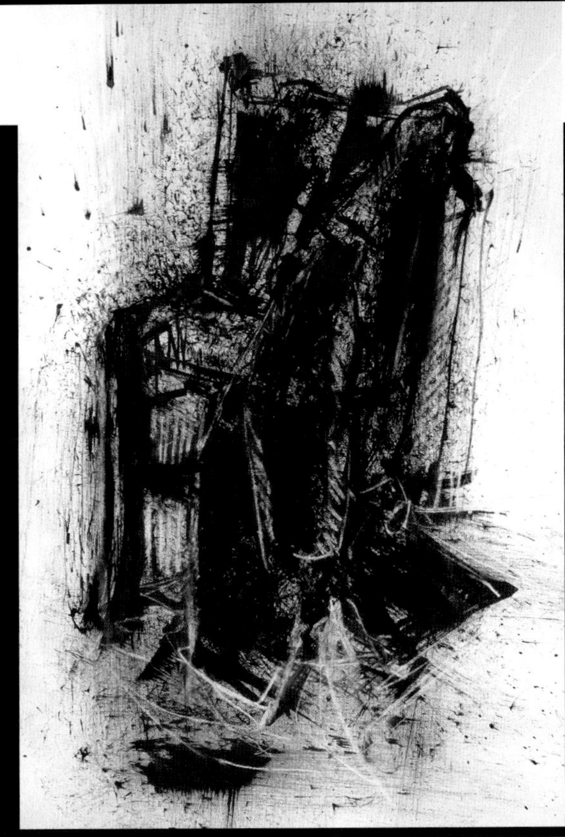

In this drawing, the protagonist is the atmosphere. The technique used is crosshatching applied in ink with a dry brush. The brush is old and worn out; the bristles are open and not charged with much ink, and the marks are made by tapping on the paper. The most defined areas are worked beforehand with a conventional brush or ink or reed pen.

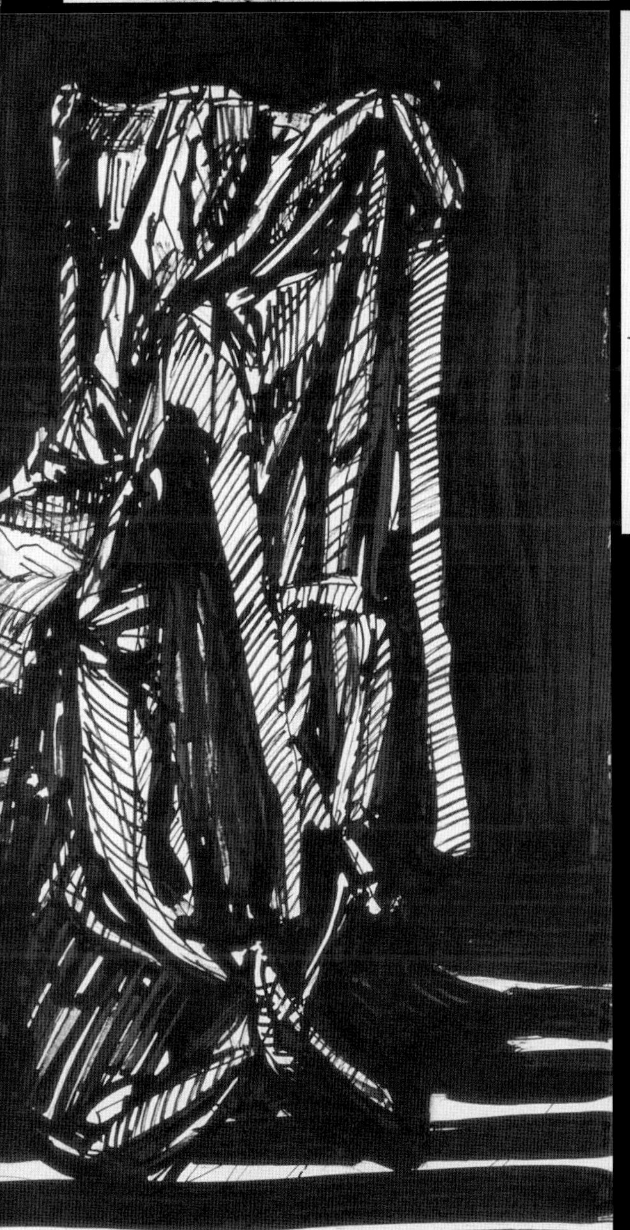

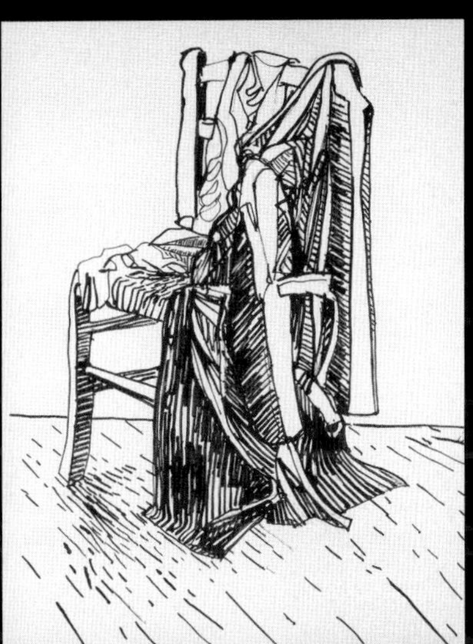

Each set of lines in this picture has been created using a fine-tip reed pen. A clean approach has been chosen, no tenebrism or atmosphere, a few lines, and no crosshatching. A basic way to define the forms accurately is to draw the lines in the correct direction, consistently with the shape of the object.

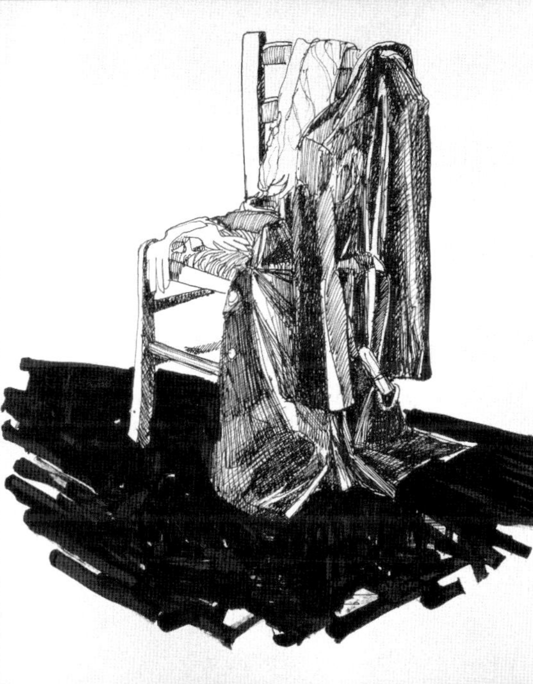

This time, two line combinations can be seen. On the floor, a heavily crosshatched set of lines was created with a very thick-tipped pen, while the very thin lines on the model were made using a fine-nib ink pen; this required great patience and attention to detail to create a perfect finish.

New approaches

Other models

This is a very different still-life theme. The artist has selected it as a variation for working with crosshatching: bowling pins, a more dynamic and informal theme than clothing, permitting the use of freer, stronger lines and contrasts. The ink pen and the reed pen in various tip sizes played a part in this exercise.

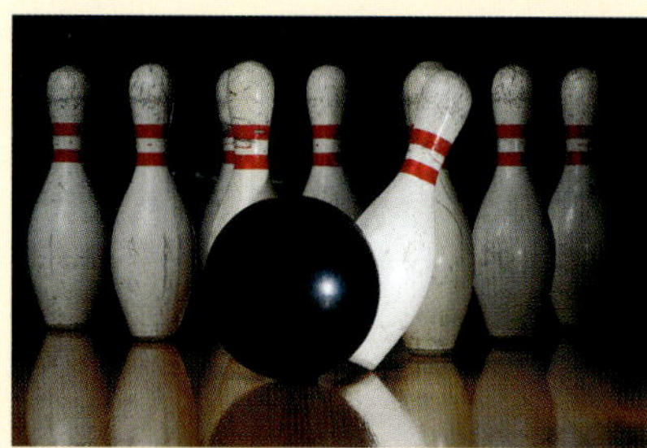

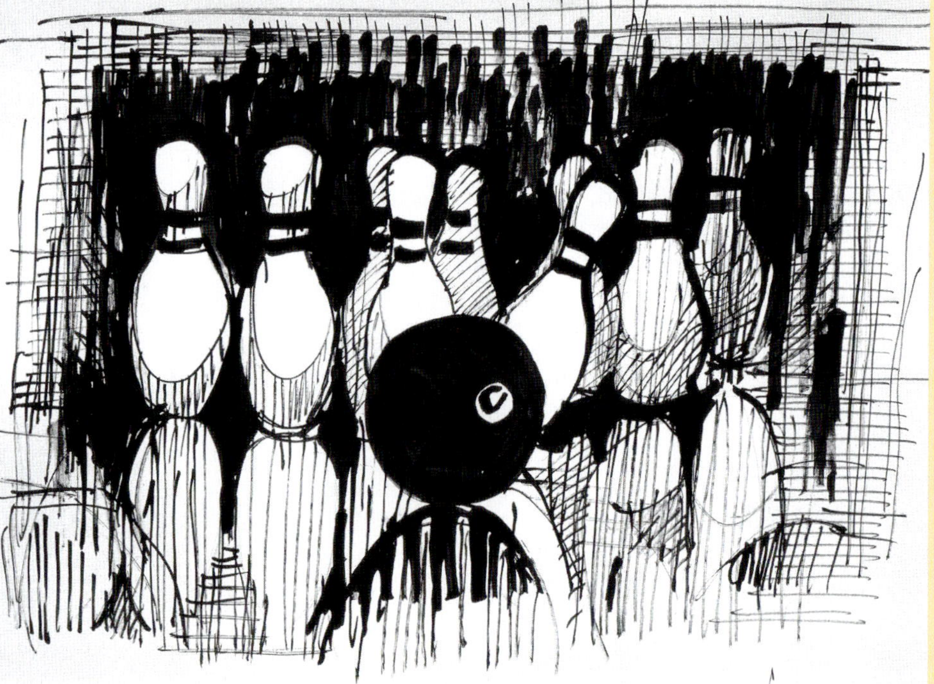

Other media

A medium that requires drawing lines when we wish to create atmospheric backgrounds and chiaroscuros with areas of color is the marker. Its opaque and dense ink does not allow creating gradations any other way than with crosshatching.

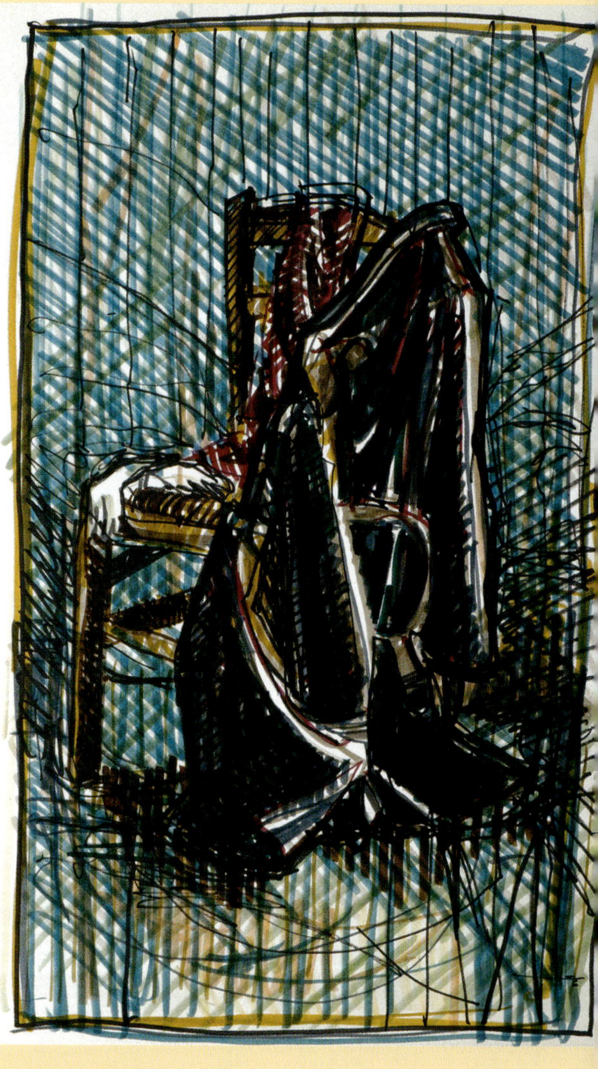

Other views

Let us look at how two very different painters use crosshatching. Joaquim Torres-García (1874–1949), whose work is difficult to classify, shows the combination of a very orderly grid structure with conventional or primitive schematic symbols, which he defined as "Universal Constructivism": art that must represent a superior reality, but without forsaking emotion and humanity. Sol Le Witt (born in 1928) does not work from symbolism but from the codes of basic language: straight lines in all four directions, geometric figures, black and white, repetition and series. Although his current work is basically an abstract grid, some earlier figurative drawings do reflect his style and sensibility.

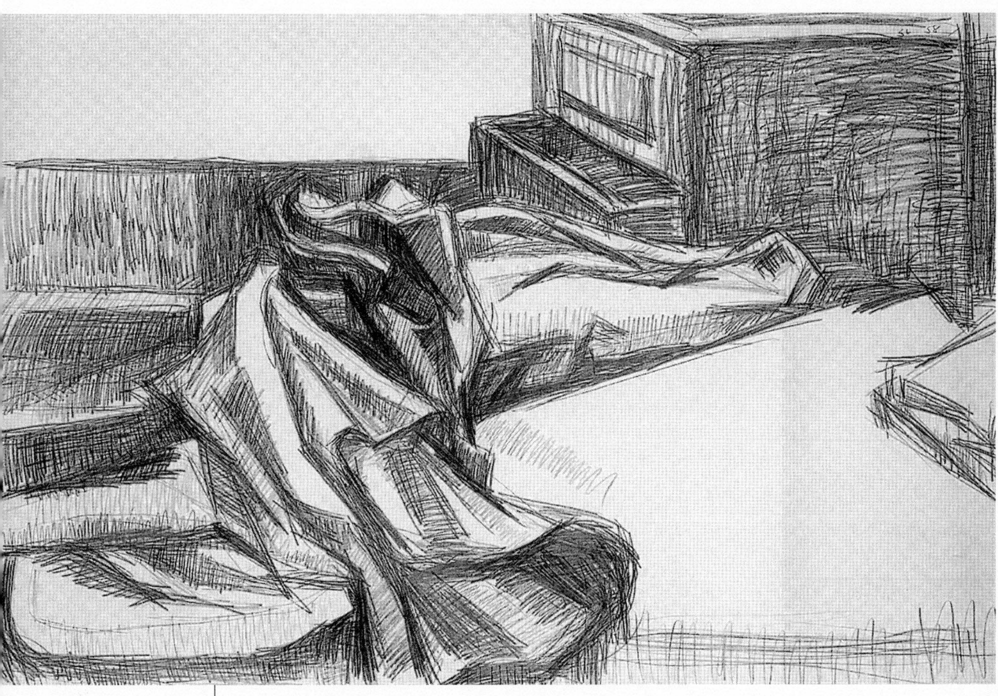

Sol Le Witt,
Bed Sheet, 1958.
New Britain Museum of American Art (Connecticut, United States)

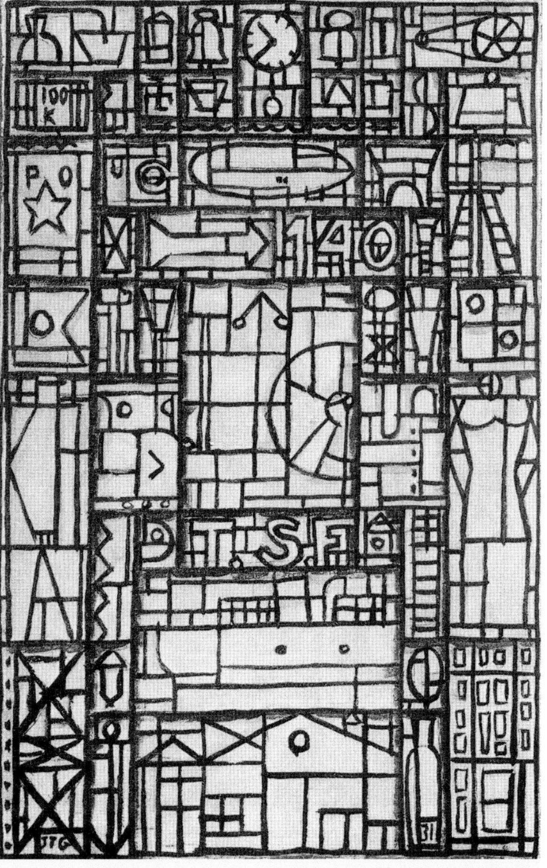

Joaquim Torres-García,
Composición Constructiva TSF/140, 1931. Private collection.

Creative approach 06

Atmospheric, diffused, and blurry textures

Sfumato is a pictorial technique that was used by Leonardo da Vinci during the Renaissance period to give images an atmospheric feeling. It consists of diffusing the outlines to a greater or lesser degree to make everything appear bathed by soft lighting. Nowadays, some painters, like Gerard Richter (born in 1932), one of the most important exponents of contemporary painting, have turned this method into a vehicle for research and personal expression. Richter's figurative representations, such as his still life *Blumen*, have an enormous atmospheric charge, some to the point at which the image is out of focus, blurred, suggesting reality yet not showing it. He deals with the line between reality and suggestion: his paintings are seen as representations of perception and not of the model. This way, the artist reflects on the act of looking itself: the out-of-focus approach blurs the image and awakens a desire in the spectator to unveil the truth behind the objects.

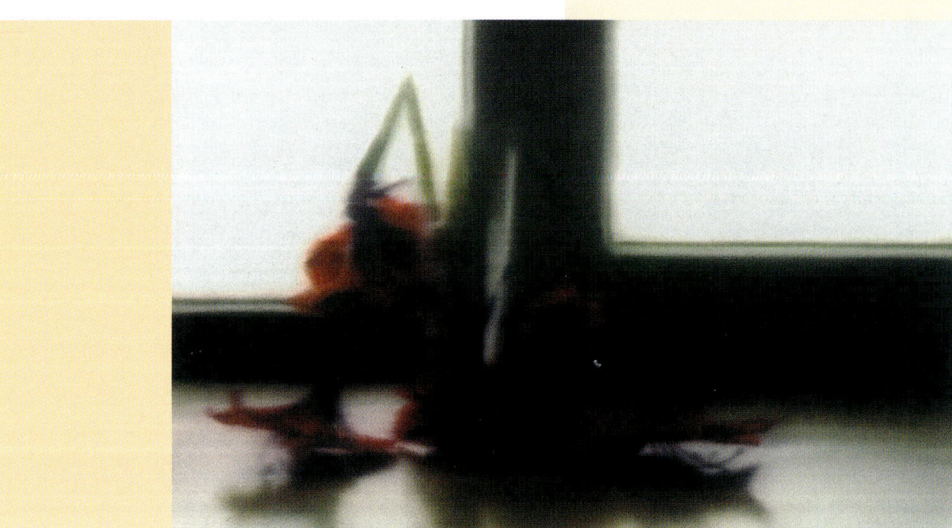

Gerard Richter,
Blumen, 1994.
Private collection.

Applying sfumato *in a simple still life with a coffee cup*

Revisiting the pictorial tradition of *sfumato*, Gemma Guasch has approached the following creative exercise using oils on canvas as the medium. The plasticity and slow drying process of oils make them ideal for creating diffused effects, from soft outlines to very blurry effects. The somber and tenebrist qualities of this still-life model are factors that help in the creation of atmospheres with contrasts of light. The objective of this approach is to experiment with various applicators to create different *sfumato* effects.

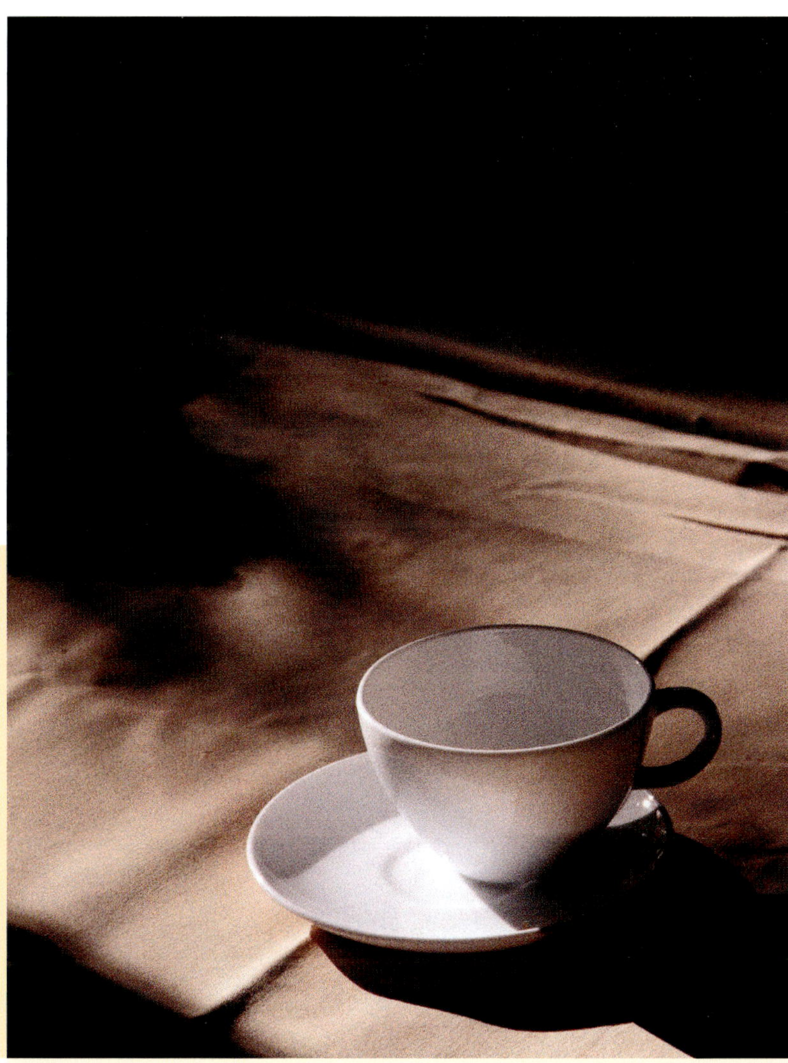

"Illusion—or rather, appearance—is my lifetime theme. Everything is present and can be seen because we perceive it, thanks to the light reflected from that appearance. Nothing else is visible. Painting has to do with appearance more than any other art (including photography, of course)."
Gerard Richter,
Notes, 1989.

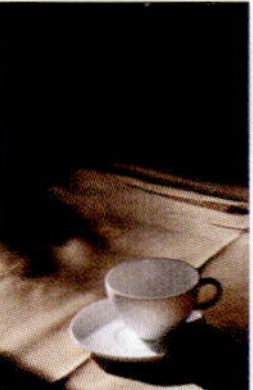

1 We paint the background with a thin layer of oil paint applied with a wide brush, blending the edges between the colors of the background and the table.

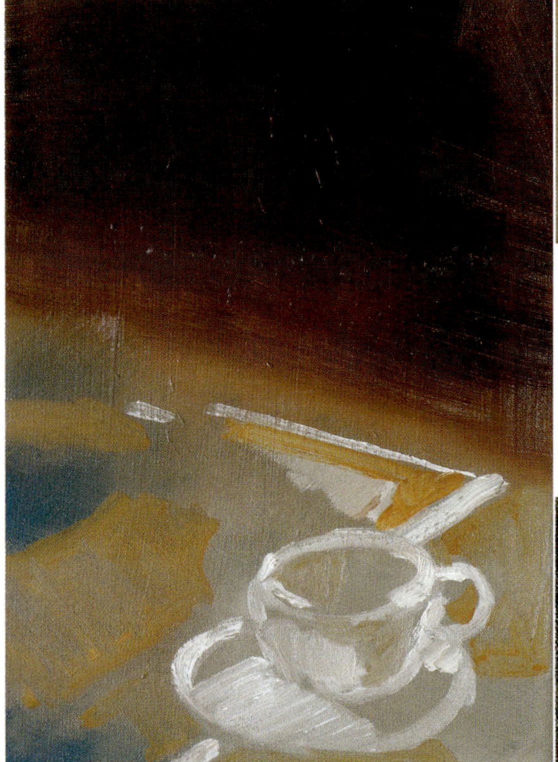

2 With a medium round bristle brush we apply the general colors of the cup and the reflections of the table. To avoid problems with thickness in the *sfumato*, it is best at this stage to use a light brushstroke.

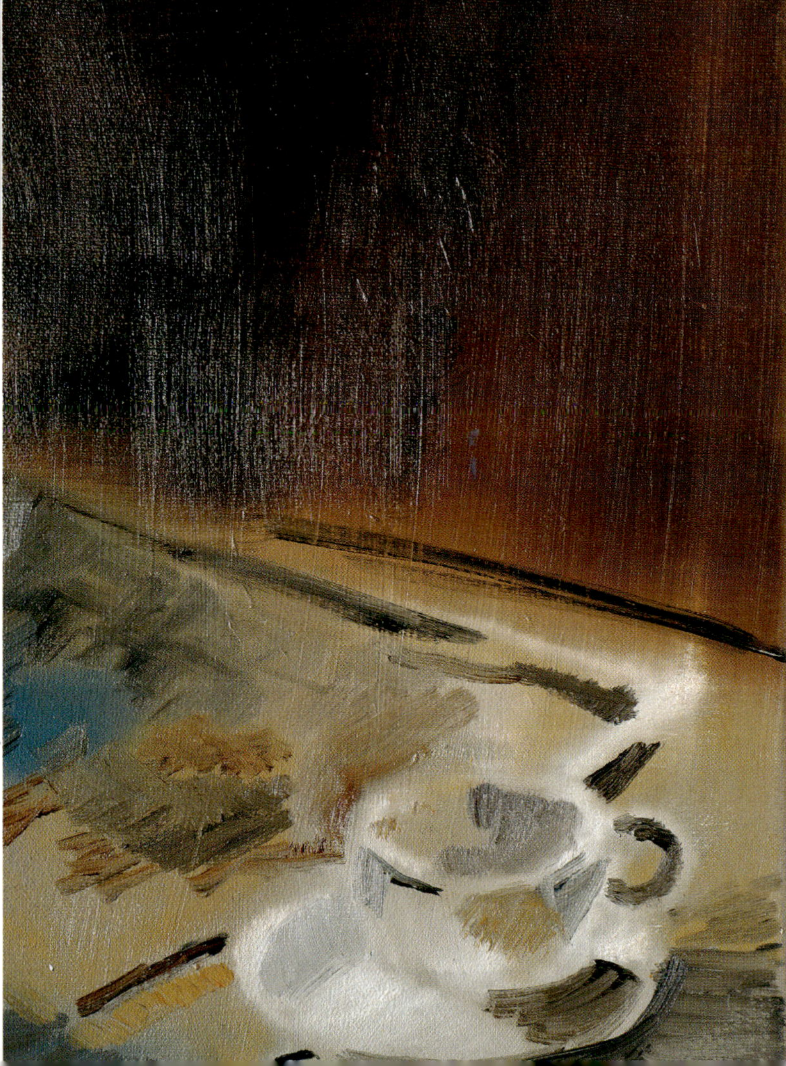

3 We blend the first color with a different bristle brush, this time dry, working in very gentle movements, as if caressing the canvas. We apply the second layer of color using a thin round brush for the dark and medium tones.

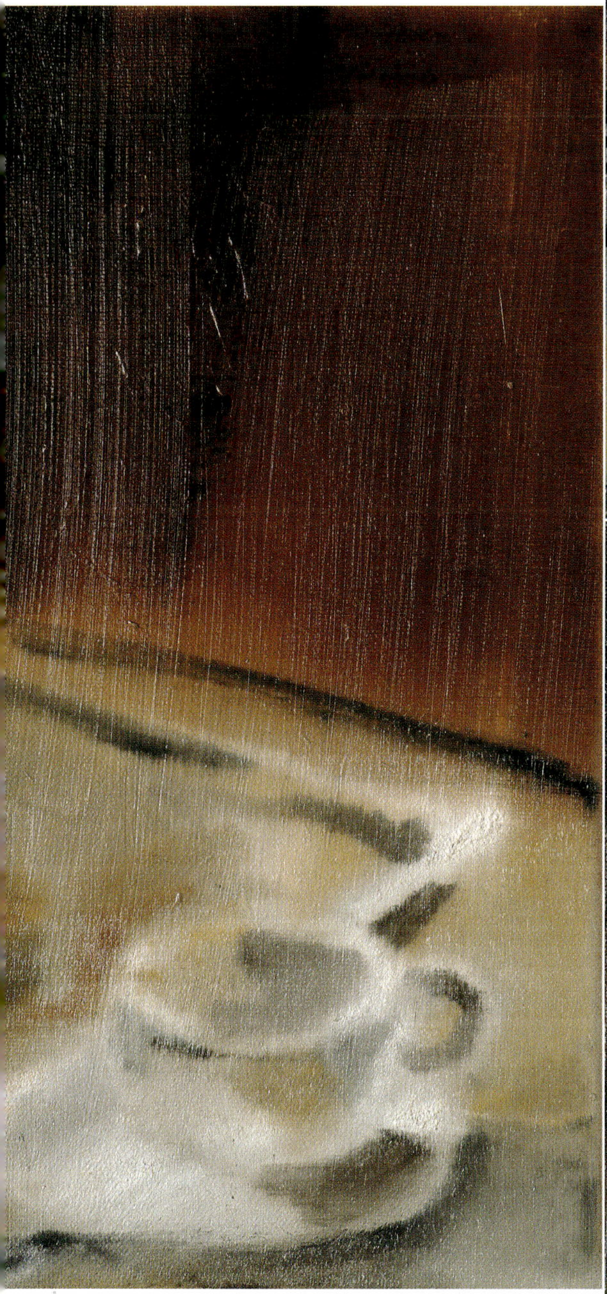

4 We blend the lines with a wide dry brush. The longer we do this the blurrier the image will become. To prevent the colors from mixing on the canvas (as opposed to what happens on a palette), it is very important here not to use solvent on the brush.

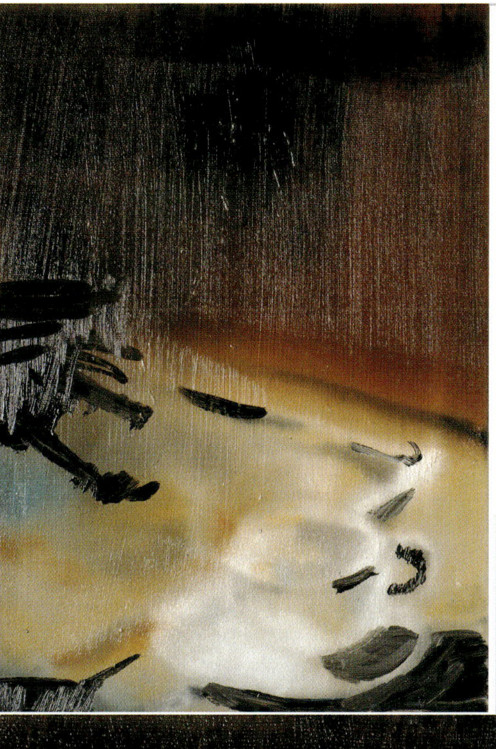

5 Over the already well-defined and diffused image, we apply the last brushstrokes with black to reinforce the contrasts of light.

6 We conclude the painting with the final *sfumato*. Although the image is very soft, it is rich in details because the first layers were diffused more than the last ones. With each pass of the brush, we lose definition.

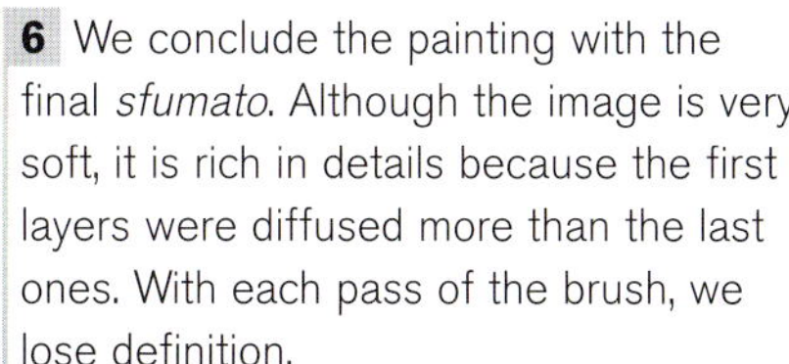

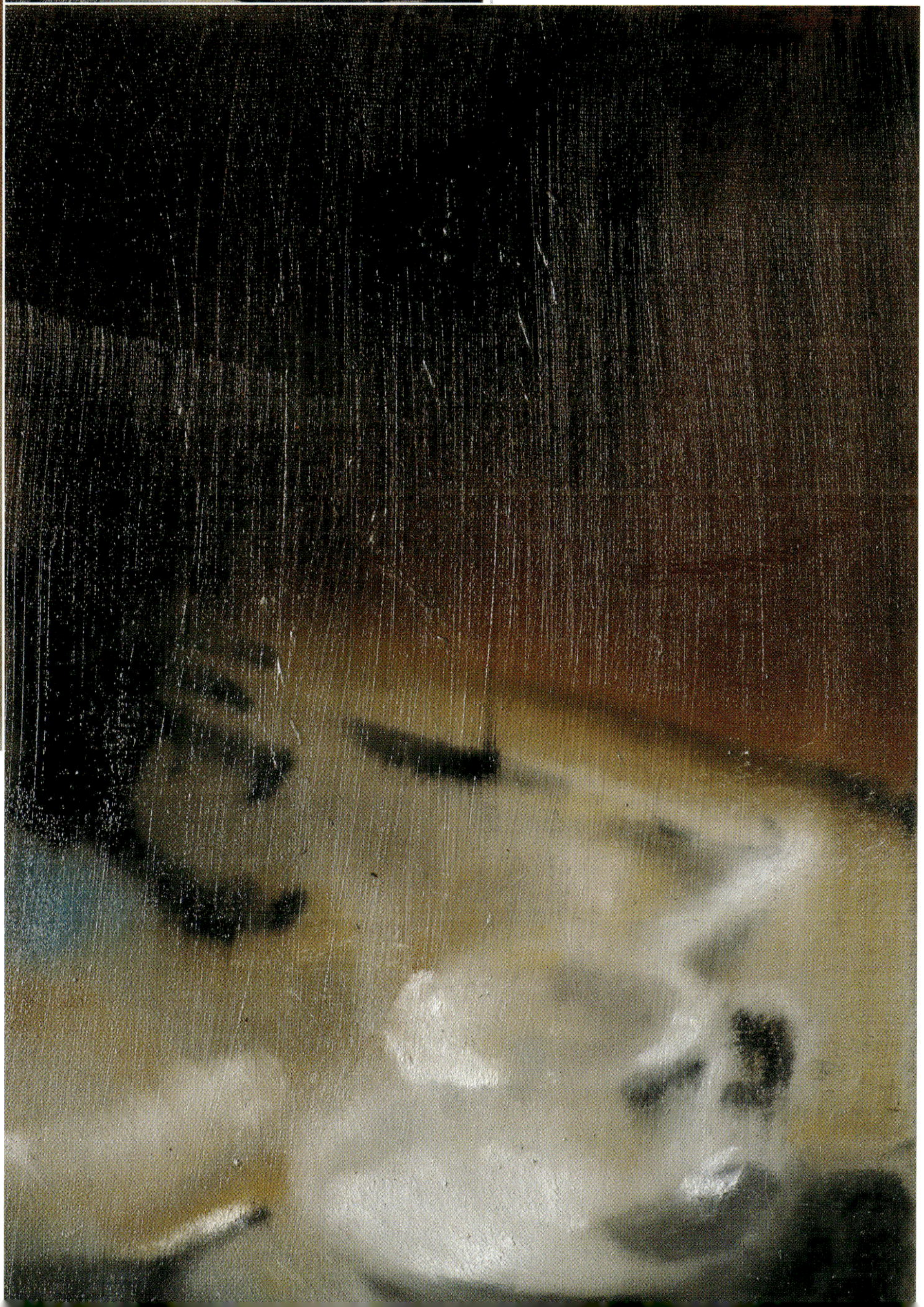

Other versions

The bristle brush is not the only applicator you can use to create good *sfumato*. A rag, the fingers, and other tools work as well in achieving the goal: diffusing the image. This gallery presents some of them.

This canvas has been diffused with a badger-hair brush, the softest and most suitable for very heavy *sfumato*. The rhythm of the final brushstroke is very controlled in a way that establishes horizontal and vertical movements to simulate a silky veil covering the image.

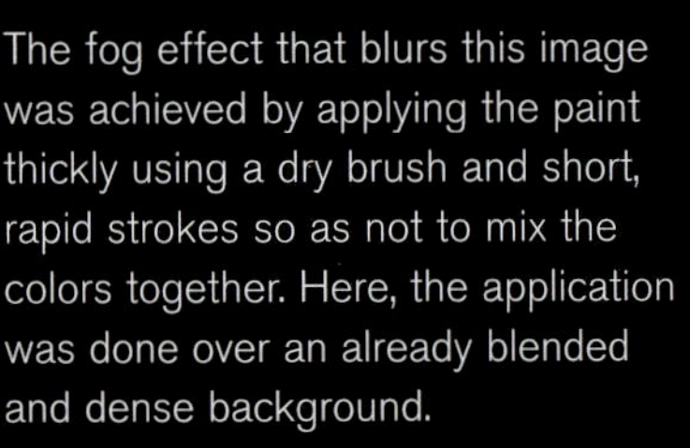

The fog effect that blurs this image was achieved by applying the paint thickly using a dry brush and short, rapid strokes so as not to mix the colors together. Here, the application was done over an already blended and dense background.

If we exploit the softness of the badger-hair brush too much, we will produce a total *sfumato*, a completely blended image, as in the case of this canvas. Because the elements of the picture are so blurred, and the dark background has such minimal contrast, the subject looks more like a reflection on glass rather than a solid form.

A rag is used not only for cleaning or erasing, but also for painting, as can be seen in this canvas. The rugged atmospheric effects here were created with a rag moistened in a small amount of paint.

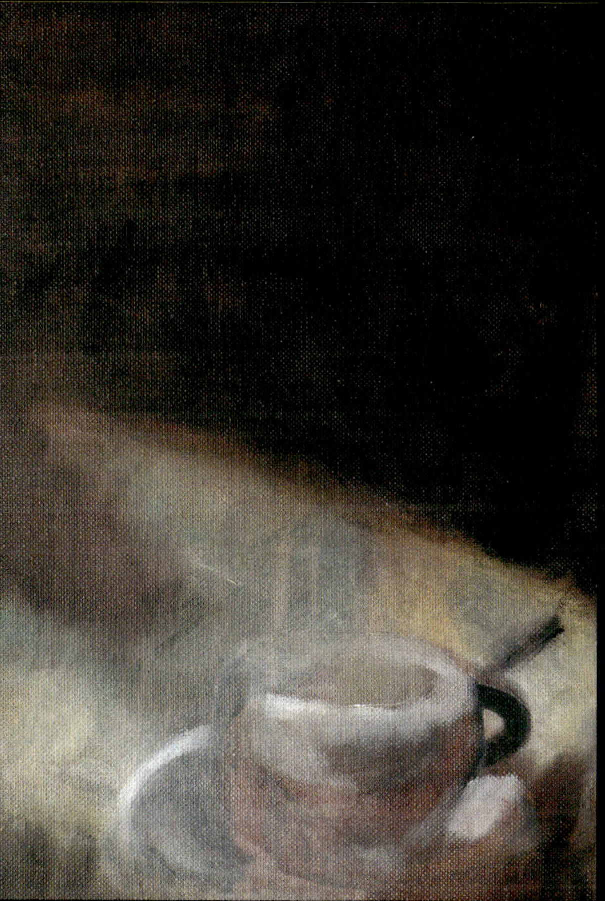

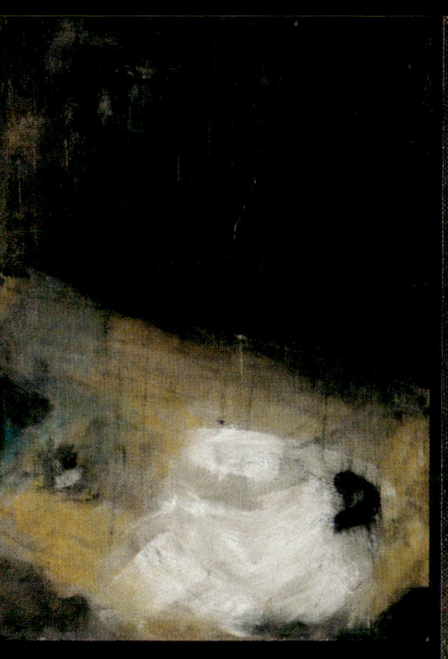

The fog effect here was achieved by applying paint thickly with a dry brush and by gently tapping the surface with the tip of the brush in a controlled manner.

The technique used to create *sfumato* in this example is glazing. The color (here, oil paint) was applied very diluted in oil and some turpentine, creating transparent layers. The surface was then wiped with a rag to remove excess paint and to create reflections.

New approaches

Other models

Pursuing the same interest in scenes of solitude dominated by a single object, the artist has repeated the experience with this simple and poetic still life. The main difference is in the light; in this case, it is not tenebrist—that is, characterized by dramatic juxtapositions of shadow and light—but clean and soft, which produces a less mysterious and more appealing result.

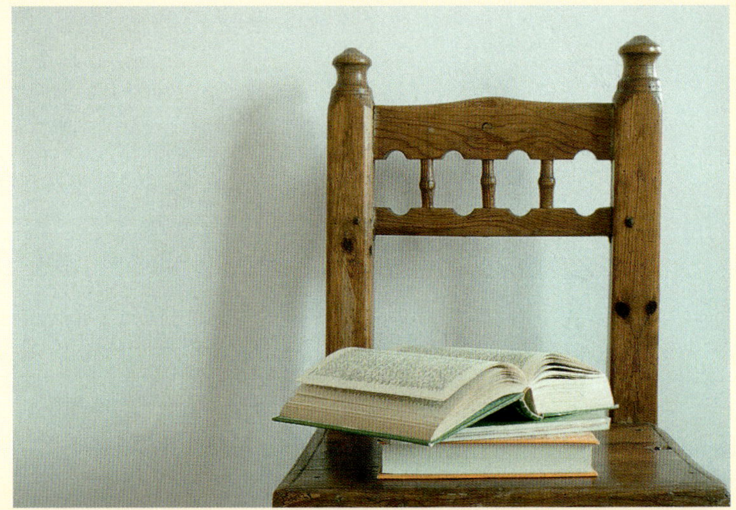

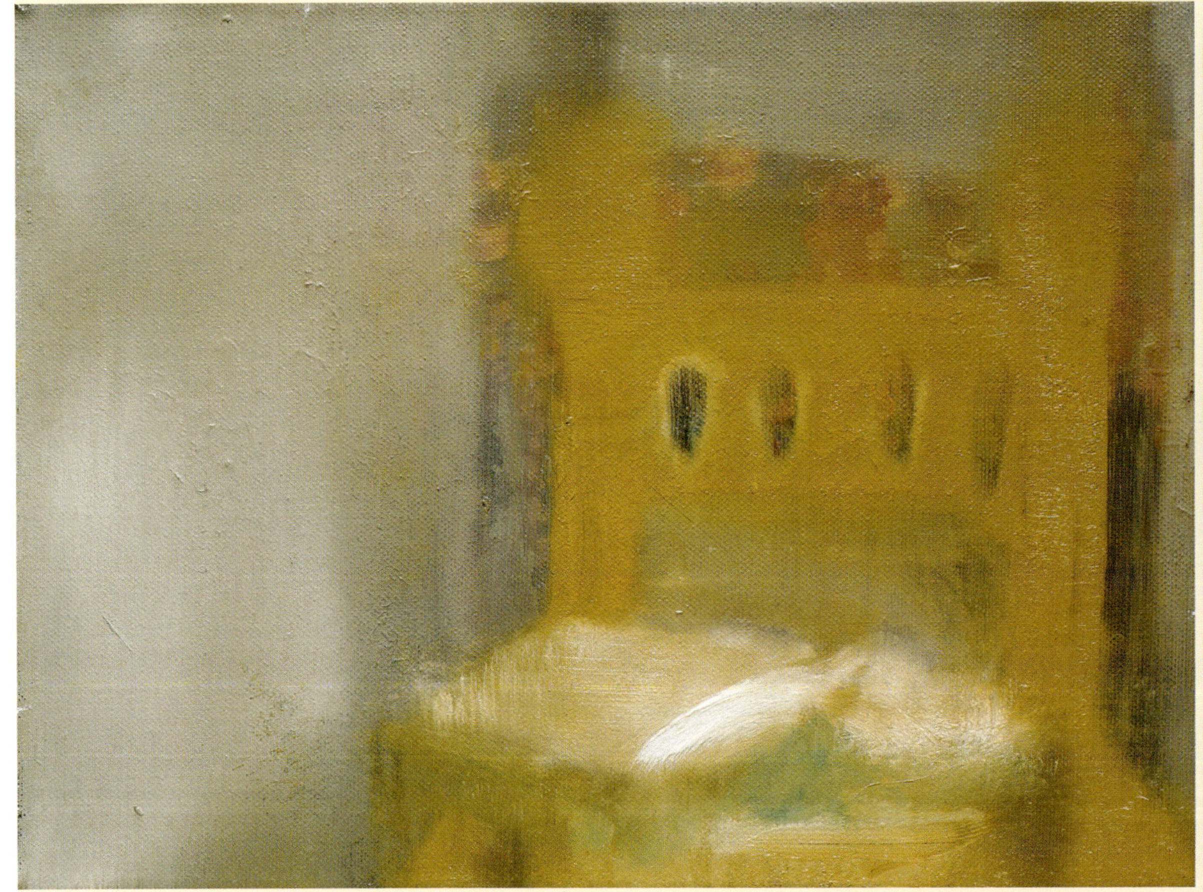

Other media

The dry medium par excellence for creating soft, diffuse effects is pastel. The artist has decided to use pastel as an alternative to the oil paints she used to depict the same subject as the one at the beginning of this section. Blending pastels is carried out with the fingers, a cotton ball, or a stamp. The result is very airy.

Other views

To maximize the effect of emptiness and silence, Fernando Zóbel (1924–1984) removed everything that was not necessary from his work. He thought that his work could not be considered fresh or spontaneous because he created the images through multiple repetitions of drawings, sketches, and photographs. The still life shown below belongs to a period in which Zóbel's paintings took a turn toward mixing the geometry of minute, thin vertical and horizontal lines with delicate luminous *sfumato* qualities.

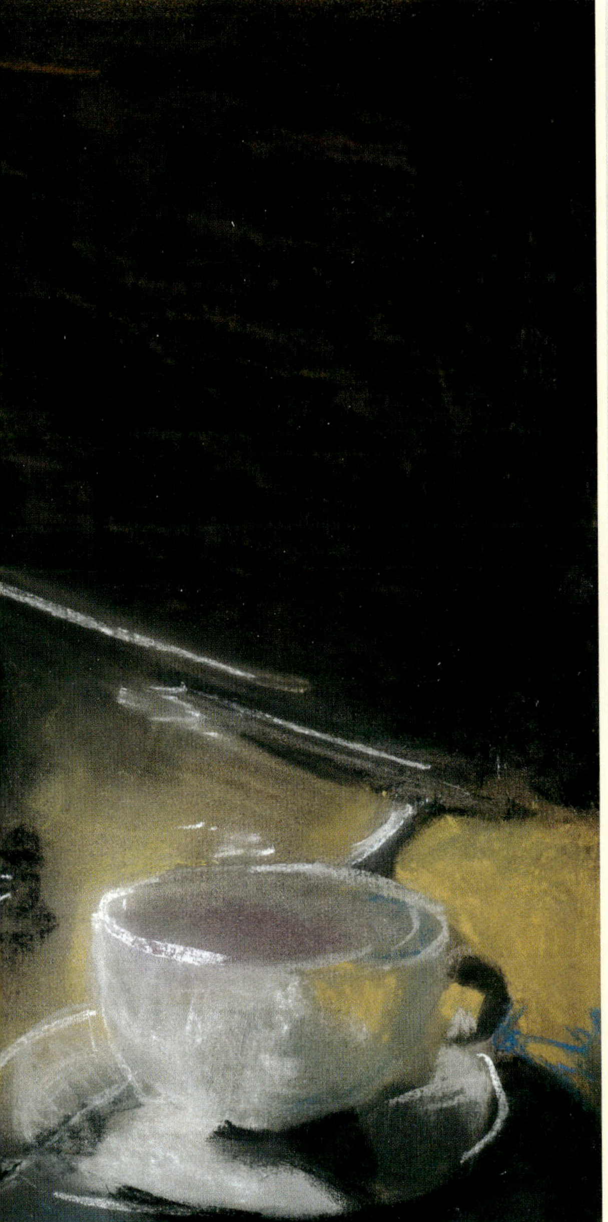

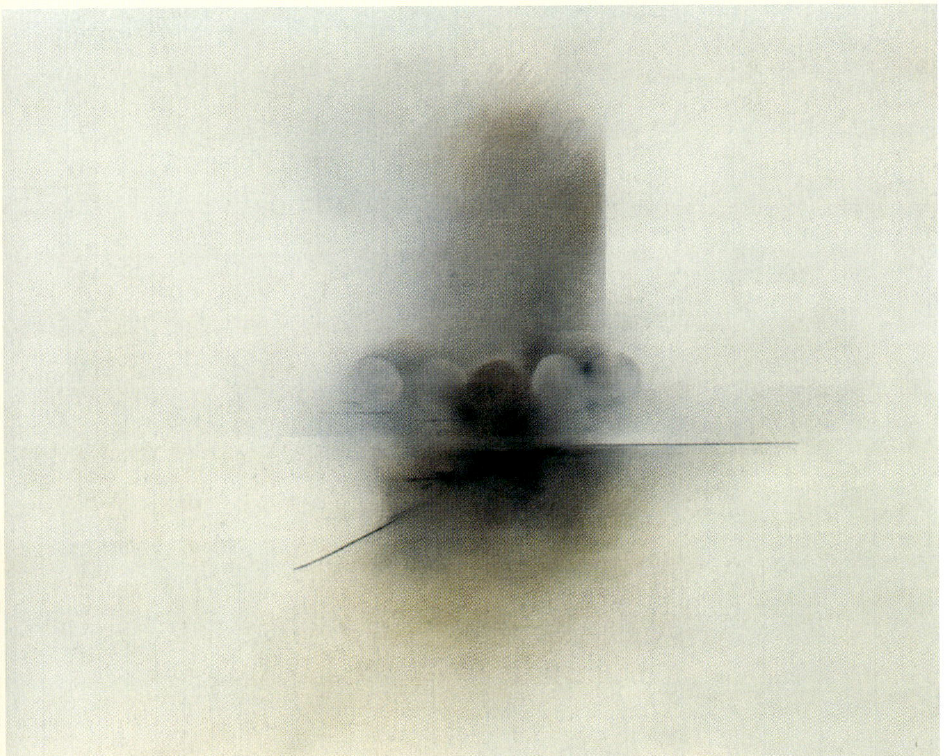

Fernando Zóbel,
Still Life, 1968.
Private collection.

Line in

Landscape paintings inevitably remind viewers of their physical contact with and connection to nature: stepping on grass on a walk through a garden or field, weighing the intense presence of ocean waves, walking on a rocky, rugged road, feeling the mist and the wind on your face before a storm—all important sensual experiences. In this section we experiment with textures produced by relief, impasto, and scraping, three characteristic effects of landscape that add expressiveness and liveliness to the representation.

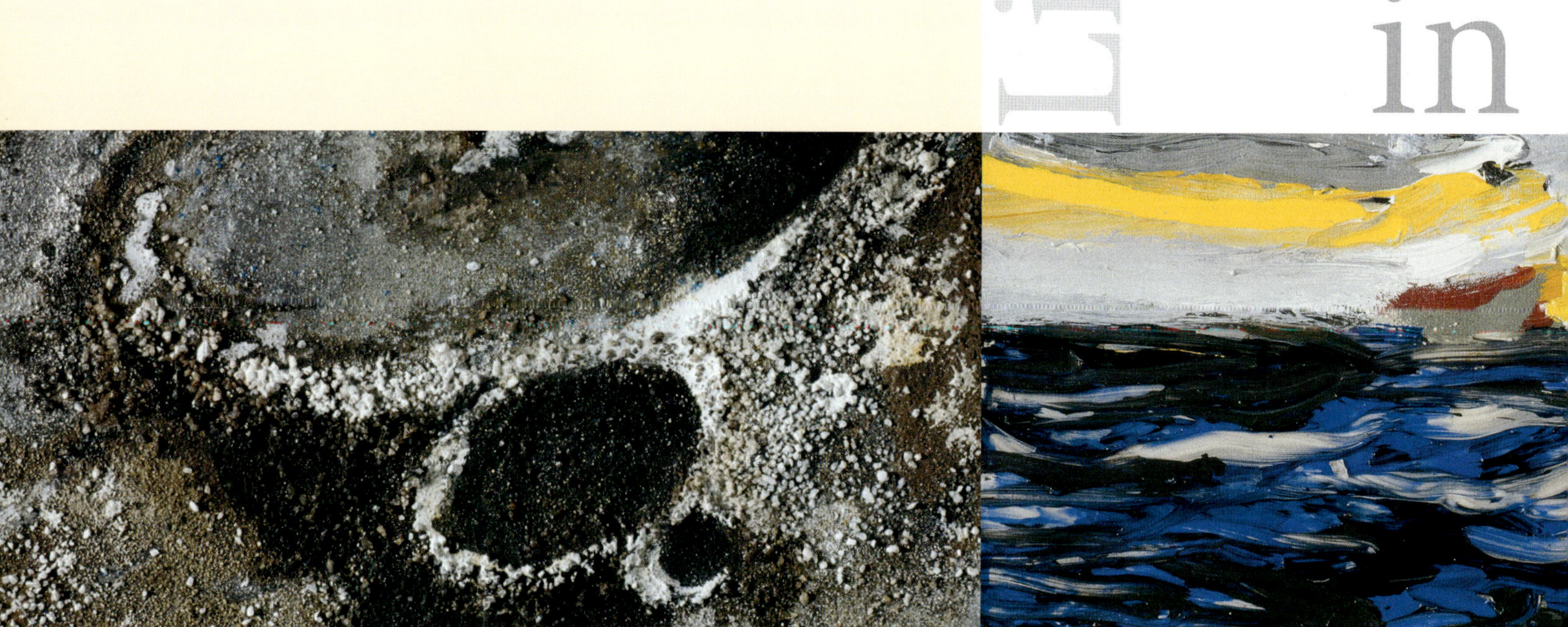

landscape

*"Being one with dust,
from that the deep identity,
the internal depth between
man and nature."*
The Book of Tao

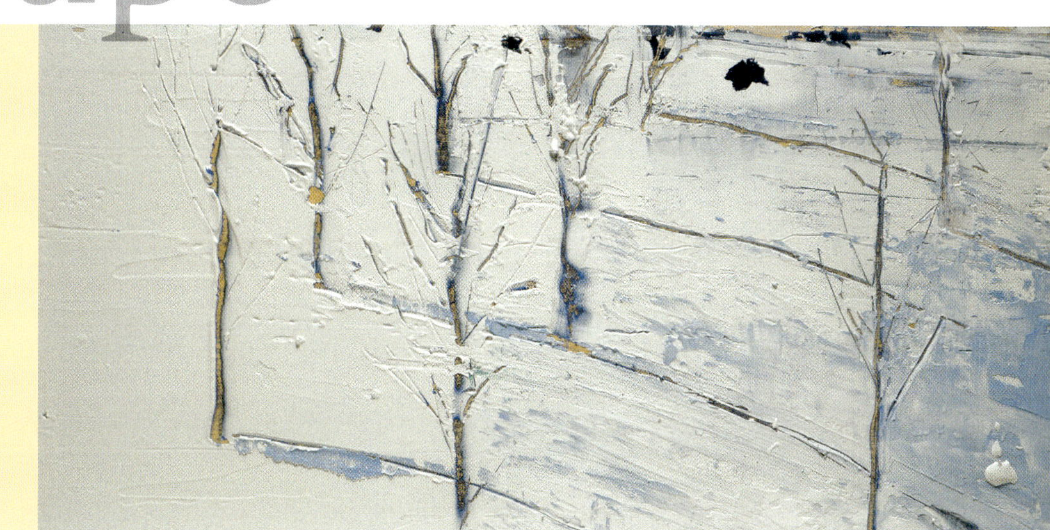

Earthy, rough, and volumetric textures

The sensual perception of landscape is an invitation to work with nature's own materials. Miquel Barceló (born in 1957) is a contemporary figurative painter who has experimented extensively with such materials. Since 1988, his stays in Africa have been a guiding force in his work, leading him to establish a workshop home in Dogon (Mali) so he can absorb all the landscape and its energy. In Africa, he has discovered an endless source of light, vast landscapes, and the importance of water as a source of life. Many of his textured landscapes are paintings of the surfaces of Mali's landscape, as in *Alrededor del lago Negro (Around the Black Lake)*, a surface like dry skin that contains the energy of the earth (water), but also the power of death. The basis of his paintings is latex, to which he adds earth pigments. He has also experimented with crayons, cellulose, mica, silica powder, marble dust, ashes, iron sulfate, decomposable organic matter . . . always looking to provoke phenomena with such physical materials.

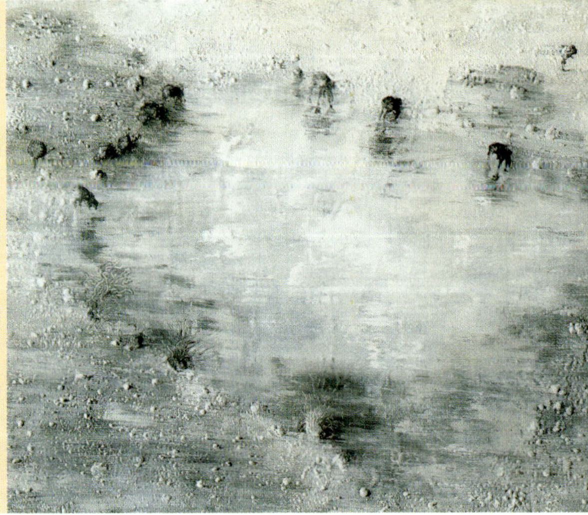

Miquel Barceló,
Alrededor del lago Negro, 1990.
Private collection.

Material painting: A lunar landscape with texture

This approach is a figurative work created with paint mixed with matter. Its artist, Josep María Ametlla, experiments with the incorporation of material on the canvas to create relief effects. The medium used is latex mixed with various substances, applied on stiff cardboard, and the object chosen is an atypical landscape: the surface of the moon, an extremely interesting textured space that lends itself to variations on the terrain.

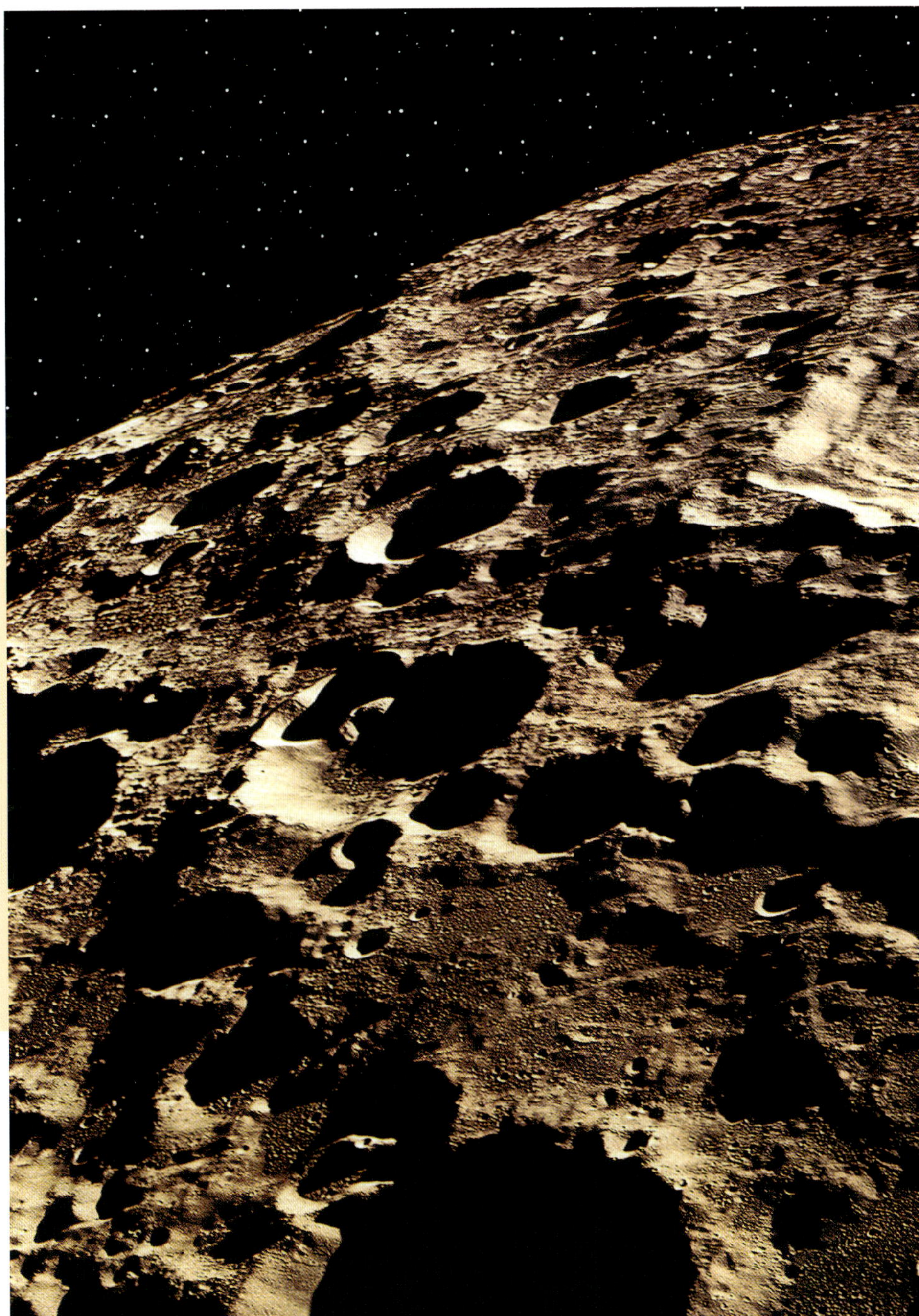

"The subject matter must adapt to the material . . . That interests me, it is the contribution between the true oyster and the representation of the oyster that becomes matter. The 'painting matter' that becomes the 'oyster matter' . . . matter alone has no meaning. My paintings represent that, images in the making."
Miquel Barceló,
Interview with Bertrand Ducourau,
1992.

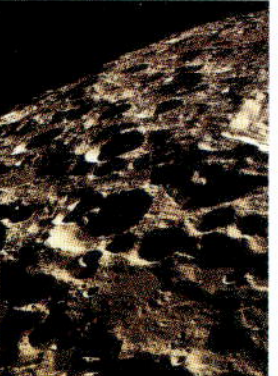

1 We prime a piece of hard, heavy pressed cardboard with a layer of latex (vinyl glue) and Spanish white as pigment to seal the pores of the cardboard and prevent future warping.

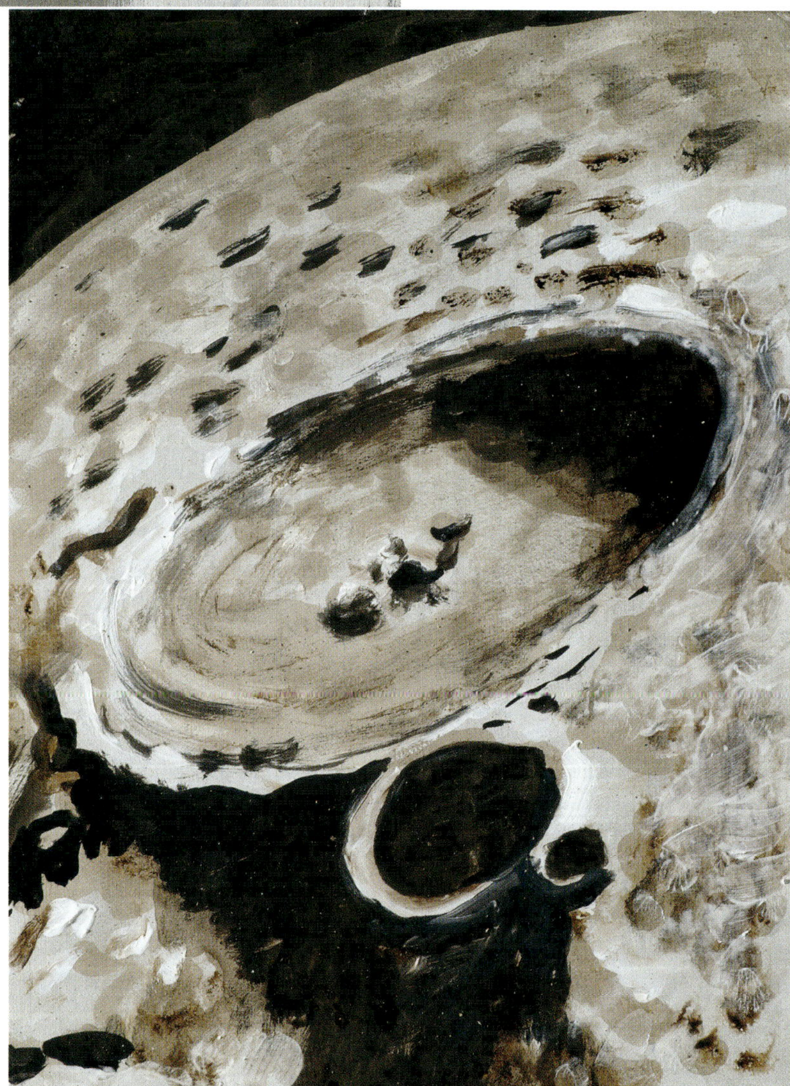

2 When the support is dry, we sketch the work by drawing directly on the surface with sienna and sepia ink.

3 The first reliefs are created by applying a synthetic paste with a spatula on the areas of volume. In this case, a type of fiberglass, normally used to fix spreading cracks, has been added to the paste.

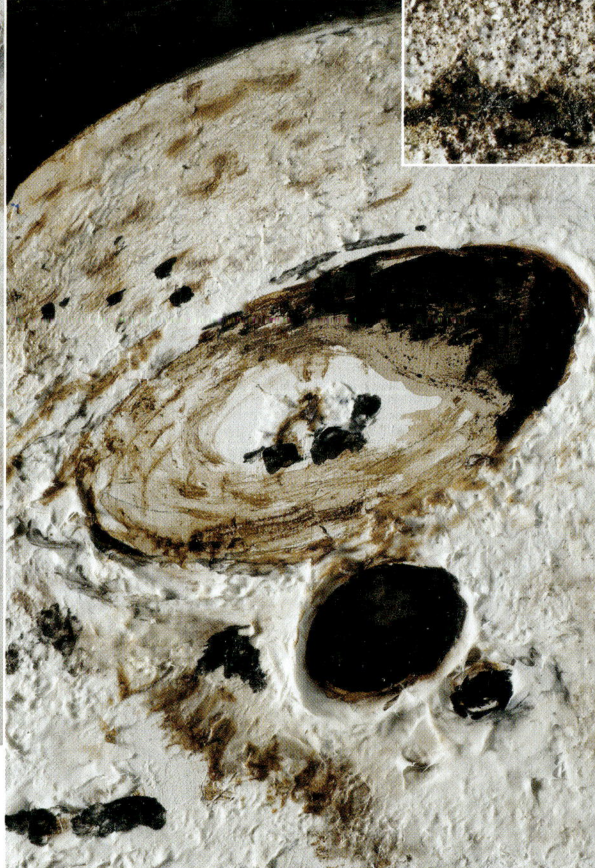

4 We create the grainy effect of the texture by preparing a solution of marble dust and river silt and natural sienna pigment. The latex must be dissolved with water into a viscous mixture, neither liquid nor thick. When everything is applied and still wet, we sprinkle some areas with iron shavings to promote natural oxidation.

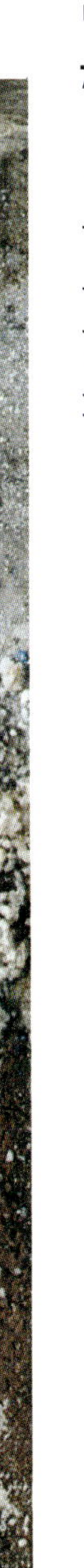

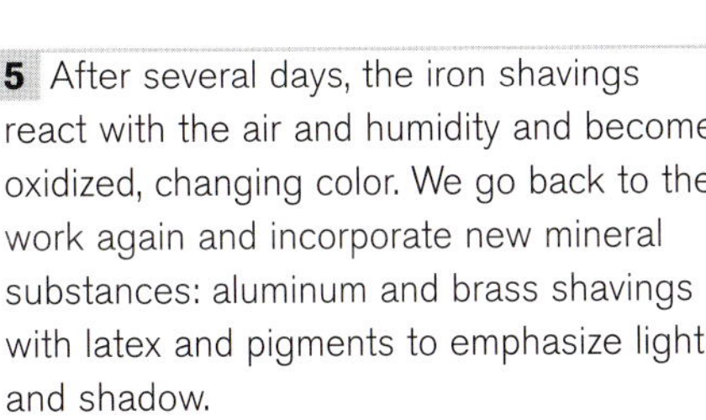

5 After several days, the iron shavings react with the air and humidity and become oxidized, changing color. We go back to the work again and incorporate new mineral substances: aluminum and brass shavings with latex and pigments to emphasize light and shadow.

Other versions

This interesting gallery is the result of experimenting with various mineral substances and inks. What all the pieces have in common is the need to observe the drying times, paying attention to the changes that the image could suffer as a consequence of oxidation and humidity.

This work was executed on stiff cardboard primed with a layer of vinyl glue and Spanish white. The textural features have been created with river silt and latex, the atmospheric effects with ink, asphaltum applied with a brush, and, finally, when the latex emulsion is still wet, Spanish white (this way the pigment will adhere to the surface while maintaining its powdery aspect).

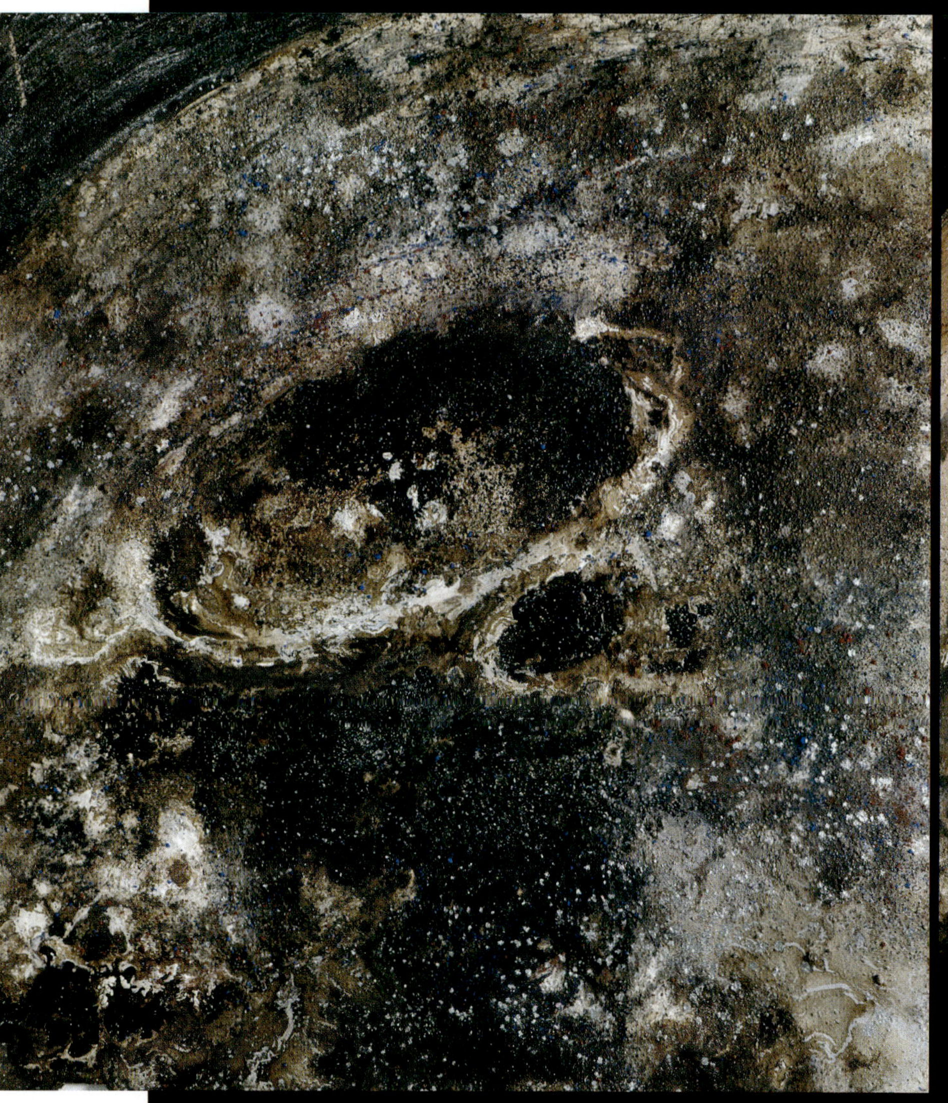

Here the support is wood, coated with two layers of vinyl primer. The textural features were created with clay and sand mixed with latex. Once dry, the surface was painted with oil enamel; then white chalk was sprinkled on to create areas of light.

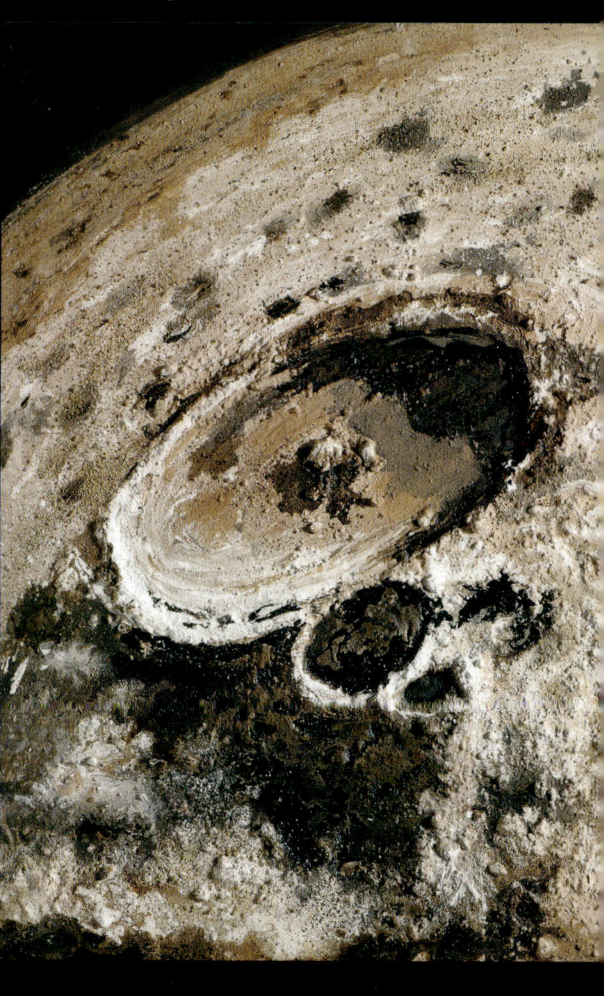

In addition to its horizontal composition, the technical characteristic that sets this piece apart from the others is the use of spray enamel paint at the end of the process. The variety of thicknesses is very interesting. The textural features were created first on primed cardboard with latex, Spanish white, and marble dust.

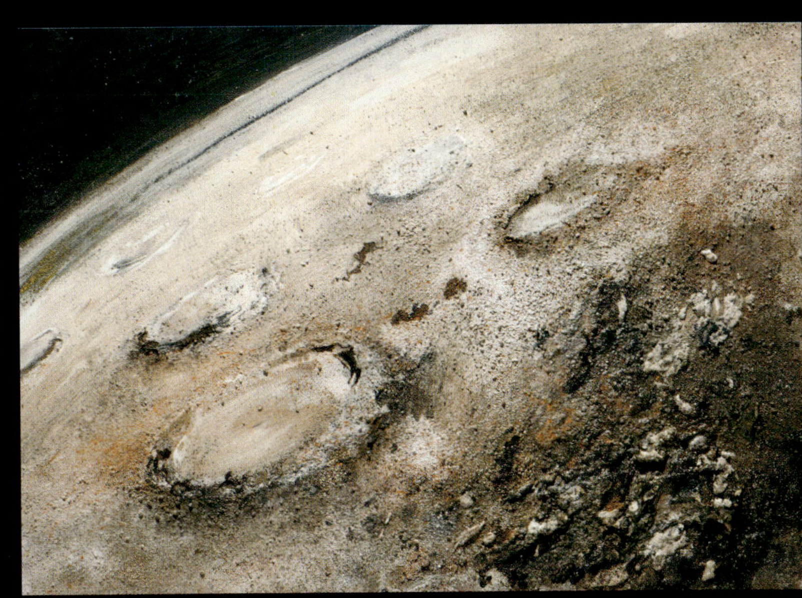

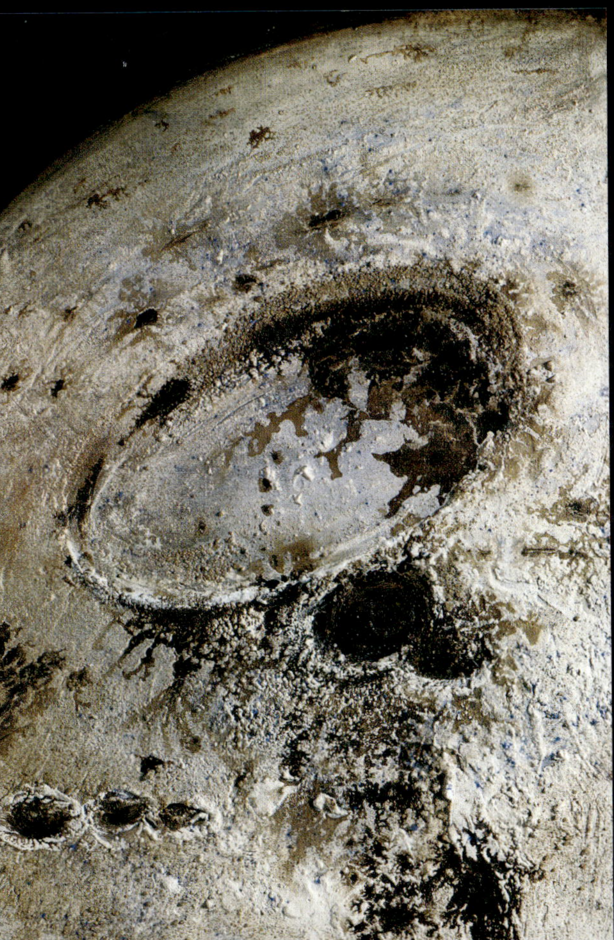

This painting has less relief and was created by mixing Spanish white, latex, and marble dust (much more refined than sand). Once the base hardened, it was painted with liquid asphaltum, over which pigments and powdered copper were sprinkled while the surface was still wet.

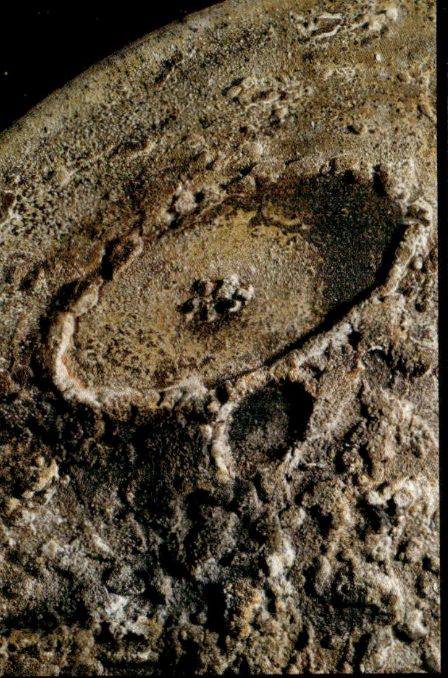

Here, on a piece of unprimed wood, the volumes were created by carefully spraying on expandable polystyrene. When this material expanded and dried, everything was covered with a primer made of Spanish white and latex. The piece was finished by applying acrylic paints with a brush.

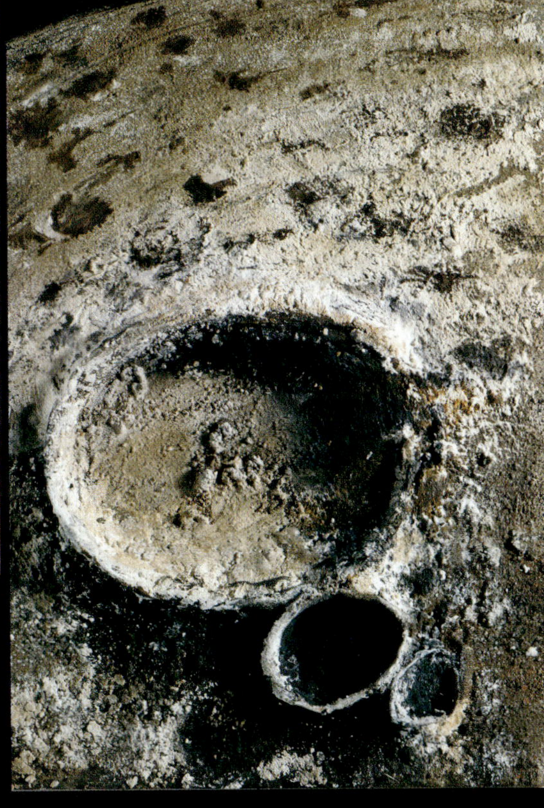

The relief features of this painting were made of cellulose modeling paste and vinyl glue (latex) applied on primed wood. When the cellulose paste is fresh it can be modeled very easily; here it was formed into small balls and thrown onto the support to create little mountains. Once dry, the piece was completed with acrylic paint.

Other models

For this variation on the theme of earthy textures, the artist was inspired by an area of marshes, the Aiguamolls de l'Empordà in Girona, Spain, a landscape he knows very well because it is where he has his studio. The painting has perfectly incorporated the natural elements: air, vegetation, and the typical features of a marsh, the water and the soil combined. The piece, executed on wood primed with latex, was made with gypsum paste (the kind used to repair cracks), acrylic paint, powdered pigments, and, finally, asphaltum.

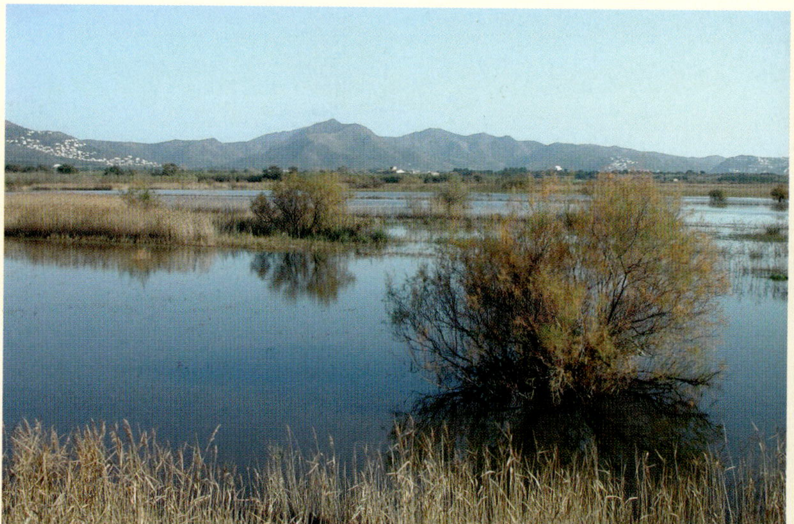

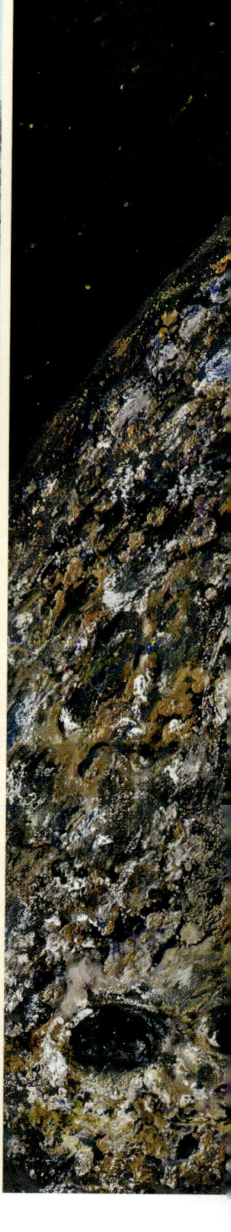

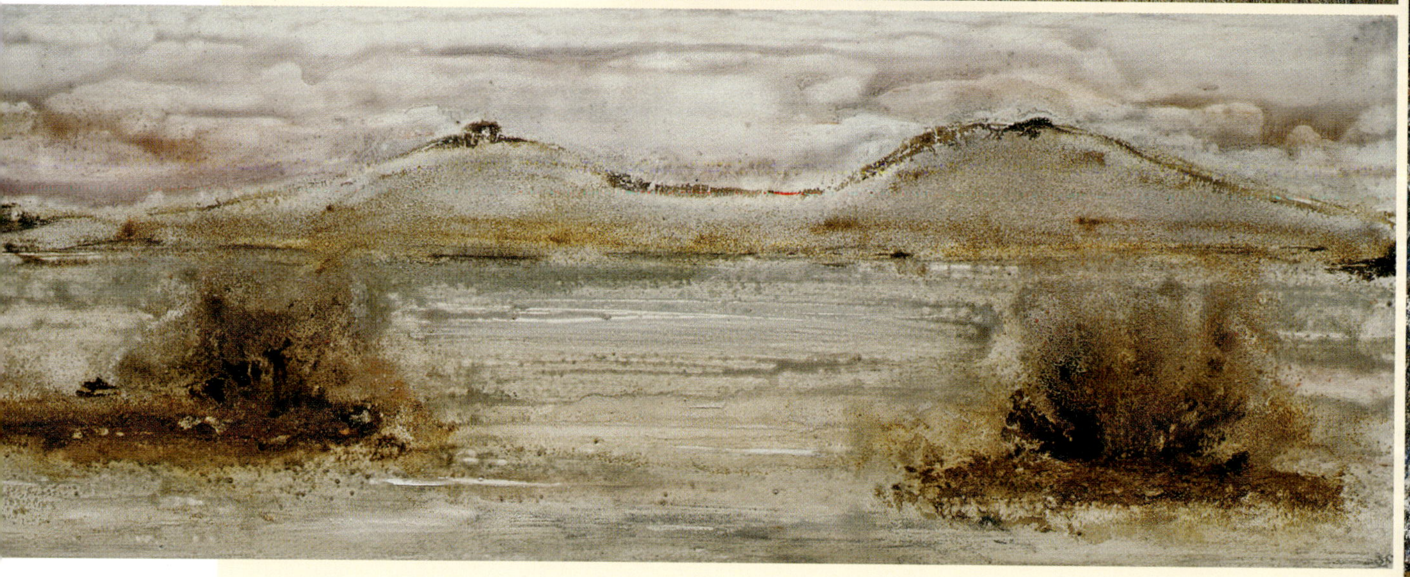

Other media

The textural work in the image below was based on substances added to the paint. To work with a medium that is already volumetric, encaustic, or wax paint, was chosen. When the hot colored wax is applied by dripping and rubbing, it leaves behind some relief. To create strong contrasts the work was executed on a wood board painted black.

Other views

Anselm Kiefer (born in 1945) is an irrefutable practitioner of material landscape painting. *Nuremberg*, a large, 152 × 112 inch (380 × 280 cm) canvas executed with acrylic, latex emulsion, and straw, is a clear example of the expressive capability of materials incorporated as integral parts of the painting. The secret of this work is in letting the materials speak for themselves rather than serve as just a technical means to create a relief. Here, the straw is very eloquent and gives realism to the piece; due to the size of the painting, the viewer feels as if he is truly stepping on the ground.

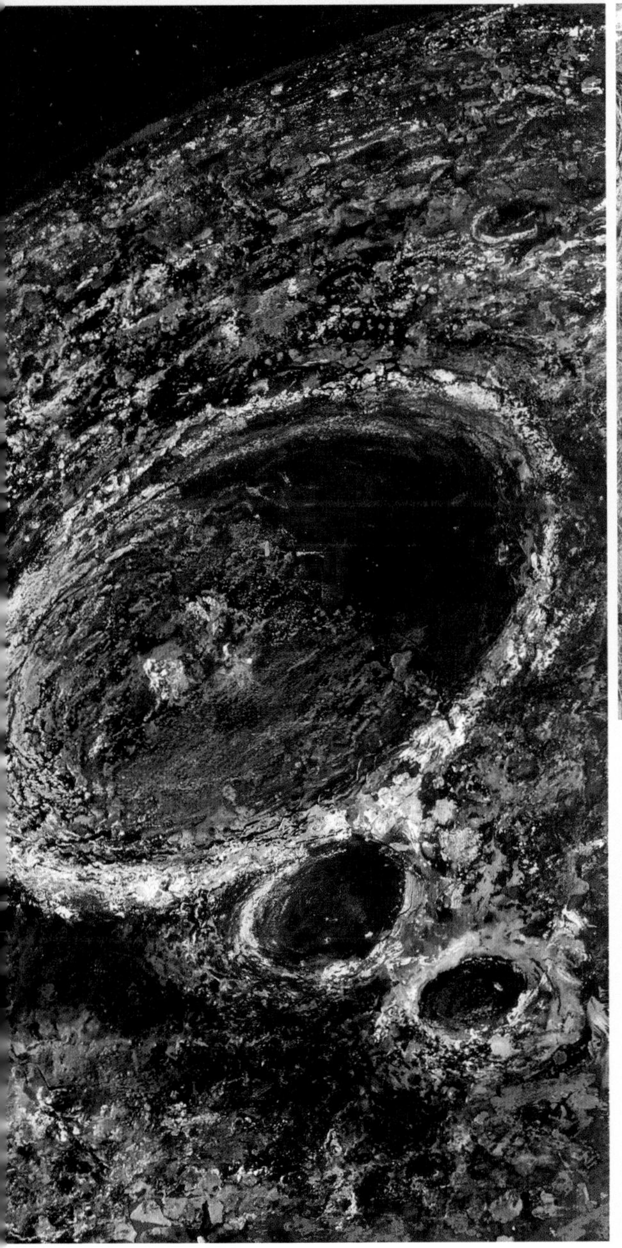

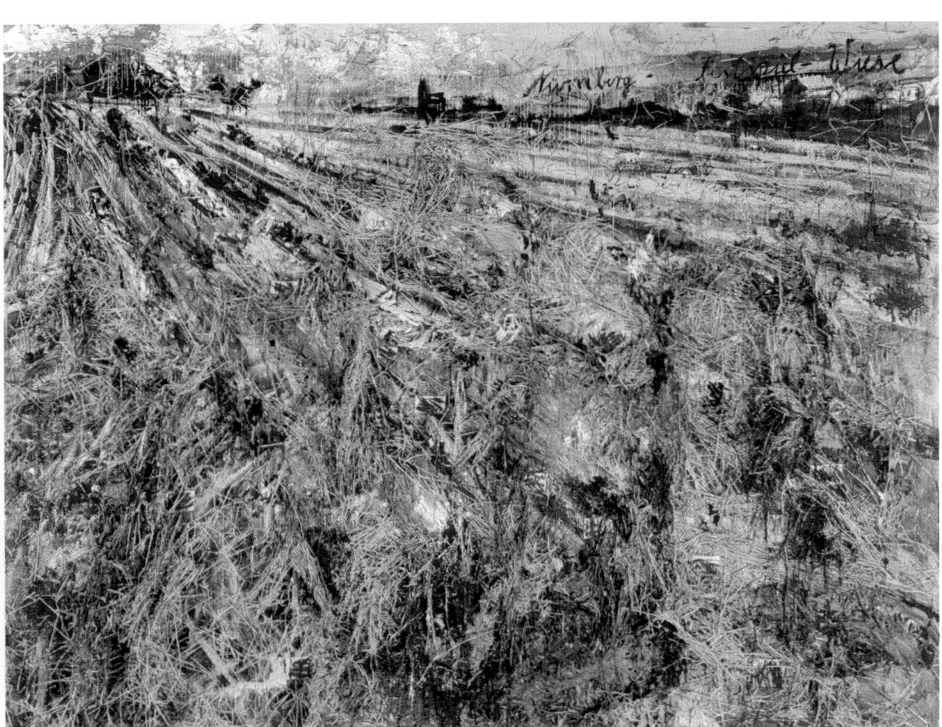

Anselm Kiefer,
Nuremberg, 1982.
Private collection.

Creative approach 08

Impasto, gelatinous, and creamy textures

With a pictorial body of work that is exceedingly modern for his time, August Strindberg (1849–1912) was better known as a playwright; he alternated his writing with painting, photography, and alchemy. He met Gauguin and was a friend of Munch, Nietzsche, as well as Larsson and Nordström, two leaders of the opposition to official Swedish art. Recently, he has been considered a precursor of American Abstract Expressionism of the decade of the 1950s and of Informalism. The central theme of his work was the landscape—an empty landscape, without human figures or known references. His emotional life was unstable, the result of an unbalanced personality; for this reason the spaces open to the viewer are always charged with anguish and inner restlessness. Strindberg always painted in his studio, although nature was a vehicle that helped him reflect upon his inner torment. With lines, planes, and impastos applied with a spatula, he conveyed an enormous expressive force, a feeling of pain and claustrophobia.

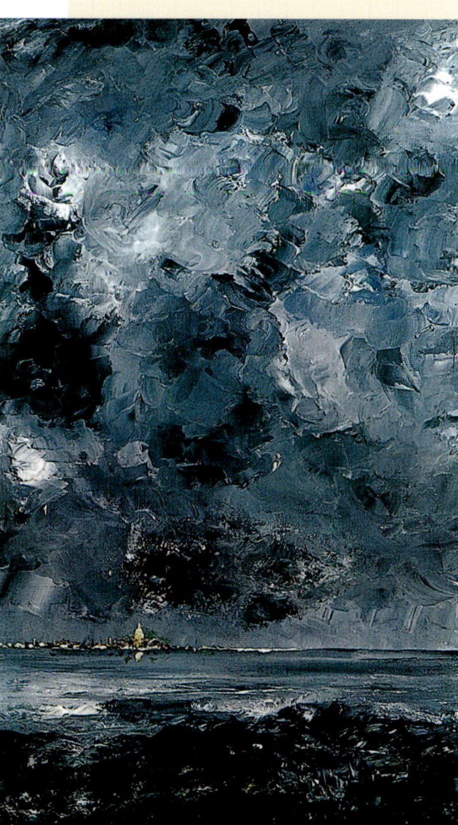

August Strindberg, *The City*, 1903. National Museum Stockholm (Sweden).

Seascape with sky effects created with gel medium and modeling paste

Gemma Guasch has chosen as a model one of the photographs she took on a trip from Stockholm to Helsinki, sailing the same waters painted by Strindberg. The view of a naked and open landscape (sea and sky) is reminiscent of the Swedish painter's work: northern, deserted scenes wrapped in a bright, nostalgic light. Acrylic is the medium used, mixed with different gels and pastes to give the painting body and thickness. The support used is canvas.

"That rage of his, those pages resulting from hard-fought struggle . . . I have not read it for the sake of reading it but to become closer to him. I feel good after reading Strindberg."
Franz Kafka

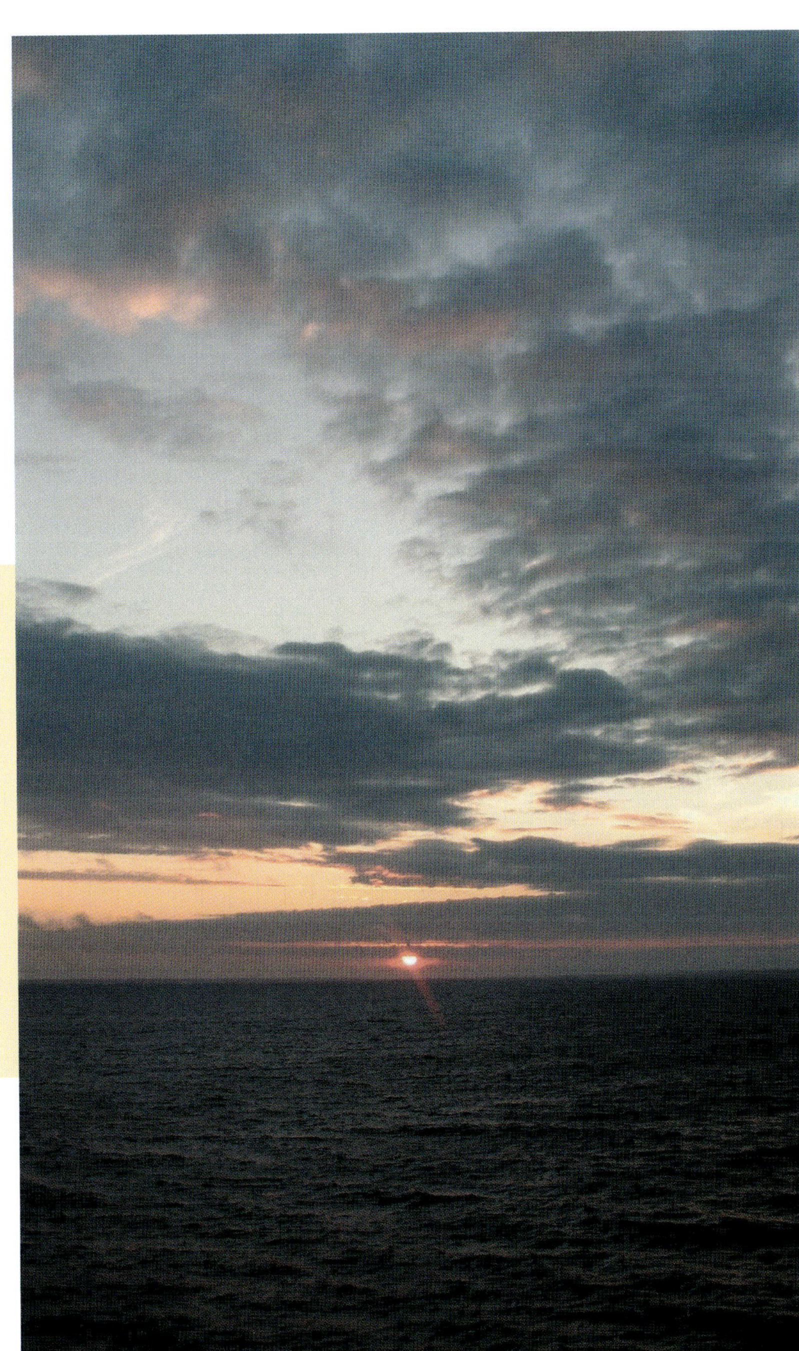

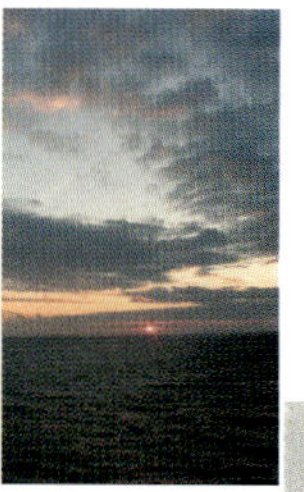

1 We apply opaque gel with a wide brush, covering the lower part of the image. Then a layer of cobalt blue is applied with a thin brush; this way we produce a heavier layer of paint that looks creamy. The lines appear to move gently, horizontally, to simulate the soft movement of the calm sea.

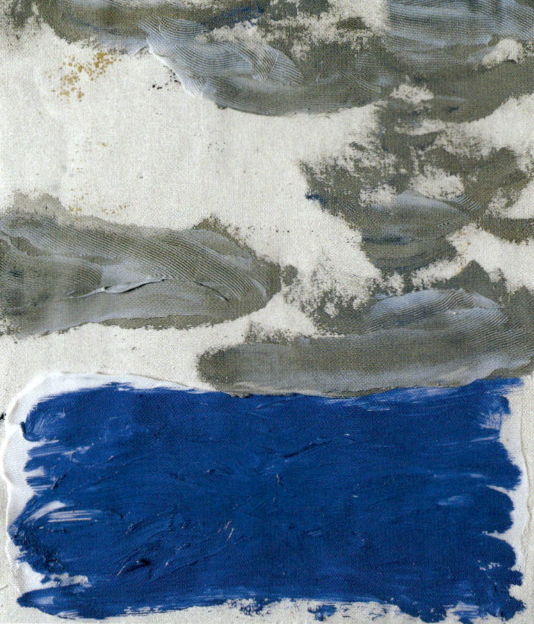

2 Next, we paint the most overcast part of the sky with gray. We use longer and more dynamic lines to indicate its heaviness. Finally, transparent gel is applied liberally over the clouds to soften the paint and give it density.

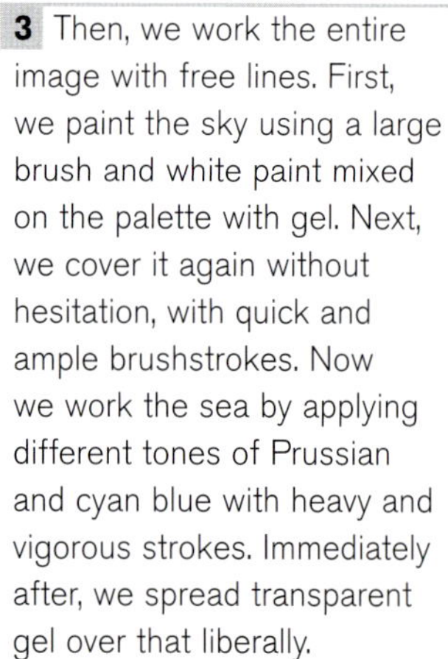

3 Then, we work the entire image with free lines. First, we paint the sky using a large brush and white paint mixed on the palette with gel. Next, we cover it again without hesitation, with quick and ample brushstrokes. Now we work the sea by applying different tones of Prussian and cyan blue with heavy and vigorous strokes. Immediately after, we spread transparent gel over that liberally.

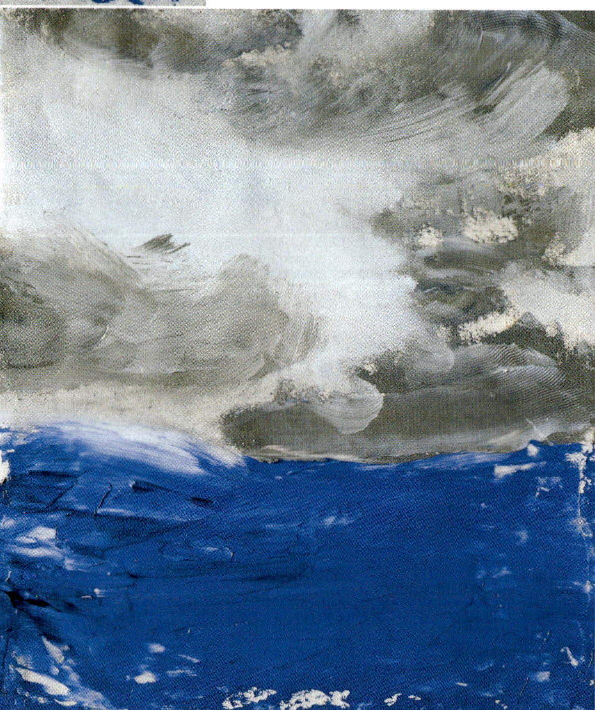

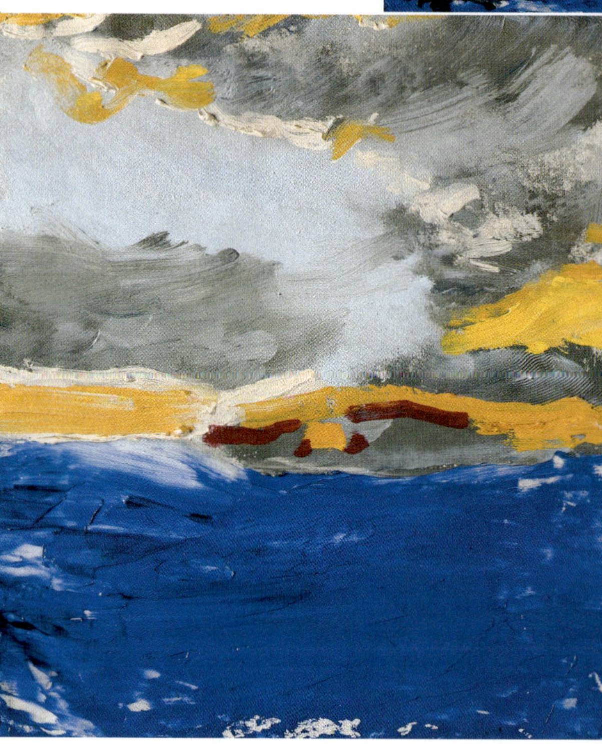

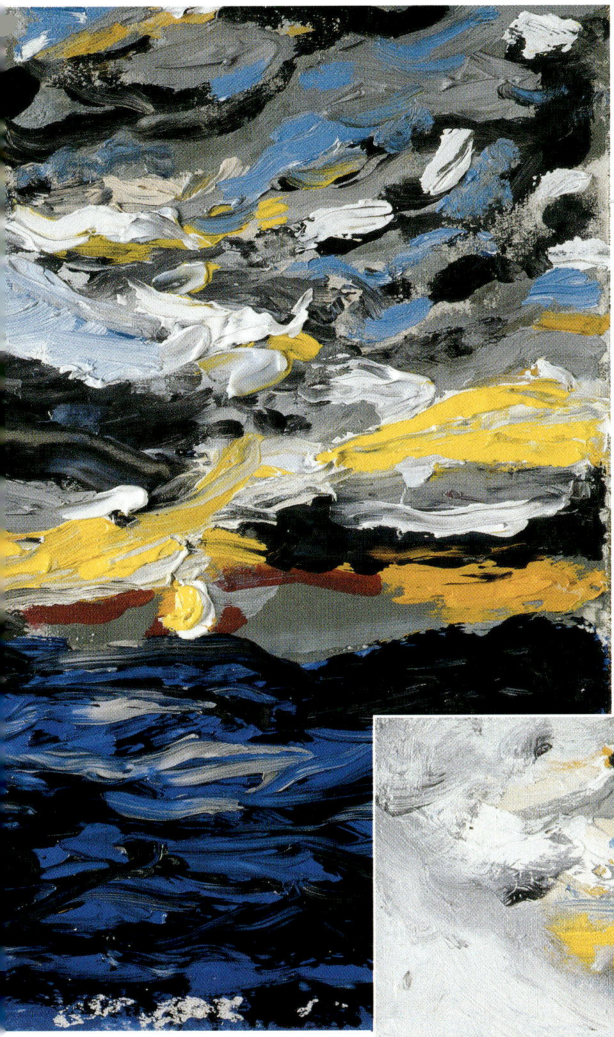

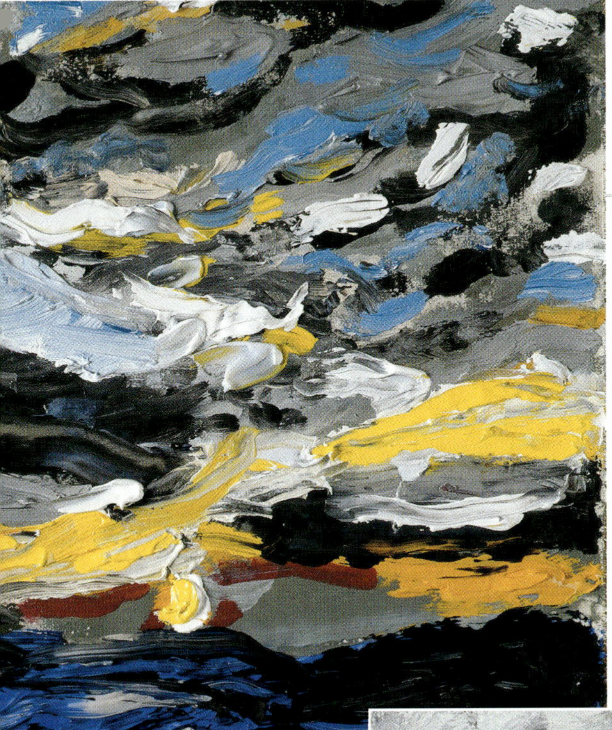

5 To enhance the dramatic feeling, we apply dark tones to the painting. The sea is painted with Prussian blue with long, undulating strokes charged with quite a bit of color, maintaining the rhythmic feeling of the waves. Then, we apply shorter and pastier brushstrokes until a heavy, dense, and thick sky of different colors (dark gray, light gray, cyan blue, yellow, and white) is achieved.

6 We wait for the surface to dry completely, since the thickness of the gel and paint make it impossible to work without dirtying the image. After a few days we apply small white brushstrokes in some areas of the sky. This way we reestablish the light and soften the image. The final work is somewhat less dramatic than it appeared in the previous step, but is has not lost any pictorial strength.

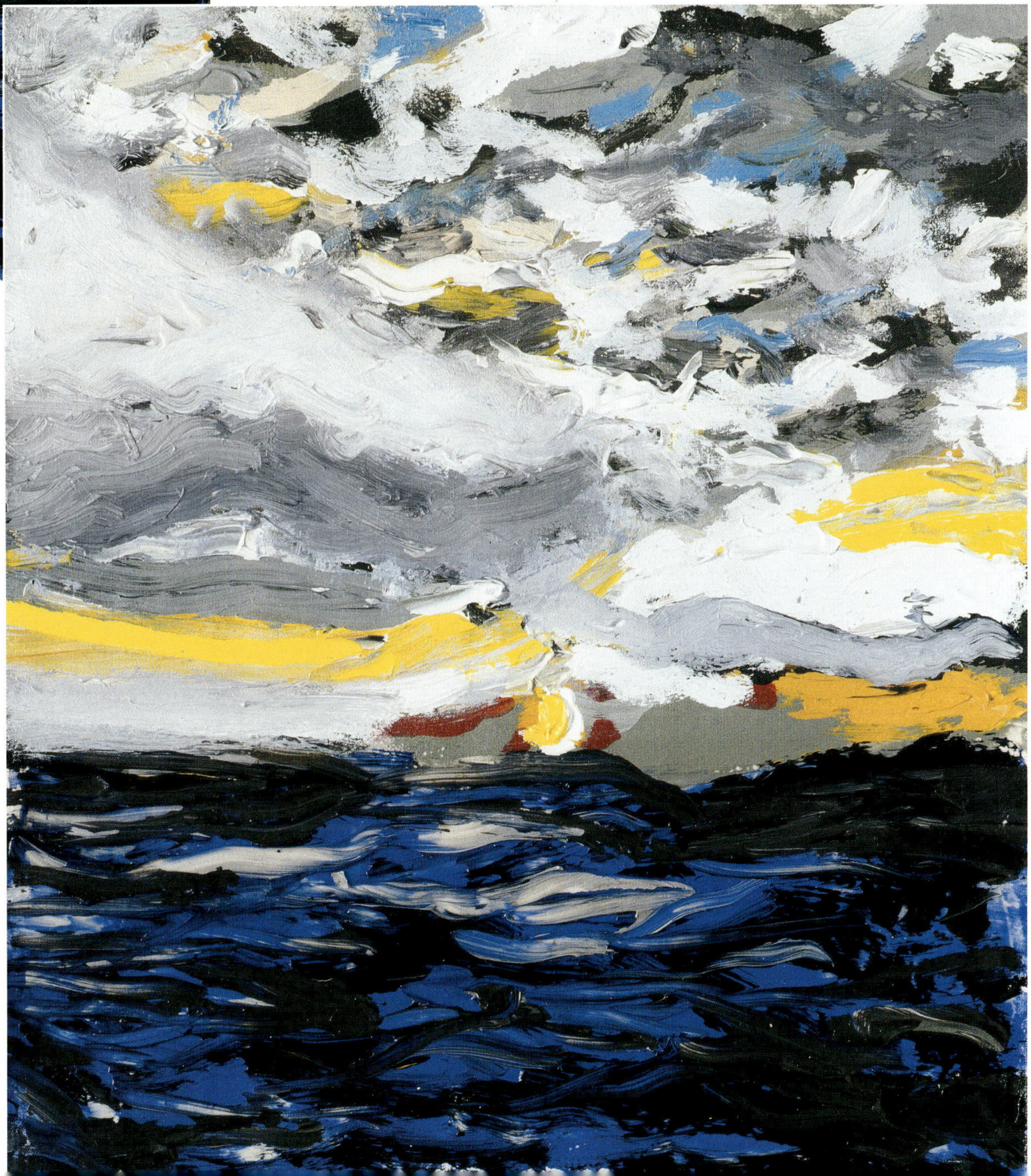

4 At this point the painting gives us a glimpse of the power of nature. Now we apply the warm tones that will define the sunset. With a thin, flat brush we apply long, heavy yellow and orange strokes in different parts of the sky. Then we apply red paint directly from the tube to prevent it from mixing with the rest and to achieve greater relief.

Other versions

Nowadays there are many gels and modeling pastes on the market for mixing with paint; these products make it possible to add body and volume to your paintings and enhance the optical sensation. This gallery was created with different kinds of gel medium and applicators to emphasize their most tactile aspects.

In this work we used an extra-dense gel medium (semigloss) mixed with abundant paint to emphasize the sea. It was applied with a wide brush, which provided a compact and gel-like look. To enhance the contrast, the sky was worked with a small amount of paint applied with a rag. The final result is very dramatic.

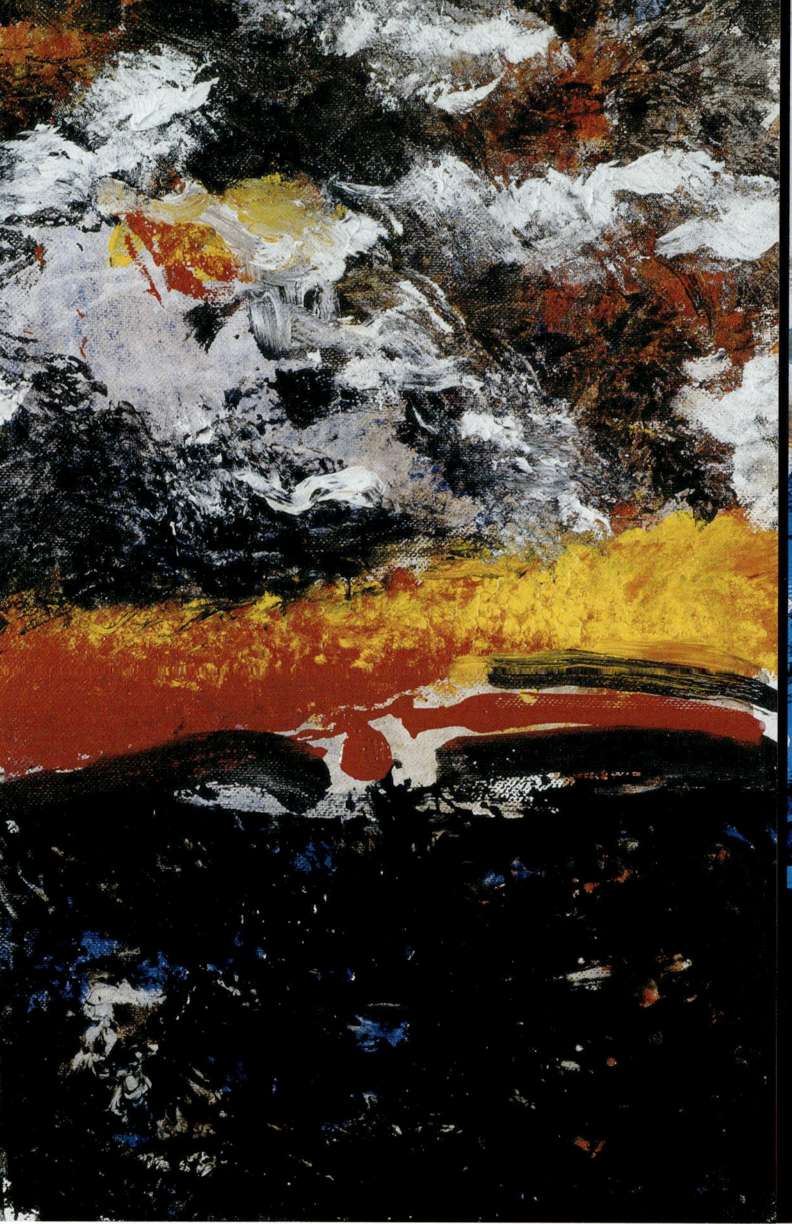

This is one of the freshest and most direct images of the gallery. It was created by applying a matte, dense gel and then painting it with a spatula, directly and liberally. Finally, a hard comb was dragged over the gel and the paint to create a striated texture.

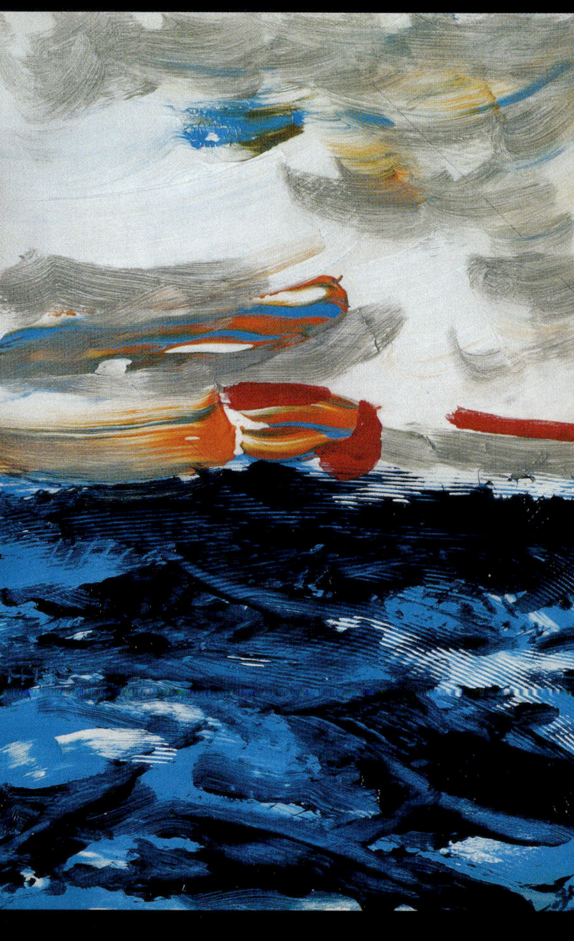

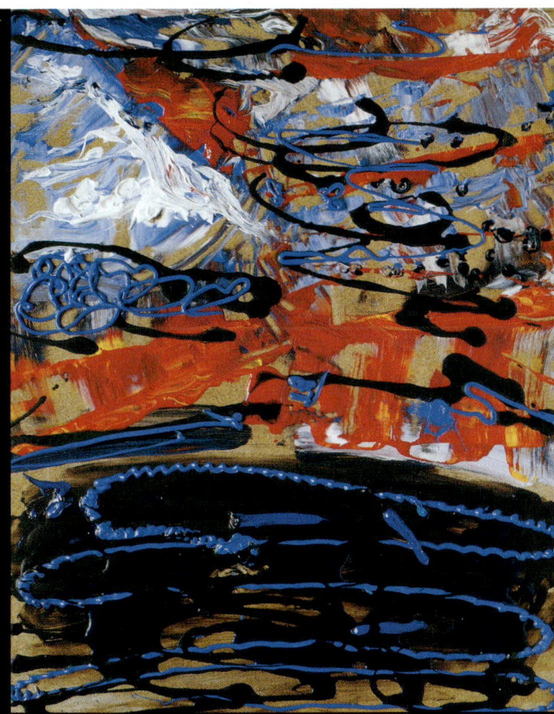

This is a quick and direct work. The support used is a piece of pressboard primed with a modeling paste. The sky was created with a large amount of paint applied with rapid movements using a wide spatula. The lines let us see through to the wood, giving a feeling of movement. To complete the work, paint was applied directly from the tube to increase the sense of volume and to obtain a dripping effect.

The mixture of many materials produced this heavy and solid result. Here, modeling paste, semigloss gel medium, and extra-heavy gel were applied with a large brush. The result achieved emphasizes the creaminess and the impasto effect of the paint.

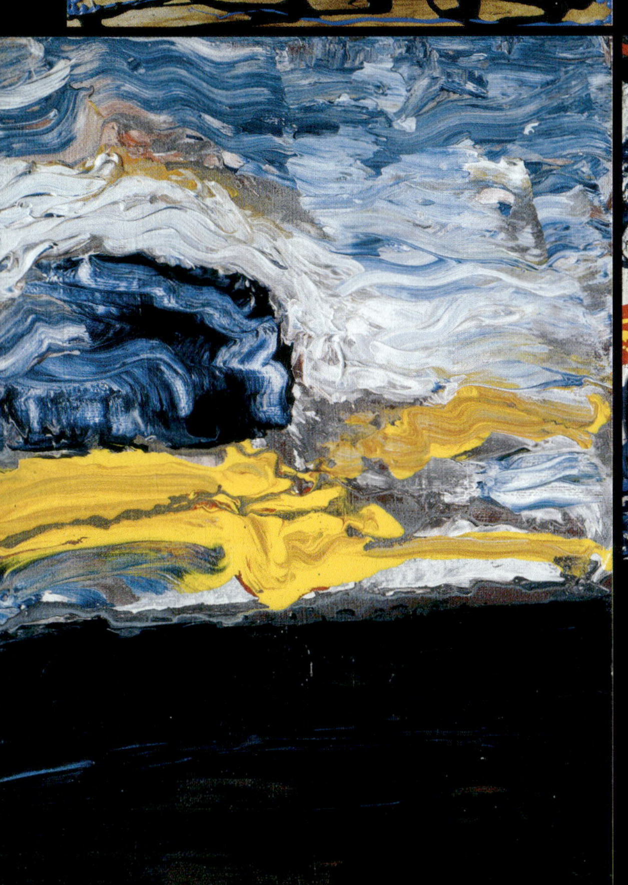

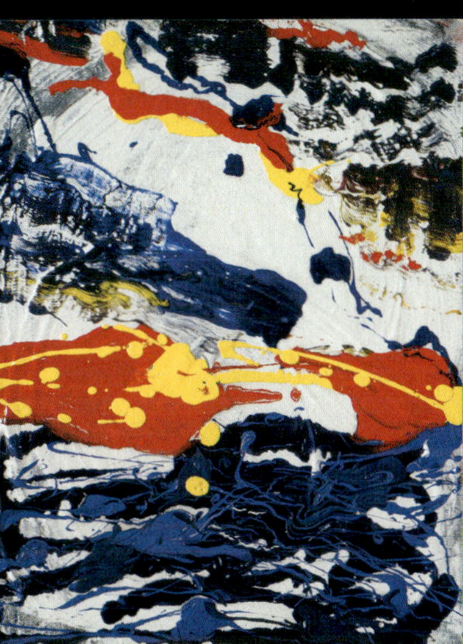

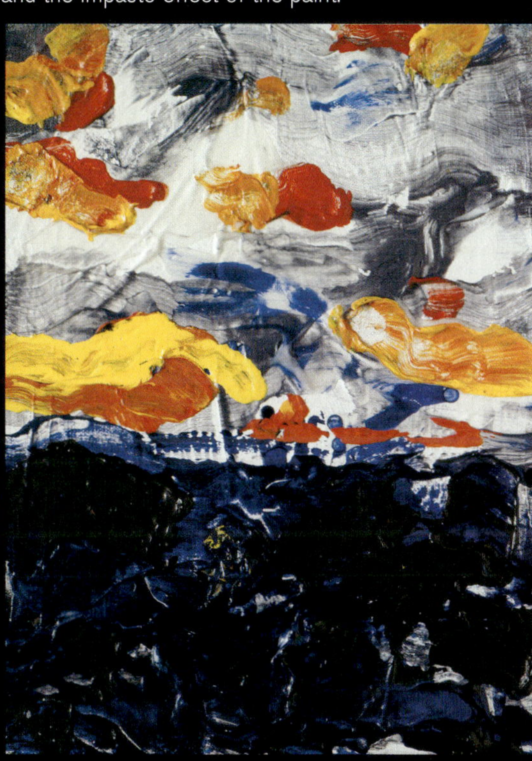

In this canvas a transparent gel, suitable for dripping, was applied to create filaments over the acrylic paint while it was still wet. The action of the gel transformed the body of the paint, making it thin and threadlike. The paint also was allowed to drip to promote spontaneity and directness in the work.

A layer of color adds warmth to this work, executed basically with soft brushes and the fingers. For the sea, the paint was mixed with self-smoothing light gel, which created a flat and gel-like texture. The final result is organic.

New approaches

Other models

We continue with the northern landscape theme, but this time the scene shows a denser sky and a small island in the middle of the sea. To create a heavy sky, Gemma Guasch worked it with a large amount of paint and a dry brush to create the impasto effect. To paint the sea and the island, she mixed the paint with a lot of self-smoothing gel medium, which produced a viscous and flat effect that greatly contrasts with the impasto sky.

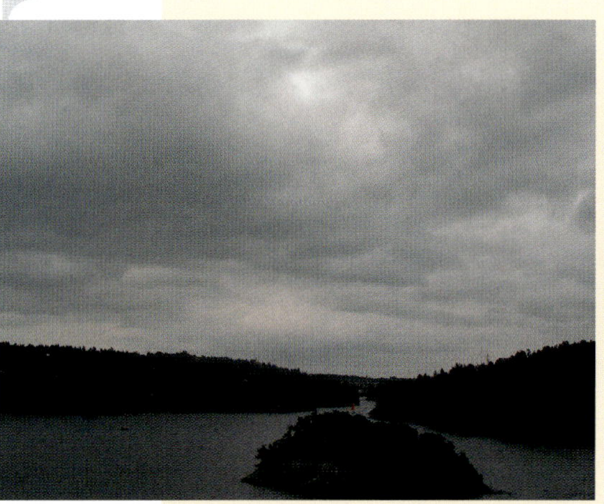

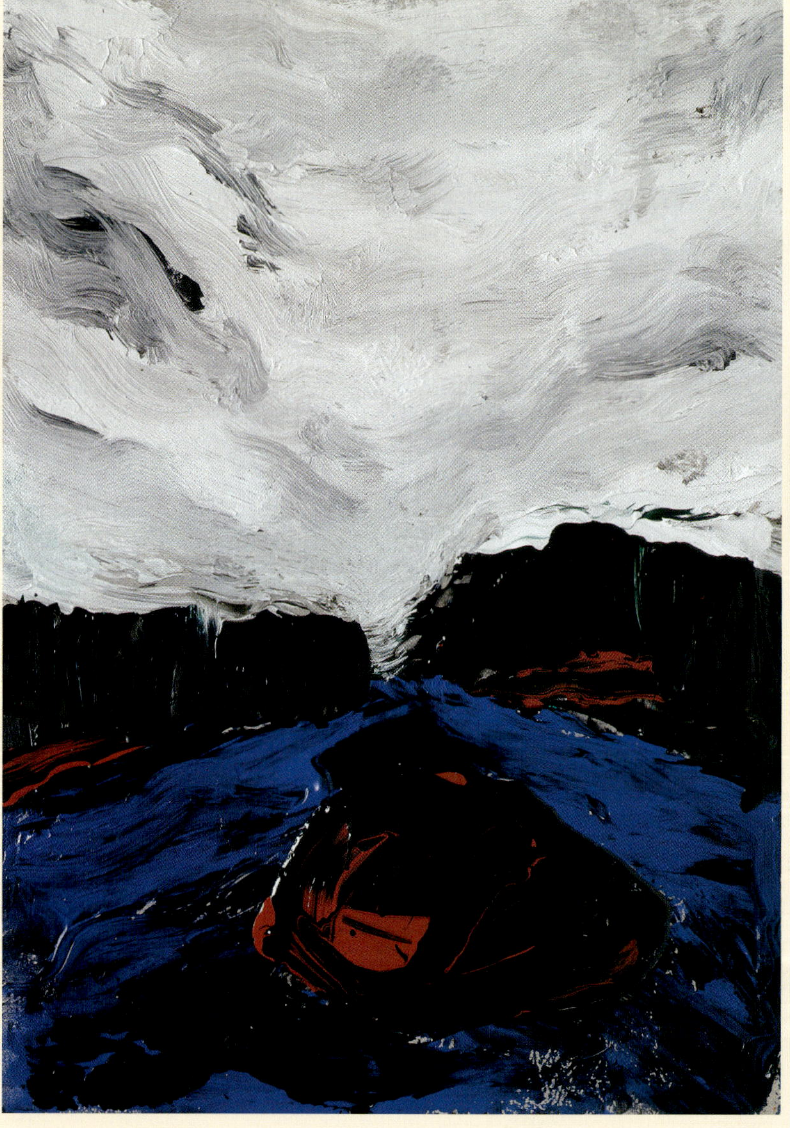

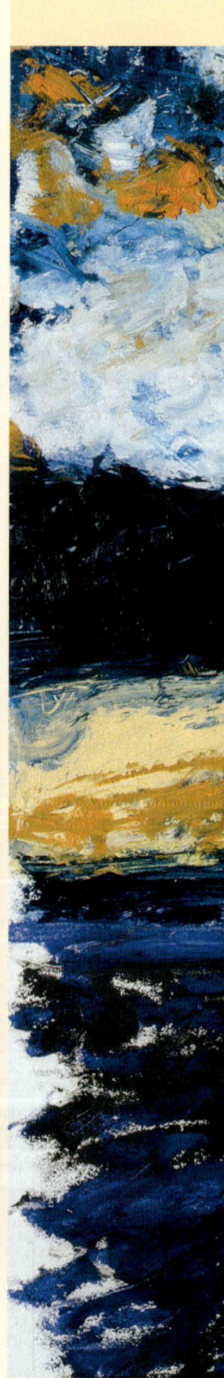

Other media

To vary the technique, pressed oil paints in stick form were chosen and applied on a piece of cardboard. Oil sticks provide a pasty and glossy line without the need for mixing with gel medium or paste. The pressure applied by hand on the support guarantees a dense and creamy result. The lines that form the landscape are short and light and provide an orderly and elegant result.

Other views

The life of Vincent van Gogh (1853–1890) was completely devoted to painting; today his work is a model of personal expression, born of passion and emotional experiences. He lived in tune with nature, trying to capture its essence and translate the impact it had on him. His line is direct, energetic, and vibrant. On several occasions he painted landscapes in which the sky turns dense and heavy, as if it were about to engulf the earth. Such is the case with *Starry Night*, in which the sky, with its undulating and vibrant strokes, forms absorbing and dramatic light swirls. Although van Gogh never used gels (they were not available during his time), he had a dense and creamy approach to oils.

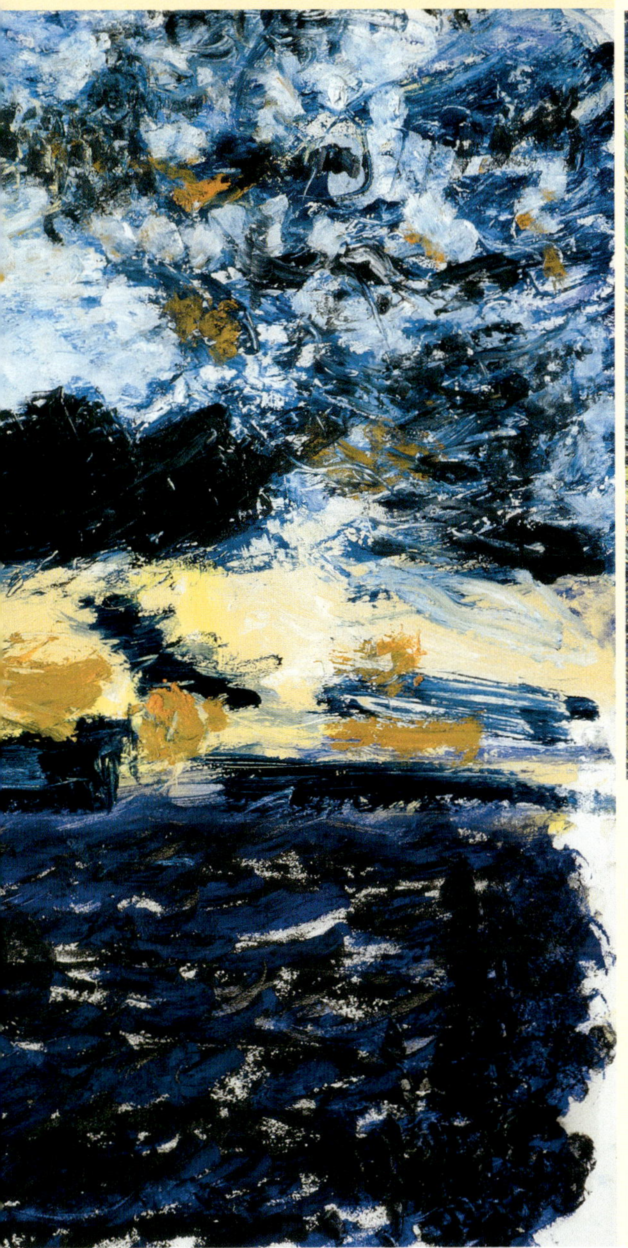

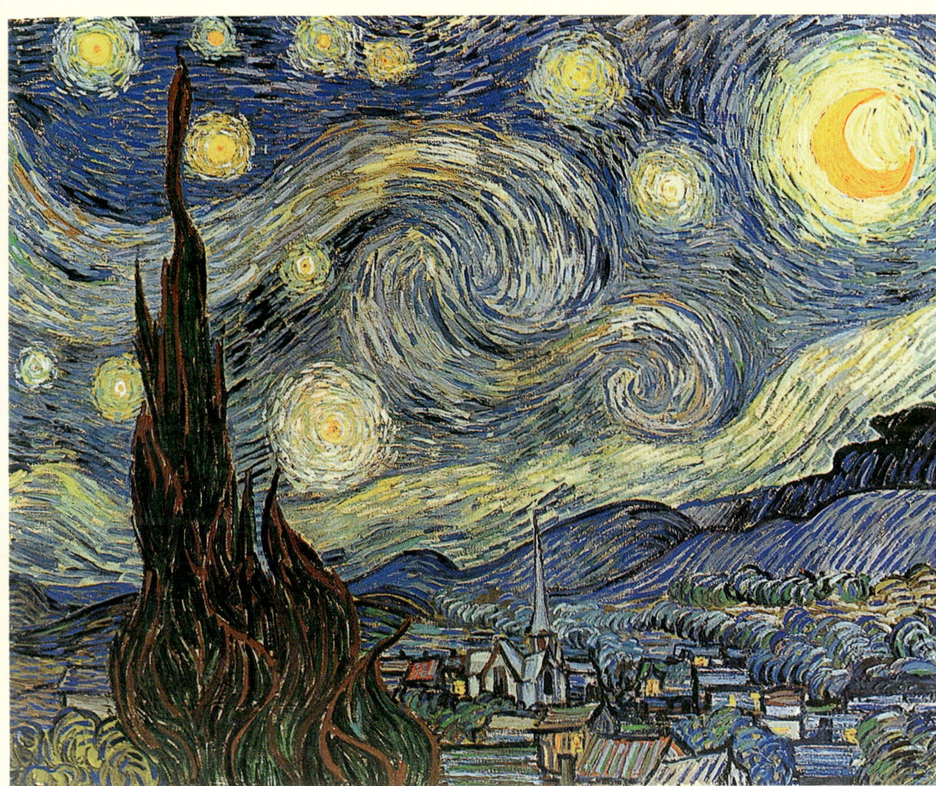

Vincent van Gogh,
Starry Night, 1889.
Museum of Modern Art
(New York, United States).

Scratched, worn, and scraped textures

"Everything that is in my painting, I have seen, I have lived," says Joan Hernández Pijuan (born in Barcelona, 1931). This painter of Informalist and Expressionist influence has a very unique style that is based on the paint's material, tactile, and sensual poetry. His pieces are sensations of a landscape, not representations of a landscape; they are personal experiences. Through a very physical relationship with the paint, which is translated into monochromatic impasto and scratched surfaces (tilled like the soil), Hernández Pijuan synthesizes the landscape's soul. He invites the spectator to submerge himself in a state of silent contemplation: a road, a cypress, a little house, a fence, the sown land—spaces cultivated by man, places where man and nature meet. The famous philosopher and historian Arthur Danto refers to his paintings as "timeless and placeless" adventures. For Hernández Pijuan, scratching the paint to reach the canvas is to speak of the physical and sensory qualities of landscapes; it is to provoke in the viewer memories of tactile emotions.

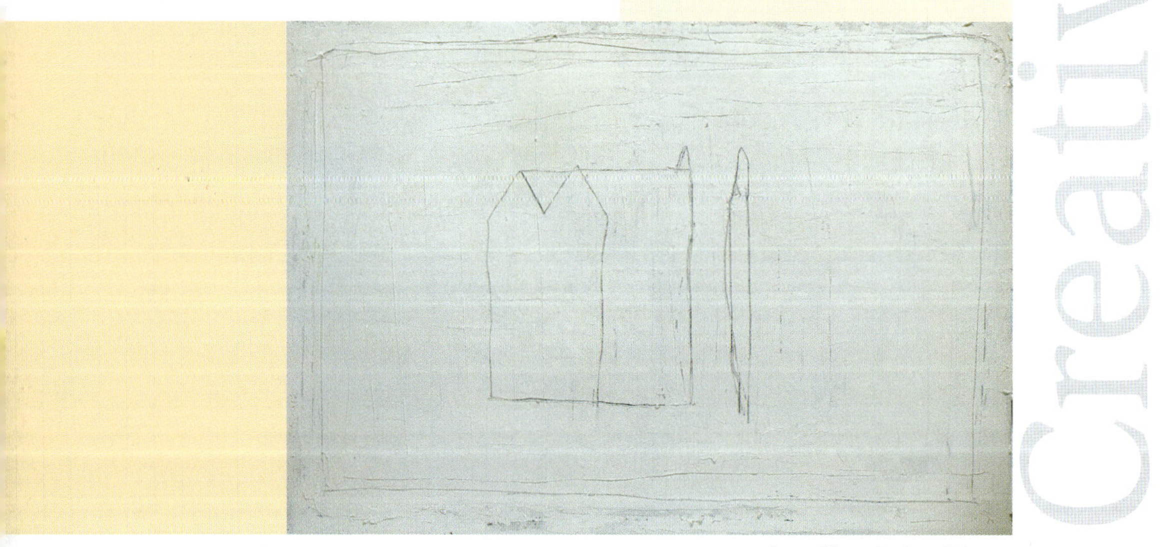

Joan Hernández Pijuan,
Casa i xiprer sobre blanc, 1989.
Galerie Von Kusph (Langen, Germany).

Experimenting with scratched lines in a snowy landscape

Josep Asunción has developed here a very poetic theme: a landscape with snow and a few trees, which project their shadows onto the pristine white. The snow is the element that has motivated him to create the image by scratching the surface, as is the case for the real landscape with snow, which shows the marks created by the passing people or vehicles on its receptive texture. The project is executed on wood with mixed media: acrylic paint and plaster or putty (the kind used to fill cracks; there are many brands available on the market in powder form or ready to use). A spatula and a rasp are used as applicators. The idea is to combine art materials with those used for home decorative purposes.

"When I walk through a sown or harvested field, I have the impression of being completely immersed in that surface and surrounded by it. Something similar to the people who used to make 'land art,' as if all that wrapped around me. And feelings such as these are the ones that, in some way, have been present through my paintings. Not in one way, let's say, representative, but as a feeling that could be described as sensual, even though this word is no longer popular. I try to approach this sensuality that can take you through a field that has been harvested with paint."
Joan Hernández Pijuan
Interview with Catalina Serra, 2003.

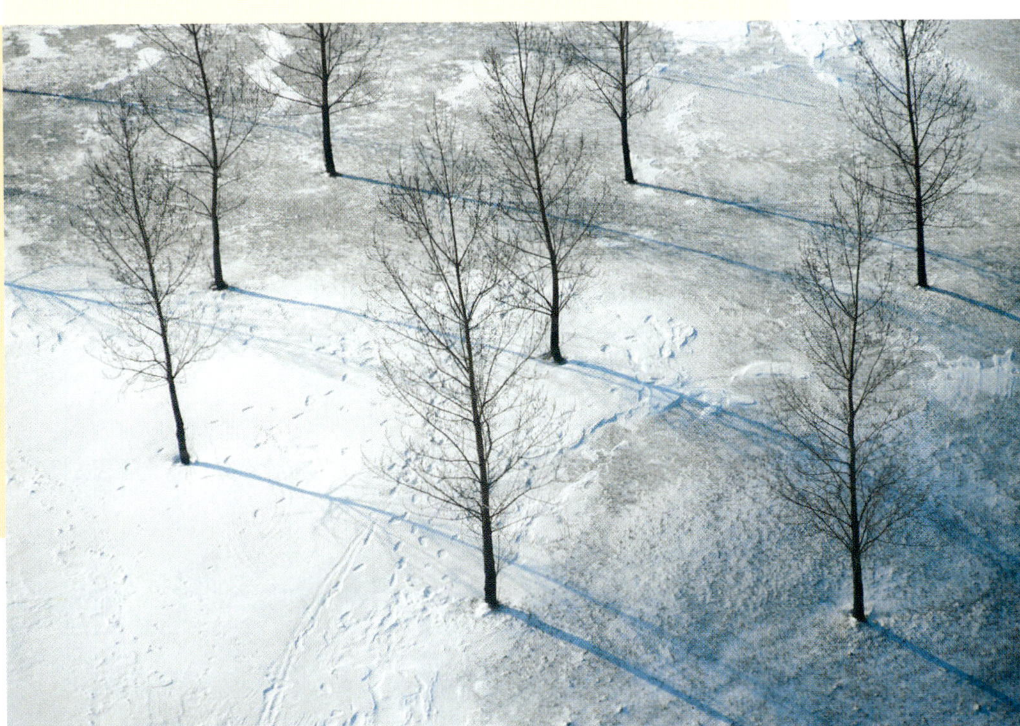

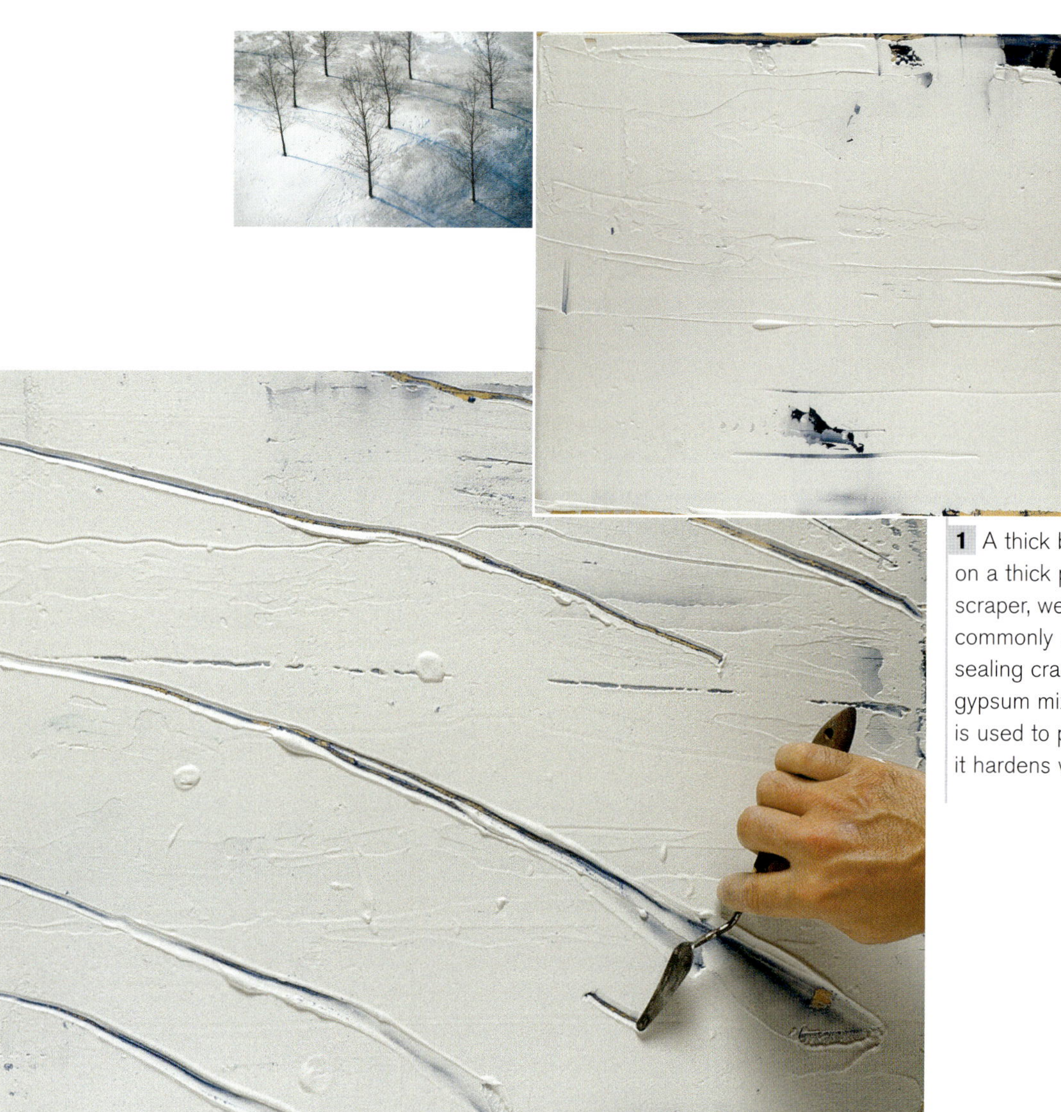

1 A thick base of dark violet acrylic paint is applied on a thick piece of wood. When it dries, using a wide scraper, we apply a second layer with a material commonly used in decorative painting: paste for sealing cracks (such as spackle). It consists of gypsum mixed with a binder of great plasticity; it is used to prime walls before painting them and it hardens when it dries, becoming water-resistant.

2 The first lines are scraped into the paste layer with a spatula. Depending on its angle, we can create a thin line or a wider band, and depending on the pressure applied we can expose the wood or the violet paint layer, or we will create a relief in the white surface.

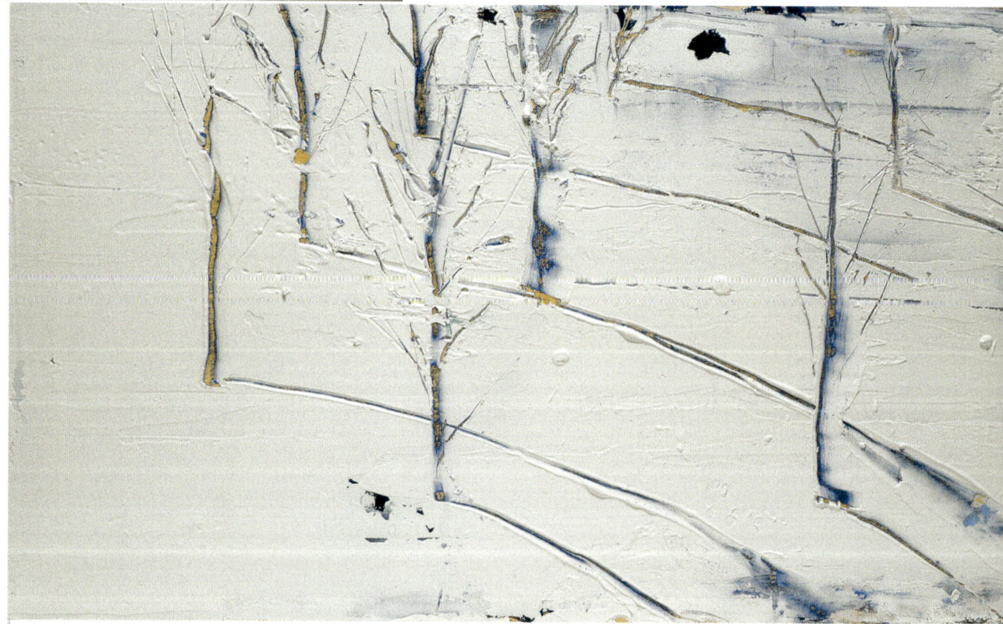

3 The construction of the image is very simple, done by creating lines of different widths and colors by modeling the scratches with the spatula. The structure of the painting revolves around the shadows and the trees, two rhythms of angle-forming lines.

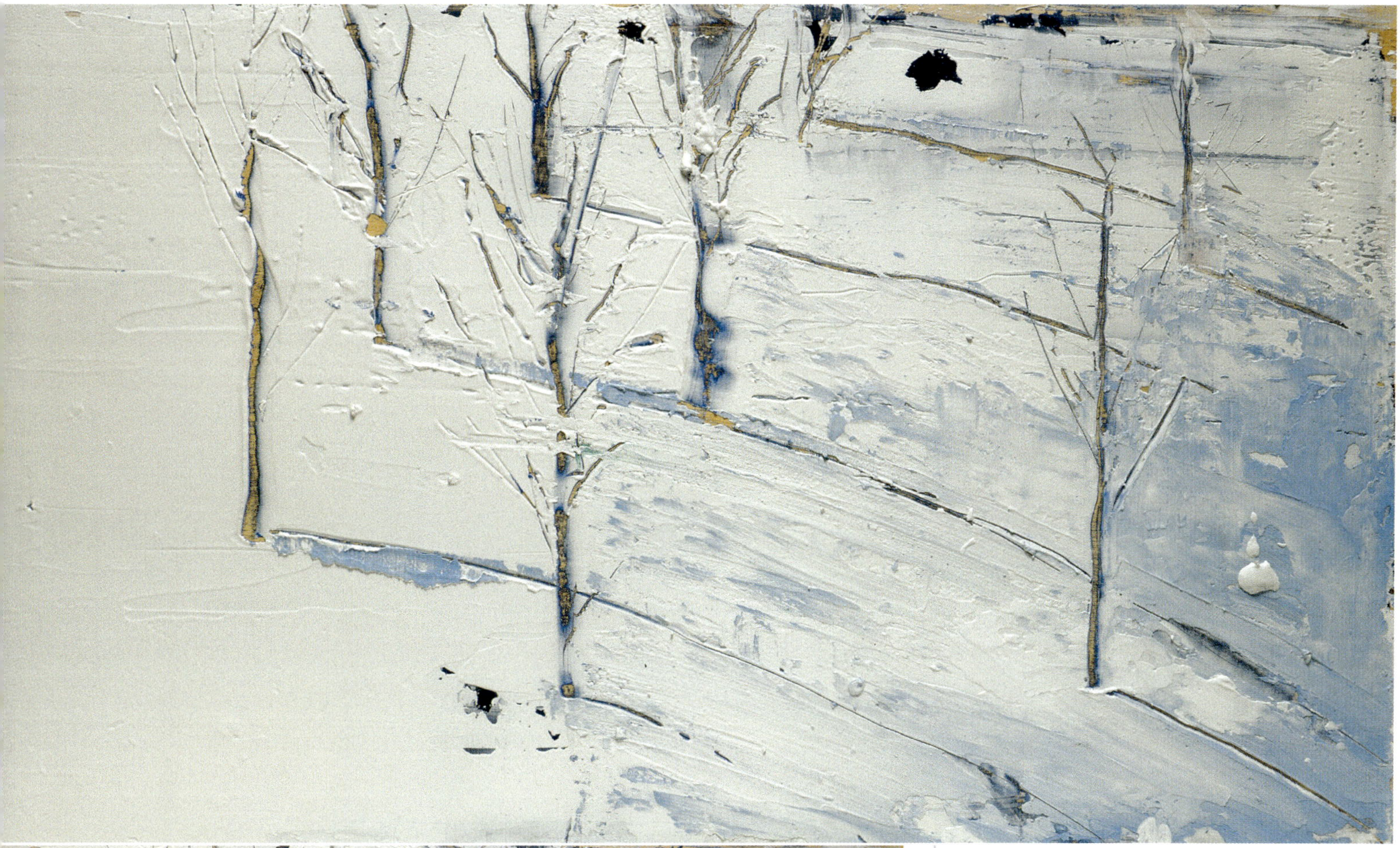

5 To finish, we go back to the fresh layer of paste with the spatula to reconstruct some of the trees that had been lost in the previous step. We complete the textured effect by dropping small amounts of paste on the fresh surface, as if they were snowballs, an effect that was applied before but that was lost in the process.

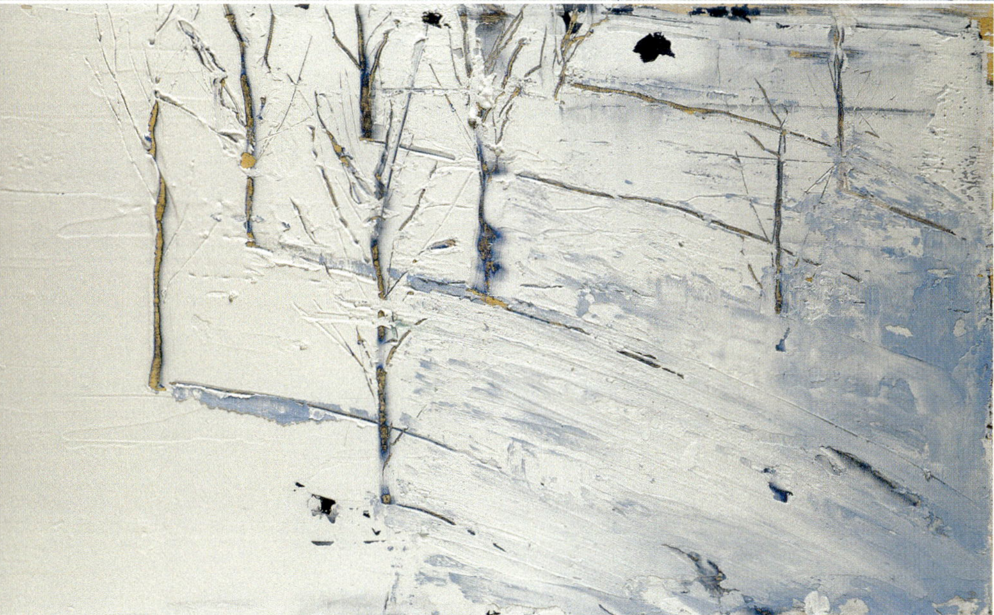

4 A second layer of paste is applied, this time mixed with cobalt blue acrylic paint, to add blues to the snow as reflections of the landscape. We apply them with the spatula in different areas, covering some previous scratches and without removing too much to avoid erasing the image.

Other versions

By changing the support material, its color, the thickness of the layer of paint, and the applicator, the artist has achieved many different faded and striated effects. This gallery shows a varied selection.

The most important feature of this work is the support: corrugated cardboard from a box. It has a smooth surface, but inside it has a series of channels that are exposed when the outer layer is removed. In this case, that removed part has turned into the line that defines the trees, whose shadows are created by applying blue paint with the fingers over the fresh paste.

This time, three layers of color have been used. The first one is carmine red, the second one cobalt blue mixed with paste, and the third one, white paste spread over the surface without completely covering the blue to give the impression of uneven texture. The silhouettes were scratched directly, without hesitation, with a spatula, leaving a striated line with two colors.

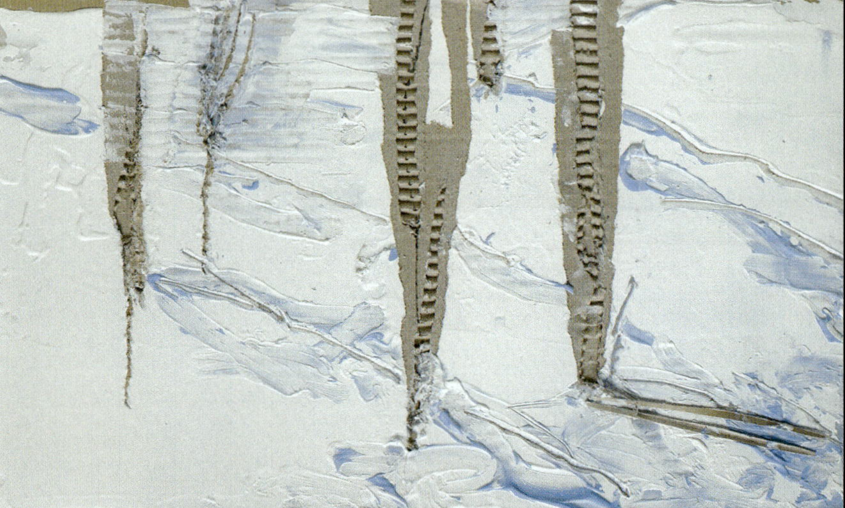

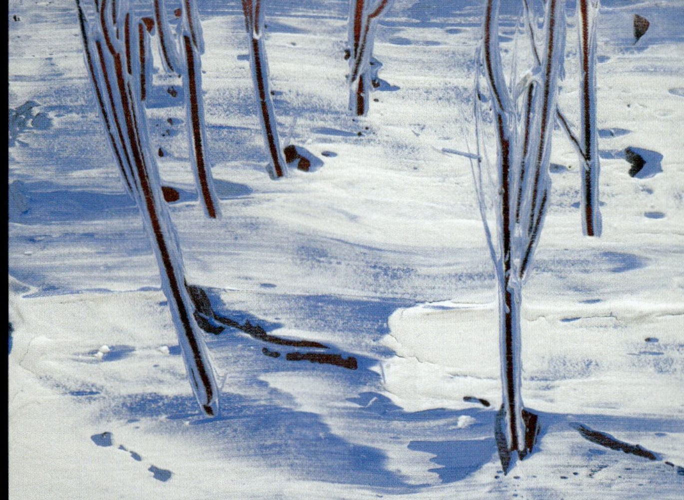

This landscape combines striated lines with dripping. The color of the first layer is burnt sienna, and the layer of paste, not very thick, has a small amount of cobalt blue mixed in. After the trees were defined by scratching with the spatula, the piece was allowed to dry completely; then the shadows were created with droplets of very diluted acrylic paint.

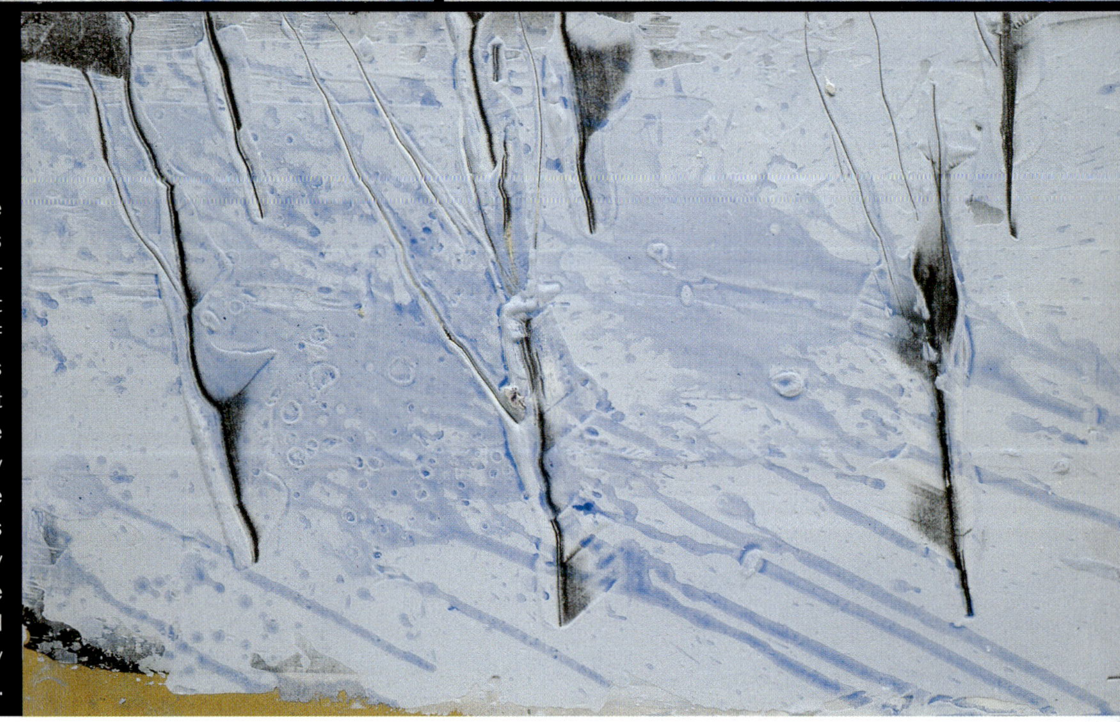

This may be the most abstract landscape in the gallery, because the scene has been so simplified that in another context the subject might not be recognized. It is also the most physically tactile work because of the thickness of the paint layer and the support, a heavy burlap canvas. The tree trunks were created by removing the paste with a finger wrapped in a rag.

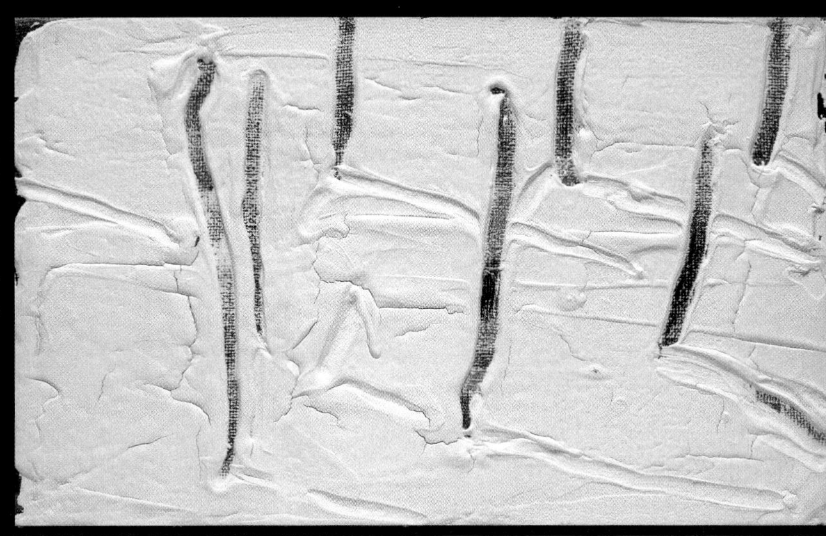

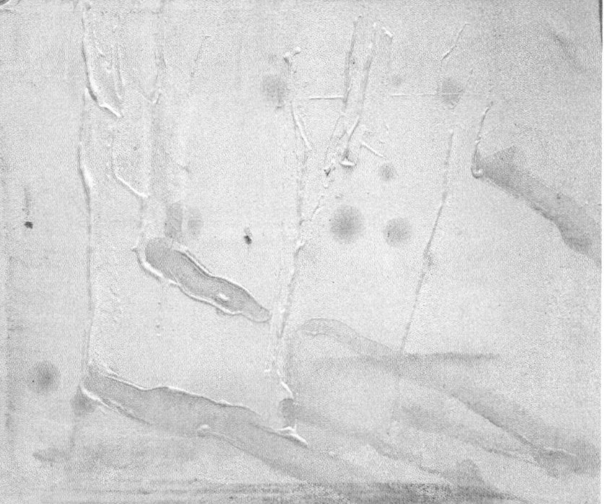

This is an extremely subtle work. The white paste was thinly spread over a wood support coated with a layer of ivory-colored acrylic. Then, the silhouettes of the trees and their shadows were scratched in with a finger, lightly and delicately, and very diluted blue acrylic paint was deposited in the grooves and dripped on in a few places.

This painting has very subtle marks between the brushstrokes and the lines. This effect was achieved by alternately removing, scraping with the edge of the spatula, and adding paste with a very wide scraper. Making uneven impasto strokes and accepting the forms they create is the secret of this work's freshness and poetry.

New approaches

Other models

The artist has chosen a thickly forested northern landscape. Over a very dark green acrylic layer, he applied a heavy layer of acrylic paint mixed with paste used for sealing cracks to evoke the thickness of the forest. While the impasto was still wet, he scraped into it with the tip and the wide part of the spatula's metal blade to make a variety of lines and areas of color, exposing the green of the lower layer. He added more paste over that and scraped again to create greater visual complexity.

Other media

To experiment with dry medium, the artist repeated the theme with chalk on blue Canson-type paper for pastels. With any dry technique, the equivalent of scratching with the spatula is erasing with a rag, and especially with an eraser. After covering the background with blue and white and a few touches of ultramarine blue (to create a subtle chromatic tension), he constructed the image by alternating erasing with making lines with the chalk (removing and adding).

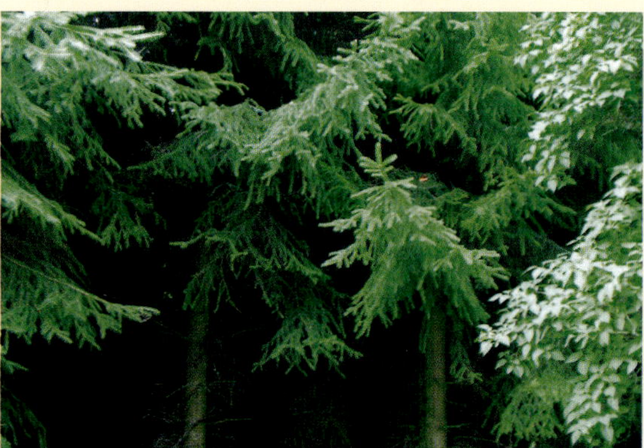

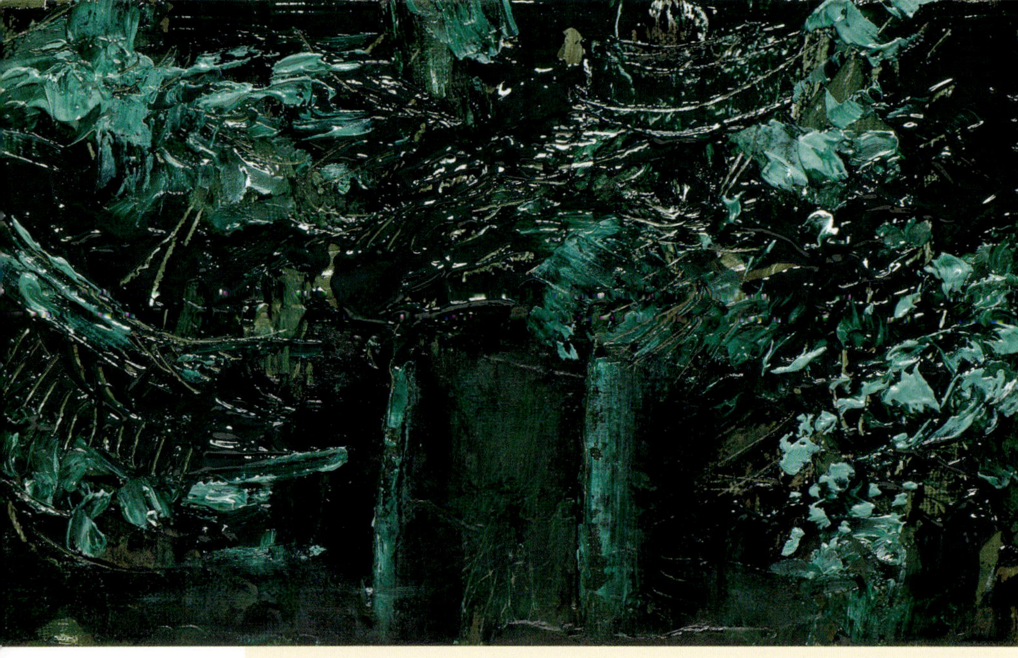

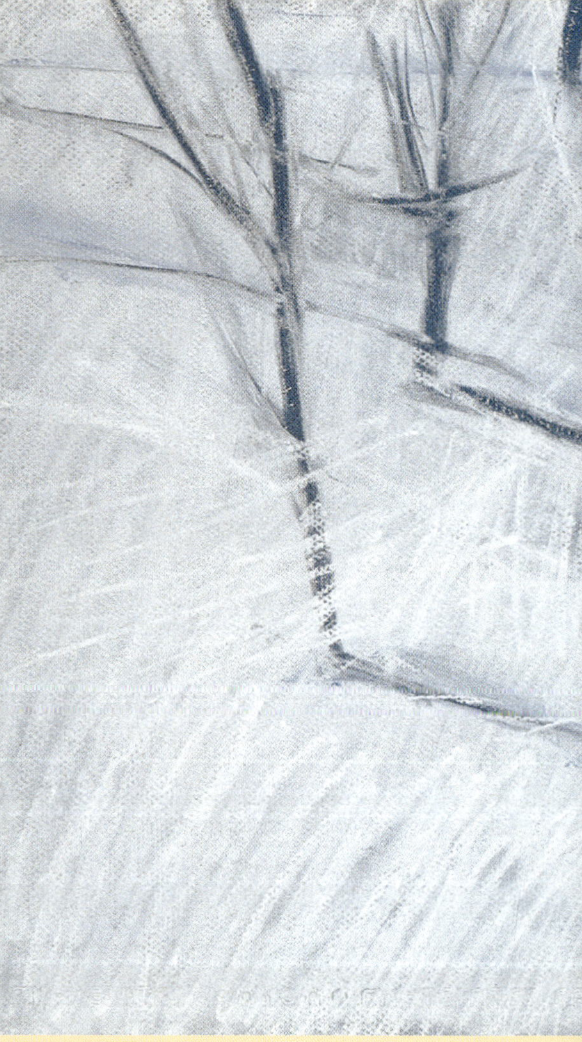

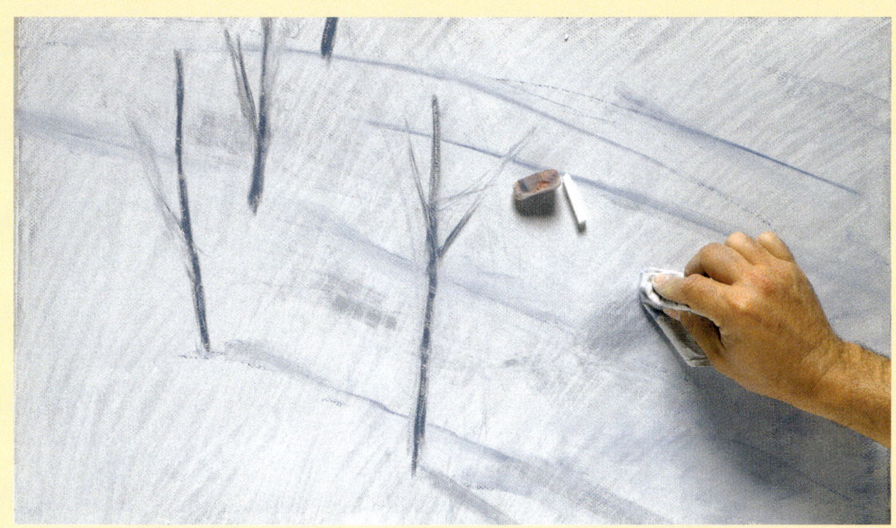

Other views

Paul Klee (1879–1940) expressed his cosmic vision through a language that could be described as poetic Expressionism. Tied to the German Expressionist group Der Blaue Reiter (the Blue Rider), he created paintings that fall somewhere between abstraction and figurative styles, reminiscent of primitive children's art. The act of physically scratching the surface of the painting (a very common technique among Expressionist painters) is a way to underline that this is an autonomous reality, independent of what is represented, which is a surface covered with pictorial material capable of instilling emotions.

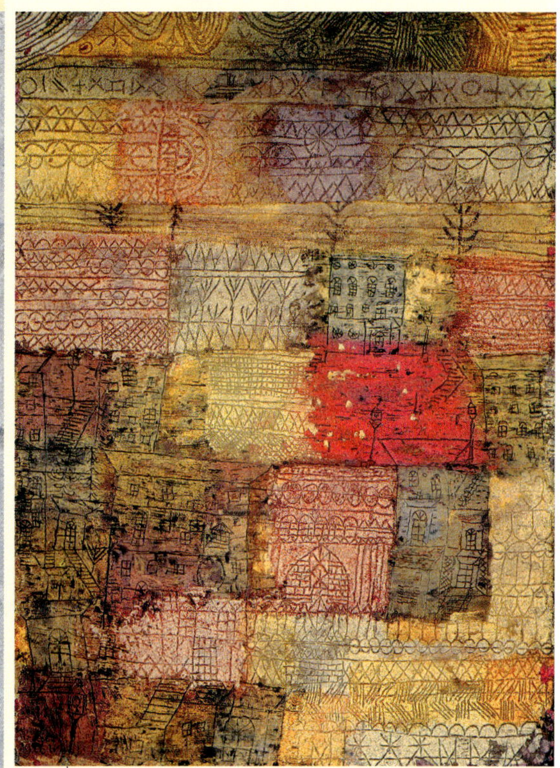

Paul Klee,
Florentine Villas, 1926.
Musée National d'Art Moderne (Paris, France).

The human body is an extraordinarily expressive tool; dance, miming, theater, and performance art are proof of that. It seems logical that painting should speak in depth about human beings, about their emotions, experiences, myths, gods . . . In this chapter are three projects about personal expression that rely on lines of different kinds to express a range of visions of contemporary man: primitive and simple gestures, passionate and very painterly gestures, and finally, flat and artificial silhouettes.

Line in

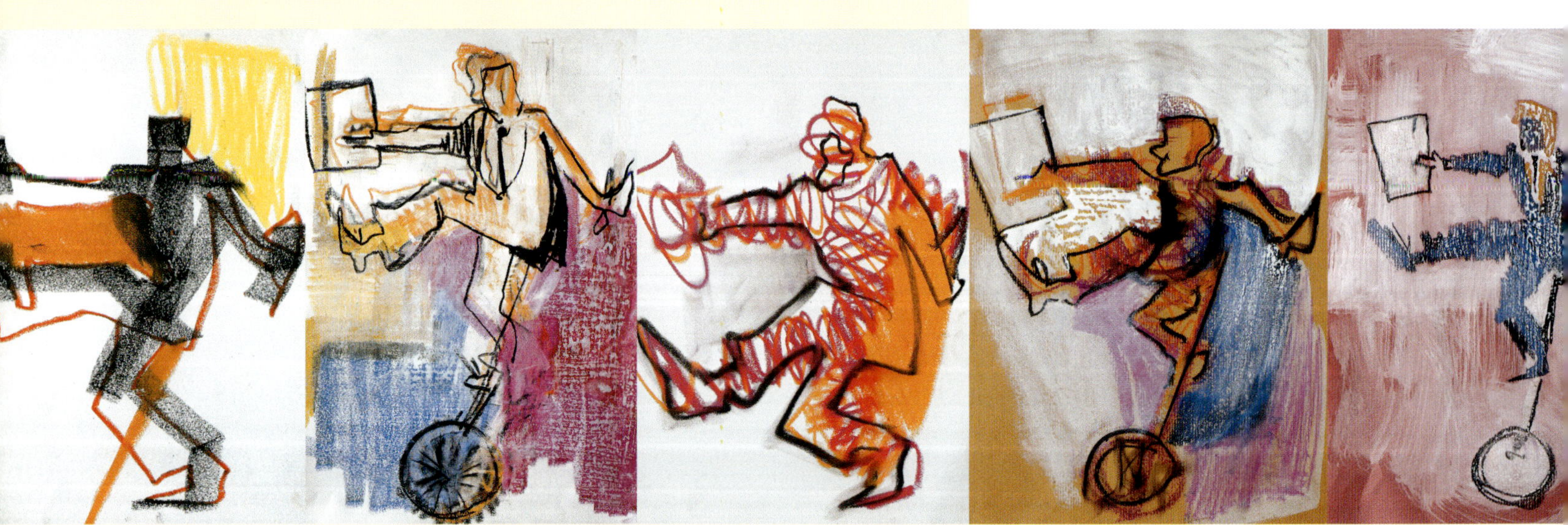

the human figure

"Having thought many times about where this grace comes from (leaving out those that got it from the heavens), I find a very universal rule (. . .) and it is to employ in all things a certain disdain (sprezzatura) *that hides the art and shows that what one says and does is effortless and done almost without thinking about it. I believe quite a lot of grace comes from this."*
Baldassare Castiglione
Cortesano IV, 59, 1528.

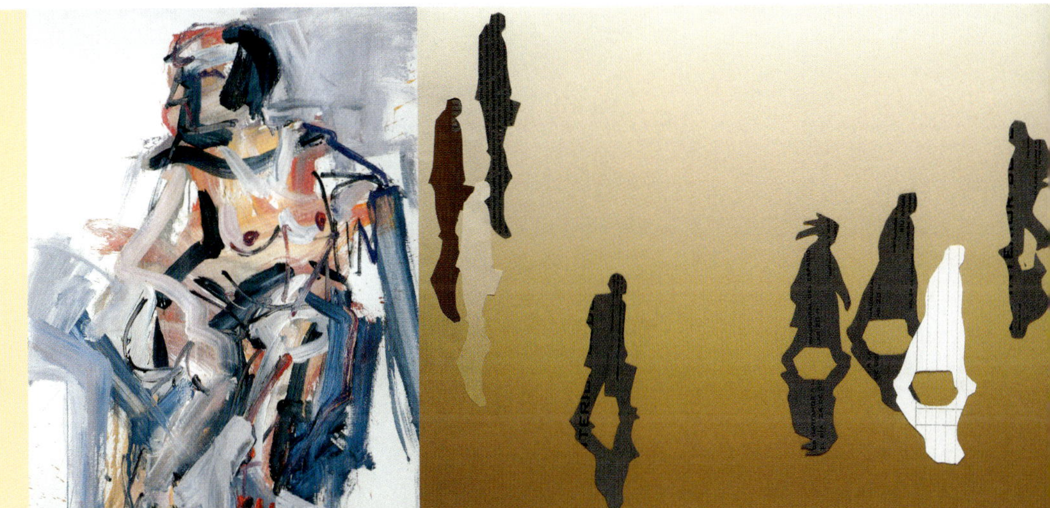

Primitive, sketchy, and basic gestures

The life and work of Jean Michel Basquiat (1960–1988) are paradigms of the art world of the 1980s. He was the first African-American painter to achieve an unprecedented worldwide fame, his work selling for unimaginable prices. He began as a graffiti artist and, under the pseudonym SAMO, left his mark all over Manhattan's SoHo and East Village. Alternating between shyness and delusions of grandeur, Basquiat was guided by a self-destructive spirit and came to a tragic end, dying of a drug overdose at twenty-seven years of age. His fame and his death made him a legend, a marginalized genius. He created his most primitive work between 1981 and 1982. Among his many sources were children's drawings, comics, human anatomy, and communications media. His line revealed his anger and rebelliousness; he sketched his characters using quick, direct, and striking brushstrokes, often adding a crown symbol to distinguish those he considered heroes and martyrs and thus honoring the man in the street and himself.

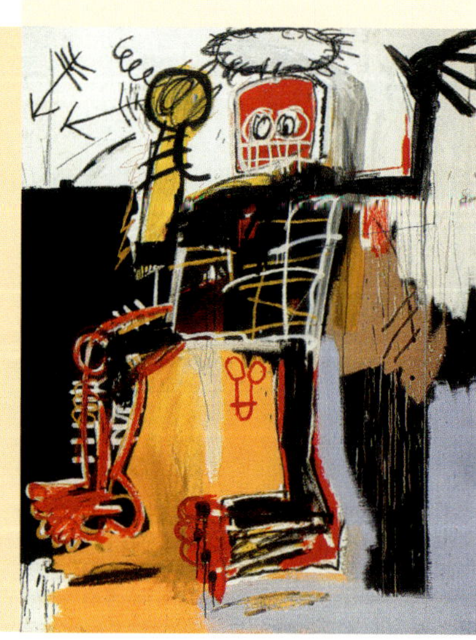

Jean Michel Basquiat, *Untitled*, 1981. The Brandt Foundation (Greenwich, Connecticut, United States).

Neoprimitivism and the urban aesthetic: Experimenting with lines from other graphic languages

Prehistoric man had the wisdom to represent what he lived using simple and expressive lines. From the beginning, artists have longed to encounter their most primitive, energetic, and expressive spirit. The need for a wild purity is reflected in fresh, raw lines. For this approach Gemma Guasch selects a dynamic model for making a direct and energetic work, free from all formal artistic ties, through which she aims to capture the visceral quality of the urban aesthetic of today's young painters. She has chosen to use a mixed-media technique for this: wax and gouache on paper.

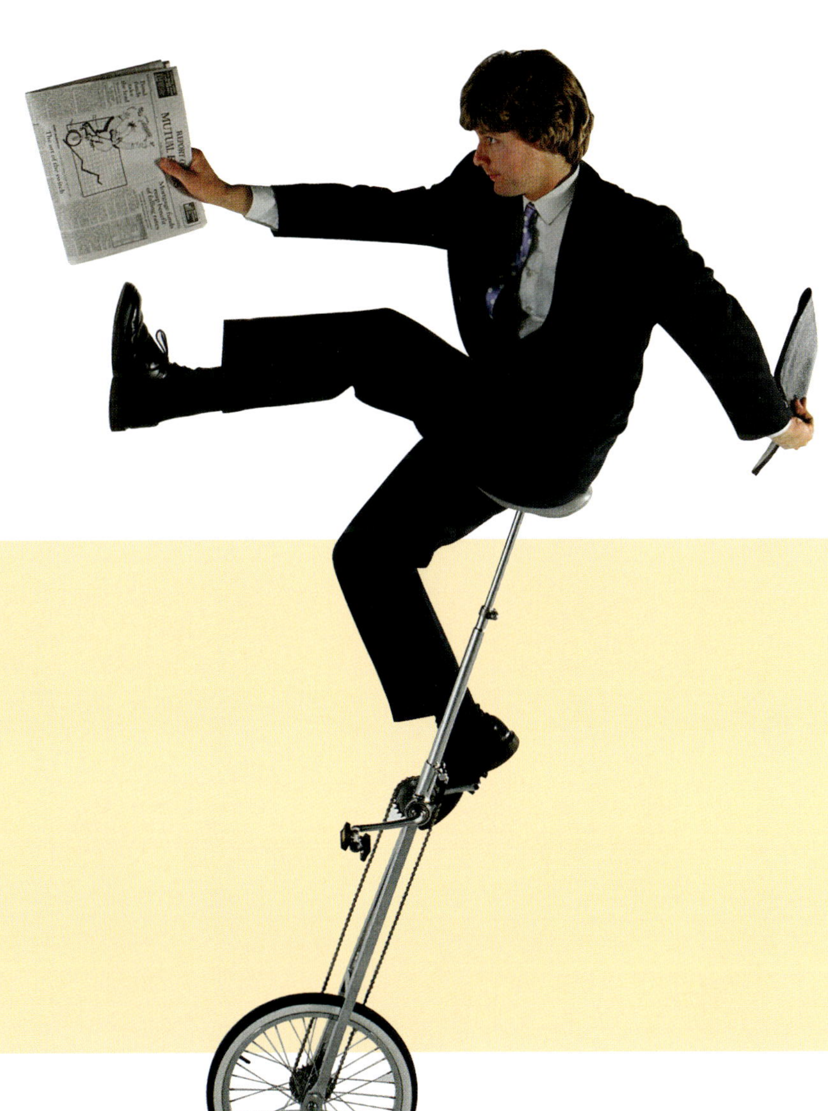

"No one has been able to create anything better than the sculptures of the primitives. Who is not attracted by the precision of cave drawings? The Assyrian reliefs still conserve the same purity of expression. This marvelous simplicity has been lost because man is no longer simple. He wished to see farther and lost the ability to see what was before his eyes."

Pablo Picasso,
Worte des Malers, 1970.

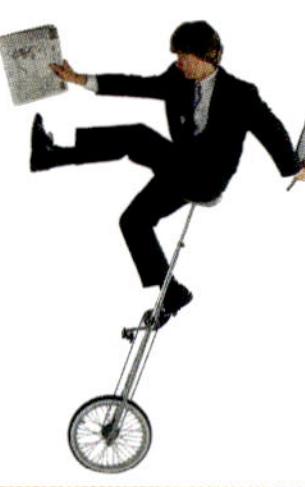

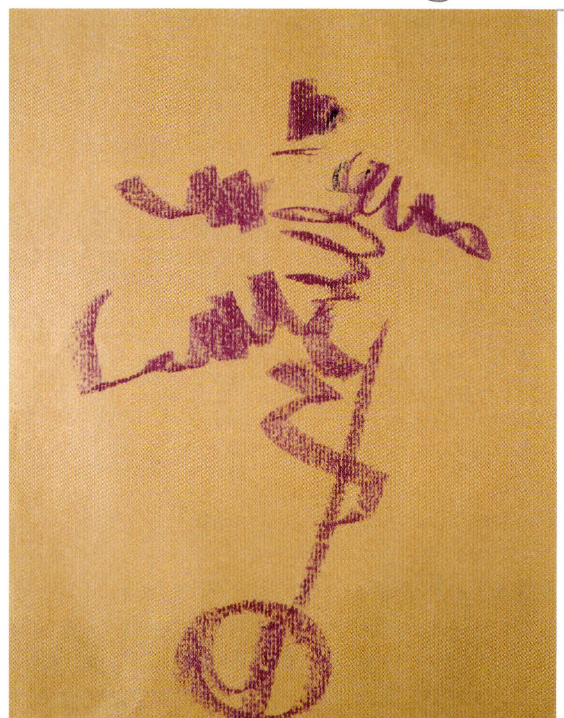

1 Using a wax crayon and kraft paper we attempt the most basic representation, establishing the young man on his unicycle with a heavy, dynamic, and quick line. The spiral line adds volume and gives the sketch dynamism.

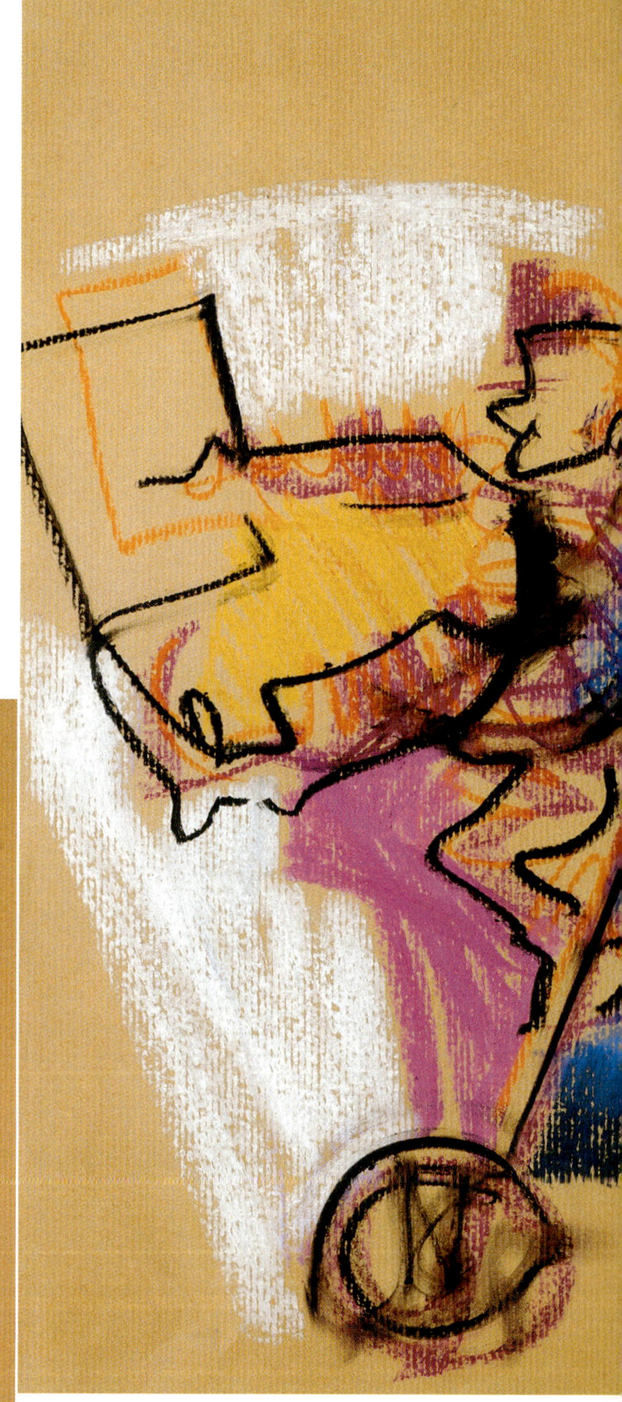

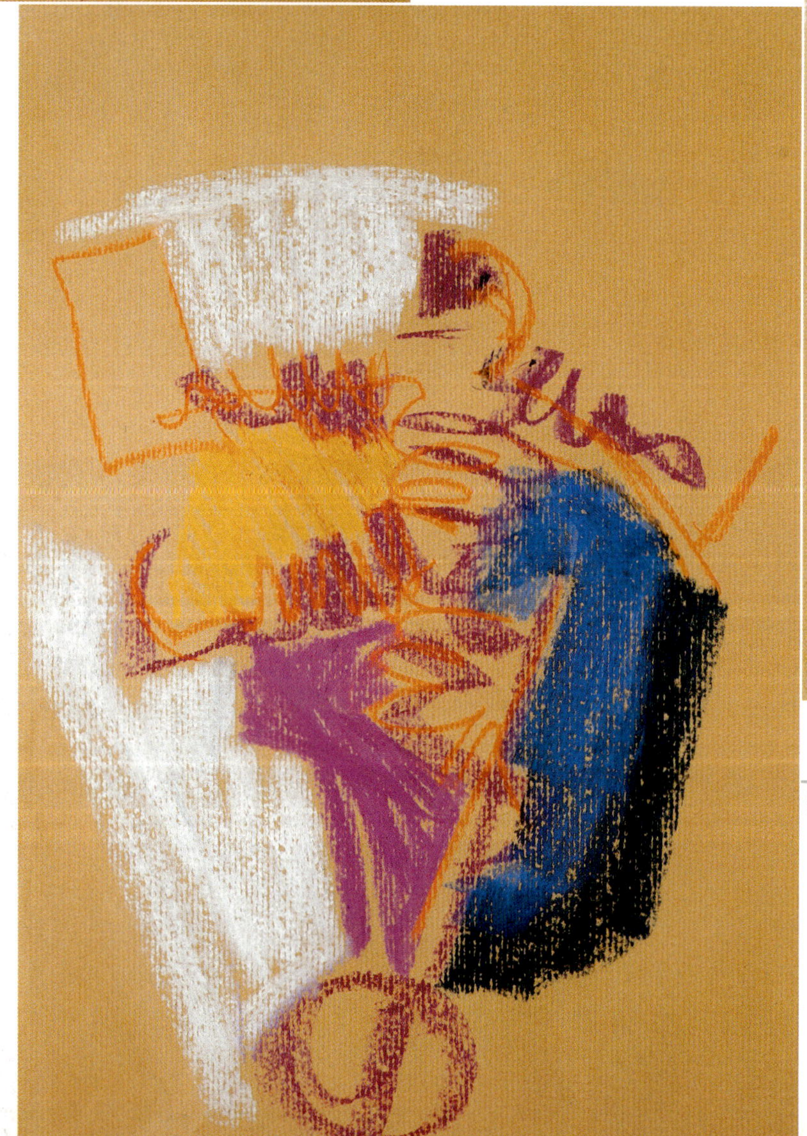

2 We use a thinner, more geometric line than the previous one to reinforce the model. The mixture of the two lines—straight and curved—reinforces the corporeality of the person. The representation of the newspaper adds an informal and relaxed feeling. To finish, we partially apply quick, wide strokes with very little pressure, adding a rough texture to the background.

3 Applying pressure with the crayon creates an oily, creamy line on the paper that contrasts with the previous ones. The use of a long, narrow line brings us closer to the aesthetics of the world of comics.

4 To conclude, we apply a layer of gouache (opaque watercolor) with a brush. The wax crayon repels the water and creates a varied and transparent texture. The final result is an elemental, fresh, and agile depiction of the human figure.

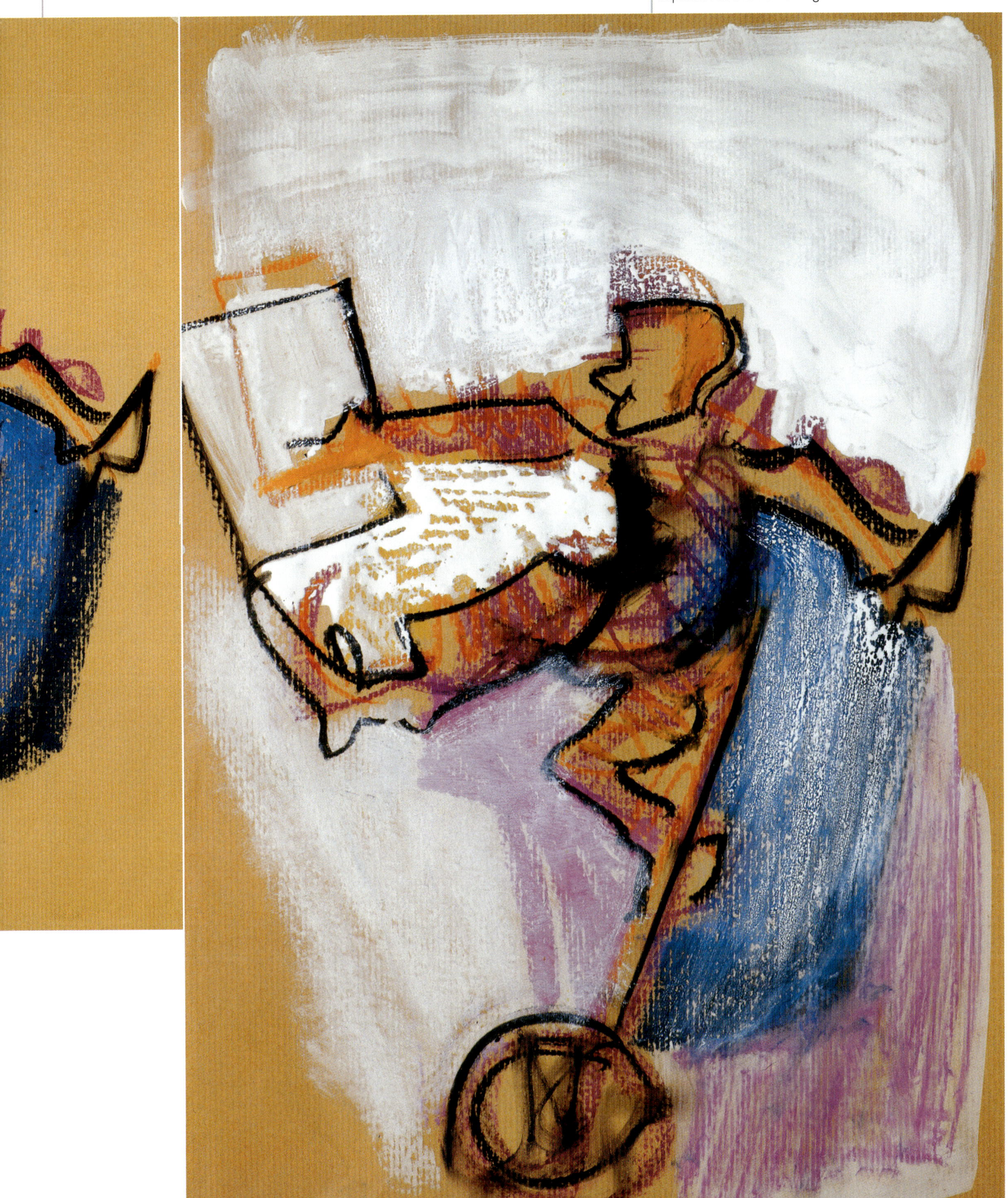

Other versions

The works shown on this and the facing page illustrate some of the ways various artists use line—consciously or unconsciously—in their compositions. The factors involved here include the media used, application methods, speed of execution, and so on, all producing a range of results.

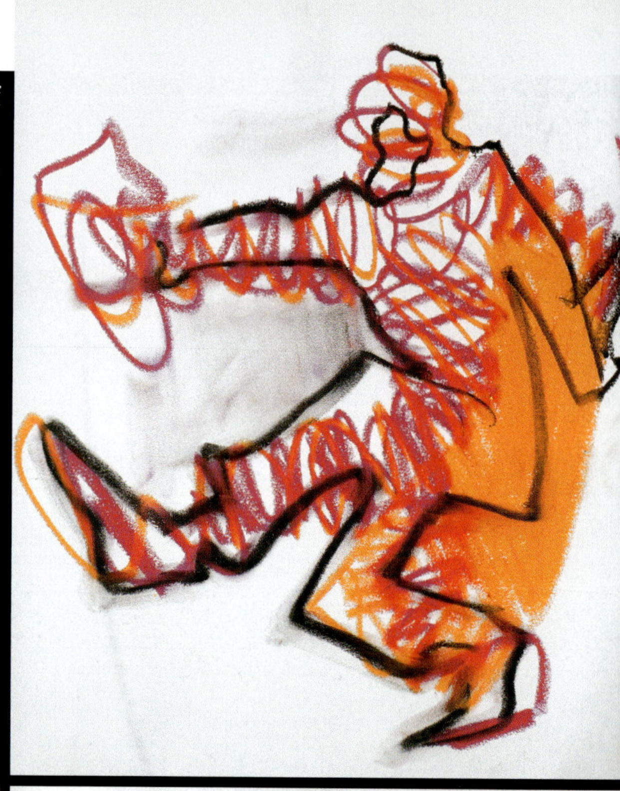

In this example, a quick and heavy line produced the most aggressive and direct representation. The line varies greatly, from rounded to heavy to thin, developing forms with energy and agility.

A more relaxed line was achieved here with a crayon used on its side and applied with little pressure. The fairly geometric outline reminds us of cut-out silhouettes and creates an effect of tranquility and repose.

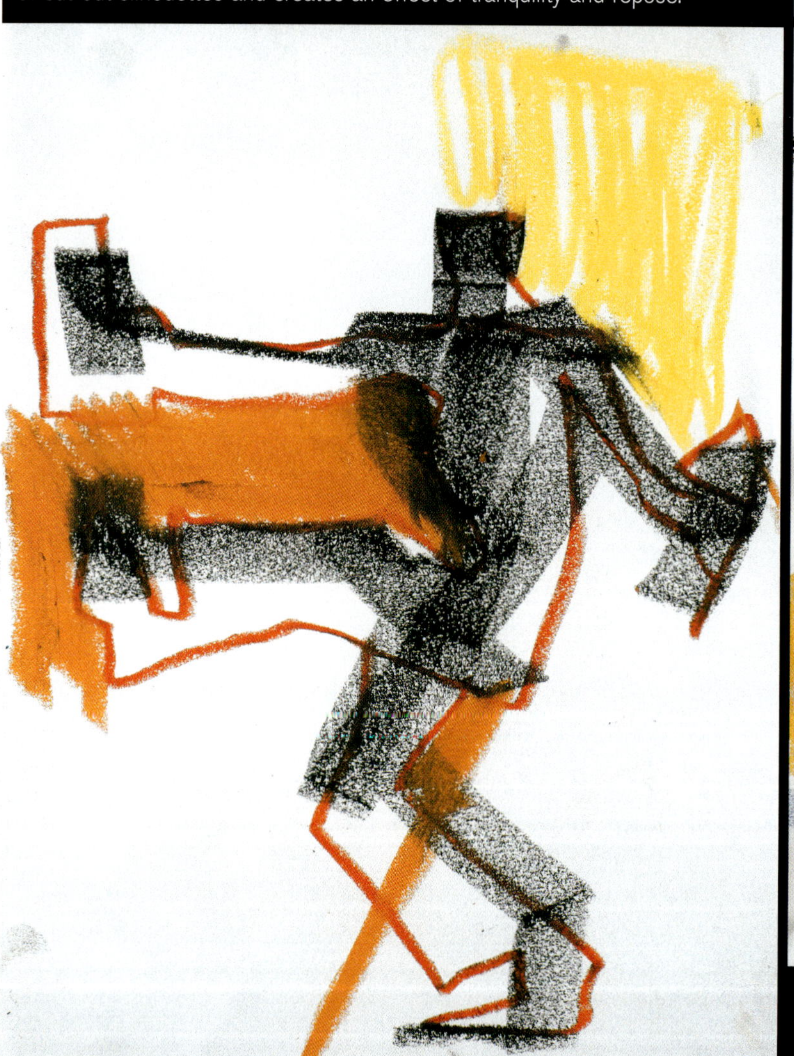

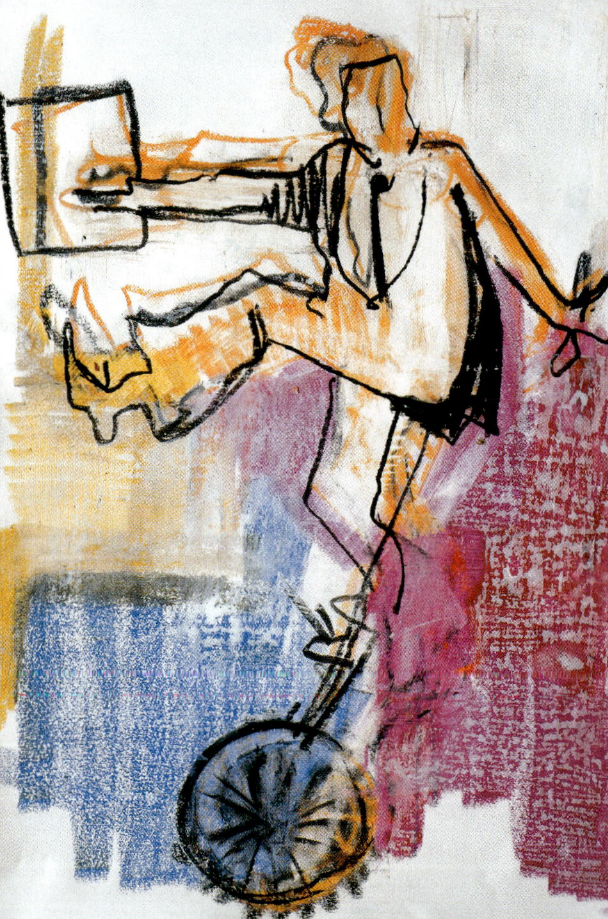

This work was created with quick, precisely drawn lines. Several outlines result from the use of repetition. The detail of the tie helps keep the representation from feeling anonymous. Gouache was applied at the end to give the work a more painterly and finished feeling.

Here various kinds of lines were used: energetic, dynamic, and direct, and mixed with heavy textures and lines. The latter were created by rubbing with an eraser or a finger, and applying pressure with these tools created a bright and smooth texture.

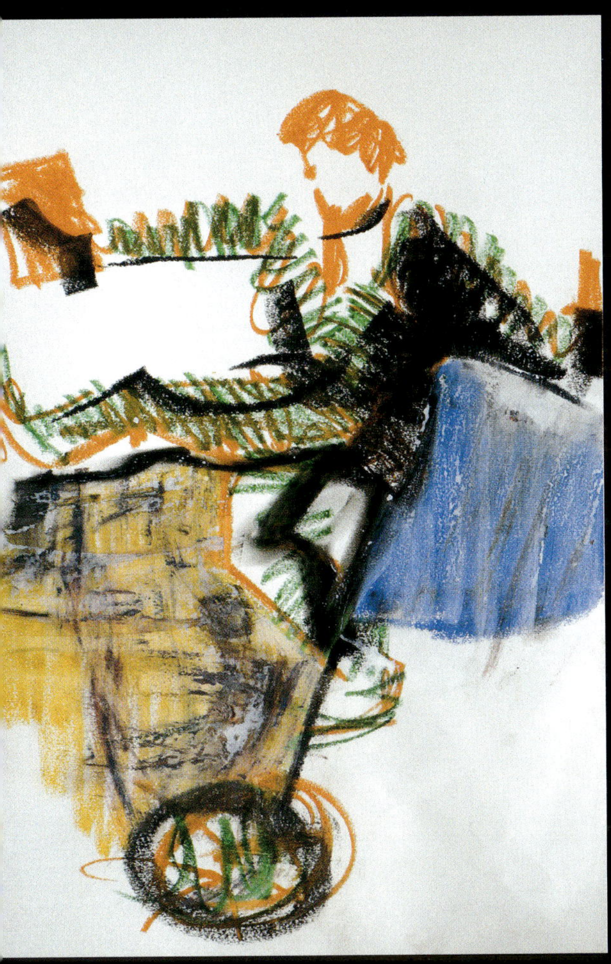

In this drawing the figure has been defined simply with a flat line. The variety in the drawing results from its texture. Gouache adds a tactile difference: in the background it is creamy, while it is repelled by the figure to create a blurry texture.

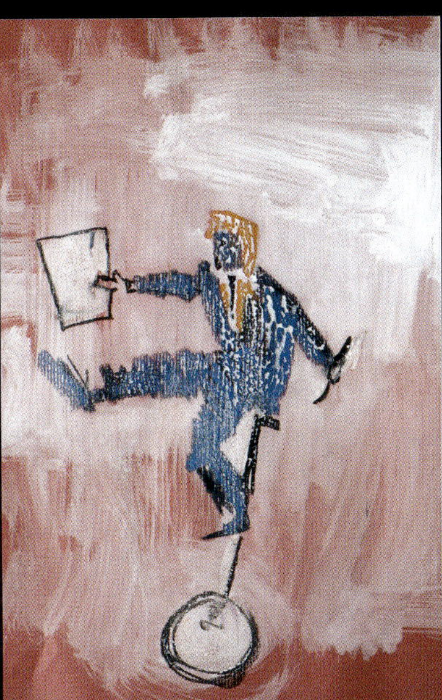

A final drawing very similar in style to comics and graffiti was executed with speed and daring using a loose, direct, and varied line that conveys freshness and immediacy. The result is an impulsive and bold work.

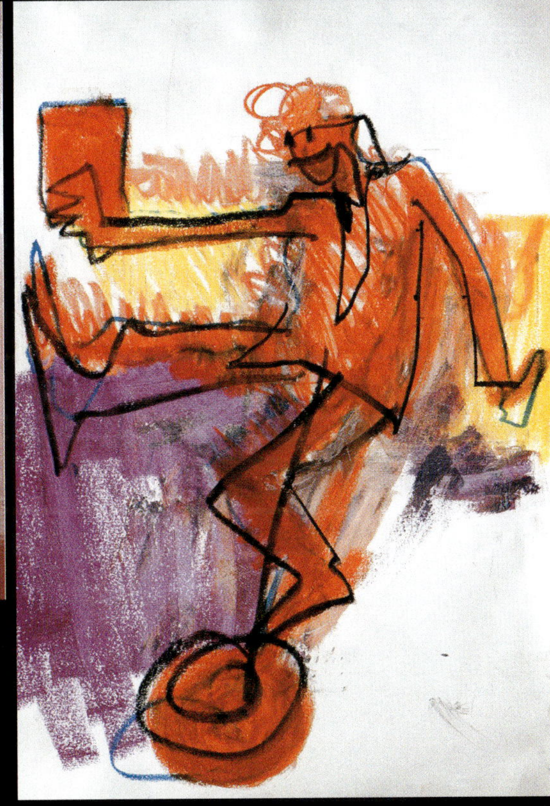

New approaches

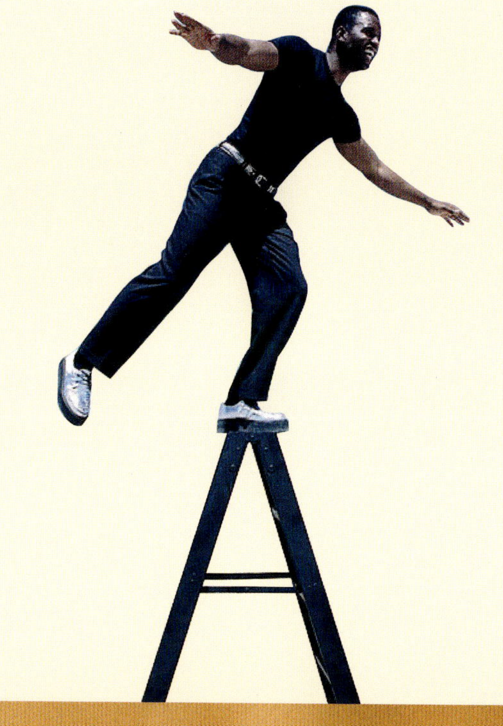

Other models

The human figure allows very rich and varied representation. A single person in movement offers a wide range of possibilities. It is possible to sketch a more reflexive or impetuous line according to what the pose suggests to us. The acrobatics of the second model are more relaxed. The resulting works have more static and less frenetic lines, even though they were made decisively and quickly.

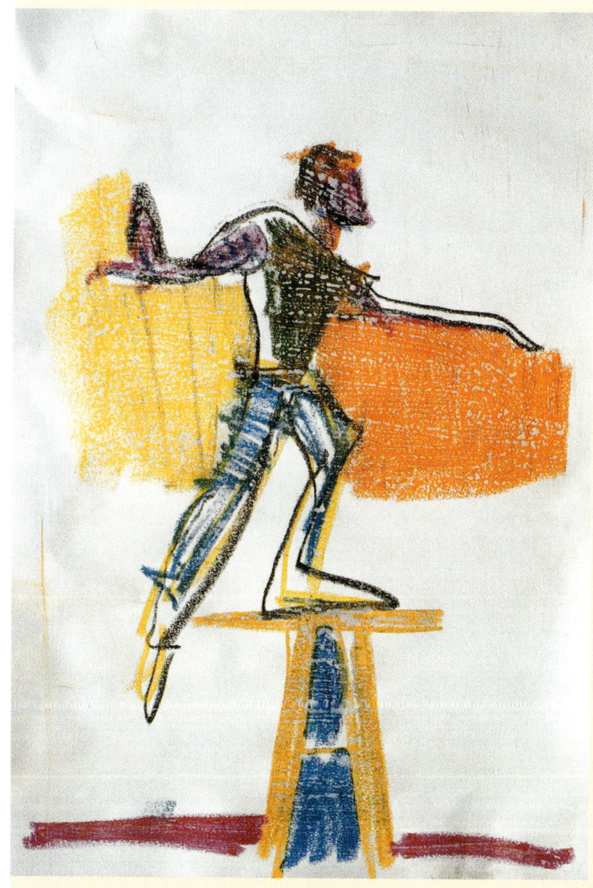

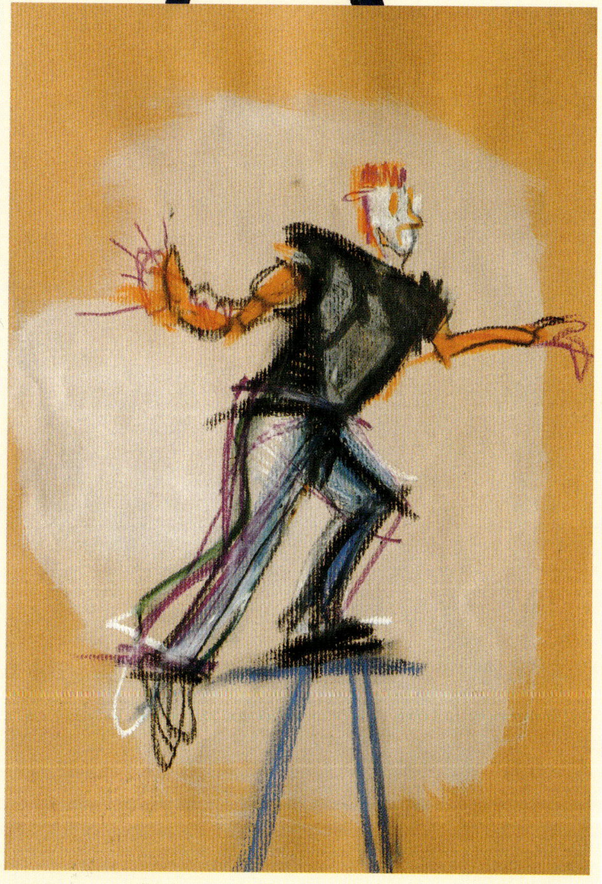

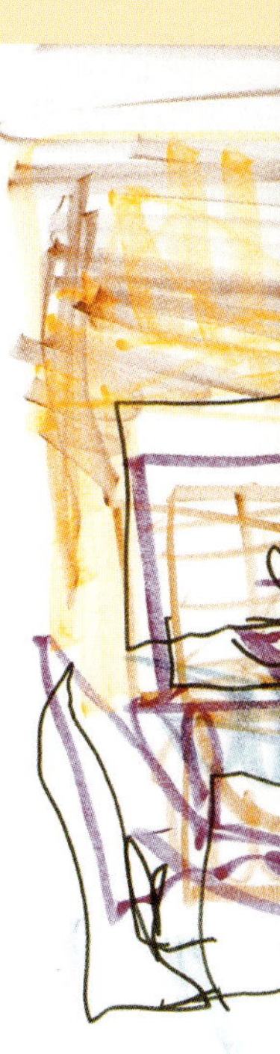

Other media

Wax crayons give us a creamy and painterly drawing and allow for an overall play of line and texture. The eclectic use of gouache and wax crayon creates different textural densities. In contrast, here we chose to use markers, a linear and hard medium that makes the line stand out and gives it immediacy and freshness because it does not allow second thoughts. The result is a direct and sincere work.

Other views

Influenced by prehistoric drawings, A. R. Penck (born in 1939), like his contemporary German neo-Expressionists, reflects them in his paintings. Symbols, simplified figures, and graphic characters appear in his paintings, executed in a wild and expressive manner. He created his own tribal and archaic universe. Keith Haring (1958–1990), who studied art and advertising design, developed a strong "graffiti-ist" or "street" painting style close to that of comics. His painting is clean, with flat and reflexive lines. In his paintings the models are very large or are repeated incessantly. His paintings offer a critical and acid reflection of the society that surrounded him. The abuse of power, xenophobia, and HIV were the subject matter of his work.

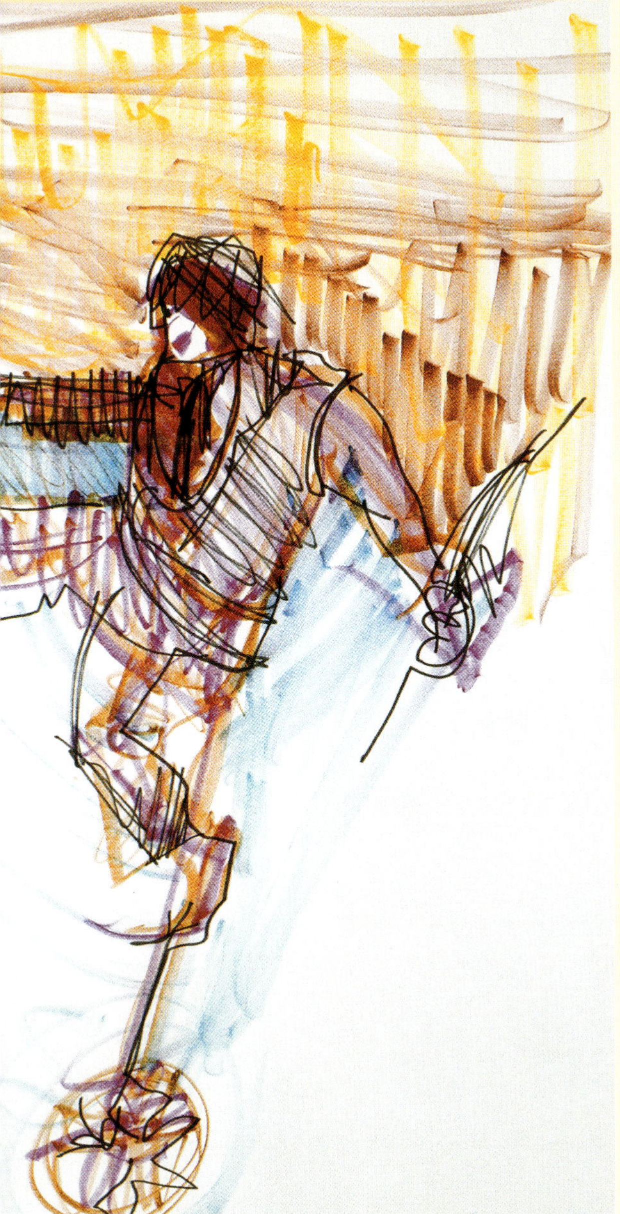

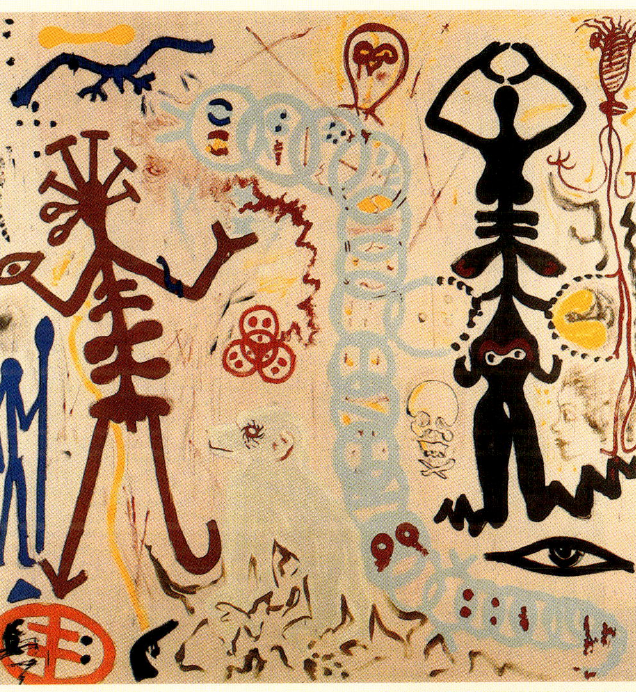

A. R. Penck,
N-Complex, 1976.
Michael Werner Gallery (Cologne, Germany).

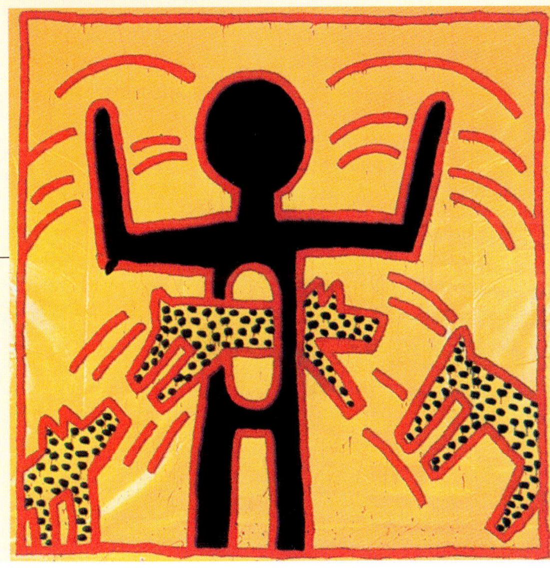

Keith Haring,
Untitled, 1982.
Private collection.

Creative approach 11

Energetic, dynamic, and passionate gestures

Broken, violent, and wild lines, vigorous, heavy impastos, and a fierce dynamism: these are the hallmarks of the work of Willem de Kooning (1904–1997), a renowned action painter. The term "action painting" was first applied by the critic Harold Rosenberg to define a group of American artists who flourished during the decade of the 1950s, for whom a painting was a space for action. The action painters valued the process more than the content, the subjective and unconscious expression, the spontaneous execution, the accident, and the chance. They were influenced by European Surrealist artists who immigrated to the United States at the onset of World War II. Willem de Kooning was the only one from the group who did not abandon figurative painting completely; his series on women are very well known. In those paintings he let the unconscious flow wild, resulting in passionate representations of the feminine figure.

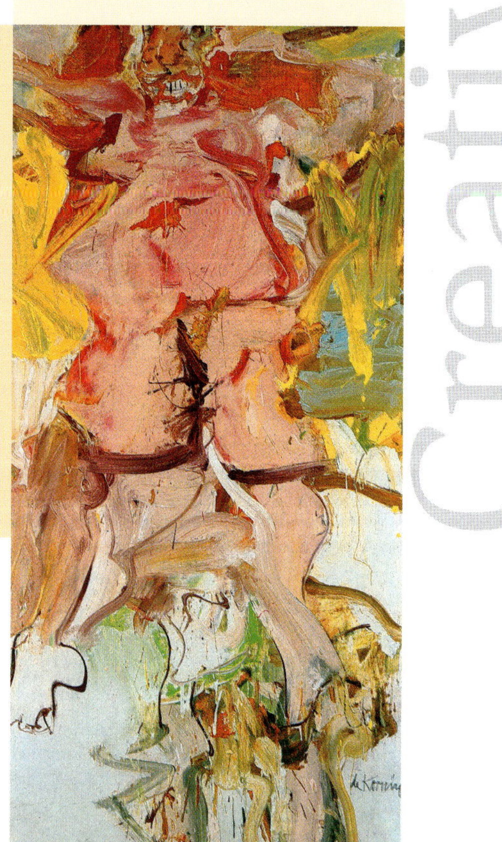

Willem de Kooning, *Sag Harbor Woman*, 1964. Hirshhorn Museum and Sculpture Garden, Smithsonian Institution (Washington, D.C., United States).

Rapid expressionistic painting of the female nude

In this creative approach, Josep Asunción has been guided by a working method based on intuition, without giving it too much thought, to achieve a result that conveys passion and energy. With a female nude as his model, he develops a series of oil paintings on canvas where the strokes flow in a quick and compulsive manner. One brushstroke calls for the next one, without any intervals, until the piece transmits its full message and is considered finished.

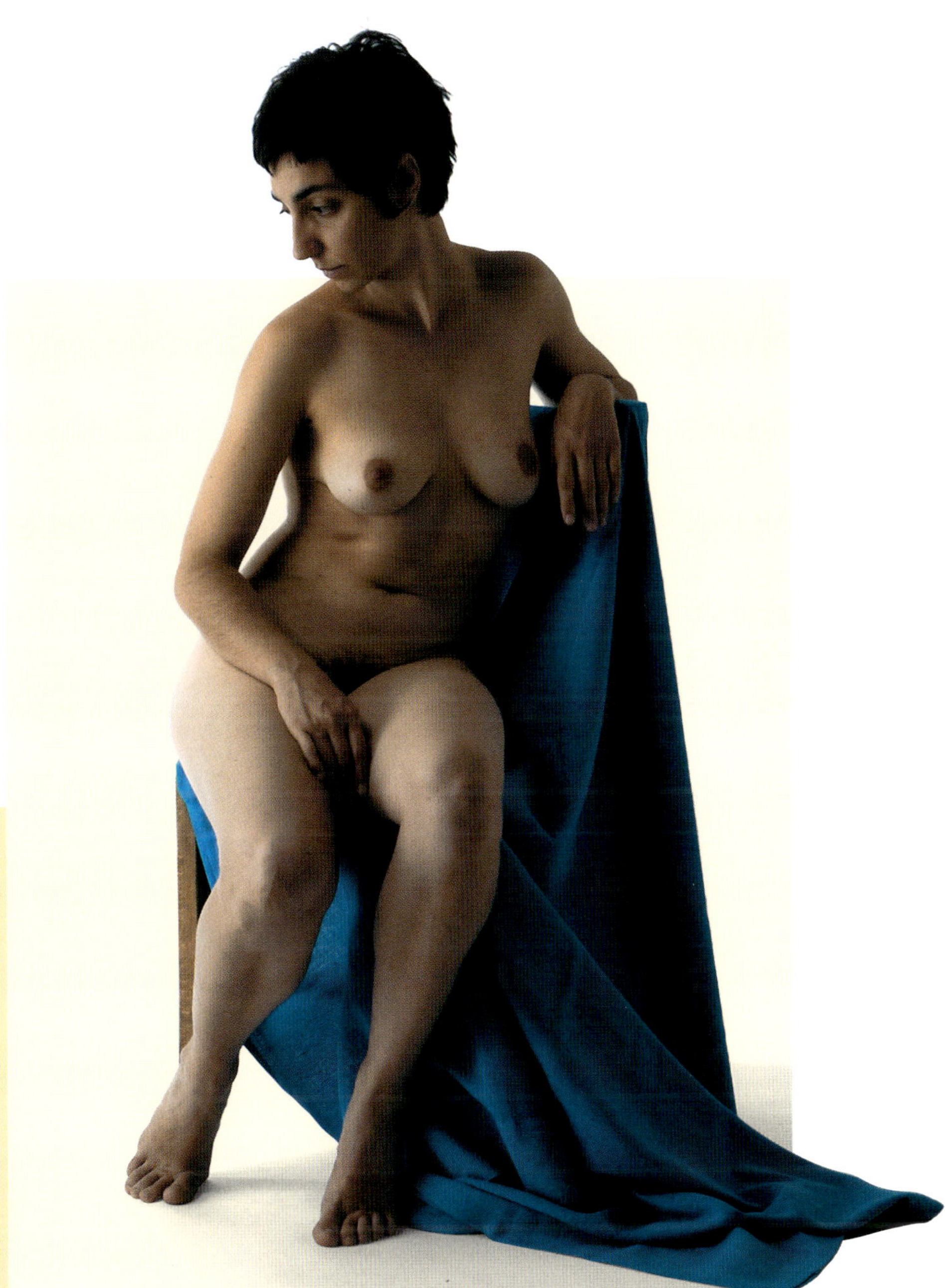

"The brushstrokes follow one another, and continue like words in a conversation or in a letter . . . One must forge the iron rod while it is still hot . . . then I continue feeling life, when I put out the work wildly . . . so alone, so isolated, I have the exaltation of certain instants, and then I let myself get carried away to excessiveness."
Vincent van Gogh
Letters to Theo, 1883.

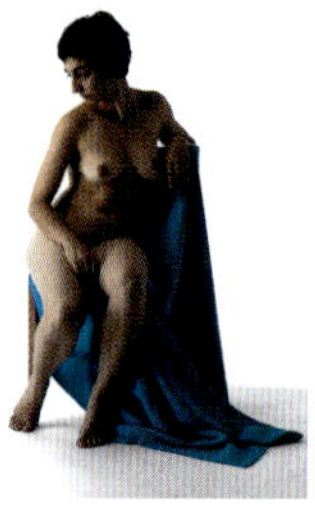

1 This project has no room for a preliminary drawing, for a small sketch or a study of form or color. There is no planning. The first step is already a step ahead in the painting; it consists of motions that must speak of themselves and of the model. One should even contemplate the possibility that the first step be the last one if that is what the painter feels.

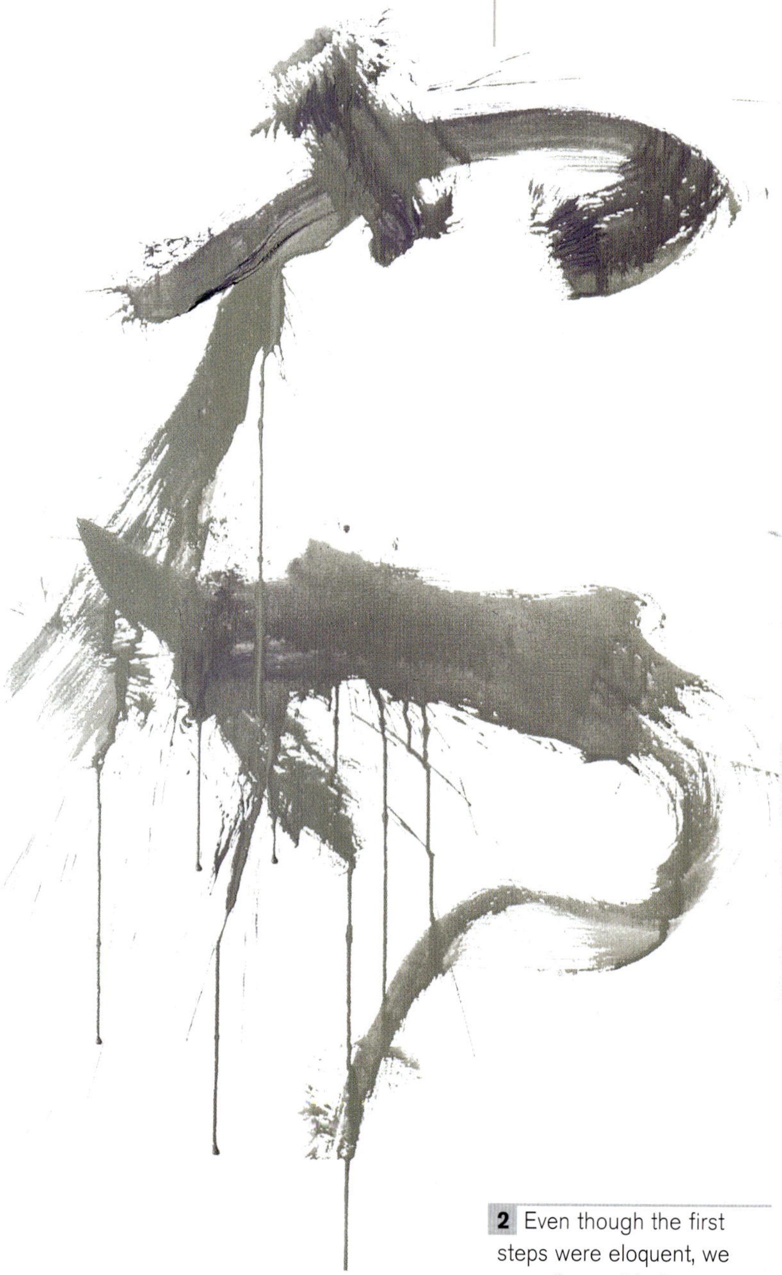

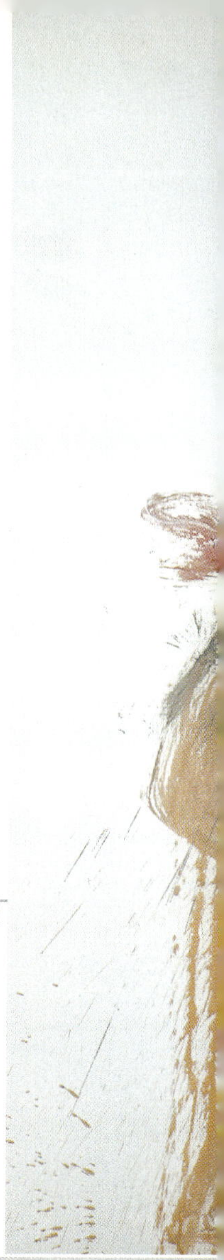

3 Next we express, with very quick and liberal strokes, our way of viewing the volume: not as a three-dimensional form, with its chiaroscuro, but through the color of the skin, as a mass.

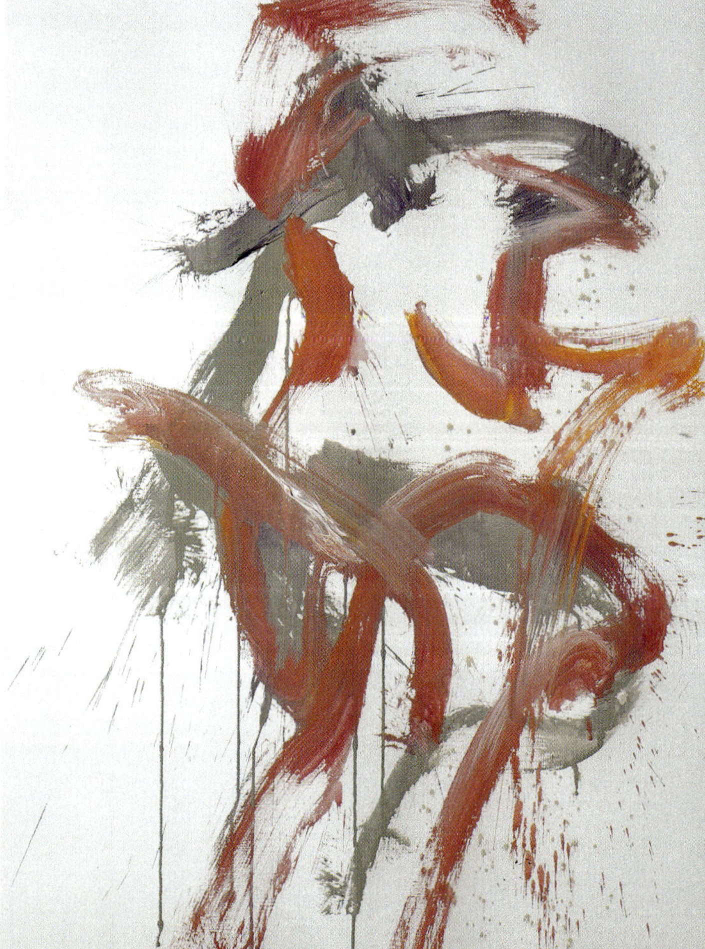

2 Even though the first steps were eloquent, we move forward in the definition of the theme. The initial brushstrokes properly express the gesture of the figure, but they have no body, they do not speak of volume or footing, which is why we decide to continue adding lines to further construct the anatomy.

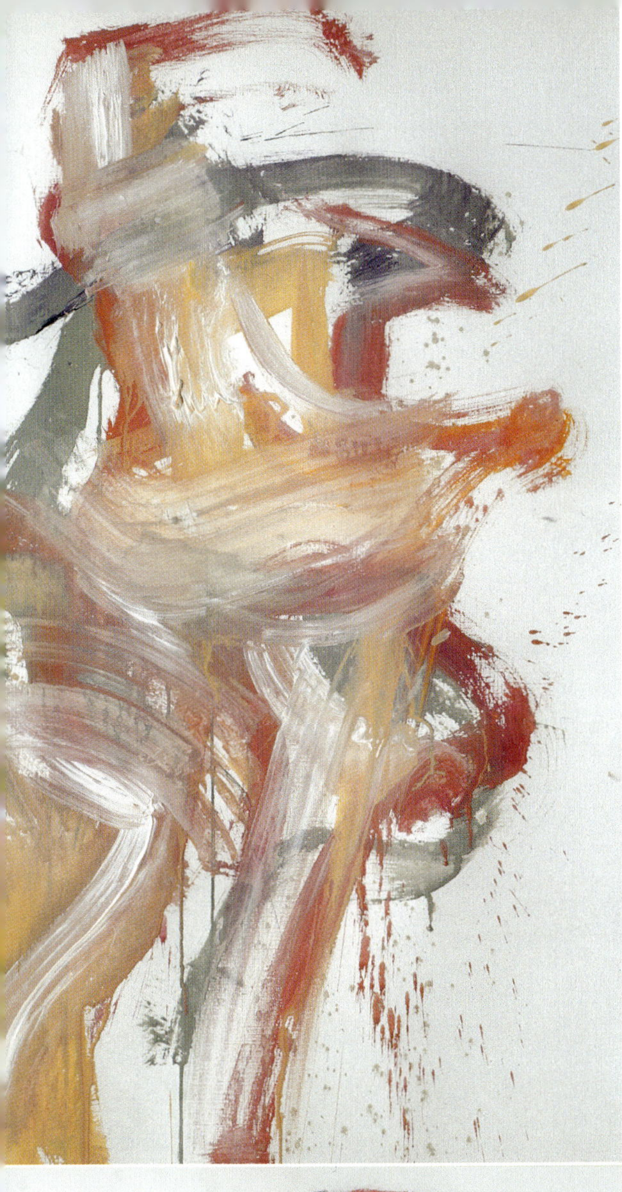

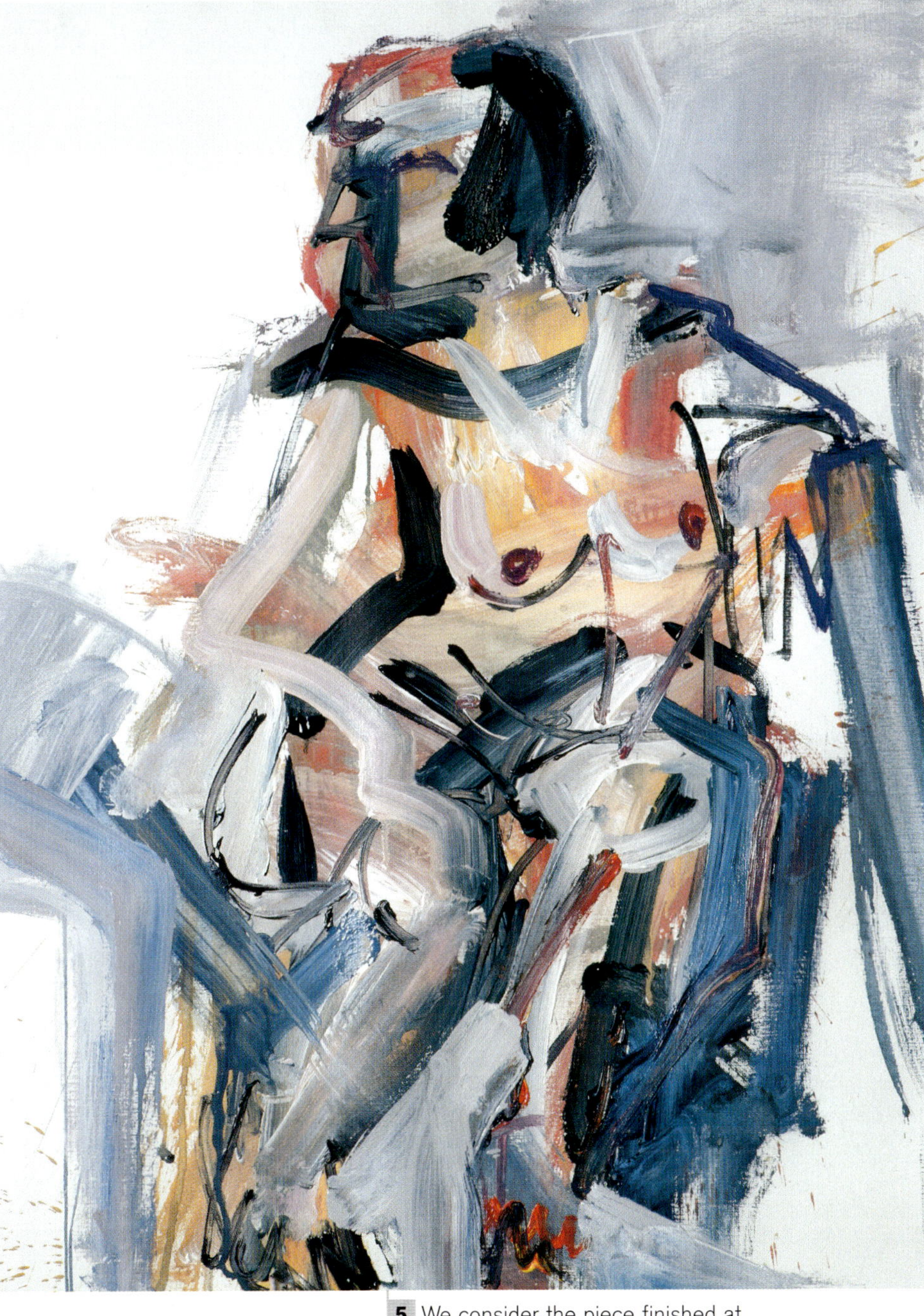

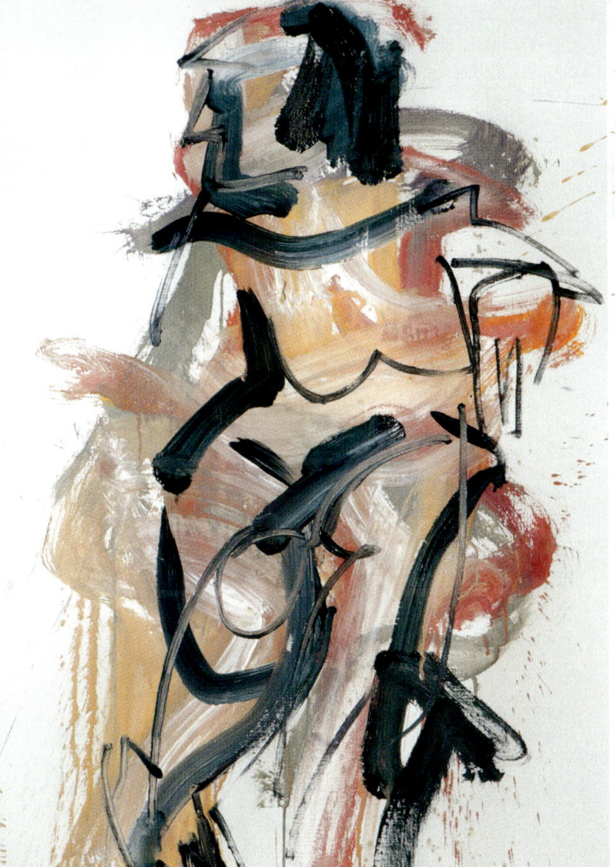

4 We emphasize the drawing of the figure with very dark strokes applied over the previous mass. The image maintains the freshness and the impetus of the first steps, but now it also has body and presence.

5 We consider the piece finished at this point because we sense that if we continue painting we will overwork the canvas with too many unnecessary elements. An excess of plastic energy can provoke a visual short-circuit by saturation. Knowing when to stop painting requires self-control, despite acting from passion rather than reason.

Other versions

Here are six variations on the same theme, in which the artist has modified the form of the line and the length of execution time. All six have in common a free and direct expression. As Fernando Zóbel said, "You either sing or shout," and an Expressionist shouts most of the time.

This oil painting concentrates the energy in the background rather than on the figure. First, a gray background was created with ample and diluted strokes of different densities. Over the latter, an outer silhouette of the body was established with red and white brushstrokes applied with a bristle brush. In the center, a few features that identify the body have been drawn.

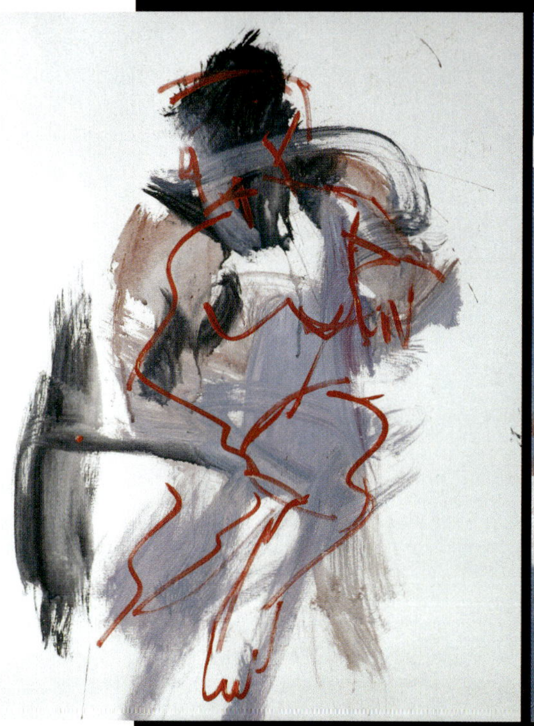

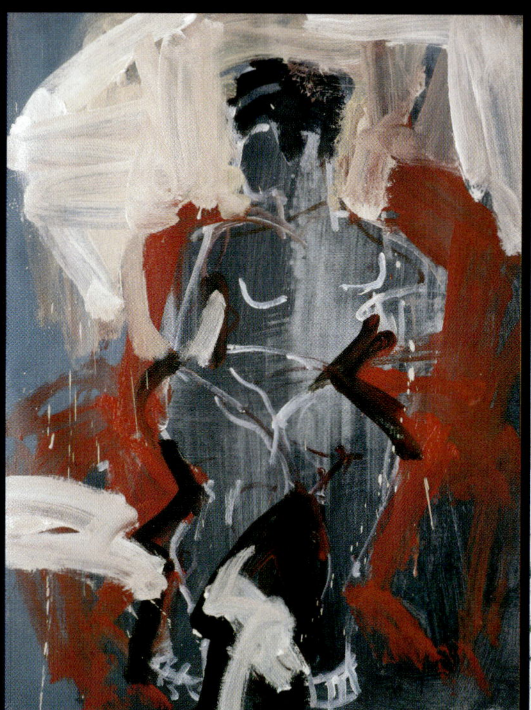

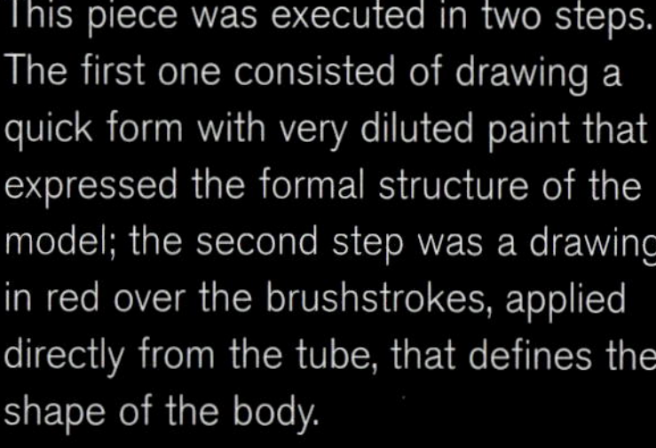

This piece was executed in two steps. The first one consisted of drawing a quick form with very diluted paint that expressed the formal structure of the model; the second step was a drawing in red over the brushstrokes, applied directly from the tube, that defines the shape of the body.

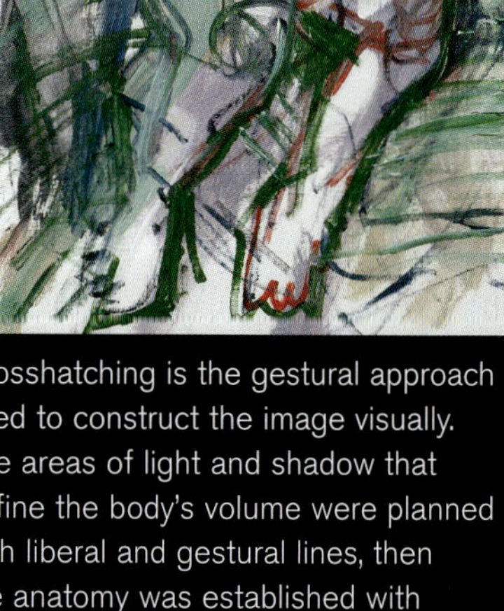

Crosshatching is the gestural approach used to construct the image visually. The areas of light and shadow that define the body's volume were planned with liberal and gestural lines, then the anatomy was established with green crosshatching.

The outlined appearance of the image in this painting was determined by the method followed to execute it. First, the model was painted with a gestural drawing, without too much definition. Next, the black background was applied, leaving the silhouette of the figure floating in the center. To finish, a drawing was made using white paint directly from the tube in quick, gestural strokes.

The gray background, distressed with a rag to create areas of light and splattered with ivory white, was the base for addressing the figure directly with a tube of black paint; the resulting drawing was pictorial, direct, and undefined.

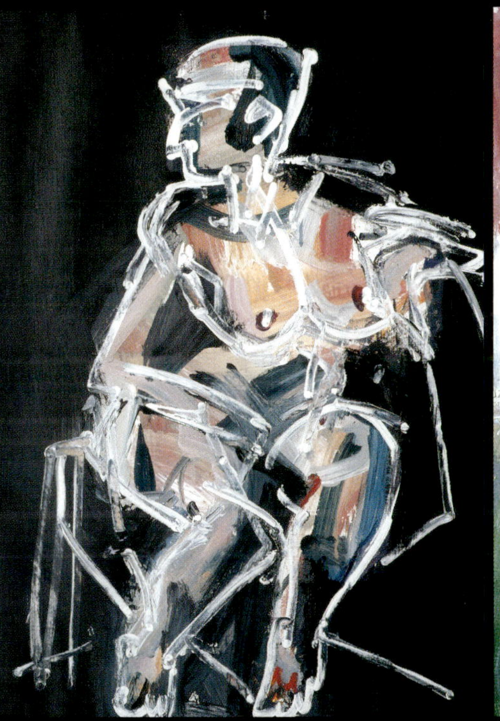

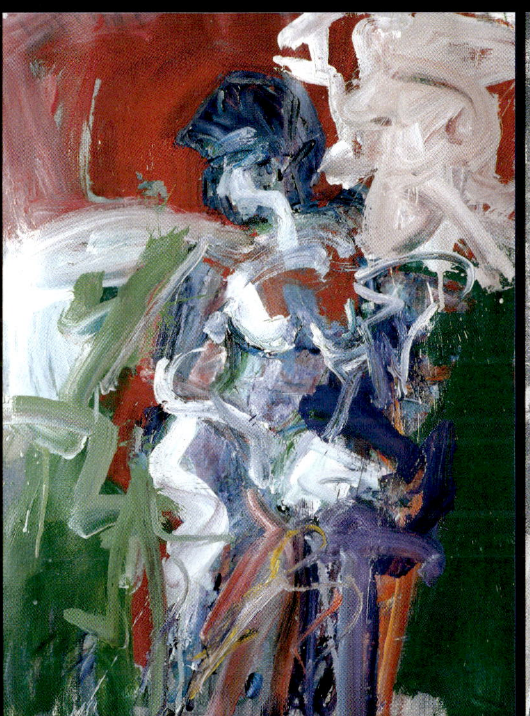

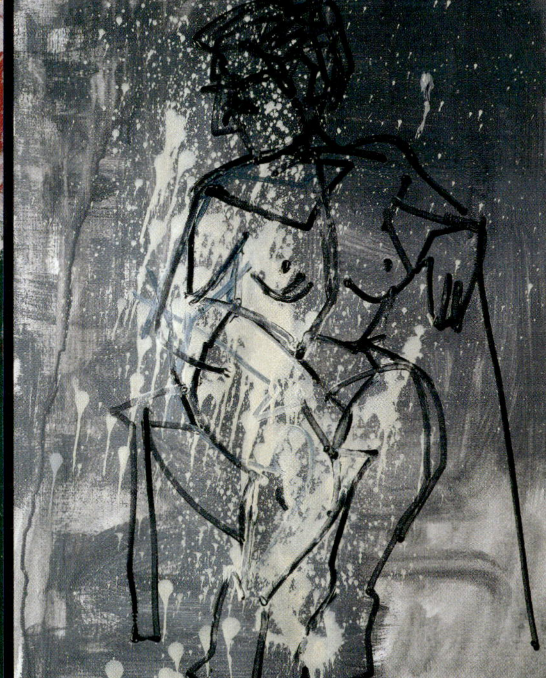

In this work, the color was allowed to blend on the surface. The very fluid and intertwined strokes give the image a look of deterioration, as if the painting were to melt from the energy applied. This method is the closest to the one used by de Kooning for his paintings of women.

New approaches

Other models

Each position adopted by the model is an invitation to a specific type of approach. This more relaxed pose inspired the artist to do a more defined and constructed drawing. The lines adjust to the chiaroscuro, which gives the painting a solid, quiet feeling.

Other media

As an alternative to oils, the artist has chosen a dry medium: chalk. The direct and energetic line of the theme is maintained but the intensity has been changed; with oils this is determined by the charge of paint in the brush, while with chalk it depends on the pressure applied on the paper. Blending was done with the fingers and a rag.

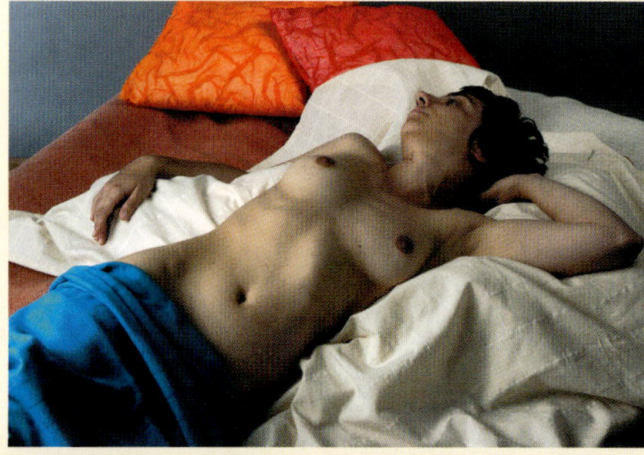

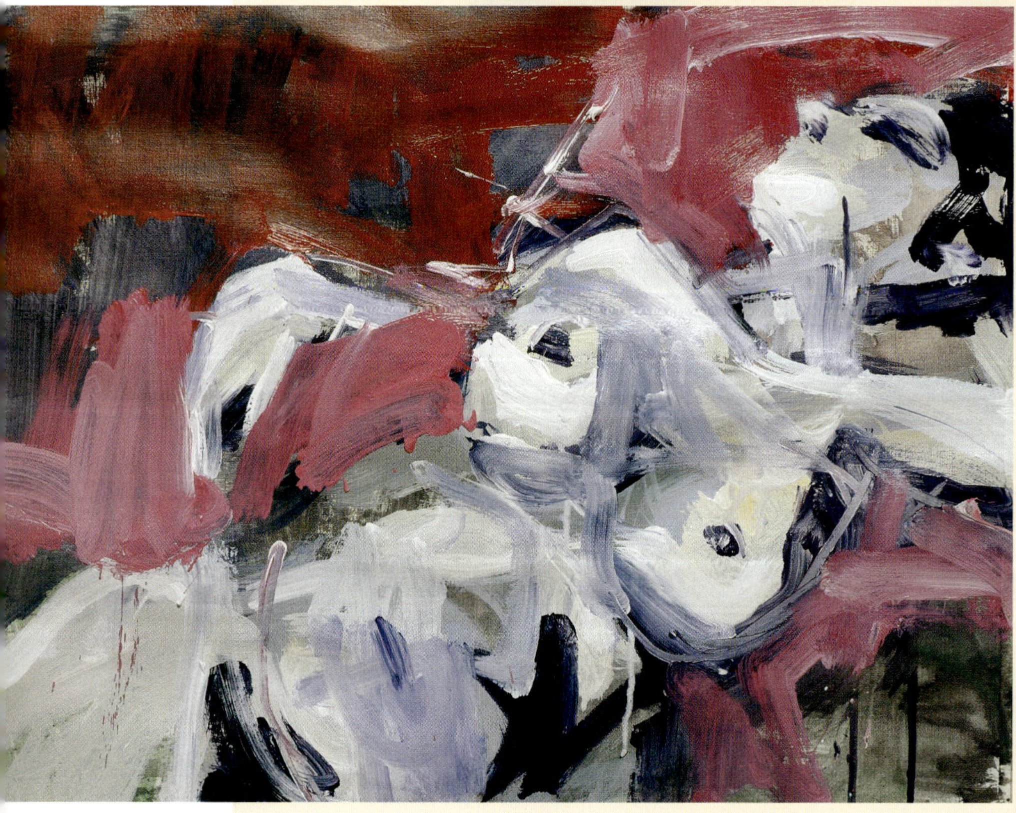

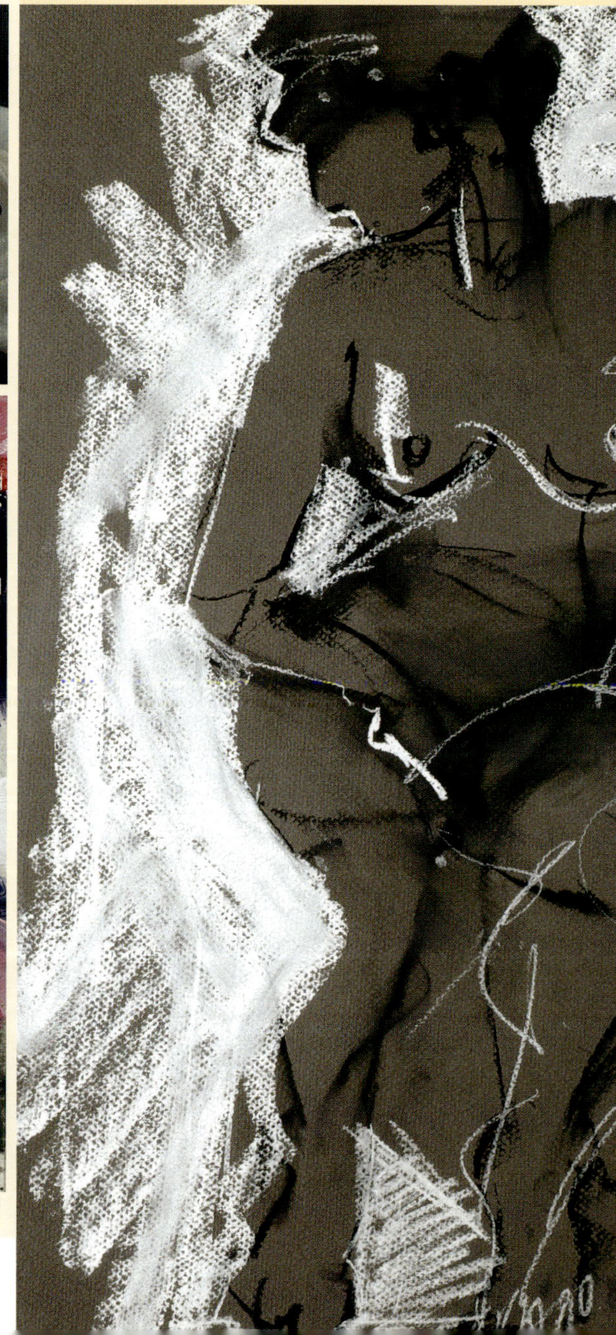

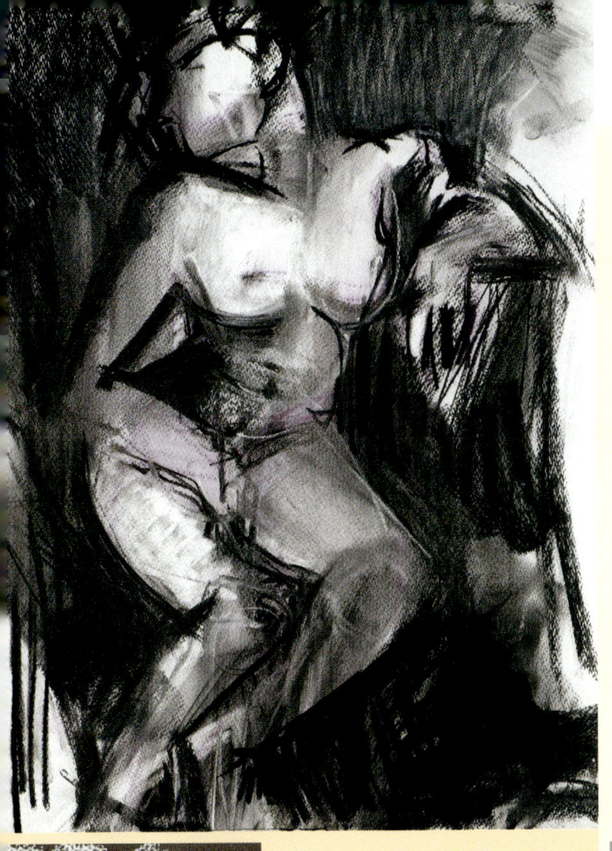

Other views

Expressionism is based on direct expression, without corrections. Throughout the twentieth century there have been many Expressionist movements; one of these was the German neo-Expressionism of the 1980s, of which Albert Oehlen (born in 1954) was a proponent. His paintings are very rich in resources (gestures, textures, structures, manipulated computer graphics, intermediate images) and his work is tied to music for its conception of art as a series of rhythmic sensations; many of his paintings bear the title of a rock or death metal group or song. Although his painting technique is defined as antivirtuosic, his paintings lead to more reflection than the work of some of the other neo-Expressionists ("I am not interested in chaos, but in order without control").

Albert Oehlen,
Without Freedom but Lascivious (detail),
1983. Private collection.

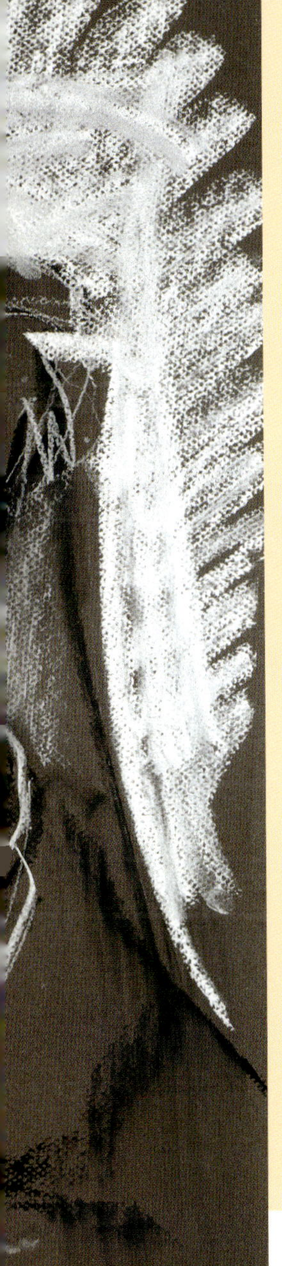

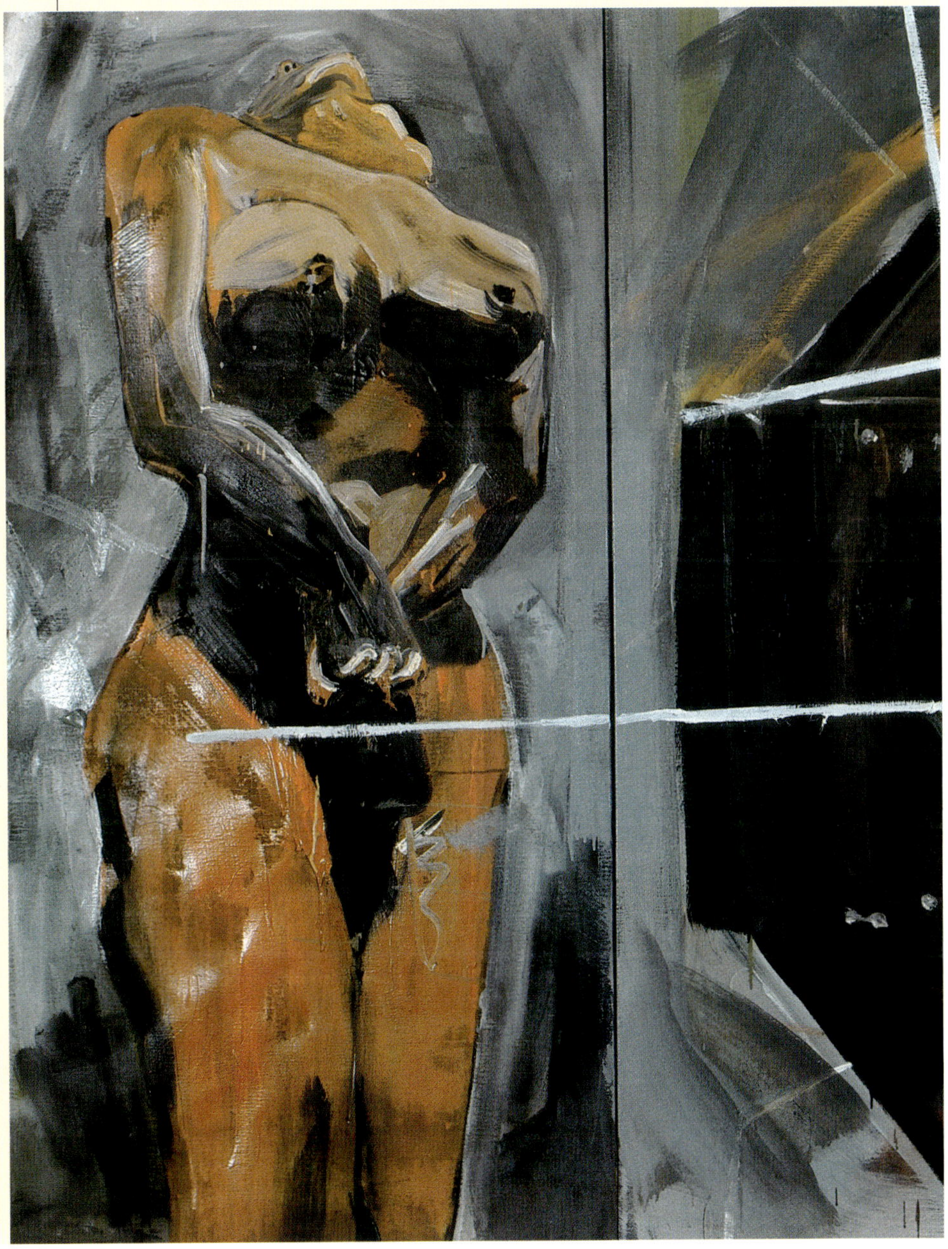

Creative approach 12

Flat, uniform, and smooth textures

When the texture is smooth, flat, uniform, we could say that it does not exist, that it is only flat; but we would fall into a semantic trap because smoothness is a tactile quality as valid as any other, and it has a specific communicative ability: the absence of surface features. Ever since Henri Matisse (1869–1954) reclaimed the flat character of painting, many artists have positioned themselves in that intrinsic reality of pictorial phenomena. Among the most outstanding is Gary Hume (born in 1962), who creates his pieces with uniform areas of color developed from materials suitable for this approach, such as synthetic resins and enamels applied on sheets of aluminum or melamine. In Hume, this smoothness, carried to extremes, is an actualization of the neoplastic principles of Mondrian. *Vicious* is a painting from a series he devoted to statues of the Olympic stadium in Rome and that summarize his intention: to create works capable of radiating beauty and affection.

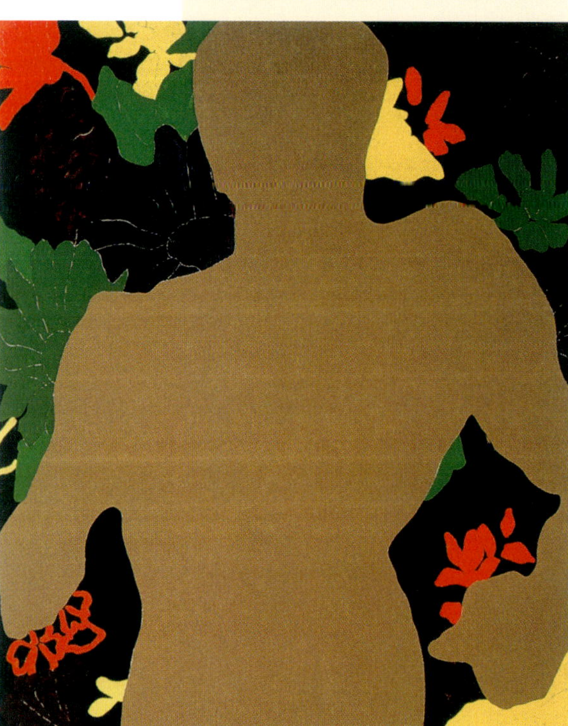

Gary Hume,
Vicious, 1994.
Private collection.

Experimenting with planes in a collage of an urban scene

This project, created by Josep Asunción, is like a small collage laboratory. The technique consists of constructing the piece by gluing paper. It provides the typical effects of flat strokes (due to the nature of the sheet of paper), depending on the characteristic of each paper and the way it is cut and glued. Here, the model is an urban scene, where the artist has created silhouettes of passersby and their shadows.

"The established concept of three-dimensional creation . . . is the way of viewing (perceiving) the past. The new way of contemplating does not stem from a determined point: its visual field is everywhere. It is limitless, without encumbrances of space and time, according to the theory of relativity. In practice, the new vision places the visual field before the plane (the extreme deepening possibility of plastic art)."
Piet Mondrian,
Plastic Art and Pure Plastic Art (articles),
1937–1943.

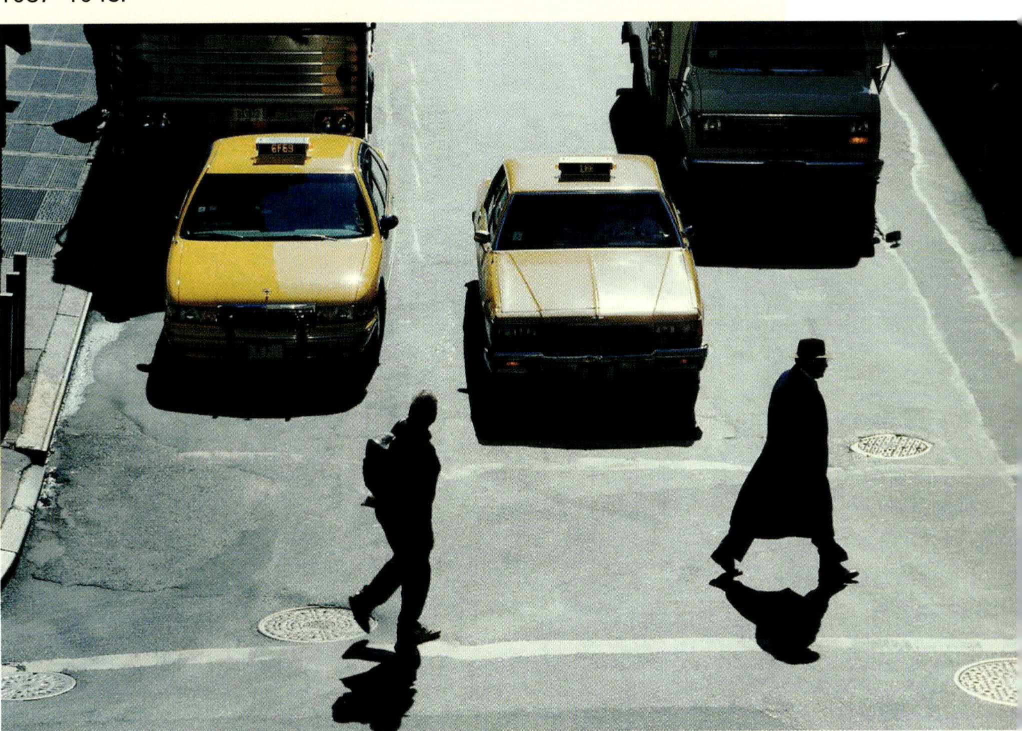

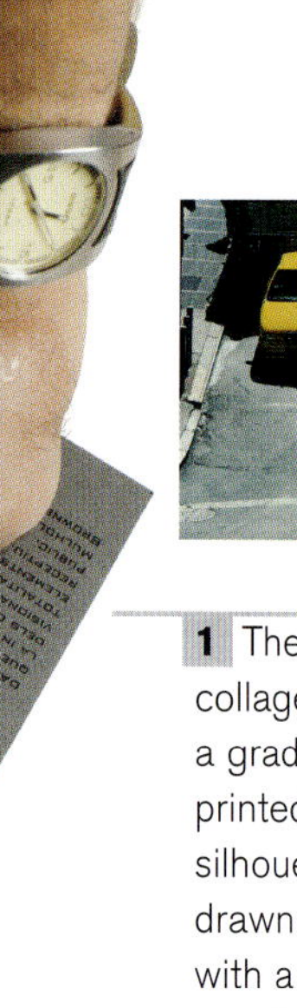

1 The material chosen for this collage is a background paper with a gradated color and pieces of printed construction paper. The silhouettes of the pedestrians are drawn with a pencil and cut out with a craft knife; we are going to use the cardboard negatives as templates to create new silhouettes if we need to repeat them.

2 The gradated background cardboard helps us perceive the space in depth without losing the feeling of smoothness. We begin to place the figures on the surface by carefully studying their distribution to create an interesting visual conversation.

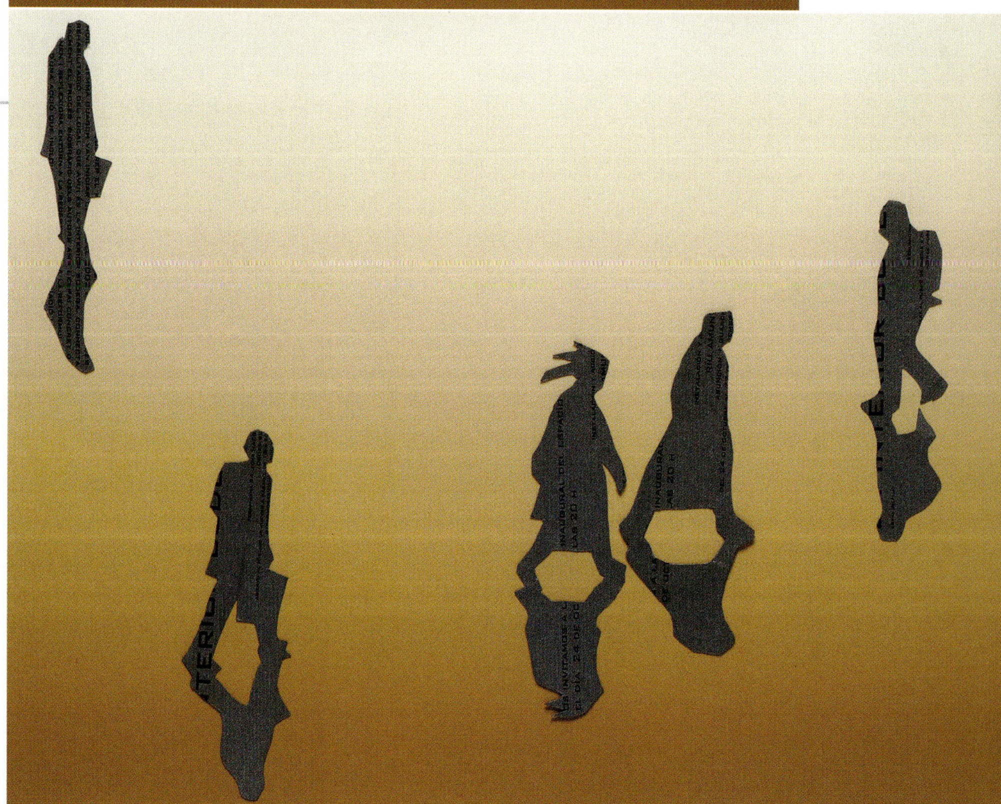

3 We remove some people from the photograph to copy the silhouettes; others are originals. We try to maintain the same point of view throughout the scene. To do this, it is important for the projected shadows of the pedestrians not to have the same proportions as the figures themselves.

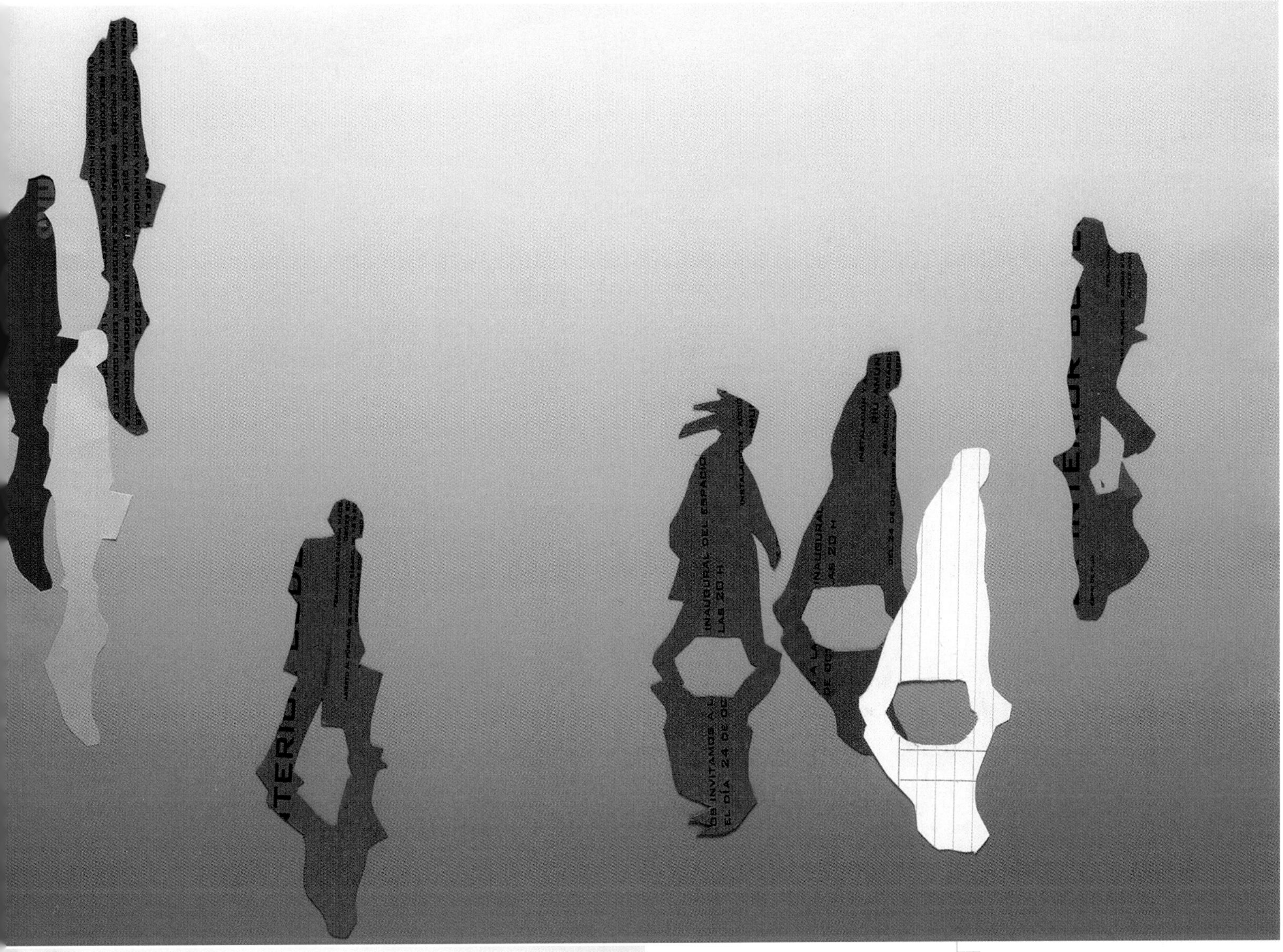

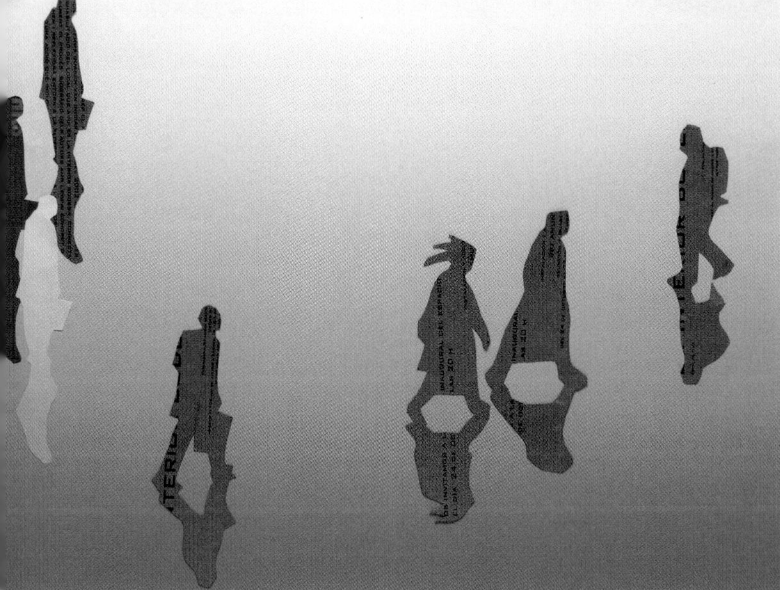

4 We duplicate some of the people, similar in terms of size but different in color and material. This helps explain the idea of alienation or multitude, which is the sense that one gets in large groups of people in cities.

5 We finish the work with a counterpoint of white light, a figure that is different from the others, made of a different type of paper and color. Although this figure is not walking against the flow, it stands out. The message is a tribute to the individual in the midst of the masses; it is conveyed in a collage through a simple change of paper.

Other views

To create interesting variations, the artist has used different papers and ways of adhering the silhouettes. He has experimented with flat but not completely smooth surfaces to achieve the goals that he has set forth.

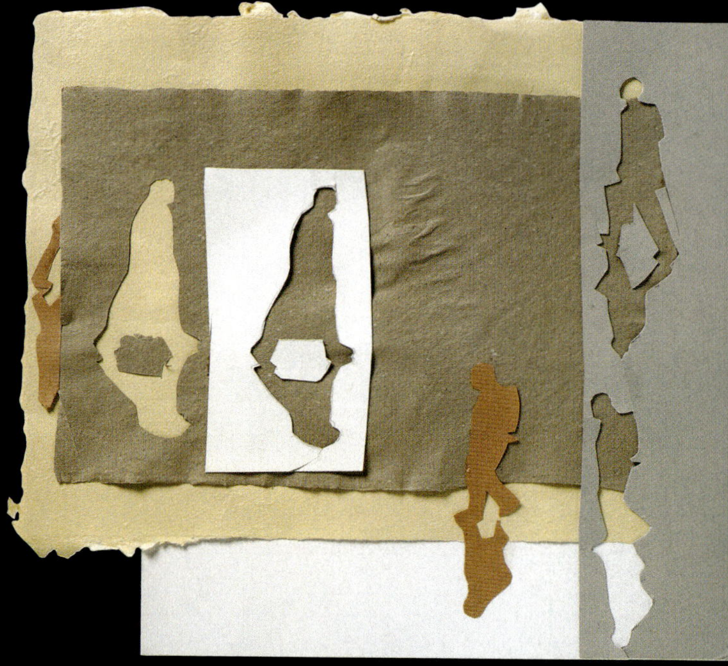

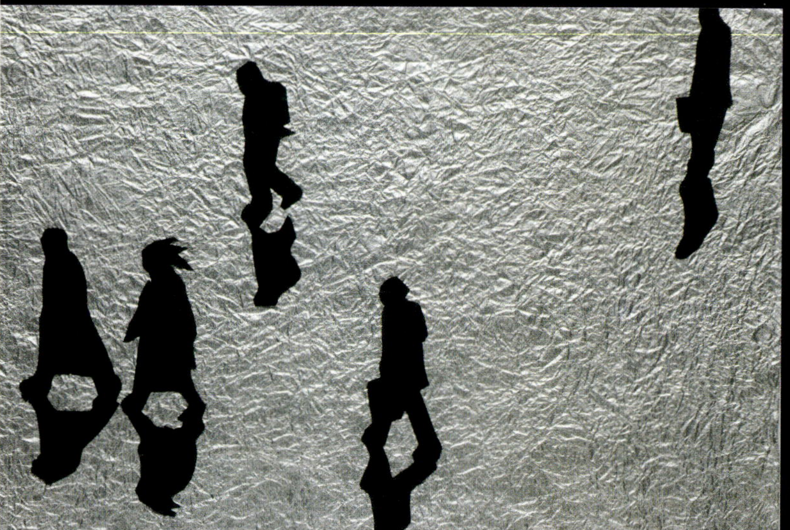

This collage is very elementary in terms of technique. It involves only two different papers: crumpled silver gift wrap and very silky black paper. The silver one acts as a reflective screen and the black one as a hole that absorbs all its light, providing maximum contrast and a striking visual effect.

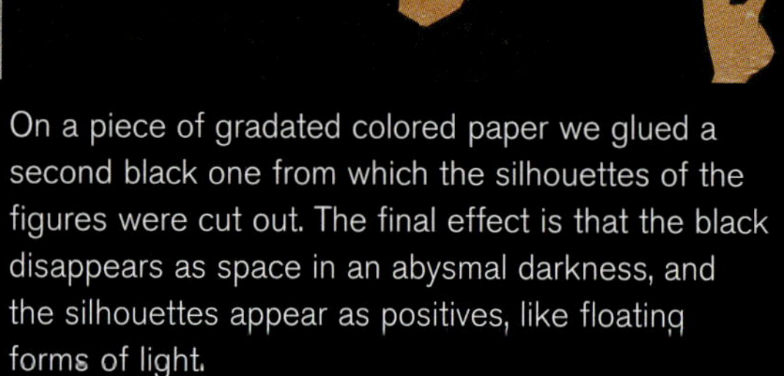

On a piece of gradated colored paper we glued a second black one from which the silhouettes of the figures were cut out. The final effect is that the black disappears as space in an abysmal darkness, and the silhouettes appear as positives, like floating forms of light.

In this piece the richness of the materials and the expression can be appreciated thanks to the combination of positive and negative silhouettes, as well as to the use of very different types of papers. In addition, the arrangement of each paper is very liberal, breaking the traditional idea of a pedestrian space.

Over corrugated paper the artist glued silhouettes of people constructed of smooth paper and slightly raised above the background. This way, the light creates shadows and makes it look as if the figures were floating, in addition to indicating that they are two-dimensional, not volumetric.

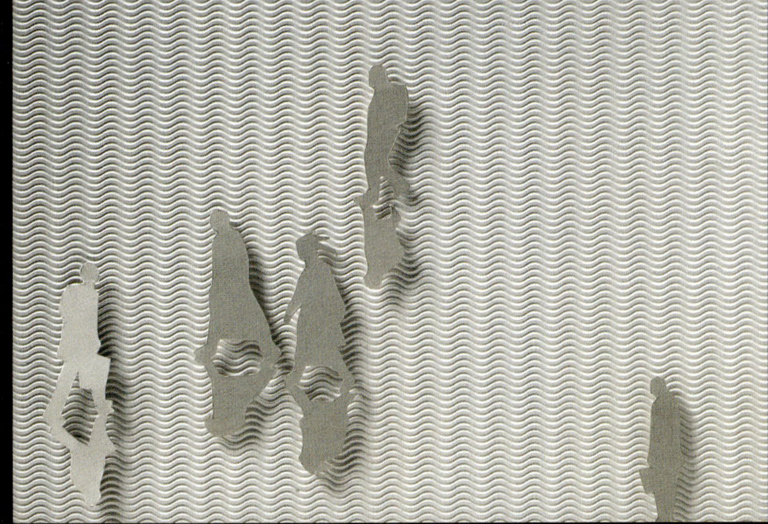

Here, the contrast is minimal. Only two papers were used and the colors are similar. The idea was to play with the subtlety of total flatness to create a poetic and simple effect.

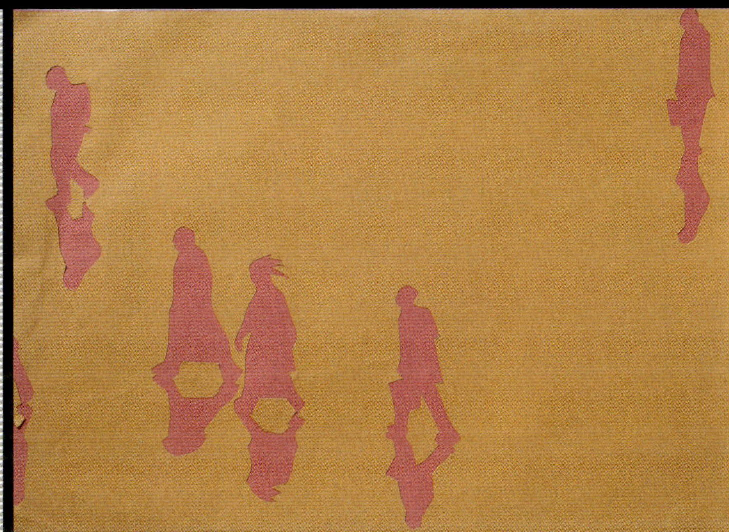

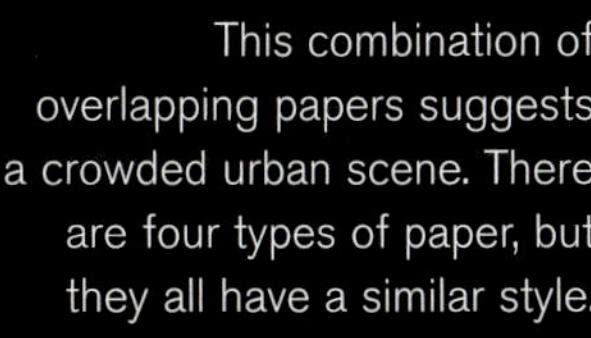

This combination of overlapping papers suggests a crowded urban scene. There are four types of paper, but they all have a similar style.

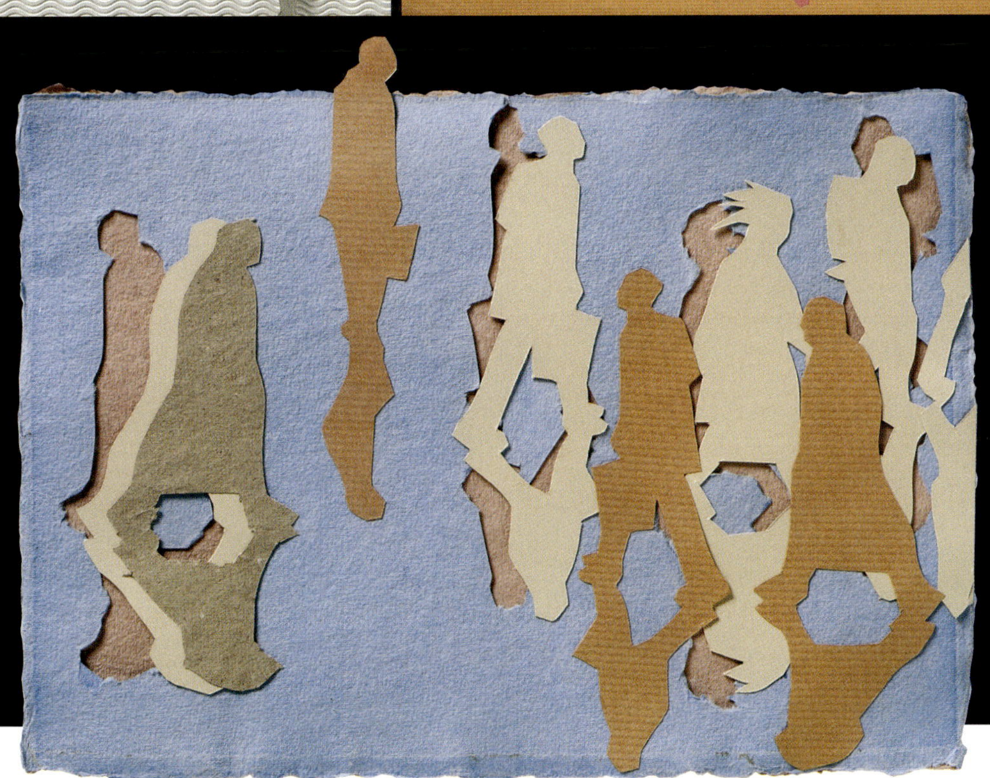

New approaches

Other models

If the previous model showed an elevated viewpoint, this one is seen from below, with strong foreshortening. This disproportionate image makes it possible to capture depth in a smooth and flat texture, where there is no relief or chiaroscuro. Using printed papers with the text visible emphasizes the fact that the paper is smooth, flat, and two-dimensional.

Other media

The artist wanted to revisit here the idea of the first Cubist and Dadaist collages, even those from Matisse's later years. First, he painted several papers with gouache, and then he cut out silhouettes and glued them to his background. This method is the oldest one; it maintains the warmth of the paint on the paper but does not lose the two-dimensionality or the effects of distance.

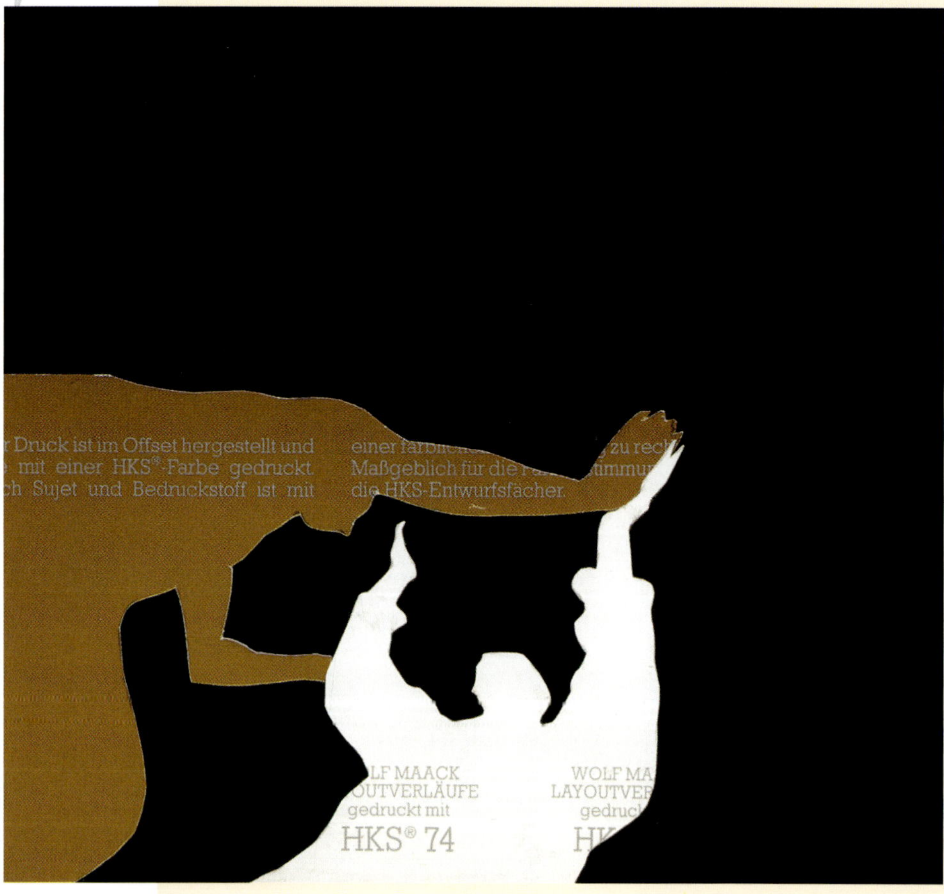

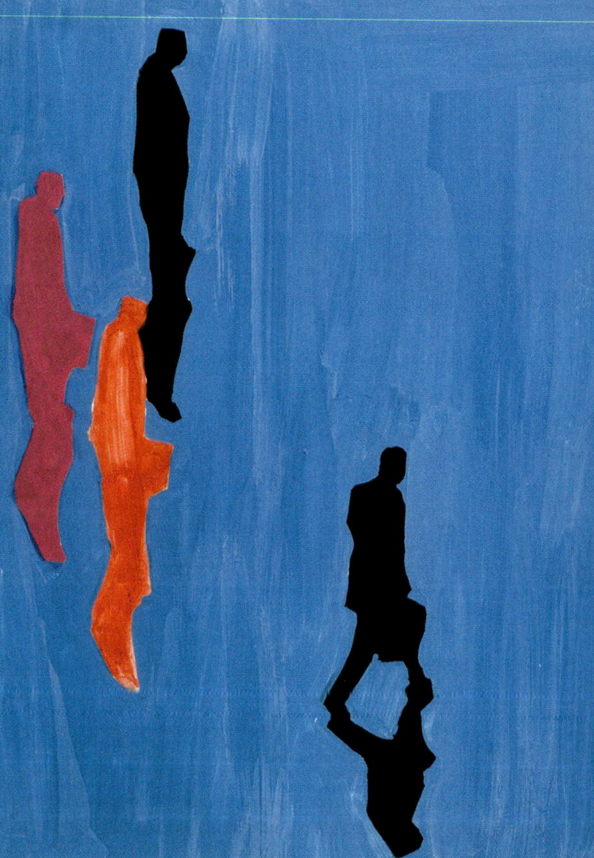

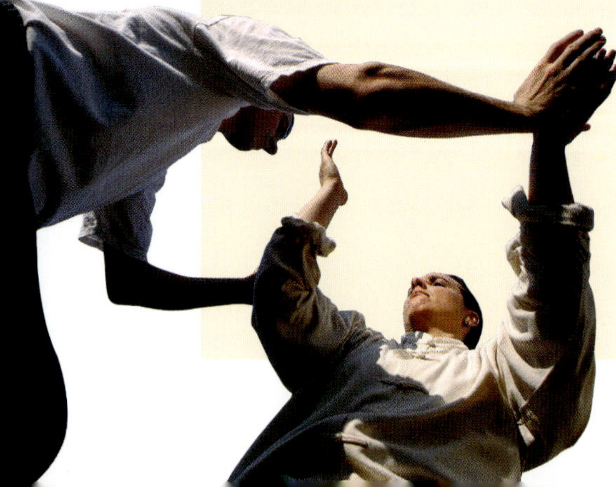

Other views

Donald Sultan (born in 1951) is a contemporary painter whose work is recognized for its compositional flatness. Unlike Gary Hume, Sultan gives his surfaces greater material sensibility, as in *Lluvia, 8 de Julio de 1982* (*Rain, July 8, 1982*), executed with oils, charcoal, and crayon on vinyl tile. His paintings tend to be large—this one measures 97 × 49 inches (244 × 122 cm)—and the supports may be rubber, vinyl, or tar, lending an industrial feeling that corresponds with his cold and direct approach to the work.

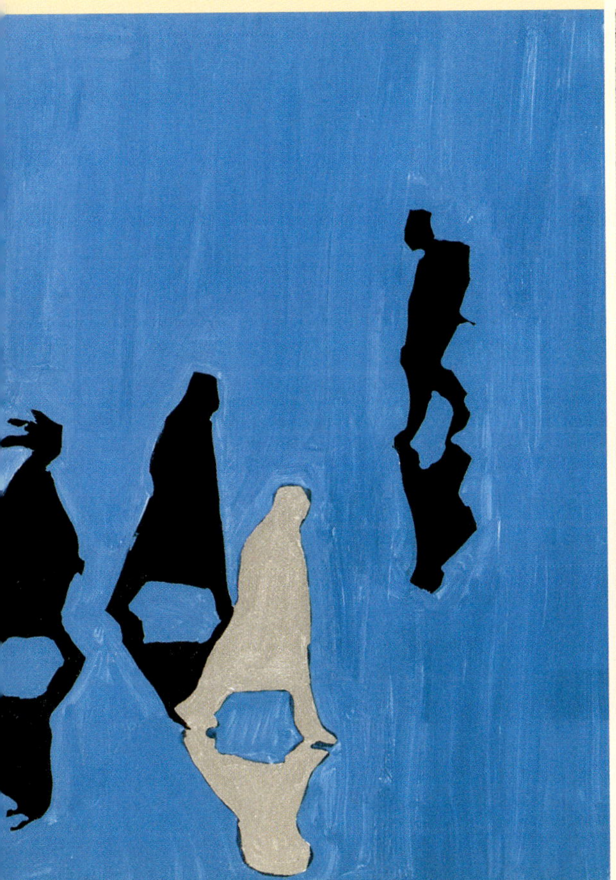

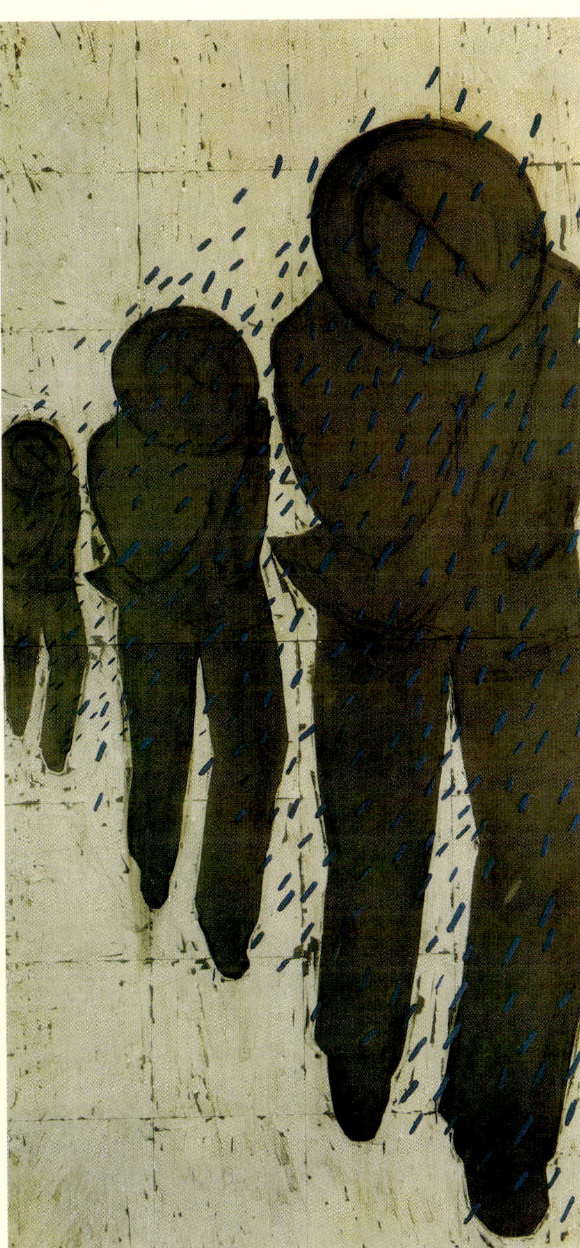

Donald Sultan,
Lluvia, 8 de Julio de 1982,
1982. Private collection.

Line in

From the onset of photography, painting set out to discover new territories other than the faithful representation of reality. Nowadays, nobody doubts that the stroke, the line, texture, or color can be eloquent in its own right; this autonomy of the line allows the painter to express himself or herself freely and intensely, without depending on an object outside the painting. In this chapter, we are going to explore three specific areas of abstract painting: action painting, material painting, and Zen painting.

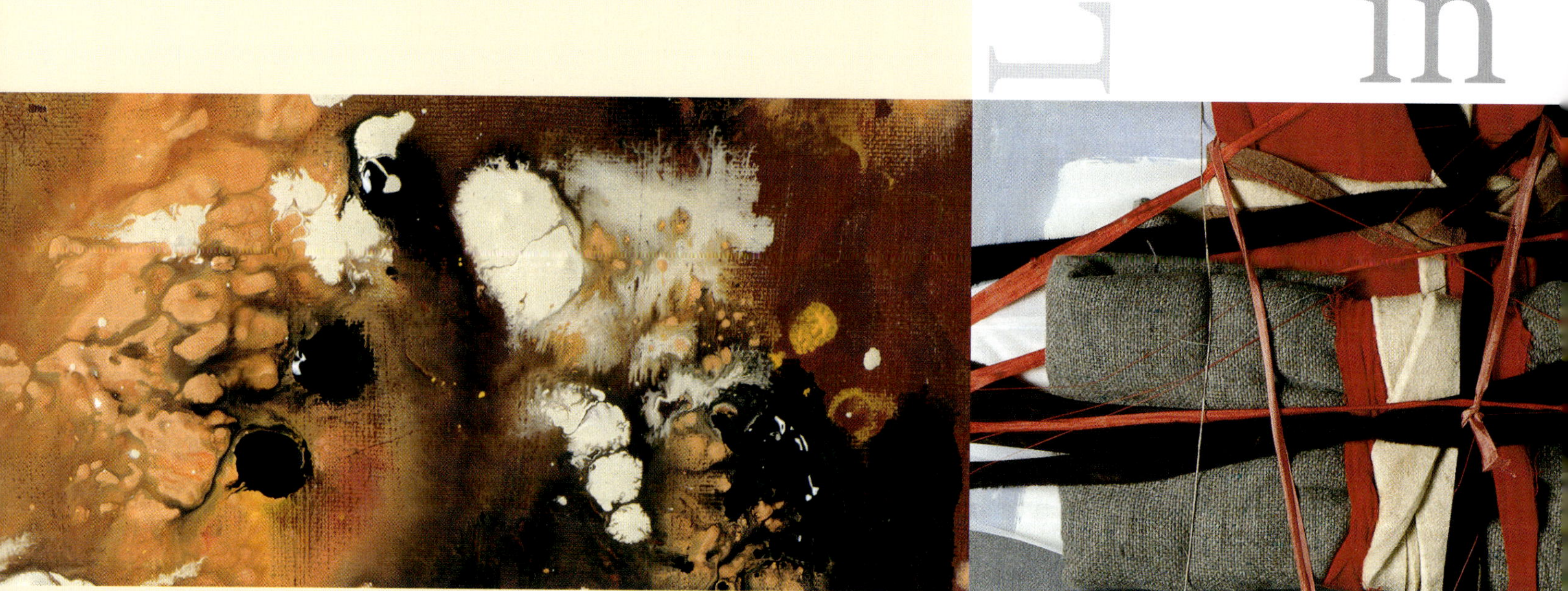

abstraction

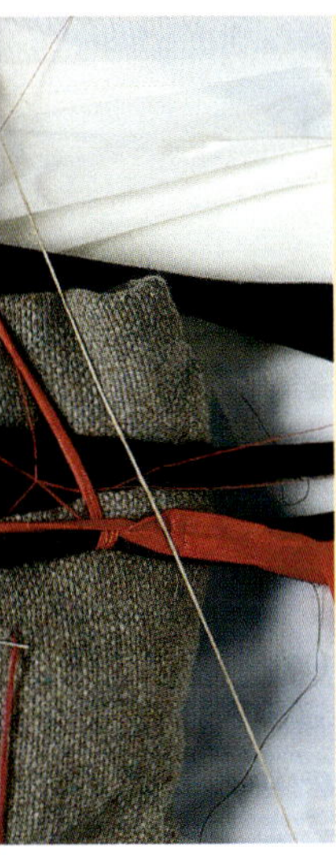

"Painting has always been an abstraction, from the cave paintings of Altamira to Velázquez to Picasso. To the fanatics of realism I have said many times that reality has never been part of painting, but is found only in the mind. Art is not a sign, an object, something that suggests to us the reality of our spirit . . . the reality shown by the eyes is an extremely poor shadow of reality."
Antoni Tàpies

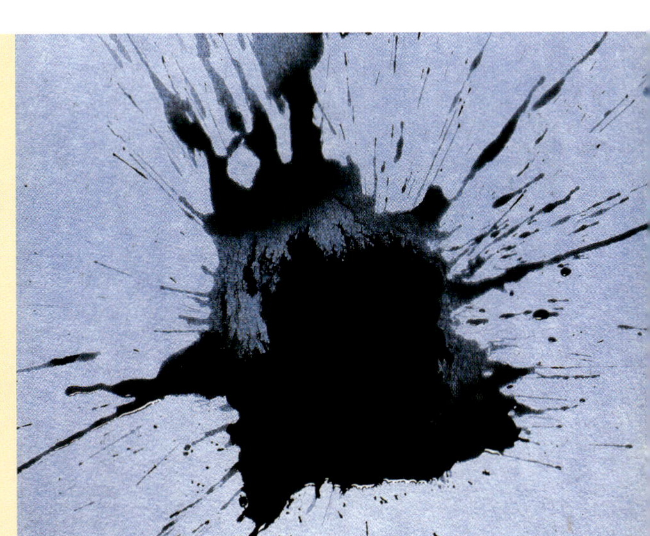

Liquid, fluid, flowing lines

In the decade of the 1950s critics labeled a group of American artists "Action Painters." The most relevant painter of this movement was Jackson Pollock (1912–1956), whose work originated from the unconscious, accident, and randomness. He was influenced by Mexican mural painters, by Surrealism, and the paintings of Native Americans. Pollock worked on canvas spread on the floor so that he could become a part of the painting and approach it from all four sides. Using the dripping technique, he applied the paint directly onto the canvas, which allowed him to liberate his unconscious and get closer to the Surrealist techniques of automatism. His paintings, because of the dripping, completely eliminated a representational approach: on the one hand, there were no longer any elements to identify in the painting, and on the other, he transgressed the traditional idea of composition in terms of a relationship between different parts. This was the birth of the field painting approach, without hierarchies.

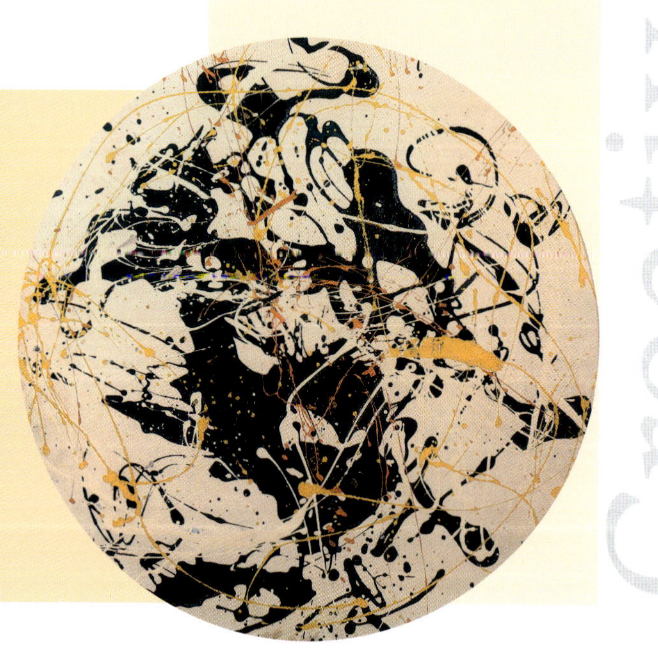

Jackson Pollock ,
Tondo, 1948.
Private collection.

Experimenting with dripping and spattering based on wood grain

Gemma Guasch has developed a work of art based on the most experimental part of painting. The support is considered a horizontal surface on which to splash, drip, dispense, dry, and layer paint. The subject consists of different photographs of knots in wood, which due to their variety, have made it possible to develop the painting with a very liberal approach based more on action than representation. Canvas and acrylic paint are the media chosen because they provide the basis for a dynamic piece, and fast drying time.

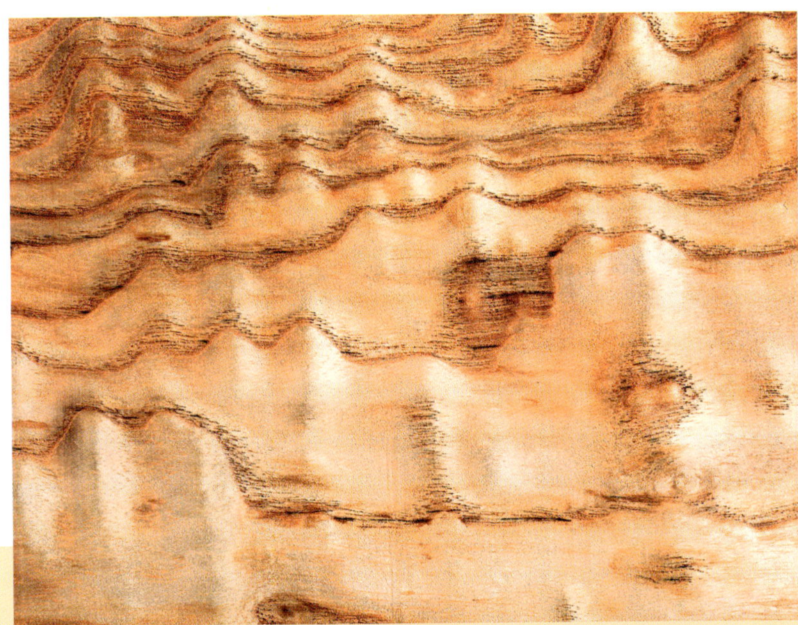

"My painting is direct . . . the painting method comes naturally from necessity. I want to express my feelings before illustrating them. The technique is nothing more than a way of saying something. While I am painting I have a general idea of what I am doing. I can control how the paint flows: there are no accidents, there is simply no beginning and no end."
Jackson Pollock
Pollock's narration for the movie *Jackson Pollock*, by Hans Namuth and Paul Falkenberg, 1951.

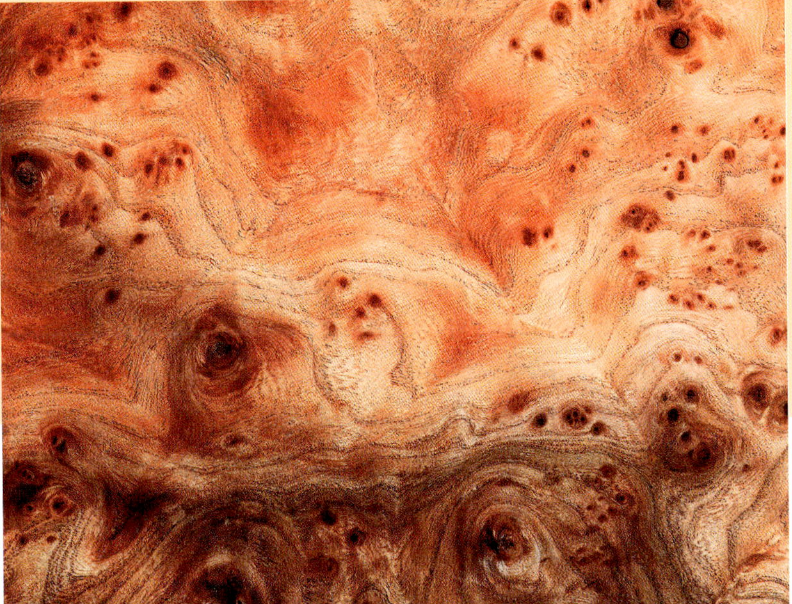

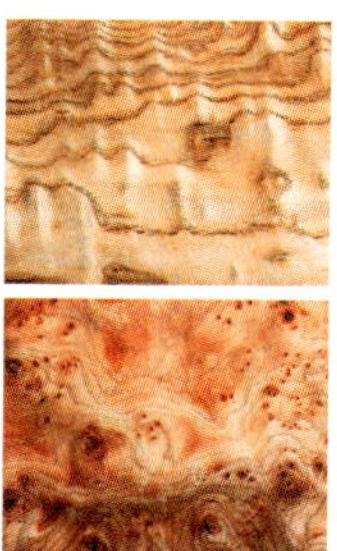

1 We begin with a tan color background. While this background is still wet, we pour orange paint liberally until tonal contrast is created. Then, the painting is washed and partially dried. The texture created provides warmth and contrast, which makes our work easier.

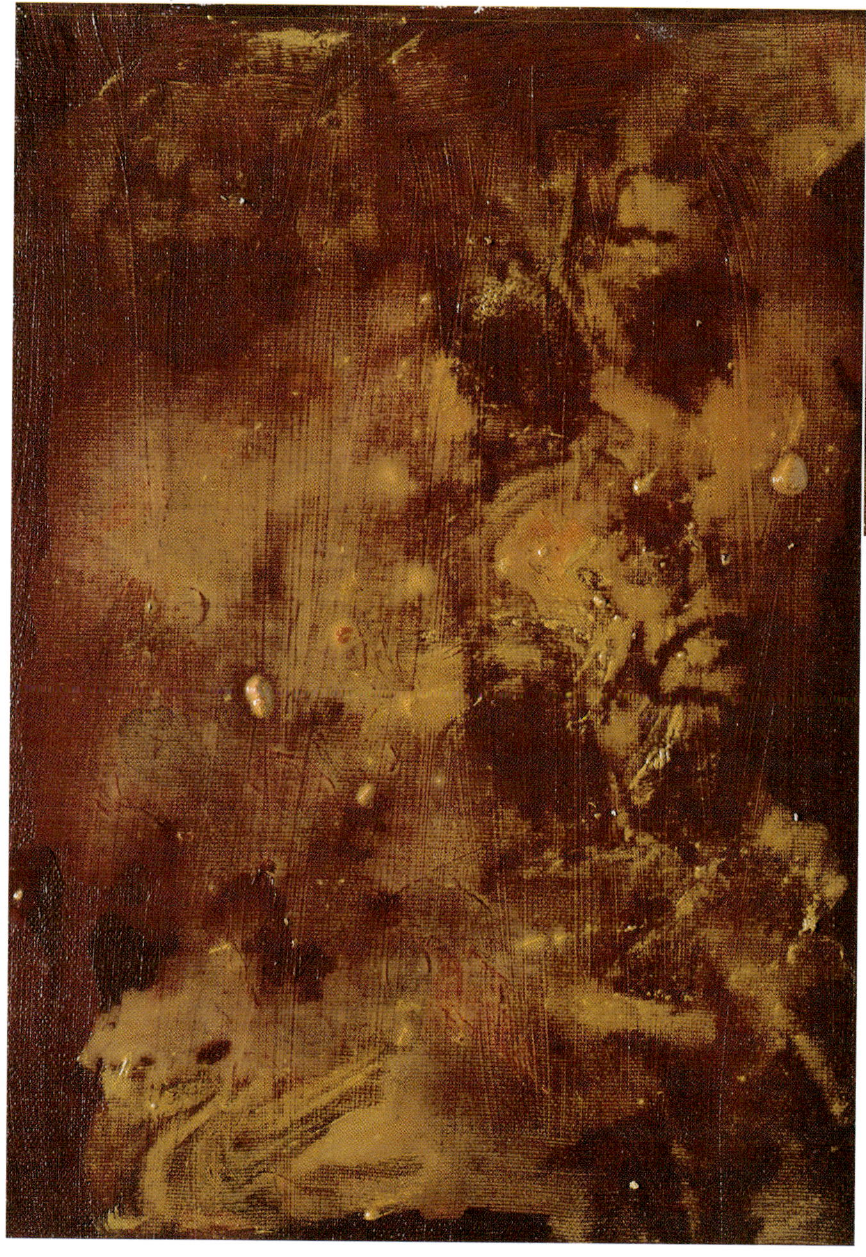

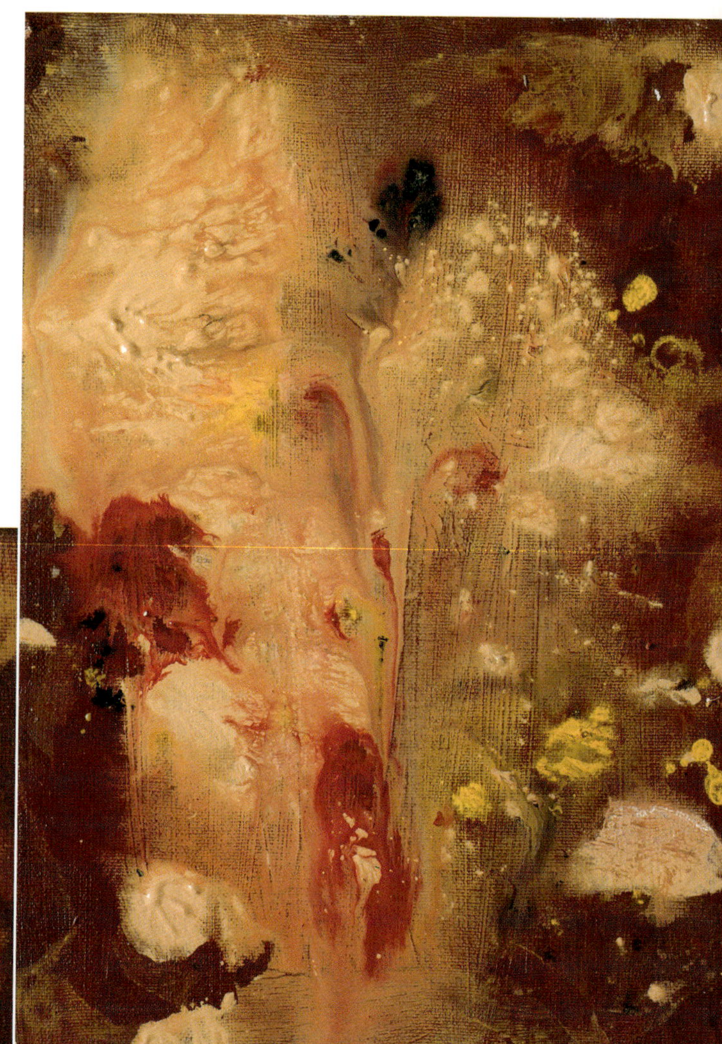

2 While the surface is still wet, we apply large amounts of paint with a spatula to produce a variety of impasto and thickness effects. Next, we spread the paint around by moving the canvas, letting the colors mix spontaneously. Through vigorous movements we create combinations that suggest the knots in the wood.

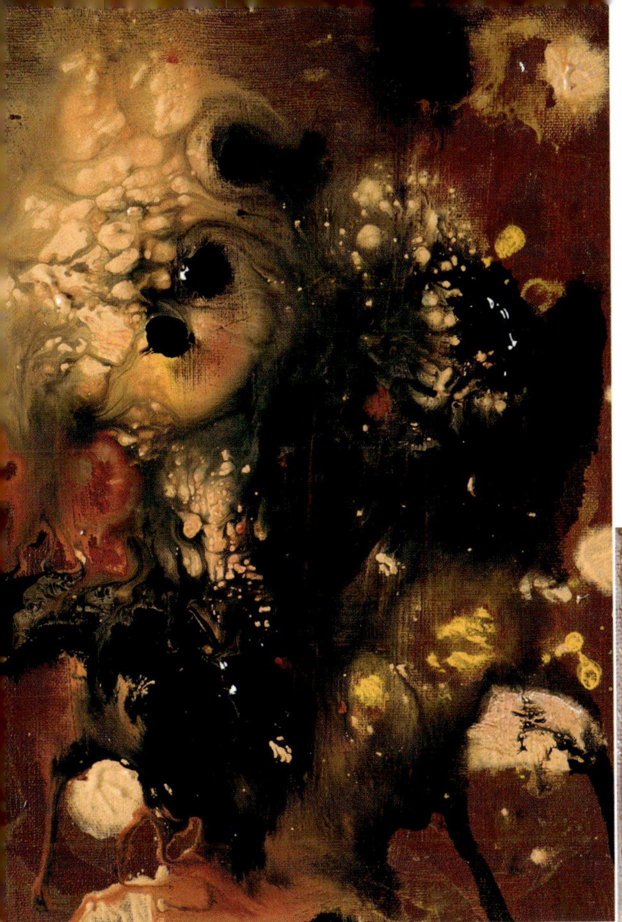

3 To highlight the contrast, we pour very liquid black paint on the center of the image and, with a rag, wipe the areas where we want to reinstate impastos and previous colors. The rag provides an interesting texture when it adheres to the still fresh paint.

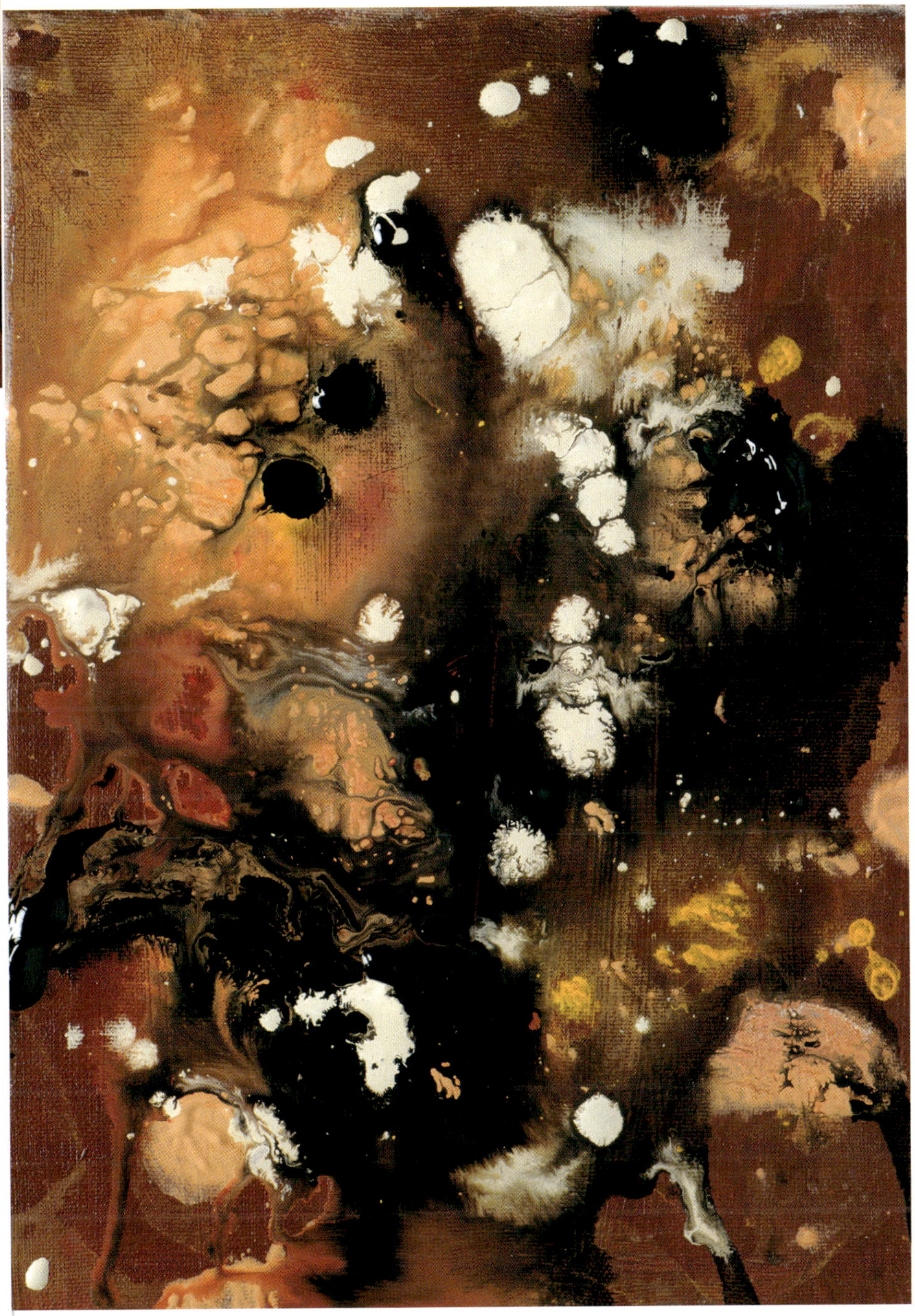

4 Finally, we drip undiluted white paint on the canvas directly and quickly; this provides several points of solid and striking light. Then, we spray water over some of the white impastos to soften the contrast and diffuse the edges.

Other views

The knotting on the wood offers an almost cosmic image due to its constant changes and contrasts. To create a varied gallery, Gemma Guasch allowed different configurations of textures and lines to result from using her medium in a fluid manner.

Over a background of tan colors, the paint was allowed to spread aggressively and harshly, producing rich impastos of different colors to create a central solid and dynamic web. The striking impasto and its textural value define this work.

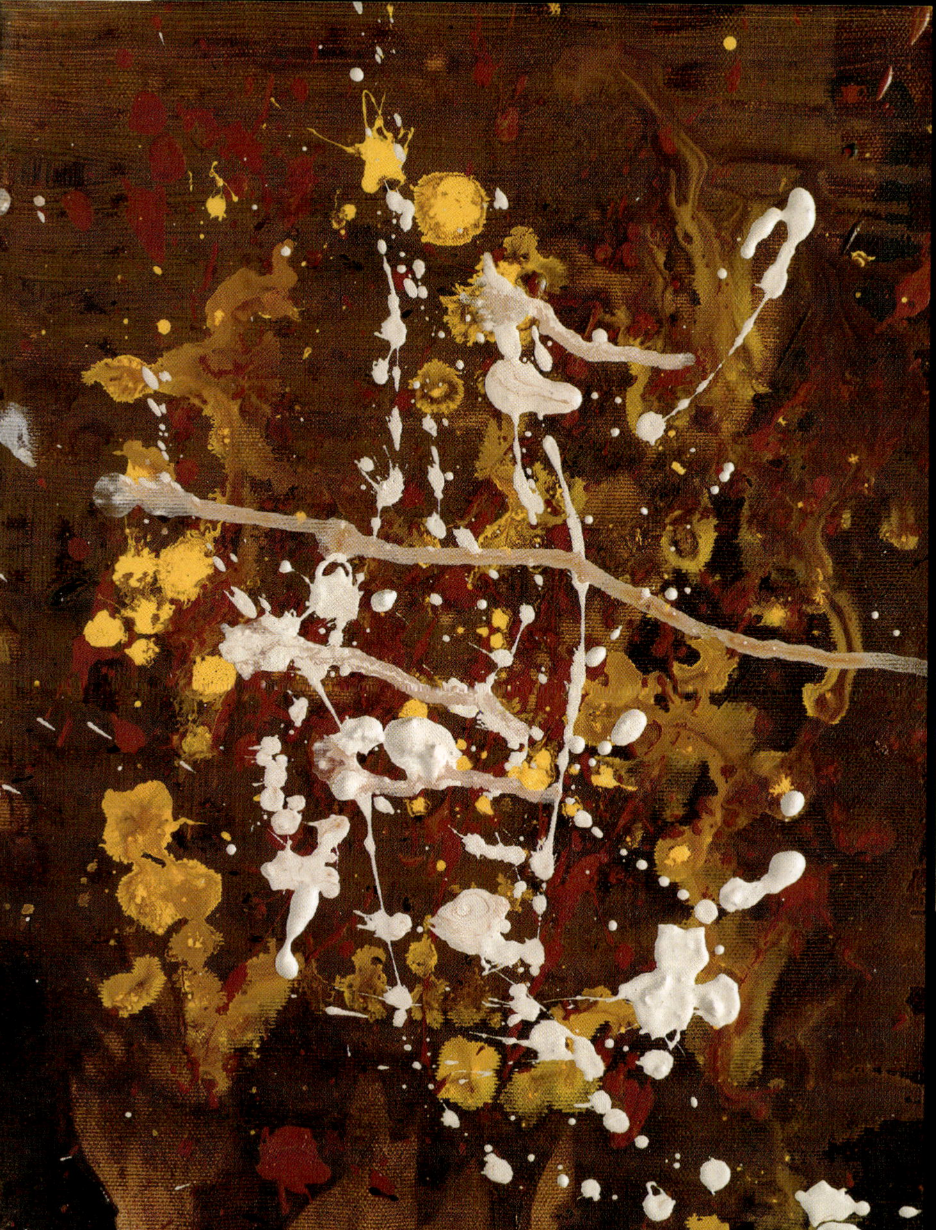

In this work we maximized the elements: the small variations of the wood's knots have been transformed into contrasting solid bodies. Over a background created with various color glazing effects, liquid red paint was deposited and then left to dry. Next, a large amount of white paint was poured onto the surface and allowed to run a little to produce an effect that looks like a skein of yarn. The contrast between the two areas (liquid/solid) gives the line an interesting variety.

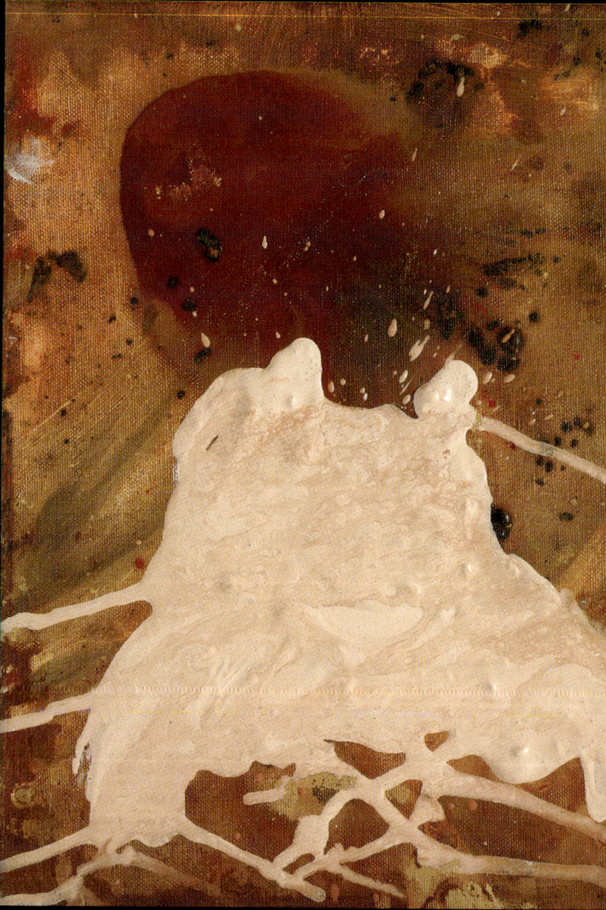

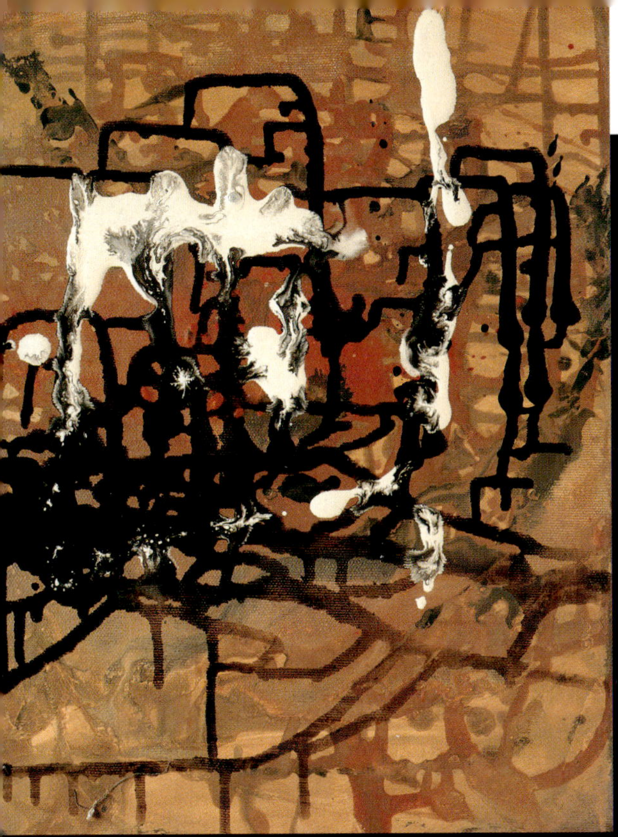

This work is defined by its layers. Underneath, the liquid paint runs and mixes; on top, a thin grid, which is formed by letting liquid paint run with very controlled and regular motions, is reminiscent of a net. The last layer, made of white paint, poured directly and vigorously onto the canvas to emphasize and contrast with the surface.

In this work we have experimented with textured effects. The paint was spread over the canvas freely and then was wiped in places with a rag to create the textural effects that look like the features of wood. The consistency of the different paints mixed together and left to dry without being disturbed produces an evanescent and soft line. This contrasts with the direct and thick applications that convey a firm and decisive attitude to the approach.

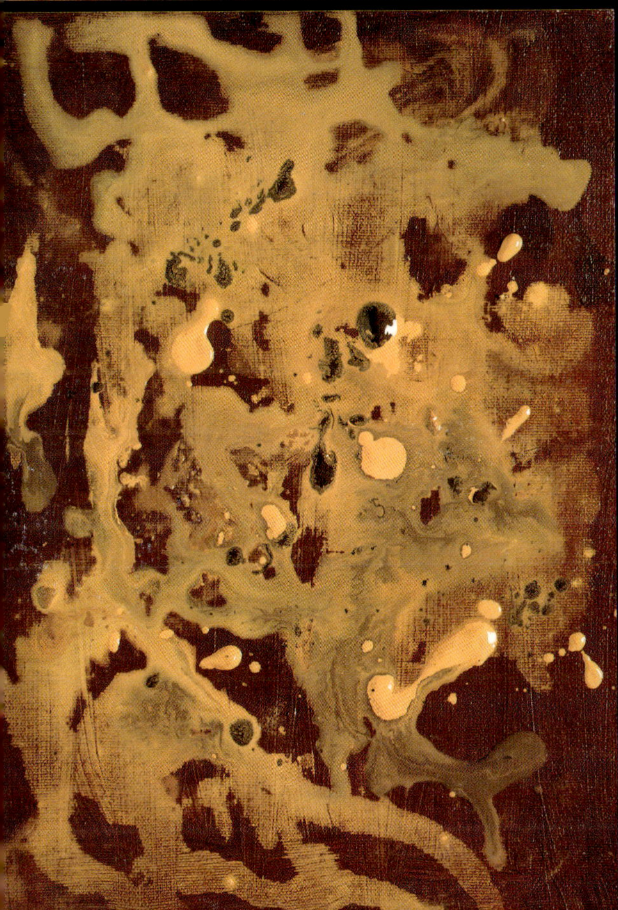

Here, we have tried to reclaim the most ethereal and liquid aspect of painting. Very liquid paint was poured over a colored background and spread whimsically over the canvas; then it was left to dry. Contrasting highlights were created with small drips of paint applied directly from the tube onto the canvas.

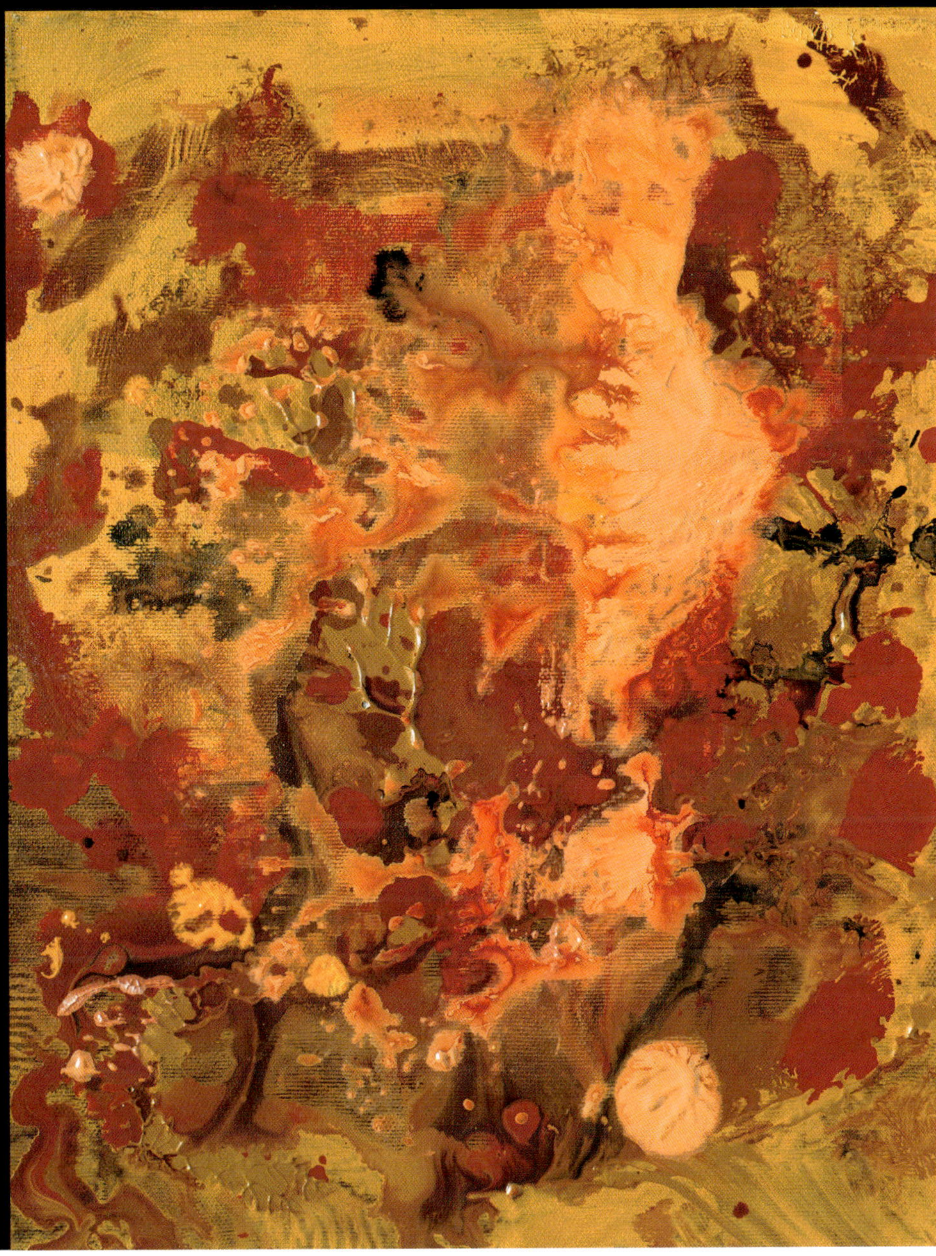

New approaches

Other models

A static model cannot be used in work where experimentation and spontaneity are valued. Gemma Guasch has decided to look for uncontrollable forces of nature, her other source of inspiration. The photograph of an erupting volcano was her reference for achieving a piece full of action, spontaneity, and energy. Over a black background she poured and spread large amounts of paint to convey the body and viscosity of lava.

Other media

To promote the effect of transparency and luminosity, the artist chose to work with inks. In the first case, she used a sponge and soft brushes, wetting the paper first to achieve soft effects when the color blends into different areas. Dripping the ink onto the paper and letting it run created a network of different intensities.

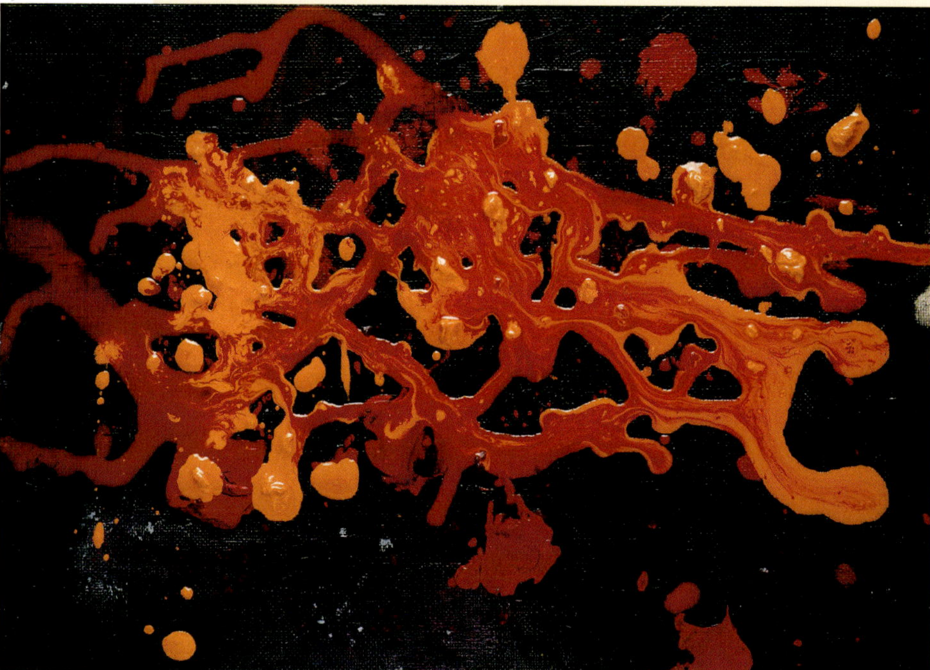

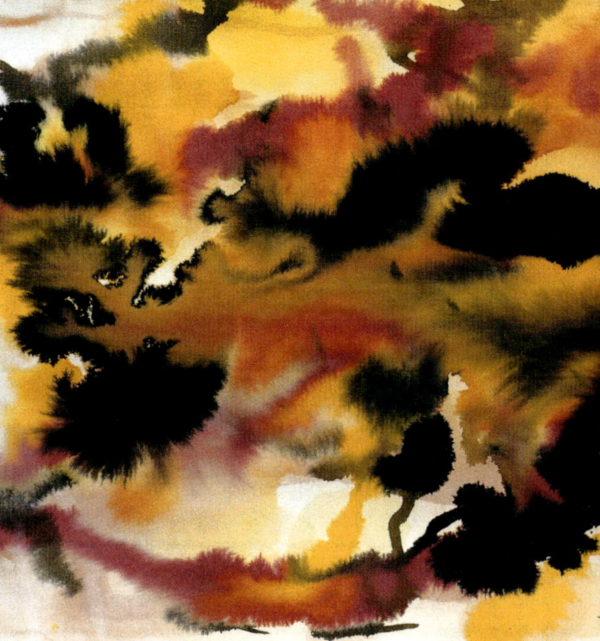

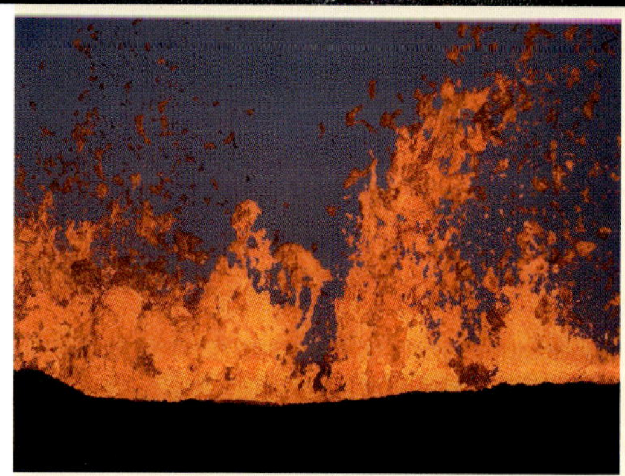

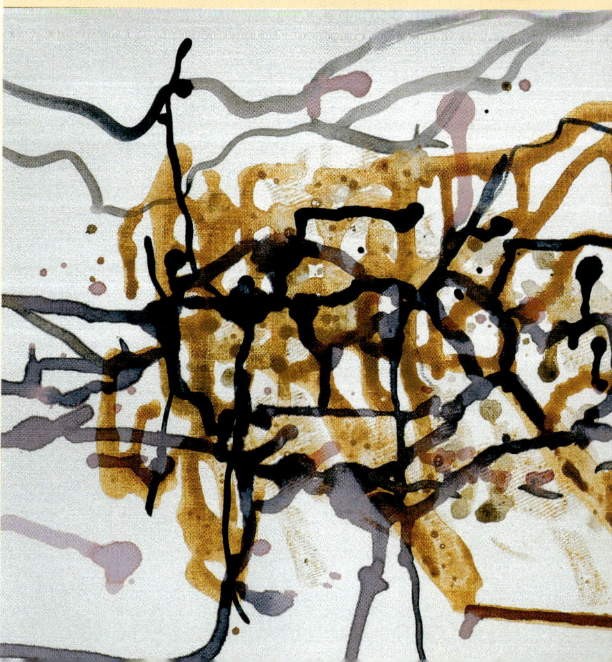

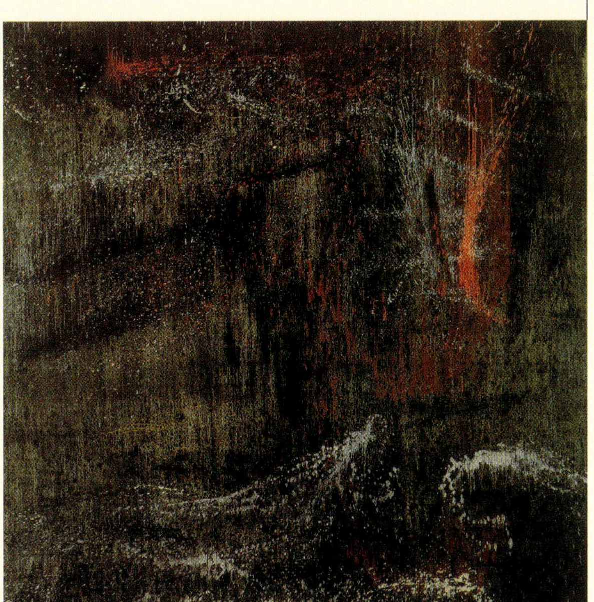

Pat Steir,
July Night, 1994–1995.
Robert Miller Gallery
(New York, United States).

Other views

With the dripping technique, Pat Steir (born in 1940) created large color curtains or cascades that range between abstract landscapes and figures. During the decade of the 1980s he became interested in Japanese calligraphy, traditional printmaking, and Chinese art, influences he reflected in his paintings by reducing the color and the different elements. Getting away from traditional methods, Bernard Frize (born in 1954) looked for new approaches and based his work on experimentation. For this he used a soft, thin brush, a type traditionally used by fishermen to decorate fishing nets and ropes, moving it gently over an infinite number of multicolor bands. Then, he applied different layers of shellac and resins until the result was cold and industrial looking.

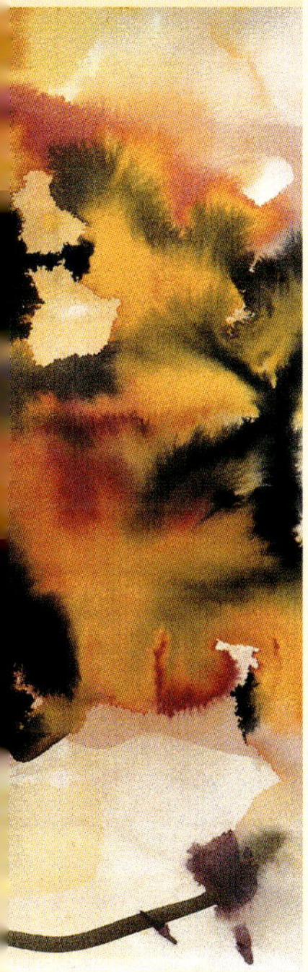

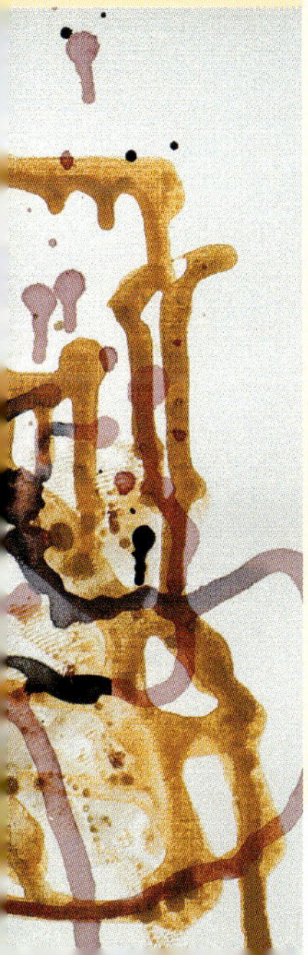

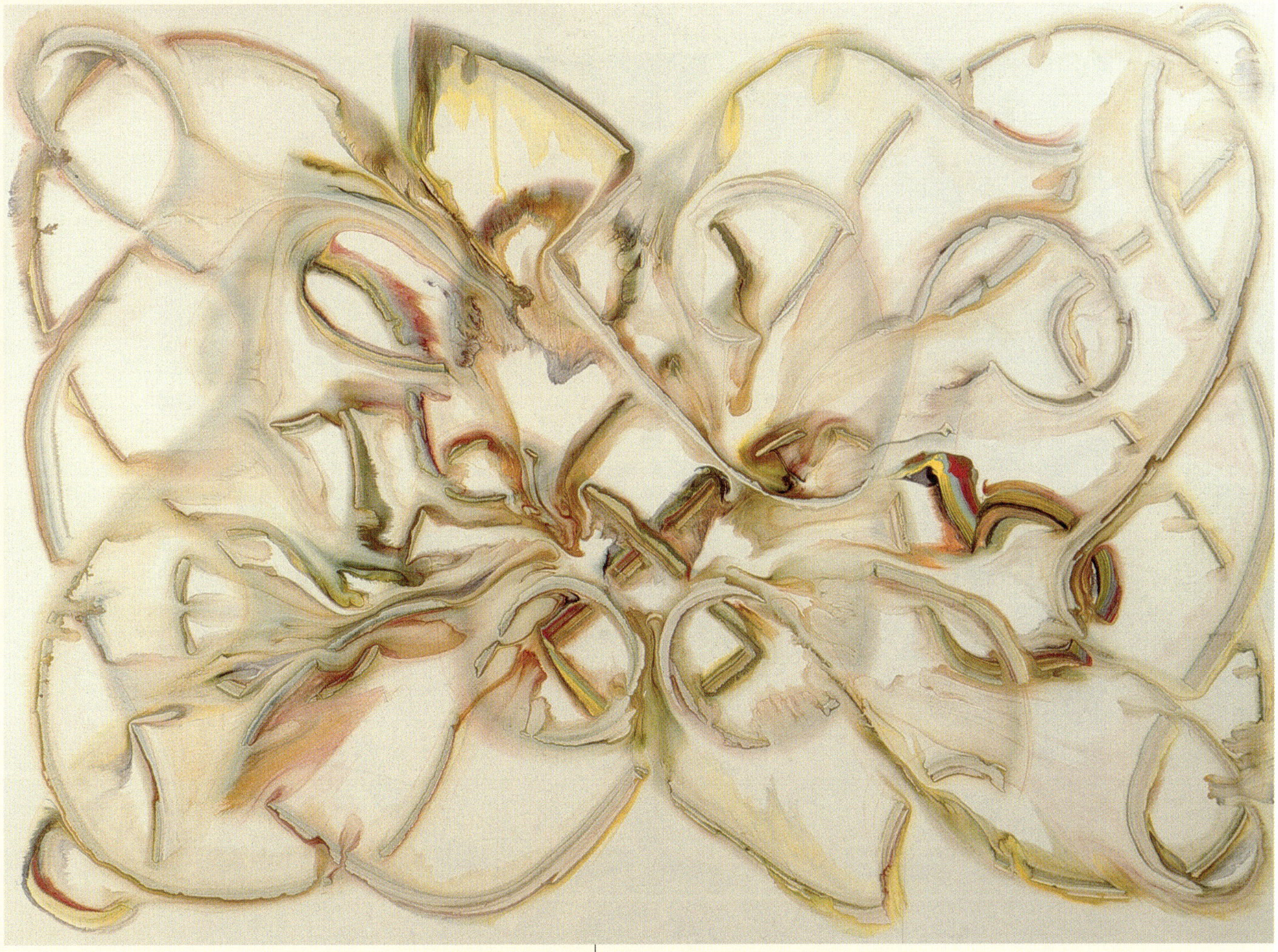

Bernard Frize,
Pacifique, 1991.
Private collection.

Real, material, and volumetric textures

In abstract painting, Informalism is a field that offers infinite creative possibilities. Working with metals, wood, sand, fabric, plastic, ropes, and other materials and making them produce a certain effect is the main working method of this approach, which made its appearance after World War II. One of its main proponents is Christo Javacheff (born in 1935), better known as Christo. Considered a conceptual artist by some and as a Pop Art follower by others, he has created his entire body of work by wrapping objects of small dimensions like this Package from 1961, or very large installations, together with Jean-Claude de Guillebon (born in 1935), his artist wife and collaborator. Christo became very famous when he began wrapping large buildings and bridges (the Pont Neuf in Paris, in 1985), surrounding islands with colored fabrics (in Biscayne Bay, Florida), or extending fabric across the landscape.

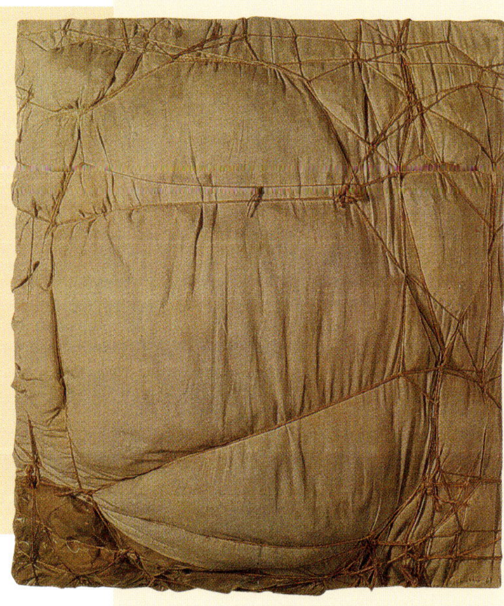

Christo,
Package, 1961.
Kaiser Wilhelm Museum
(Krefeld, Germany).

Using material in a volumetric collage

The following approach to abstract creation comes from the language of the material itself, which results in a group of pictorial works. Josep Asunción considers the idea of calling the collective a painting, even though paint hardly has a place in it, since the work stems from the pictorial alphabet and syntax of composition, color, form, textures, gestures; the fine line between painting and sculpture has not been crossed, even though the results may have some three-dimensionality. The medium is the materials themselves and the technique is assemblage (a volumetric variation on collage). The starting point or source of inspiration is the wrapping or package, considered an art in some cultures, like the Japanese.

"I wrap things simply because it is pretty. Art does not hide any messages . . . or do Cézanne's apples possibly have a message? True art lacks any meaning."
Christo

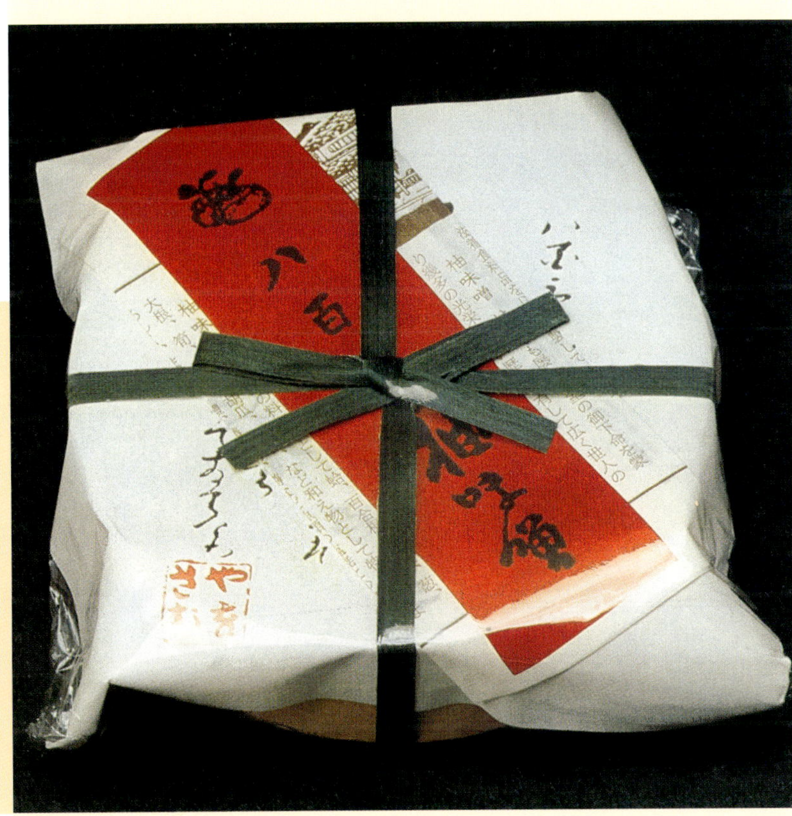

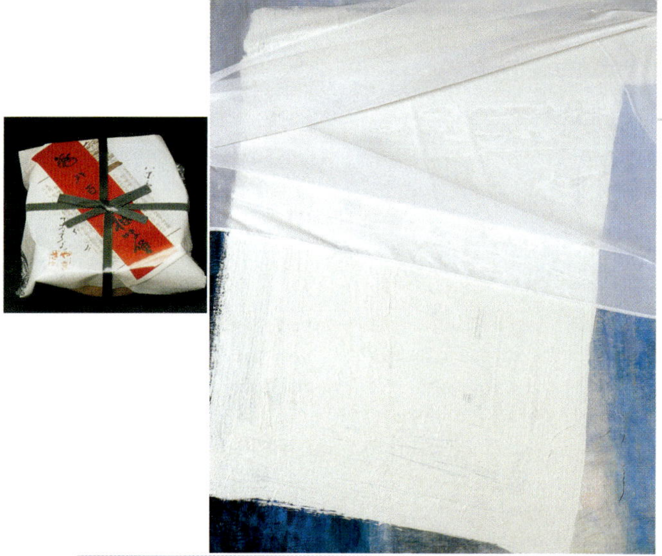

1 We begin with an old canvas that we no longer need and recycle it by covering it partially with white paint. This rectangle is the skeleton of the composition and marks the overall tone of the work. Next, we begin to cover it with a piece of translucent nylon.

3 The first package is a box wrapped with gray wool fabric and strips of red cotton and white felt. We center the red and white strips and tie them in place with a long band of dark cloth.

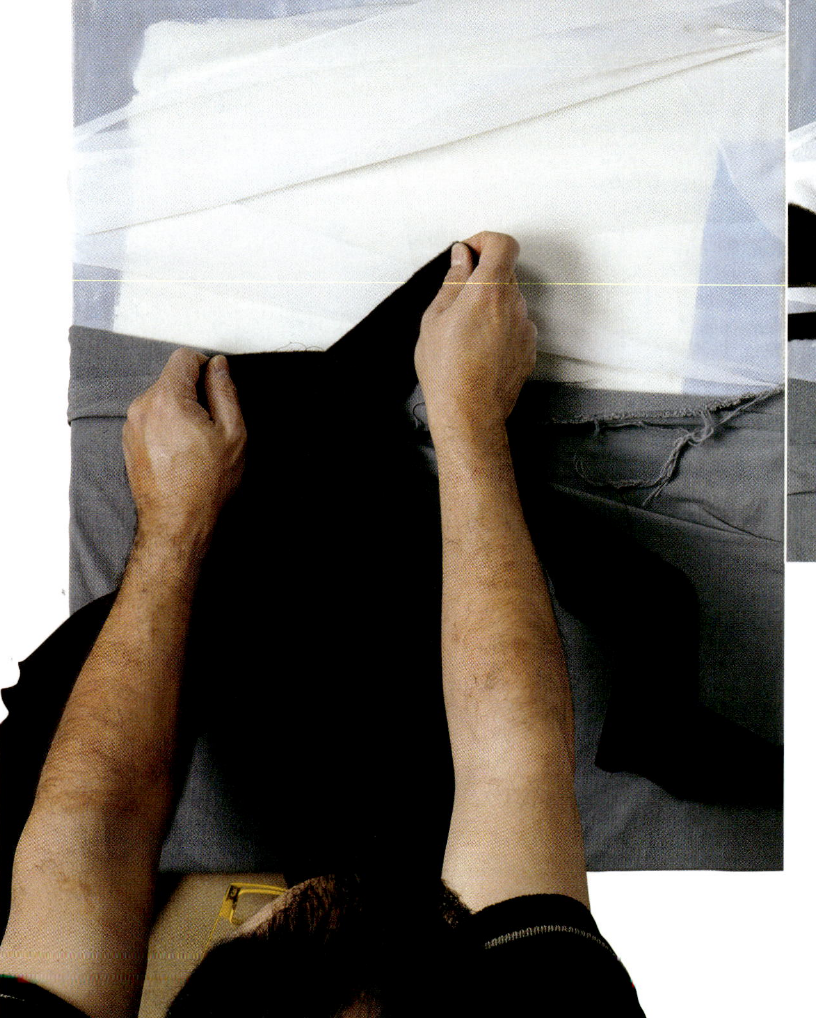

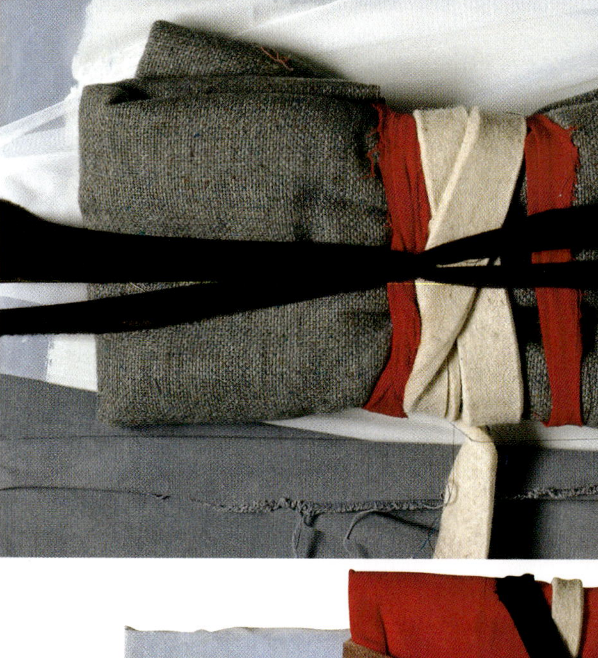

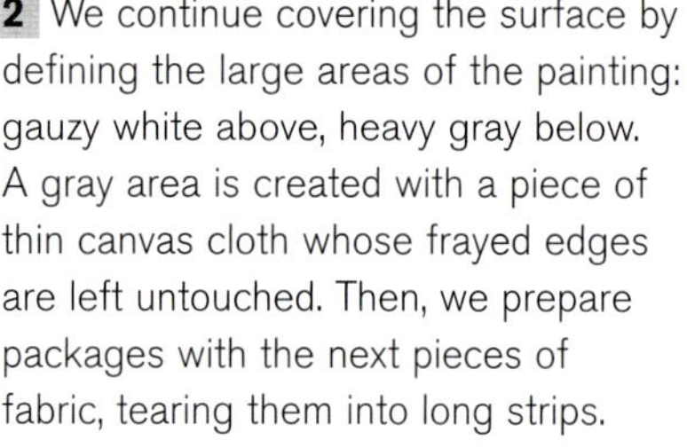

2 We continue covering the surface by defining the large areas of the painting: gauzy white above, heavy gray below. A gray area is created with a piece of thin canvas cloth whose frayed edges are left untouched. Then, we prepare packages with the next pieces of fabric, tearing them into long strips.

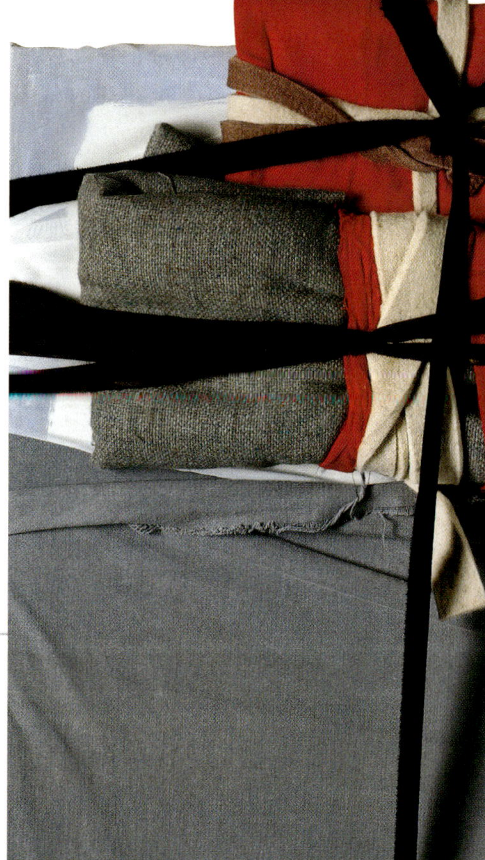

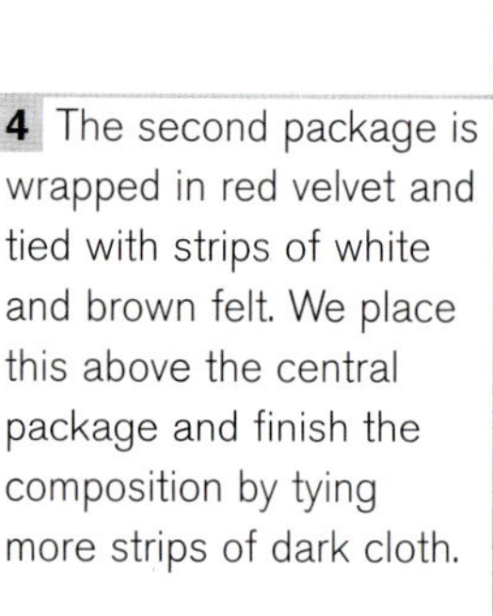

4 The second package is wrapped in red velvet and tied with strips of white and brown felt. We place this above the central package and finish the composition by tying more strips of dark cloth.

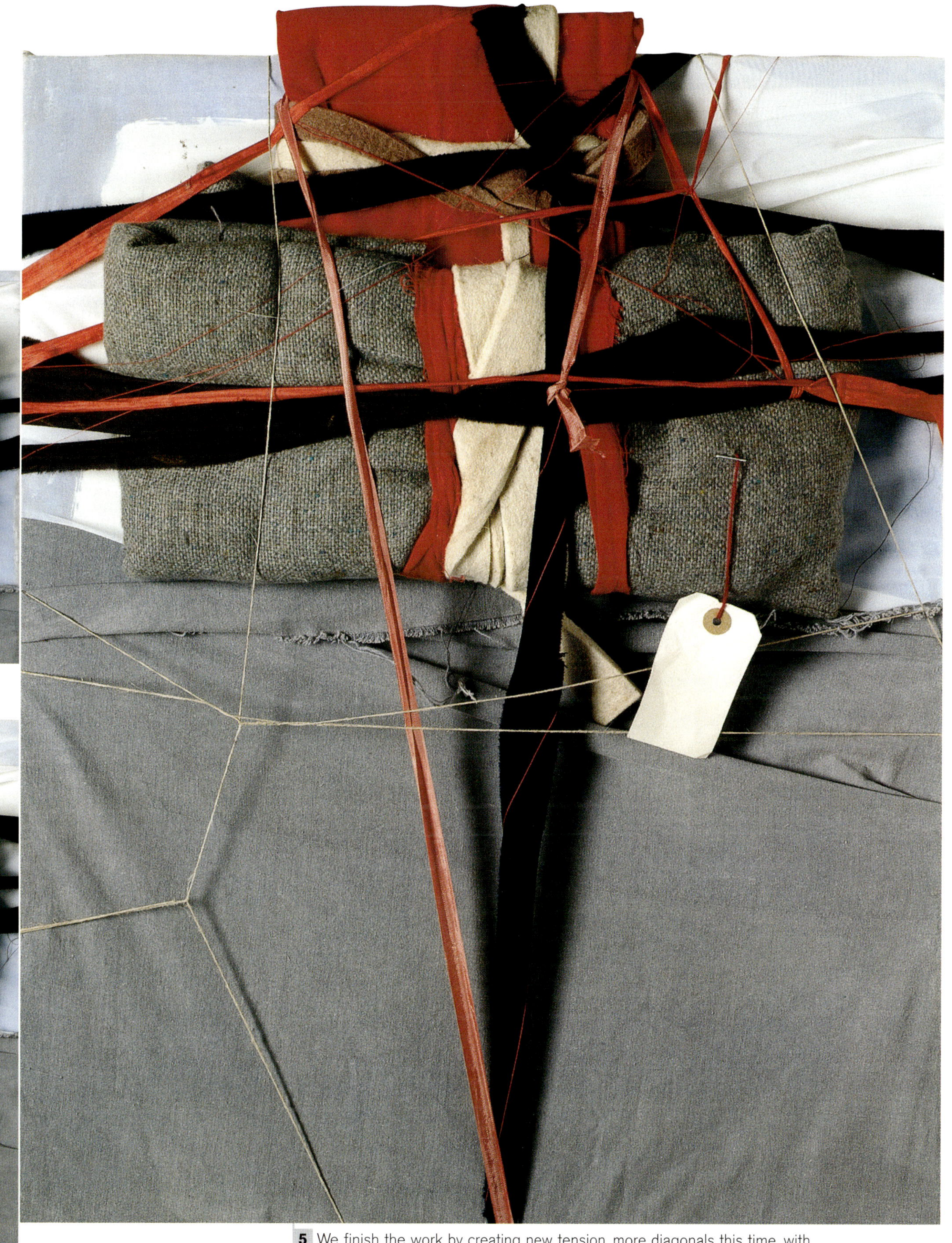

5 We finish the work by creating new tension, more diagonals this time, with red silk ribbon and linen cord. We add an old-fashioned label that came with the cloth. The result is a piece rich in textural qualities: nylon, silk, velvet, dark cloth, canvas, cord, paint . . . and great visual beauty.

Other versions

By varying the materials involved and their arrangement on the fabric, the artist has created a series of different pieces, all following the same concept. They all begin with recycled canvas covered with white paint, but their individual approaches express different emotions and messages.

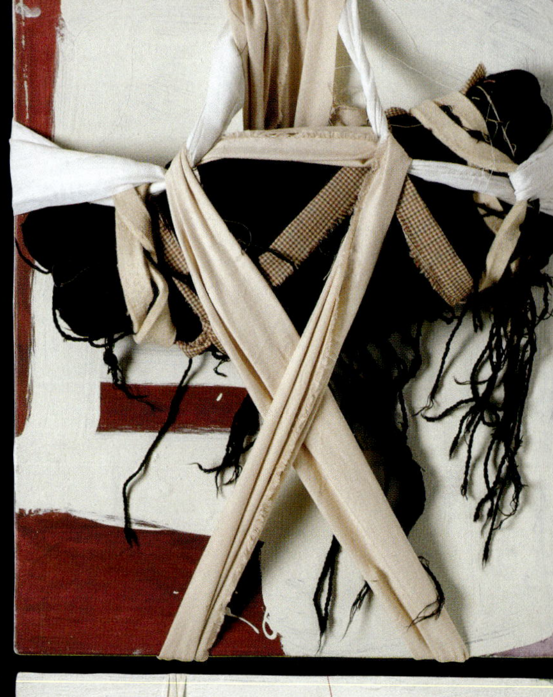

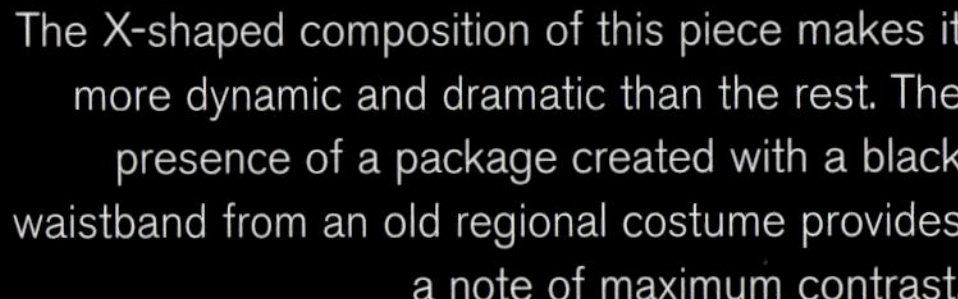

The X-shaped composition of this piece makes it more dynamic and dramatic than the rest. The presence of a package created with a black waistband from an old regional costume provides a note of maximum contrast.

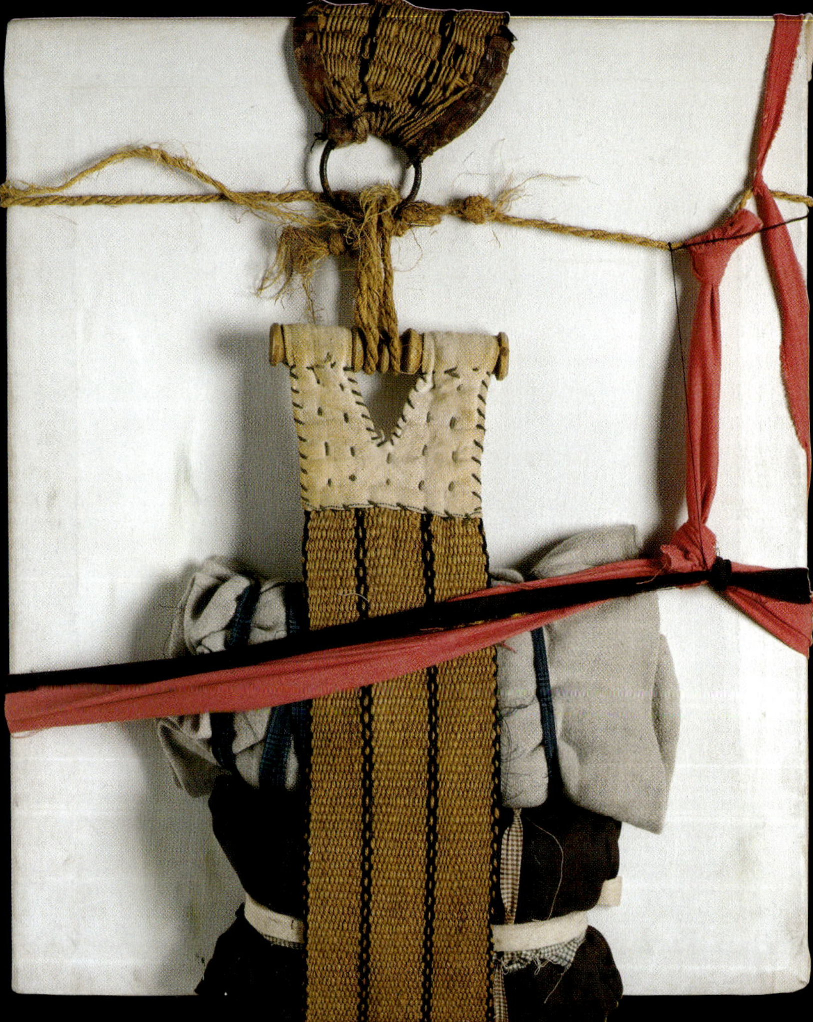

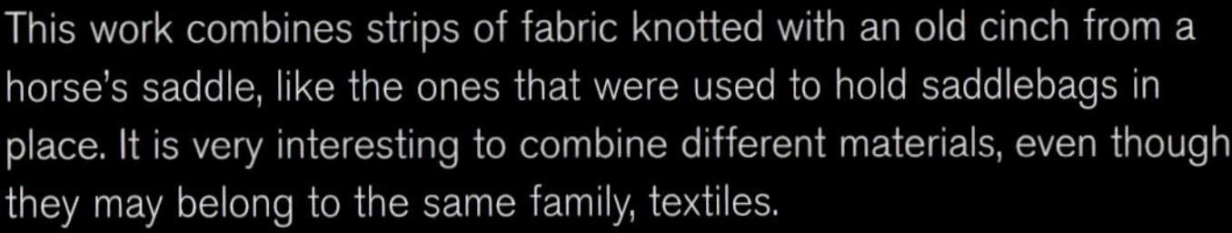

This work combines strips of fabric knotted with an old cinch from a horse's saddle, like the ones that were used to hold saddlebags in place. It is very interesting to combine different materials, even though they may belong to the same family, textiles.

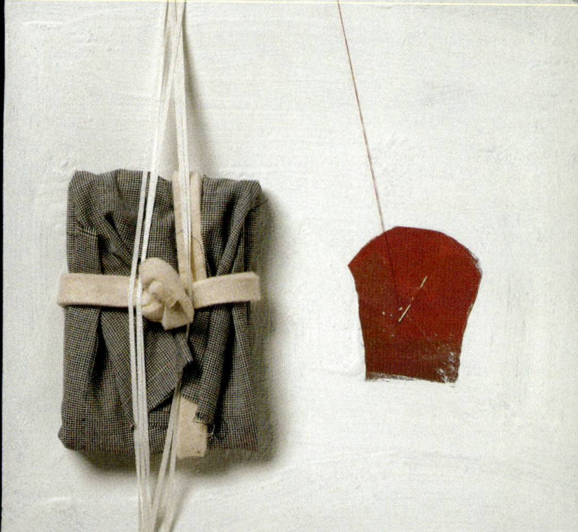

The dimensions of the package with respect to the rest of the painting are important. In this case, the blank space (with the exception of the red uncovered window in the background) that surrounds the package stands out much more for its volume. The package is surrounded by white felt and elastic bands. In addition, a needle threaded with red thread pinned down on the center of the piece speaks eloquently of the world of textiles.

This work conveys a feeling of imprisonment due to the abundance of wrapped knots and cords that prevent the package from slipping off the canvas. Despite the excess binding, the work does not appear excessively dramatic, since the package is very appealing visually.

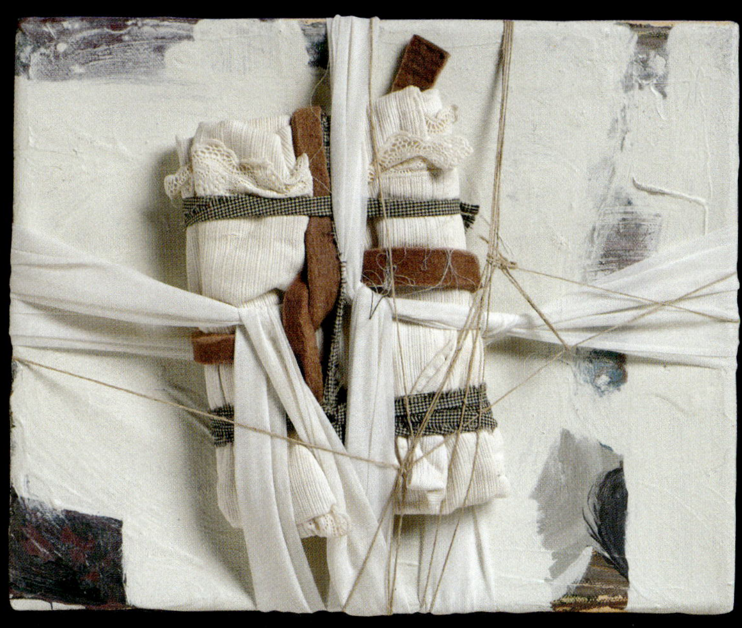

A unique red velvet and white felt package is trapped here by a web of strips of silk and a few elastic bands. The overall perception of the piece is that of a net or a web, a fabric that covers another, heavier, fabric, the clothing.

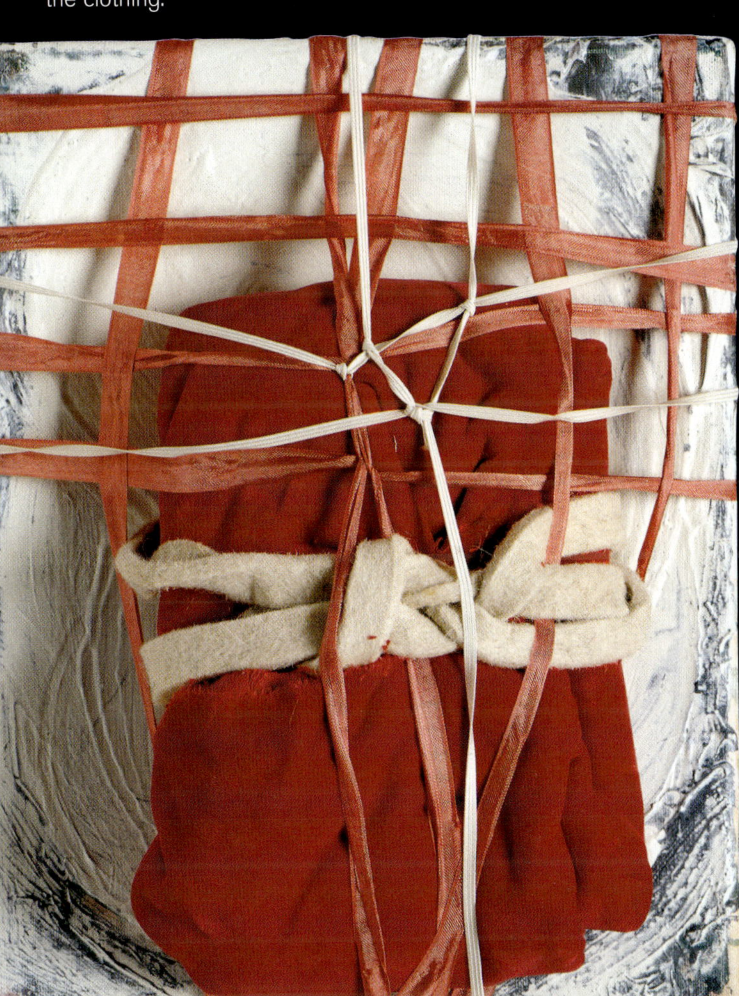

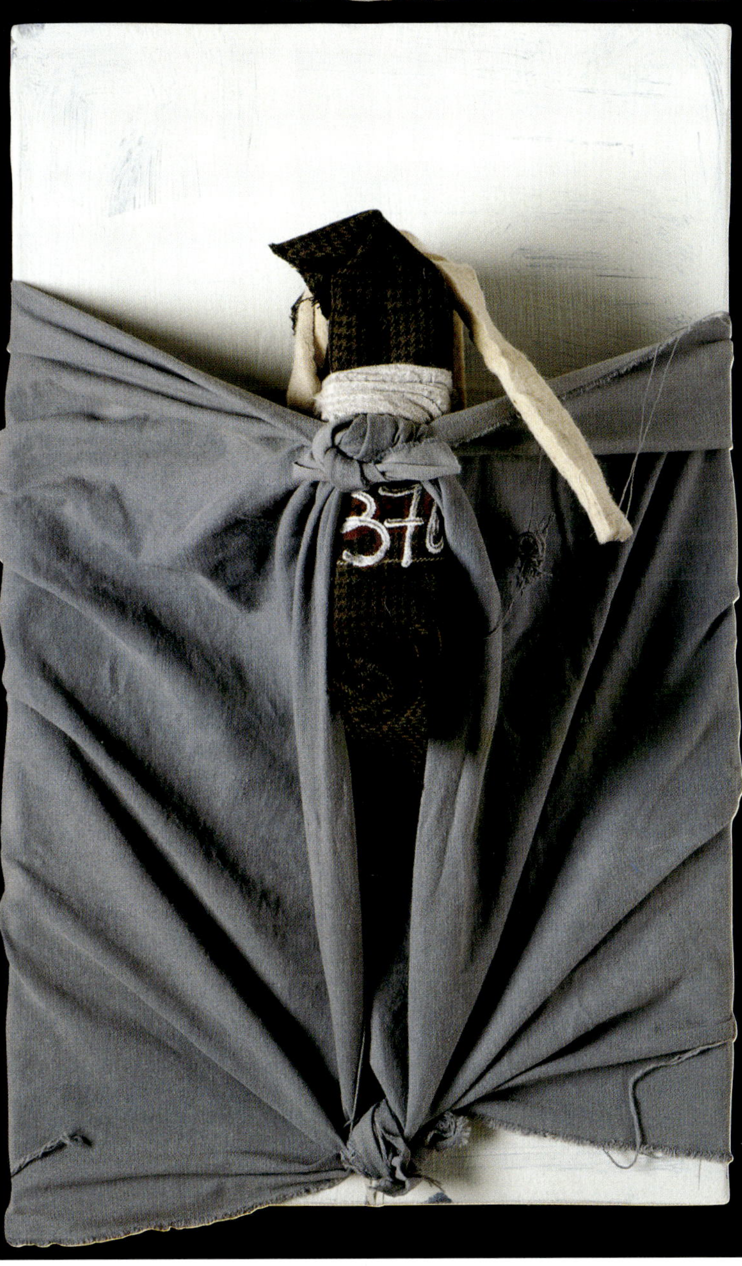

The visual power of this painting resides in the knotting of the fabrics that wrap around the canvas and, at the same time, holds the package tightly in place and perpendicular to the painting's plane. This work is the most volumetric of all; the three-dimensional effect is very pronounced and the play of wrinkles and folds makes it look more like a sculptural piece.

Other models

The conceptual basis of this project is the idea of a wrapper, of a covered object from which we perceive the volume inside and that allows us to create tensions derived from the act of wrapping. Josep Asunción, working together with Gemma Guasch, begins with the concept of emptiness, a space that has nothing inside, and that is discovered upon opening a door. A space that is free of furniture, poor, rustic, old . . . like the piece of cut and folded fabric chosen for this interpretation of human poverty created for the series *The Fecundity of the Absent.*

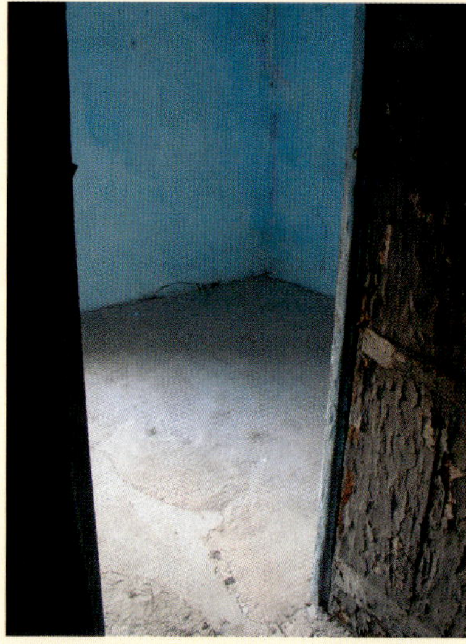

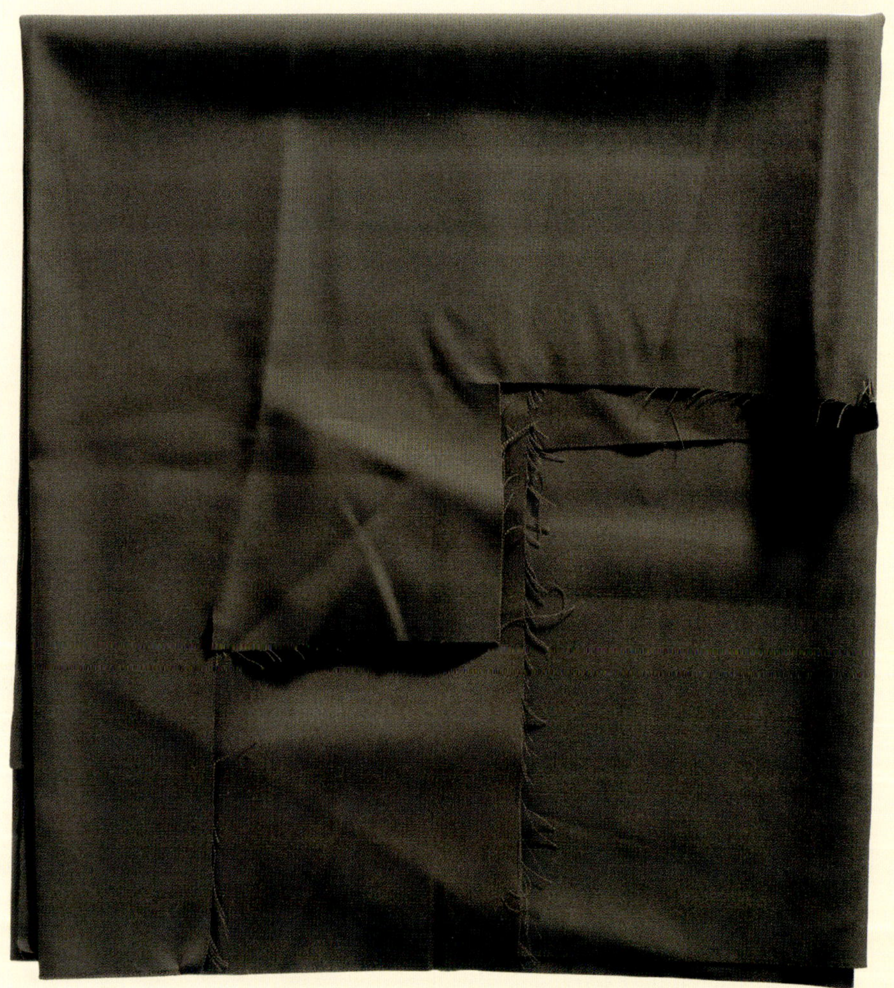

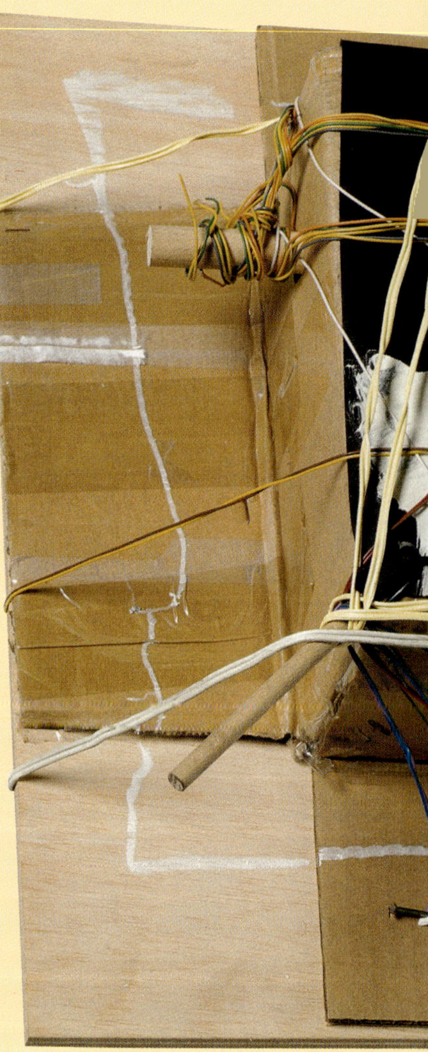

Other media

The poetry of fabric results from the human dimension of this material. Clothing is an element intimately tied to humans. Here, the artist has created an abstract interpretation of the theme of the package using disposable materials: pieces of electrical cord, adhesive tape, cardboard . . . the result is a piece that begins with the concept of a container, represented by the box—much more rigid and volumetric than fabric, which in principle is flat and ductile.

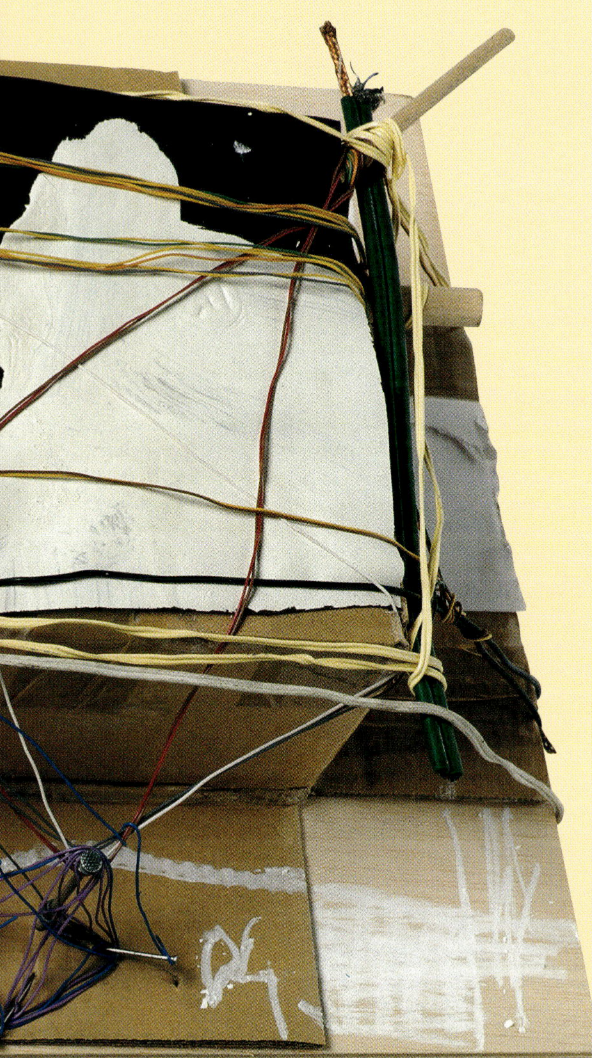

Other views

Alberto Burri (1915–1995), one of the most important precursors of European Informal art, has a different approach to working abstractly with fabrics. His beginnings conditioned his language and the way he worked. He started painting in 1944, during his days as a prisoner of war in Texas. His first burlap pieces, as well as others made with rusted iron and burned wood, are reminiscent of the bloody bandages of members of the military and other battlefield materials. His work became a perfect mixture of drama and poetry, because he was able to extract a true ode to beauty from the poor and faded condition of the materials he used.

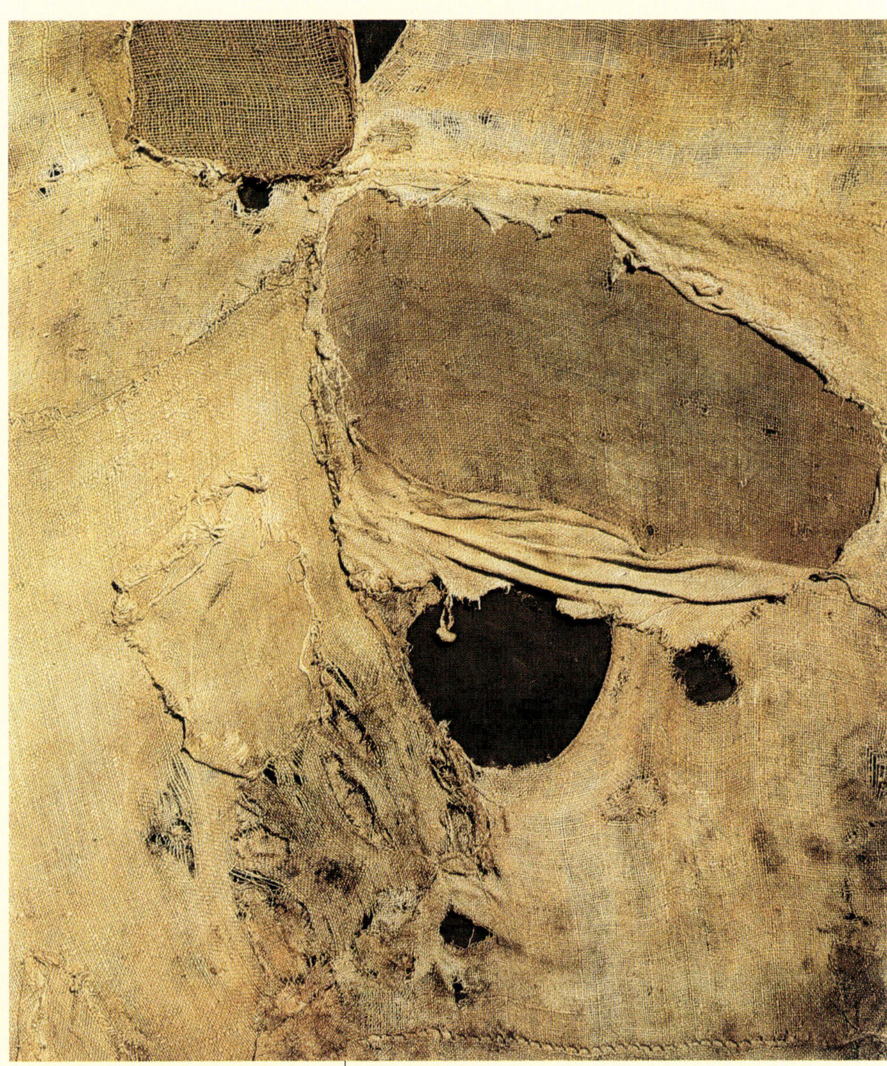

Alberto Burri,
Sacco, 1956.
Private collection.

Minimalist, essential, and reflective gestures

One of the twentieth century's painters who made the most use of gestural lines was Joan Miró (1893–1983). Although mostly abstract, Miró's work maintains a claim on reality ("Each line on the canvas corresponds to a concrete representation in my mind"), a reality transformed by his poetic vision. In his work there are different styles opposing each other; on the one hand, he made studies based on the transformation of real elements, characterized by bright colors, planes, forms in profile, experiments with materials and known archetypical images; and on the other hand, he created open, ethereal, and abstract paintings, where a soft line or a few signs blend in the empty space. Such is the case with *Pintura sobre fondo blanco para la espera de un solitario,* a triptych representing the prison cell of a person condemned to die, a person who has lost contact with the reality outside and knows only the inner reality of the mind, of the spirit, and imagination. These two styles correspond to two aspects of Miró's personality: the extroverted and active and the introverted and meditative.

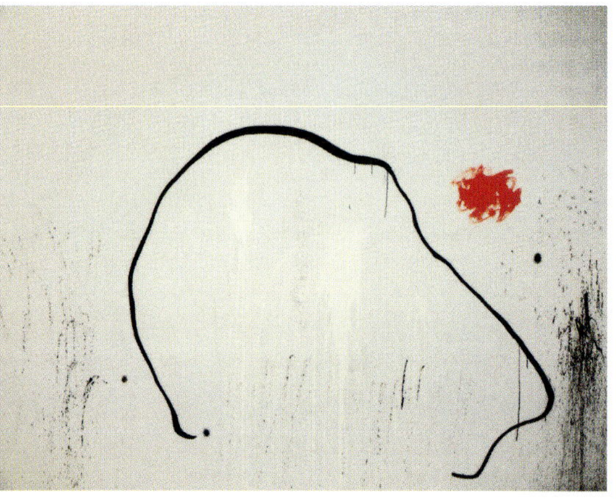

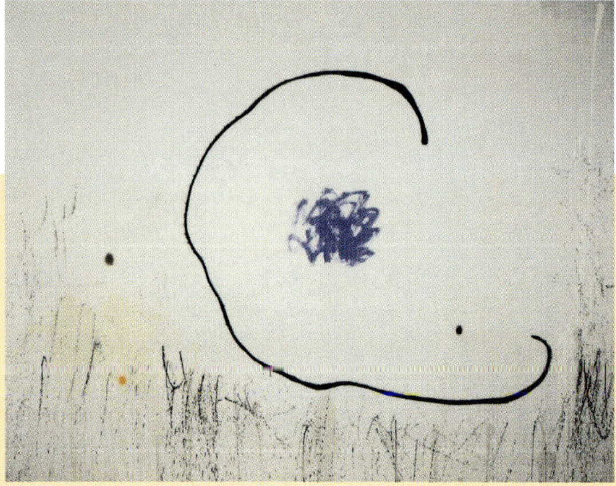

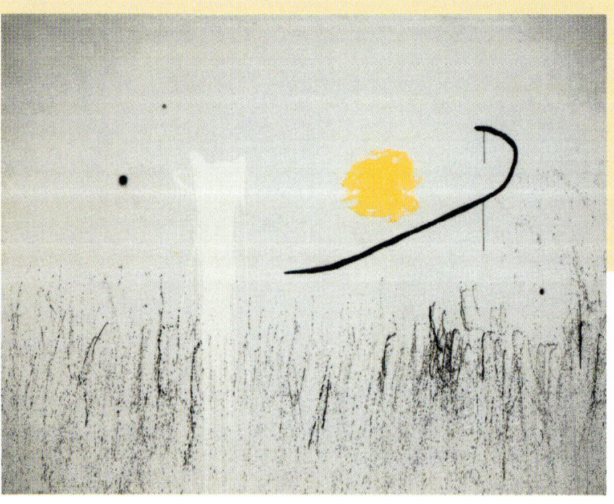

Joan Miró,
Pintura sobre fondo blanco para la espera de un solitario, 1974.
Fundación Joan Miró
(Barcelona, Spain).

A Zen painting experience: Abstraction based on a drop of water

Everybody knows the importance of calligraphy in Eastern writing, as well as *sumi-e,* which searches for the synthesis of forms through few but well-modeled lines. The last creative approach of this book focuses on another area of Eastern art: Zen painting. It is characterized for being direct (it does not allow corrections), synthesized (the fewer the interventions the better), natural (it does not incorporate design; each line is new), spatial (it values empty spaces especially), and vital (the artist concentrates the energy in his hand, letting it flow all the way to the tip of the brush). Beginning with the photograph of a drop of water in motion, Gemma Guasch experiments using ink on paper with four basic techniques of Zen painting: frontal attack, dragging, syncopated cadence, and colors without borders.

"These three paintings are for me the decoration of the life of a lonely man: they could adorn the cell of a prisoner condemned to die. This simple line is for me the indication that I have conquered freedom. And for me, conquering freedom is conquering simplicity. . . . I sketched this line with charcoal for a long time, I thought about it, with innumerable revisions. I started it over for years. . . . One day, before a last try, uneasiness abandoned me, it gave way to happiness. I took a brush and, with a single stroke, I made a line. But I did not accept it as final until after an entire month of new silence."

Joan Miró,
Cited in an article by Pierre Bourgier in
Les nouvelles littéraires, 1968.

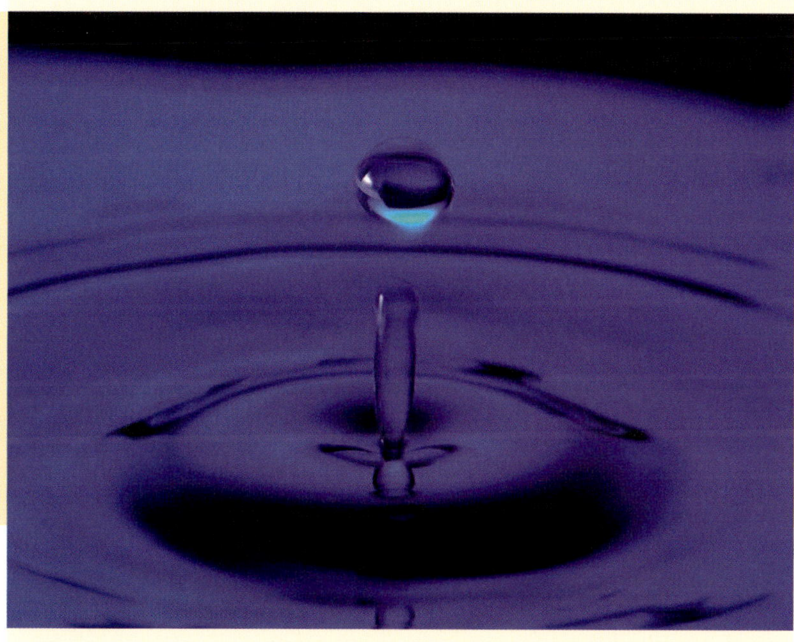

This time we analyze the development of four gestural pieces of work with Zen influence and only two steps, since they require minimal intervention. We accompany the captions with comments related to Zen painting extracted from conversations of masters of this spiritual art.

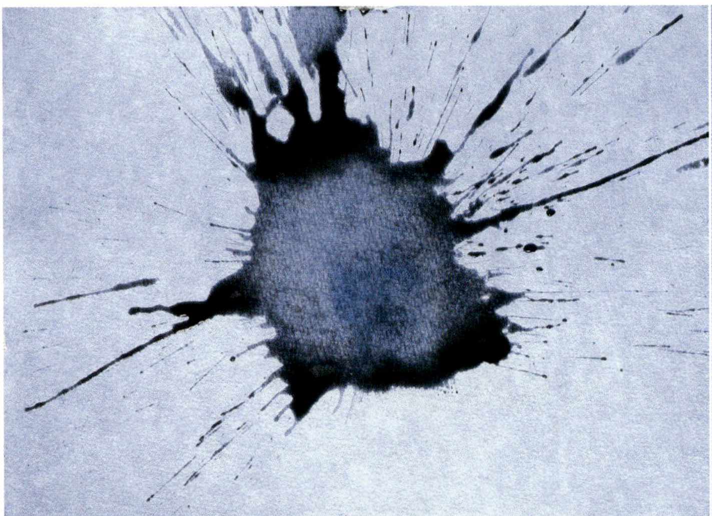

1 "To empty oneself, to silence reason and the mind pushing them to the confines of the absurd, to arrive at a direct experience of reality." A single frontal attack (*zheng feng*) is sufficient to create a drop of water that holds a world of sensations.

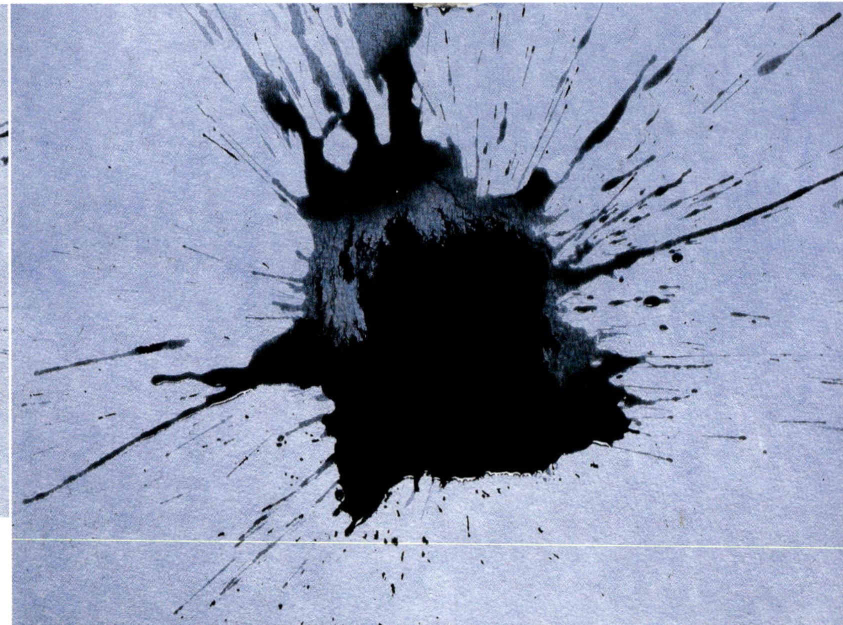

2 We continue with two movements: filling/emptying, charging the brush with ink and absorbing excess water. We repeat the movement to intensify the impulse, like the beating of a heart.

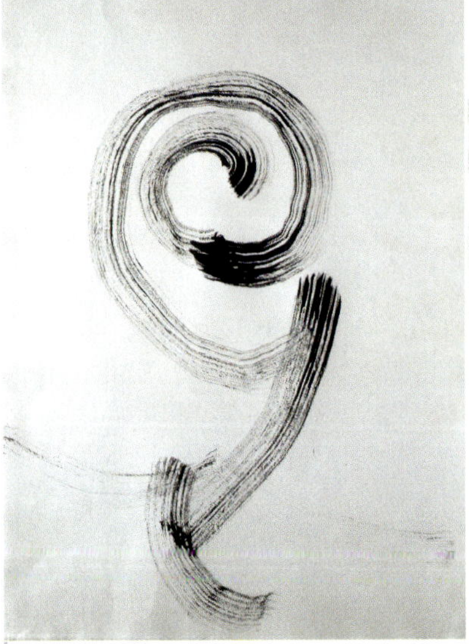

1 "Pause and meditative movement takes us to *tuo* (dragging line)." We wet the tip of a wide dry brush with ink and, slowly, with little pressure, we draw a spiral dragged line (*tuo*).

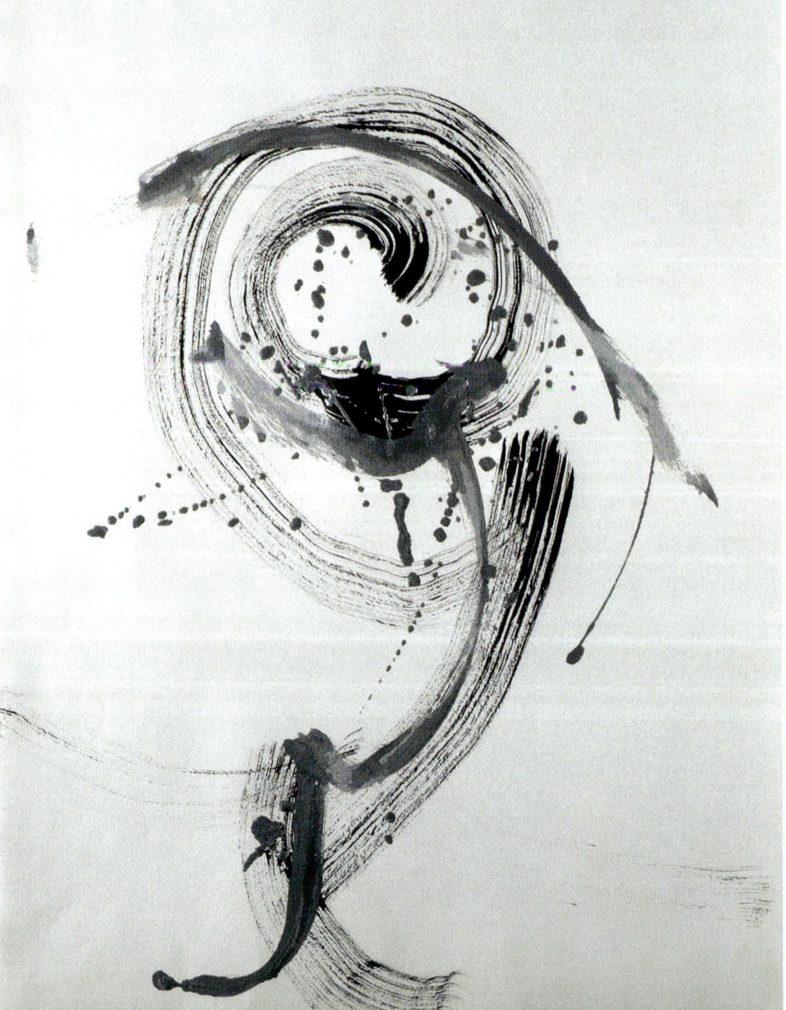

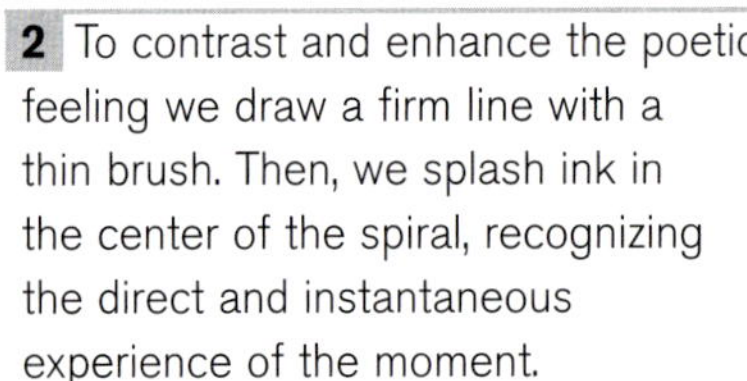

2 To contrast and enhance the poetic feeling we draw a firm line with a thin brush. Then, we splash ink in the center of the spiral, recognizing the direct and instantaneous experience of the moment.

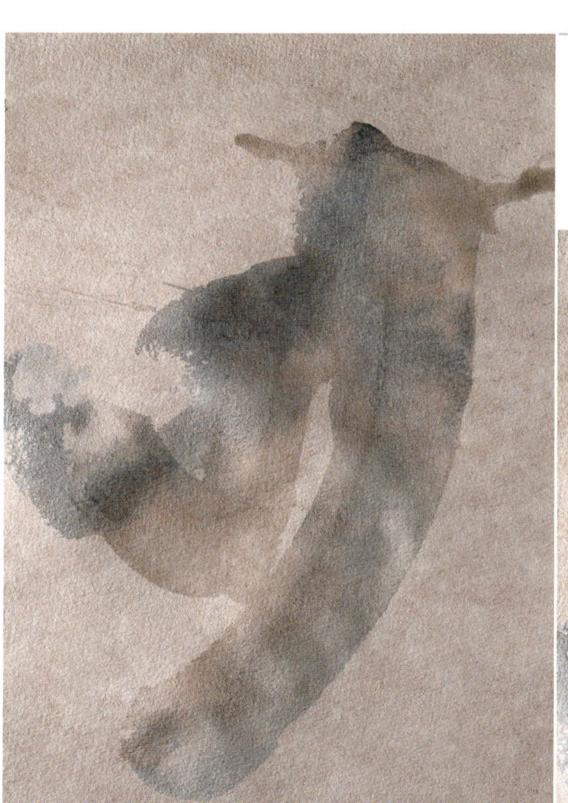

1 "The brush is an extension of the arm." With a thick brush, dampened only with dirty water, we draw a firm line, allowing the paper to absorb it. With this we create an area of color without an outline (*pomo*).

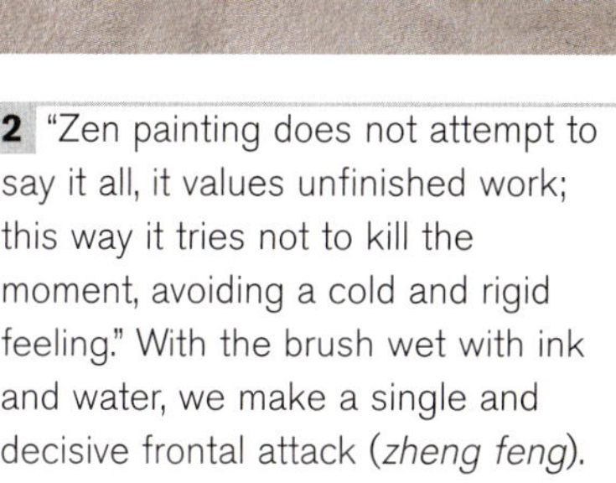

2 "Zen painting does not attempt to say it all, it values unfinished work; this way it tries not to kill the moment, avoiding a cold and rigid feeling." With the brush wet with ink and water, we make a single and decisive frontal attack (*zheng feng*).

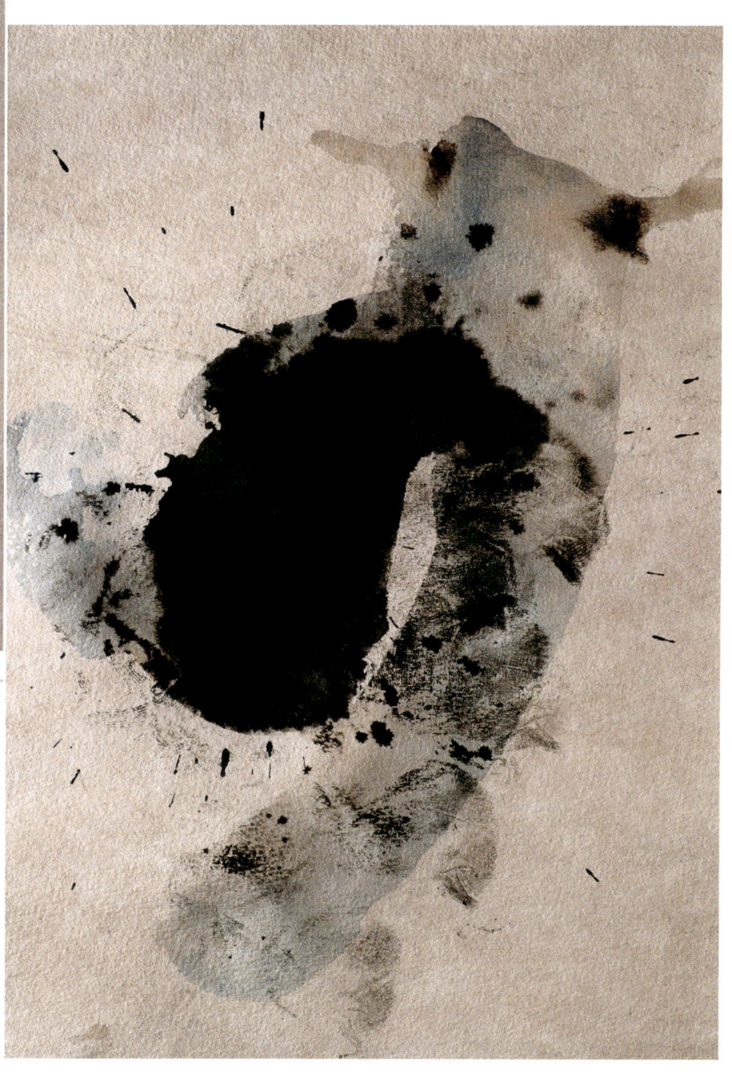

1 "Zen painting is similar to a cosmic dance where the figures emerge on the paper." Visualizing the movement of the drop of water as if it were a dance, we charge the brush with ink and let the arm dance, rubbing the paper until a fluid line is achieved by using the dripping method.

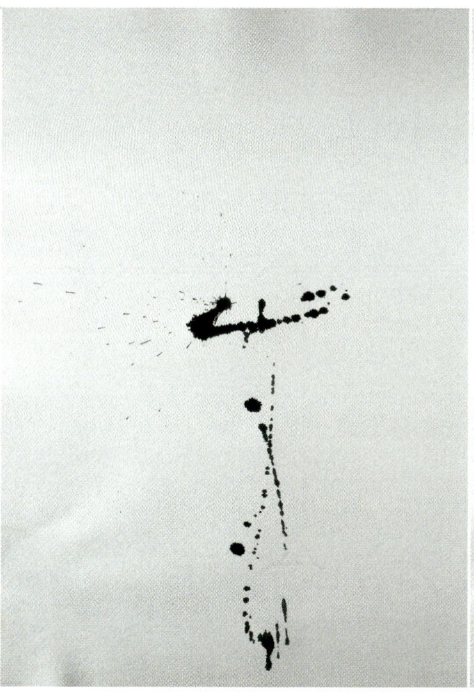

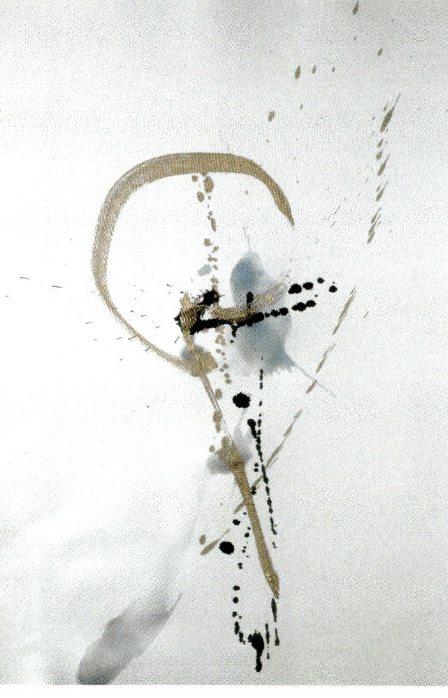

2 "We must let the line speak to create based on what has been created, valuing the empty space and the moment lived." The previous step "asks us" to establish a delicate gestural dialog with new lines that contrast with each other. With a thin round brush we make a direct line with precision. We finish the piece with a new frontal attack (*zheng feng*), which we execute with a thick round brush dampened in dirty water.

Other views

"In sumi painting, there is something that is painted with a brush, but nature cannot be painted when one begins to understand nature; it lives on the paper." For this gallery, Gemma Guasch let herself be guided by contemplation and tried to live as the drop of water, giving it a life of its own on the paper.

A blue splash of color without edges (*pomo*) spreads freely over the paper, describing a circle. Its contemplation evokes the freedom and freshness of water. Then, it receives power and concentration through a dragged line (*tuo*), which does not drown it, but invigorates it.

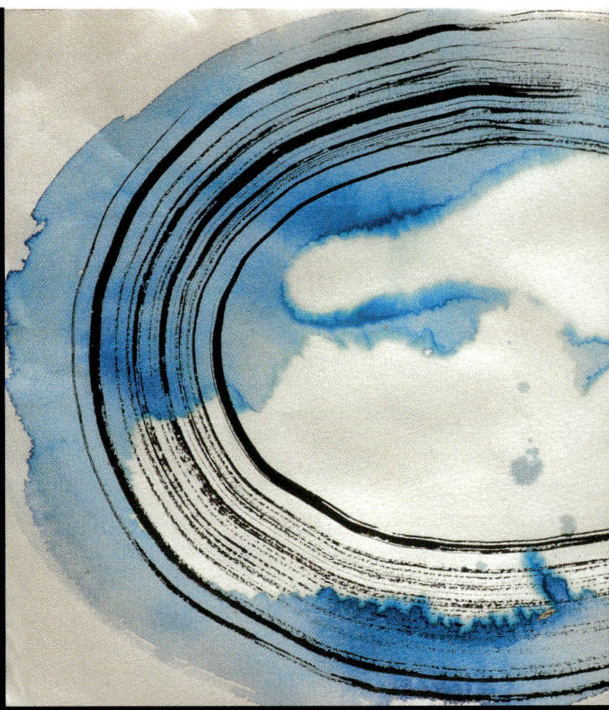

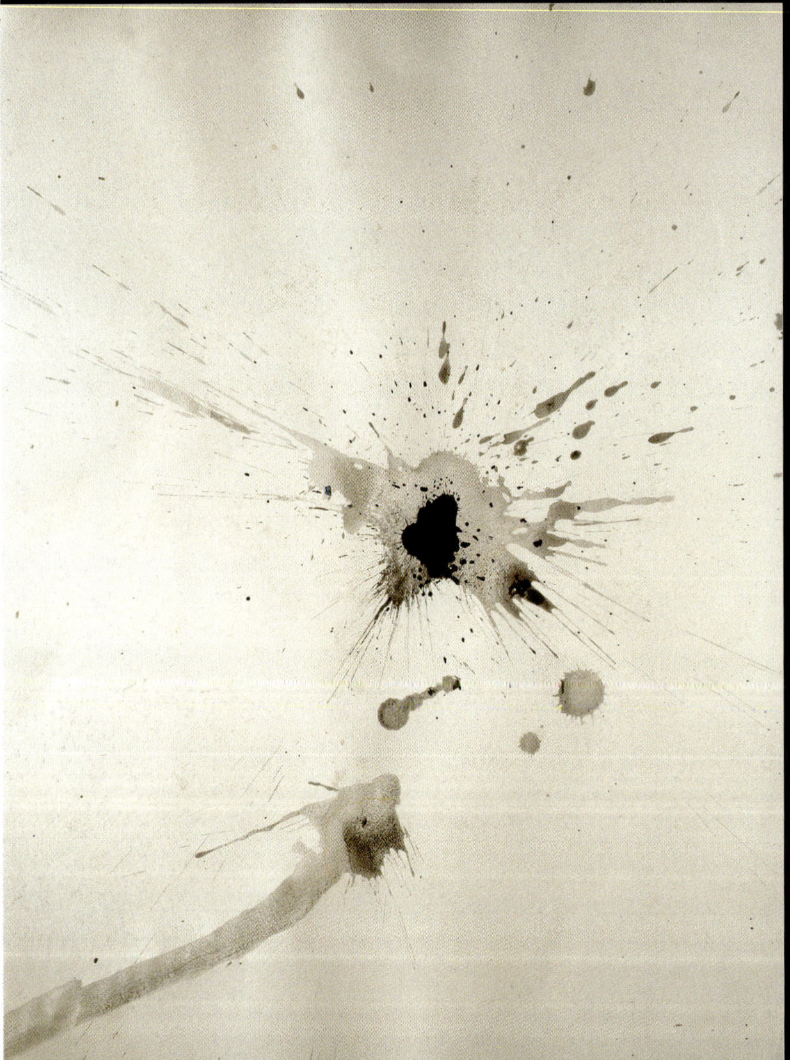

With a frontal attack (*zheng feng*), a quick line was drawn, without corrections. The appreciation for empty space, the spontaneity of the line, and the unfinished look help us see the drop of water in its mutable nature.

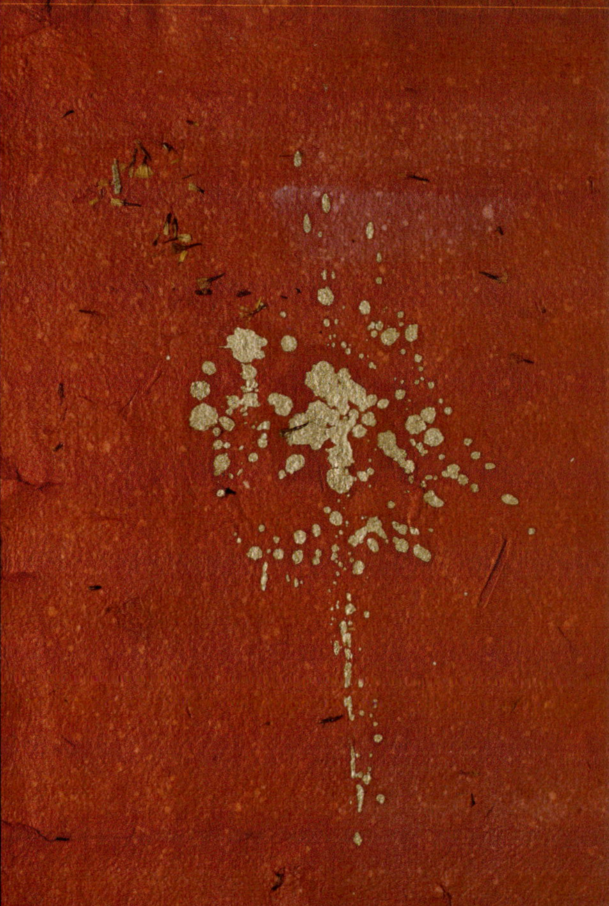

We let gold paint drip on a piece of handmade paper. With a slow and concentrated line we created an intimate, small, and beautiful mark on the support that invites us to contemplate a drop of water and its imprint on the delicate paper.

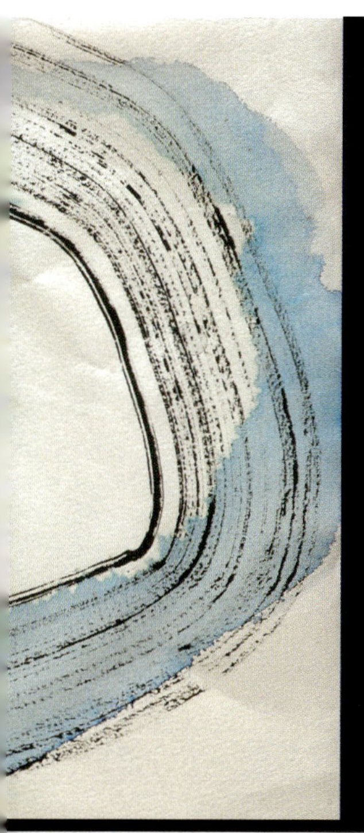

Dragged lines and direct lines form a fuller and more complex end. The movement is always accompanied by other movements, which generate new forms that go beyond what we perceive. Concentric, compressed, and dense lines show the presence of water as a strong and powerful element.

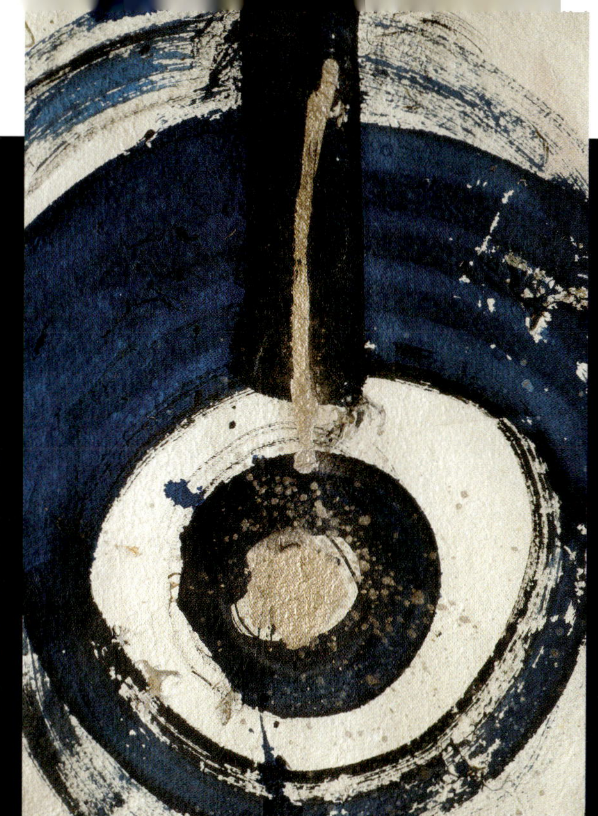

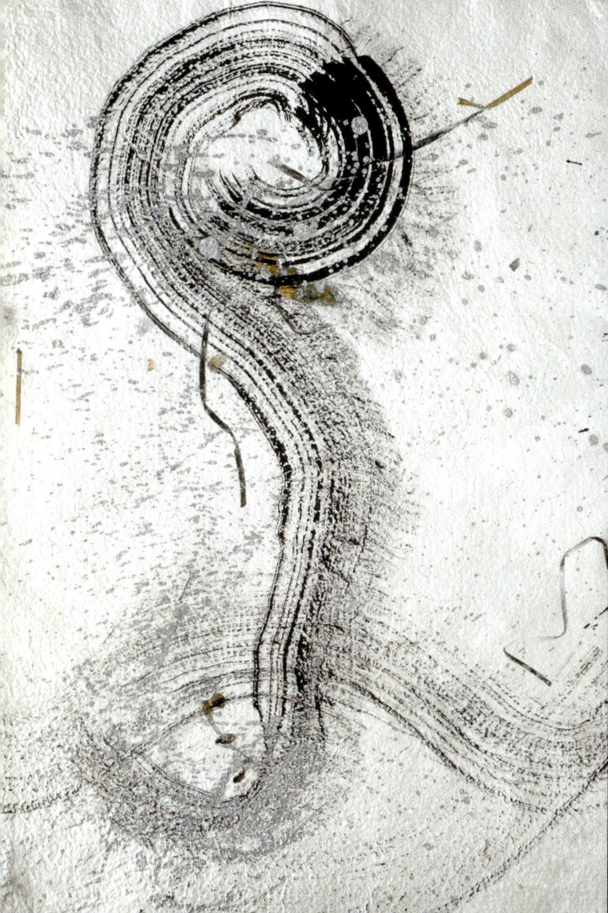

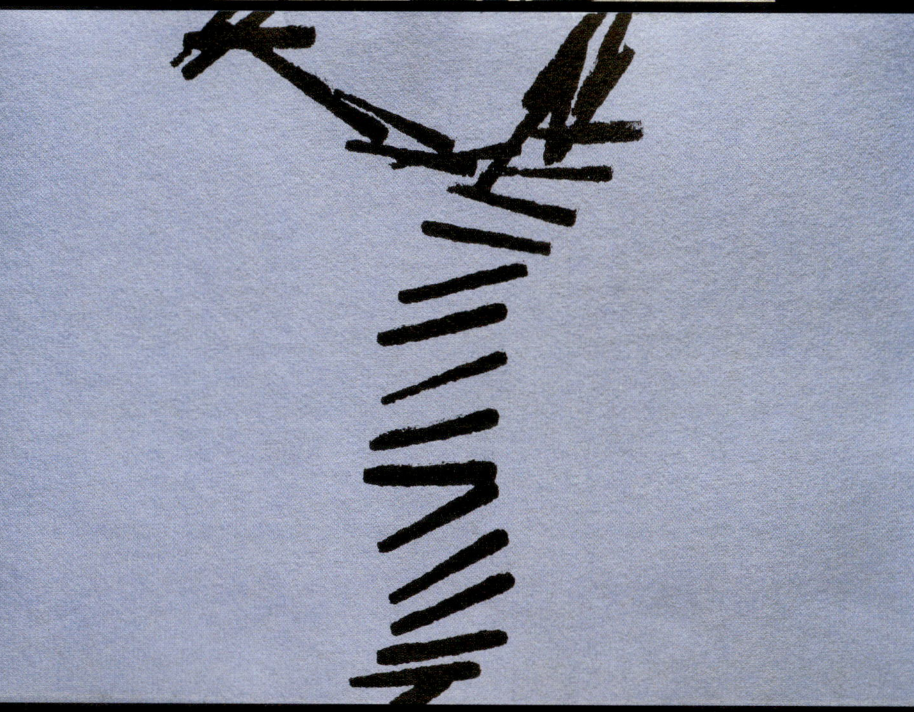

The most abstract view is provided by a line of syncopated cadence (*duncuo*). The vertical movement has become static and heavy; it looks as if it has stopped time and the drop of water has frozen.

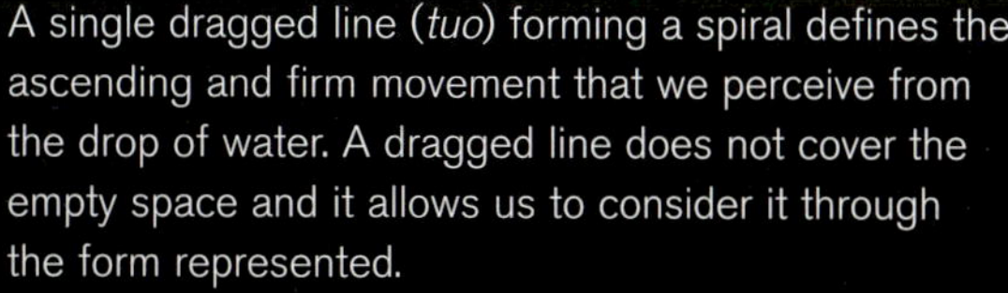

A single dragged line (*tuo*) forming a spiral defines the ascending and firm movement that we perceive from the drop of water. A dragged line does not cover the empty space and it allows us to consider it through the form represented.

New approaches

Other models

A fallen branch on the snow awakens a world of visual emotions as a result of its delicate and vulnerable aspect. The artist has painted this new subject on two sheets of handmade paper. On one she has emphasized the branches by dragging a brush with ink, adapting the stroke to the extremely horizontal format; and on the other, she has focused on the withered fruits, creating circular forms with very liquid metallic enamel.

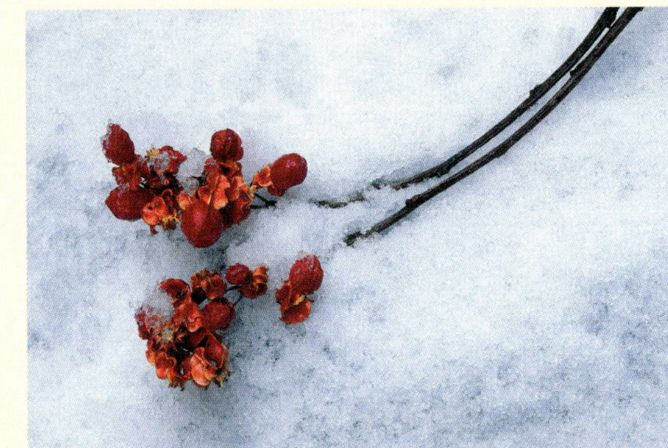

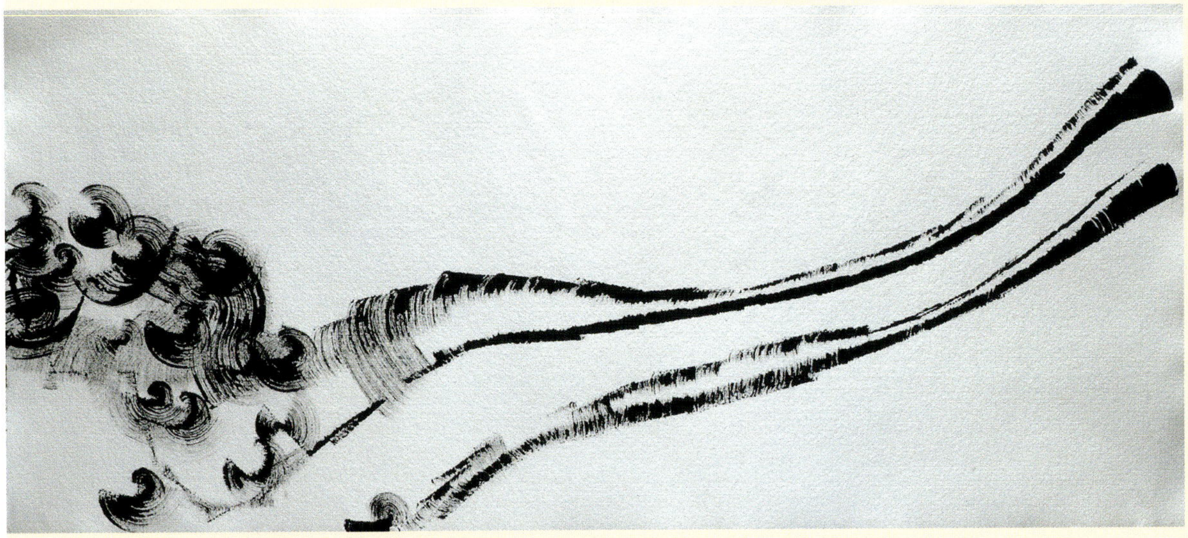

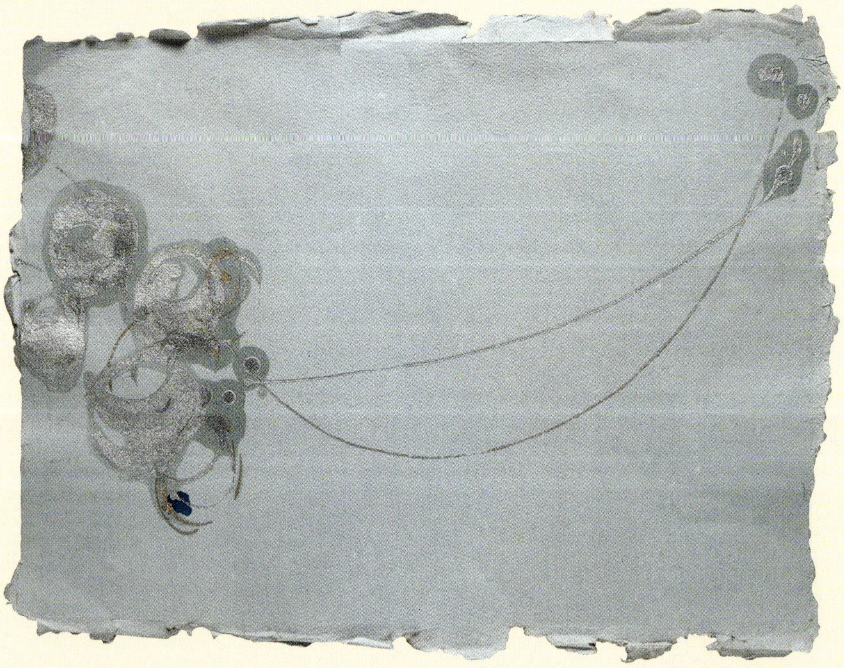

Other media

Zen painting incorporates the natural reactions of the materials on the support. It is open to splashing, dripping, rough edges, and accidents, because it is a basic principle of this type of work to accept whatever happens, without corrections or disguises. The artist has experimented with the direct gestural approach using oil-based shellac on a sheet of metal, a medium that produces variable results, creating rough edges and amazing water effects.

Other views

Here is how an Eastern visual artist, Dai-Bih-in (born in Taiwan in 1946), expresses himself through gestural line. His work can be classified between painting and paper art, and both his paintings and his handmade papers display a great dose of energy and poetry. Often, he approaches empty spaces with a single straight, clean, direct, and energetic line, or with a multitude of drips where the brush never touches the paper, as is the case with this ink piece, inspired by the mountain of Montserrat in Catalonia (Spain), which instills a state of openness and receptivity, like the soil in the rain.

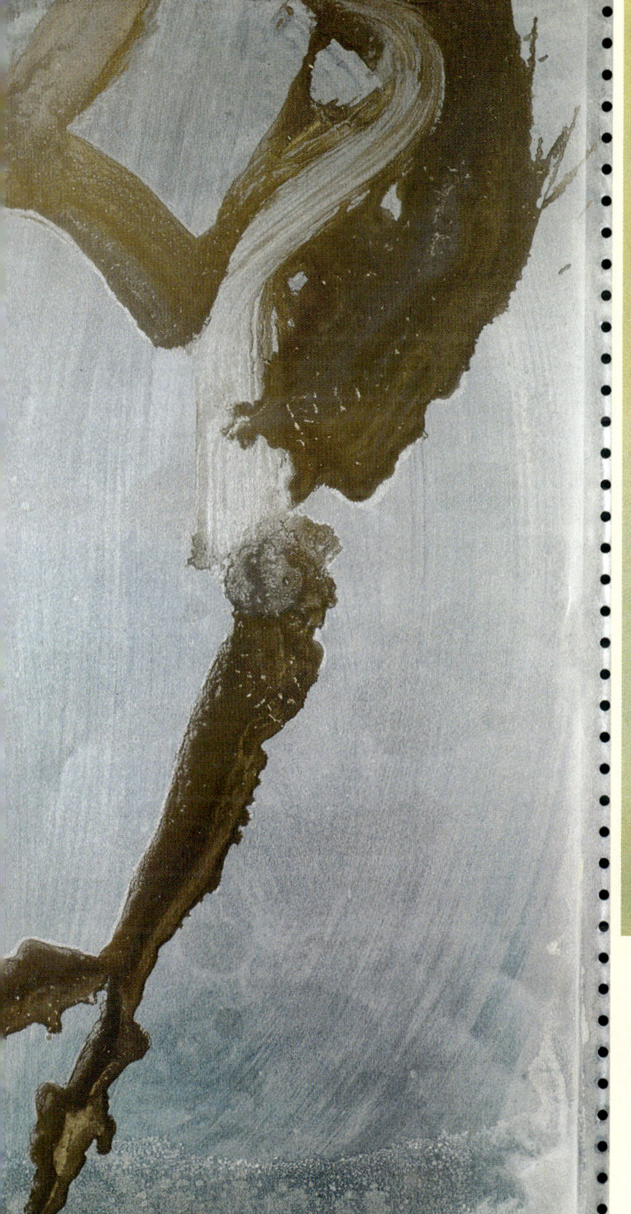

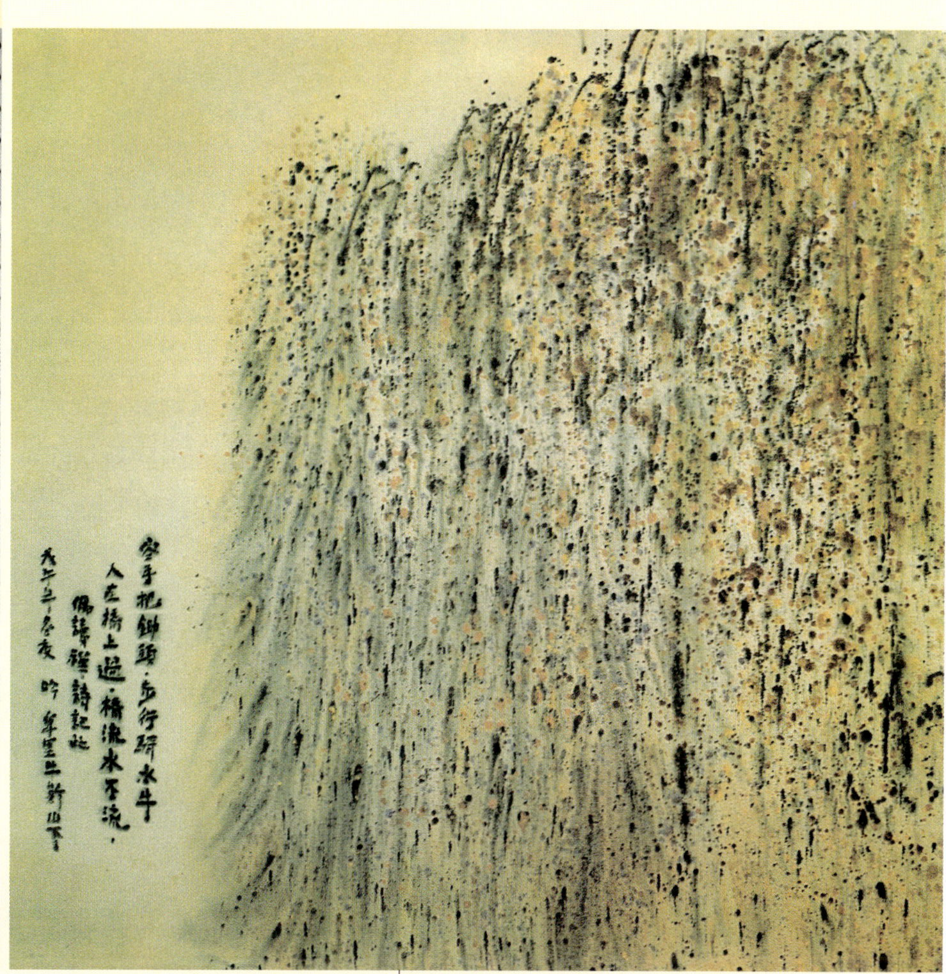

Dai-Bih-in,
Untitled, circa 1982.
Private collection.

The following pages include the basic concepts related to the media, the supports, the applicators, and the techniques used in the creative approaches outlined in this book.

Wet media

These media are composed of a mixture of pigment, binder, and solvent. They are classified in two groups according to solvent: water-based and oil-based.

WATER-BASED MEDIA

Regular tap water, or distilled water, which prevents granulation, is used as a solvent for this type of medium.

Acrylics

Acrylics are made with pigments bound with synthetic resins. They are known for their fast drying time and the fact that they do not turn yellow with the passage of time. They are very versatile, offering the advantages of watercolors when diluted with a large amount of water, or the thickness of oils if used without water. Acrylics have a soft and creamy consistency, very similar to oils, making them ideal for painting impastos. They can be diluted with water or an acrylic medium. The mediums—glossy, matte, and gel—can be used to increase the glossiness and depth of the colors. We can delay the drying time by adding glycerin or a retardant medium. Acrylic paint has a uniform, matte finish, but we can restore the glossiness by applying a thin, transparent coat of acrylic varnish. This should be applied over the paint when it is completely dry, so it is a good idea to wait for a day. The varnish can be matte or gloss, or the two can be mixed to create a semigloss finish.

Acrylic paints

Acrylics are available in tubes of different sizes or in cans at very reasonable prices. It is a very durable medium that can be painted with any type of applicator on almost any support.

Watercolors

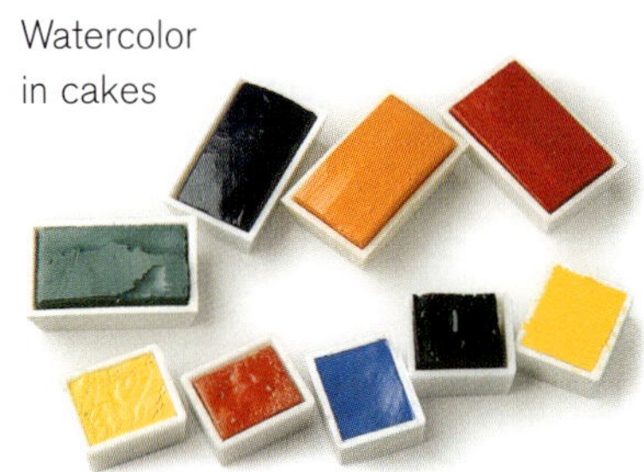

Watercolor in cakes

Watercolors are made of finely ground pigments mixed with gum arabic, which acts as a binder, and another substance, such as honey or glycerin, is added to give it plasticity. They are sold in the form of cakes or tubes of different sizes, and can be purchased in boxes of assorted colors or individually.

Their main characteristic is transparency. Mixing the pigment with water reduces the intensity of the colors and increases their transparency and luminosity. White does not exist in watercolors. When white is required, the paper can be left unpainted, or an opaque watercolor like white gouache is painted over the watercolors.

Because of their softness, sable-hair brushes are ideal for watercolors, although today synthetic brushes create similar effects and are less expensive. Washes can be applied with sponges, rollers, or paper towels. The ideal support is watercolor paper, which is available in different weights and textures. It can be worked dry or wet; in the latter case the paper must first be stretched on a board with adhesive paper tape.

Ink

Ink can be permanent or soluble in water. If it is not soluble in water, it contains lacquer, is denser, and has a glossy finish when dry. Water-soluble ink does not contain lacquer and is used for making line and hatched drawings with a nib or reed pen, and for washes applied with a brush. It has a matte finish when dry because it penetrates deeper into the paper. It is available in different colors, although black is the most commonly used.

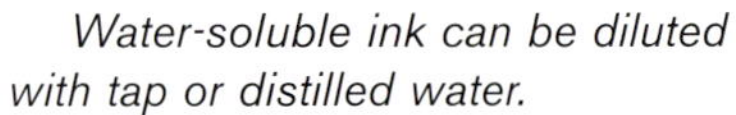

Drawing inks

Water-soluble ink can be diluted with tap or distilled water.

It is an ideal medium for mixing with other media to achieve very special effects.

It is best applied with round brushes because they hold more water. Drawing effects can be achieved using nib or reed pens. Pens are available with different nibs that can be used to draw fine or wide lines. The handcrafted reed pen is more primitive, and makes irregular and more expressive lines. Smooth or satin paper with a certain degree of durability is recommended as a support.

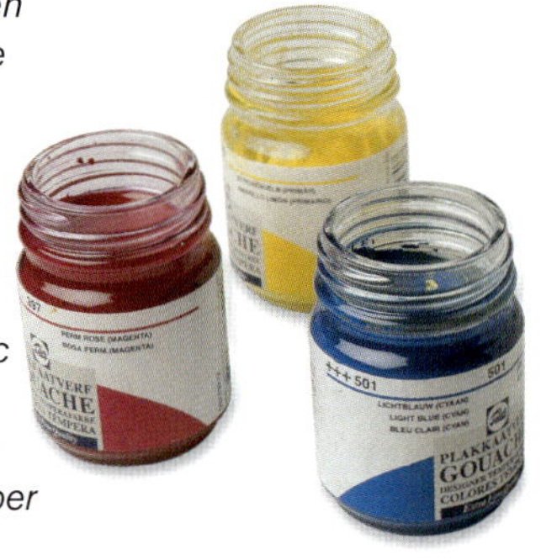

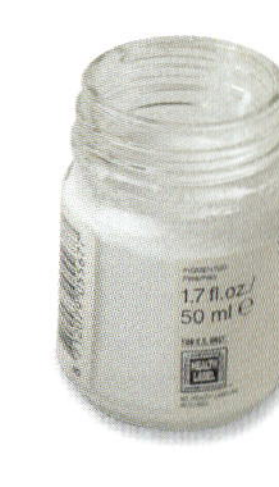

Gouache

Gouache

This is also known as "tempera," "gum tempera," and "opaque watercolor." Composed of pigment and gum arabic, it can be diluted in water. Like watercolor, it is applied on paper, but it is a thicker medium, and therefore more opaque. The opacity allows it to be painted over dark papers. It can be applied with a brush or a roller in a creamy consistency, no impastos or glazes, so that after it dries the brushstrokes are smooth, uniform, and brightly colored. This finish makes it a perfect medium for posters, illustrations, and backgrounds for other media. It is sold in tubes and jars.

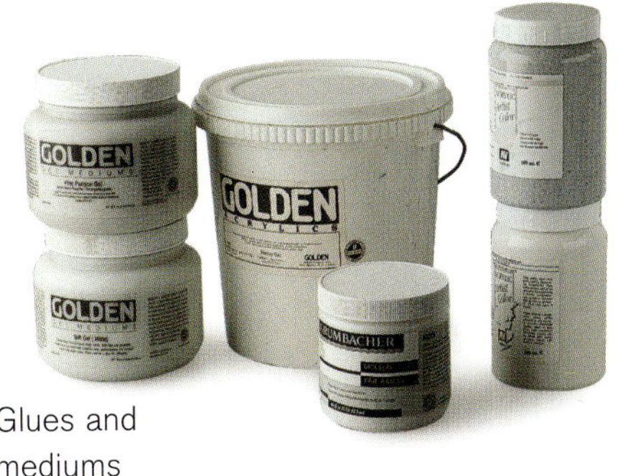

Glues and mediums

Glues, Mediums, Fillers, and Paste

Glues are binders that help the paint adhere to the support; they can be of vegetable or animal origin, or vinyl. The latter are the most common ones nowadays because they are easy to use and because they do not need to be mixed; the most common is latex. Mediums and fillers are substances that can be added to the paint to increase its volume or to change its appearance. A medium can also be a gel or modeling paste because of the way it looks, very similar to vinyl glue but much thicker. Normally it is added to acrylic paint, since it is soluble in water, to increase the volume without losing its color. Mediums are sold in bottles ready to use and they can produce a wide range of effects: light, heavy, glossy, satin, matte, and so on. Filler is a substance that can be added directly to the paint to change its appearance and its texture. These are usually sand or minerals (marble, pumice, garnet) that adhere to the paint as a result of its natural binding properties, although sometimes it is a good idea to add a binding agent to the mixture if more filler and greater adherence are desired. A third option is to acquire bottles of medium already prepared with filler; the advantage is that the amounts of filler and binder are well proportioned and ready to use.

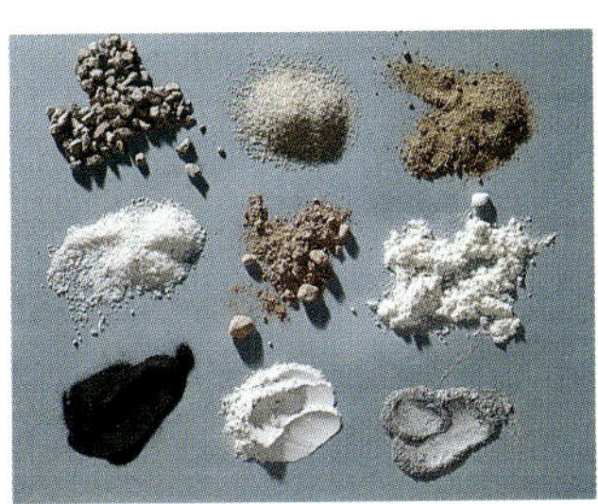
Fillers

A paste already contains a mixture of a binder and some mineral substance (gypsum, kaolin, pigment) that hardens when it dries. As its name indicates, a paste has volume, a reason it is used in home decorating as filler for cracks and holes. In art, pastes are used to create volume in paintings, since they are already compatible with acrylic paint, although it can change its final color.

OIL-BASED MEDIA

The solvent used in oil-based media is an essence, which can be of either vegetable or mineral origin. The vegetable essences are: essence of turpentine, which is more refined, and paint thinner, which is less. The mineral essence derived from petroleum is mineral spirits, a substitute for paint thinner.

Oil

Oil paint has been one of the most valued media in the history of painting. It has an oily and pasty consistency, made of tints or pigments mixed with a binder: walnut, poppy, or linseed oil. It is preferably diluted with turpentine or paint thinner. It is available in tubes of different sizes from 1¼ oz. to 8 oz. (5 to 200 ml) or in one-gallon (4-liter) cans. The prices can vary a lot according to the initial cost of the pigment. The earth tones are the least expensive, while the cadmiums can cost four times as much. Today, less expensive colors have been created, substituting synthetic pigments for natural ones.

Oil paint has a very slow drying process; this permits the forms to be blended and retouched, and allows more time for working on the painting. The colors are bright and intense, and lose little brilliance in the drying process.

Canvas, wood, or hard cardboard supports are recommended for use with this medium.

The most appropriate brushes are those with real or synthetic bristles; the spatula is recommended for use with impasto.

Wax crayons

Crayons are made by mixing pure pigment with animal oils and waxes. Then they are formed into sticks of different colors that will make a thick and creamy mark.

Their tones are intense and bright, and can be mixed on the support by rubbing with cotton, a paper towel, an eraser, or the fingers, which will create a smooth, bright, and oily texture. The colors can also be diluted with a brush or a paper towel impregnated with turpentine or thinner to create a transparent effect.

Wax crayons can be melted by heating them in a metal container on a burner and applied with a spatula or poured directly while liquid. This method is called encaustic.

Paper and cardboard are ideal supports. It is recommended that you fix the artwork by spraying it with lacquer or a fixative when it is finished.

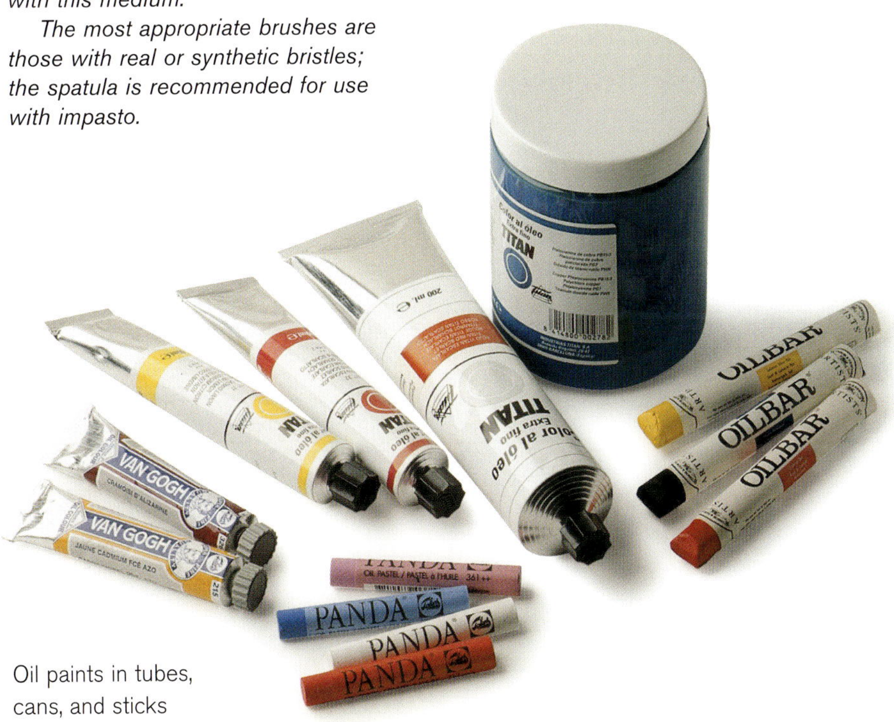

Oil paints in tubes, cans, and sticks

Dry media

These media are usually applied without a solvent. They can be monochromatic or polychromatic.

MONOCHROMATIC MEDIA

These are media of a single color, which are gradated to achieve an extensive range of values.

Vine charcoal

This is made of sticks of grapevine, beech, or willow, carbonized at high temperatures in an airtight oven. They are sold in boxes of several sticks approximately 6 inches (15 cm) in length and in different hardnesses and widths. The softest charcoal lends itself to rubbing and blending; the hardest is ideal for drawing lines and details. It is a very fragile medium, and it is recommended that you draw with shorter pieces broken off the stick. Various gray tones can be achieved by wiping with a rag or the hand. Charcoal should be used with a textured paper. When a drawing is finished it should always be protected with a final coat of lacquer or fixative.

Vine charcoal

Graphite pencils

These are very thin sticks known as leads, whose degree of hardness is determined by the amount of hardener (clay) mixed with them when they are manufactured. A universal system was adopted for identifying the different hardness of pencils. The letter B is used for soft pencils, and H for the hard ones, preceded by a number or coefficient. Hard pencils range from 9H (the hardest) to H, and the soft ones from 9B (the softest) to B. The HB and F grades fall between H and B.

The soft pencils produce darker tones than the hard ones, making them ideal for shading and blending, and rendering expressive results.

The hard pencils are more suitable for technical drawings because they make precise lines and details and have a lighter tone. Generally, several grades of hardness are used in a drawing to achieve a range of tones and expressiveness.

The universal support is paper; its weight, texture, and tone are chosen based on the desired effects. Normally, graphite can be used with any type of paper, except waxed or very glossy papers. It is a good idea to apply a fixative or lacquer when the work is completed, especially if very soft pencils have been used.

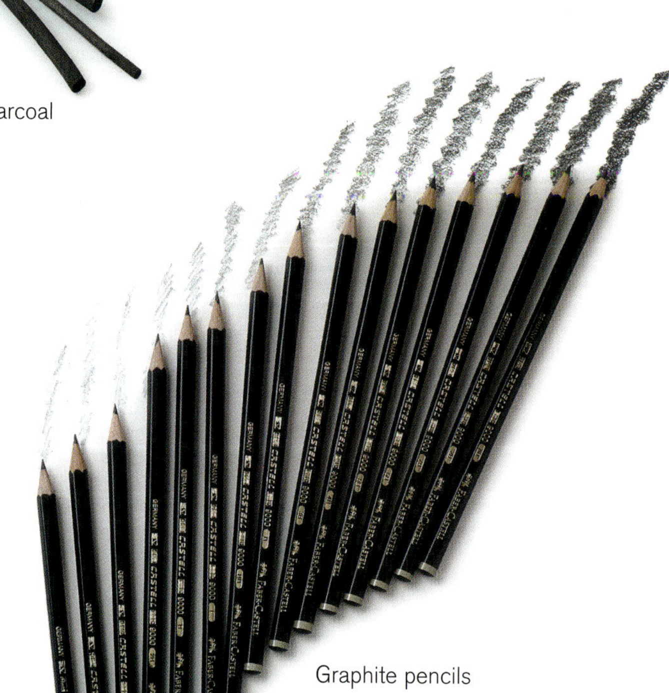

Graphite pencils

Sanguine crayon

This is a terra-cotta-colored crayon made from hematite (an iron mineral) that has its own outstanding personality. A single color provides a full range of reddish tones. We can create excellent blended effects by rubbing with a rag or the fingers, achieving softer and more luminous effects than those obtained with vine charcoal. Vigorous erasing will produce watercolor effects. Sanguine crayon can also be combined with other drawing techniques (pastels, vine charcoal, graphite). The most appropriate support for this medium is one that has a little texture or that is velvety. A fixative or lacquer should be applied when the work is finished.

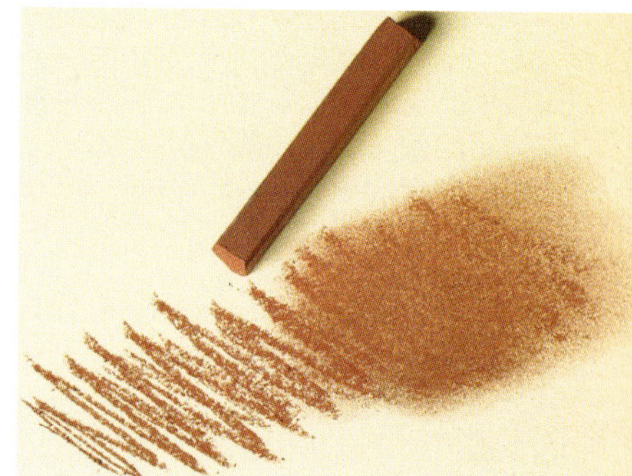

Sanguine crayon

POLYCHROMATIC MEDIA

These media are normally used in combination with other colors, although they can also be used monochromatically, thanks to the large range of tones available.

Pastels

Pastels are made from pure pigment mixed with a base of chalk and bound with glue. They are mixed to form a stiff paste, which is then cut and molded into sticks and left to dry until they harden.

There are hard pastels and soft pastels. The soft pastels have more pigment and less binder, which causes them to break easily. They create magnificent bright, saturated, and velvety tones that are ideal for rubbing and blending.

The hard pastels have less pigment and more binder. We can use hard pastels for making a preliminary drawing and for details and finishing. They are the perfect complement to soft pastels.

They are sold in boxes of assorted colors or individually. Prices can vary considerably. The high cost is due to the quality of the pigment; the more expensive it is, the less chalk in the mixture and the purer its tone.

This is a very painterly and versatile medium, and it allows working with line, glazing, impasto, rubbing, and blending. The artist can work with the side of the stick, with the point, or with the powder that comes from the stick, spreading it with a brush, the fingers, or a cotton ball.

It should be used with supports that are rough or that have a heavy texture to hold the pigment, and on resistant papers that can stand up to blending, corrections, and creating effects with an eraser. When the work is finished it should be preserved with a fixative or lacquer.

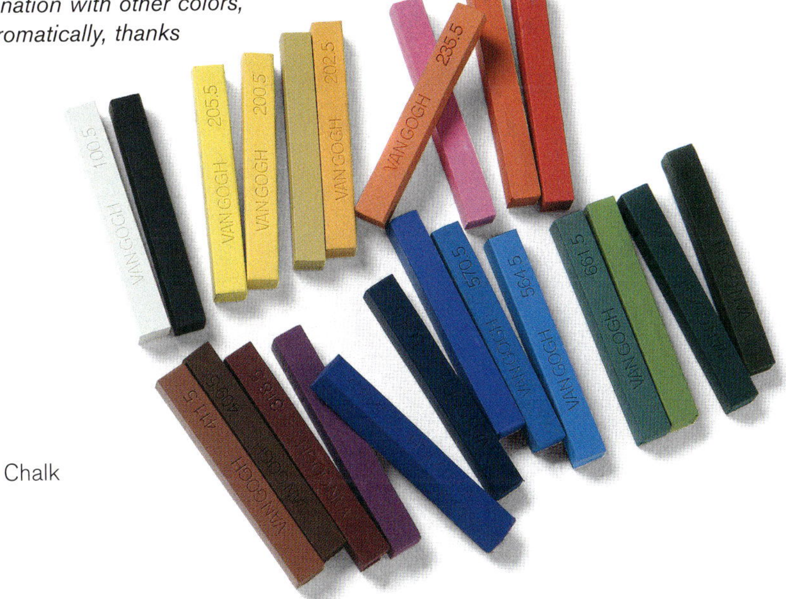

Chalk

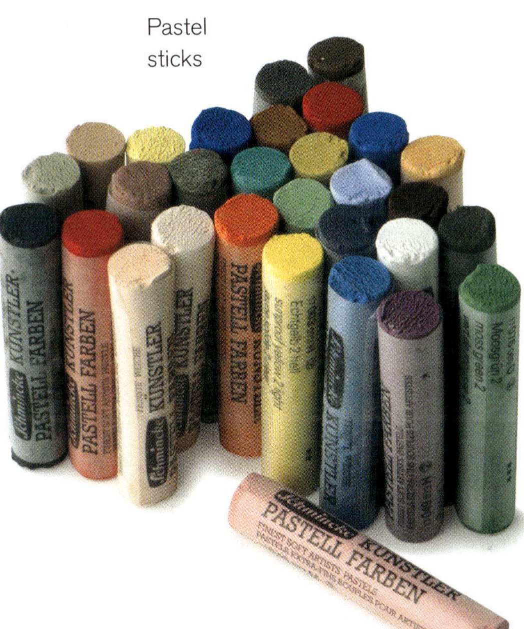

Pastel sticks

Chalk

This is the name for pastels that are of a greater hardness. The composition is the same as that of soft pastels: pigment with glue, but usually hardened with resin. The most common chalks are white, black, sanguine, and sepia, but there is a wide assortment of colors available. The finish of chalk is very graphic because it is applied as hatching and blended on the paper. It can also be applied to unsized lightweight fabrics, making use of their porosity, although this is not as common. When the painting is completed it should be fixed with lacquer or fixative.

Markers

Although the composition of the colored substances in markers is wet (usually an alcohol soluble ink), they can be categorized as dry media, because they are applied directly to the support without using a solvent. The color in the marker passes to the support through a fiber point that must always be kept damp, which is why it is recommended that the caps should not be left off markers for long periods of time. The most common support is paper and the most commonly used technique is hatching.

Color markers

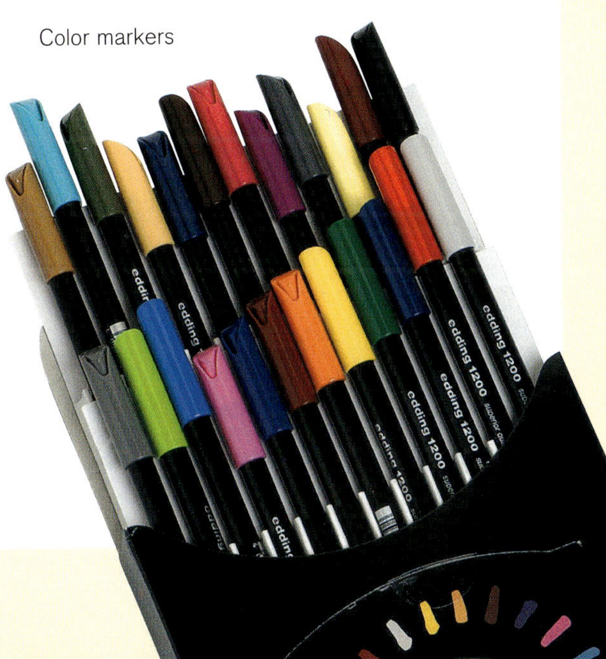

Supports and applicators

SUPPORTS

Wood

Wood is suitable for almost any media. It must be prepared according to the medium that is to be used. First, the wood is selected, making sure it is dried and cured, with no resin, knots, or nails. It is best if it is not too well sanded. Then it is prepared, neither too much nor too little, as either extreme will make the adhesion of the paint to the support difficult, and the final result will be fragile and difficult to conserve. The porosity of the wood should be controlled with the appropriate product. Various materials like gesso, casein, rabbit-skin glue, latex, or latex diluted with water can be used, depending on the painting technique we intend to use. Both sides must be prepared so that the board will not warp.

Canvas panels

Boards and canvas panels

These are made with a cotton fabric primed with acrylic and mounted on a rigid support. They come in a range of standard sizes and in several textures. They are light and easy to transport.

Canvas

The canvases that are traditionally used for painting are made of vegetable fibers like linen, hemp, jute, or cotton. They must be prepared to reduce their absorbency, but not so excessively that they lose flexibility, because a heavy preparation would cause the paint to crack. They are prepared with a primer. Primed canvas is available in rolls by the yard, or mounted on stretchers of various kinds, sizes, and formats. The sizes of the stretchers are international, each number corresponding to a specific length and width.

Paper

Paper is made of intertwined vegetable fibers, the most common nowadays being cellulose. The best is made with cotton, after which comes eucalyptus or pine (kraft paper), which have woody fibers that deteriorate more easily over time. There are papers that are ideal for wet techniques and for dry techniques, sold under a wide variety of brand names.

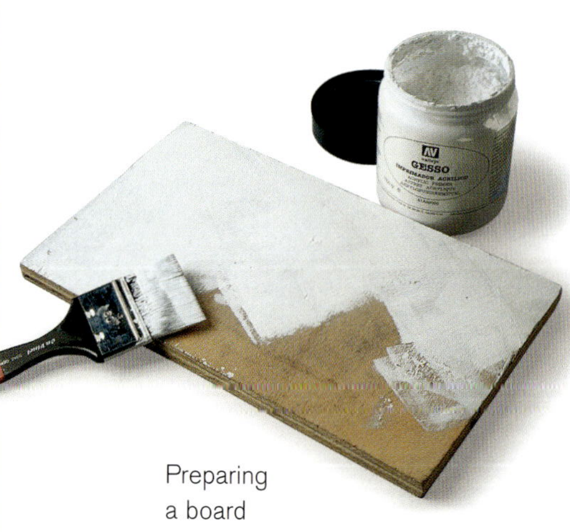

Preparing a board

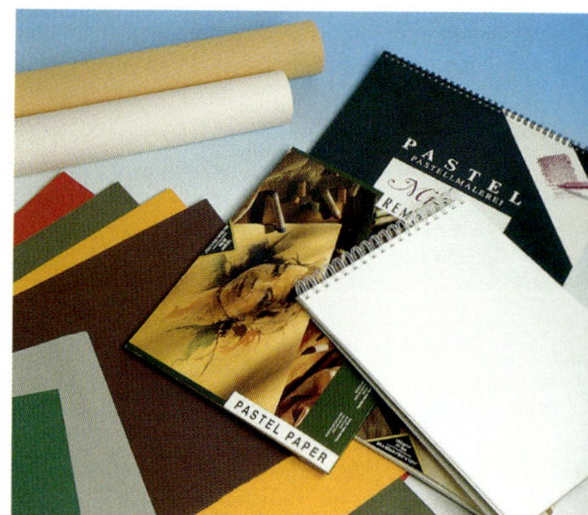

Papers

Canvas

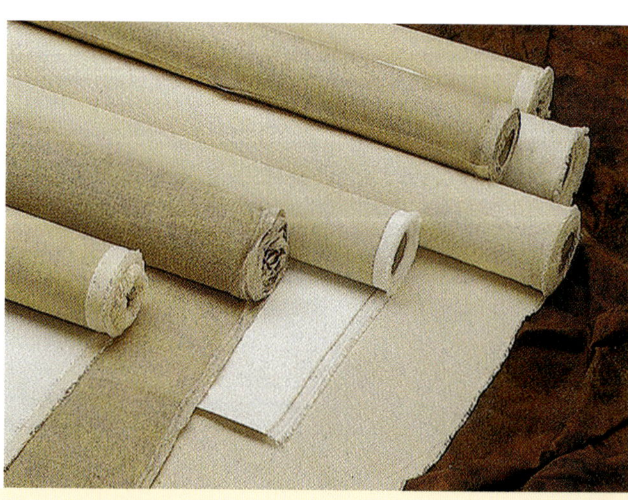

APPLICATORS

Brushes

Brushes are composed of three parts: the hair, the ferrule, and the handle. They are available in several shapes and sizes. The choice of brush will be determined by the medium that is being used.

There are brushes with fine hair and stiff hair, and each group includes flat, round, and other shapes (filberts, brights, fan blenders, and so on). Each group has different sizes indicated by numbers. The types of hair used to make the fine brushes are sable, ox, otter, squirrel, and badger, used for doing subtle blending.

Stiff brushes are made with hog or boar bristles. Nowadays there are also brushes made with synthetic fibers.

Round brushes are usually made of fine hair and they are most suitable for water-based media because they hold water better. The best-quality round brushes end in a point. Flat brushes usually have stiff hair and are most appropriate for oil-based media.

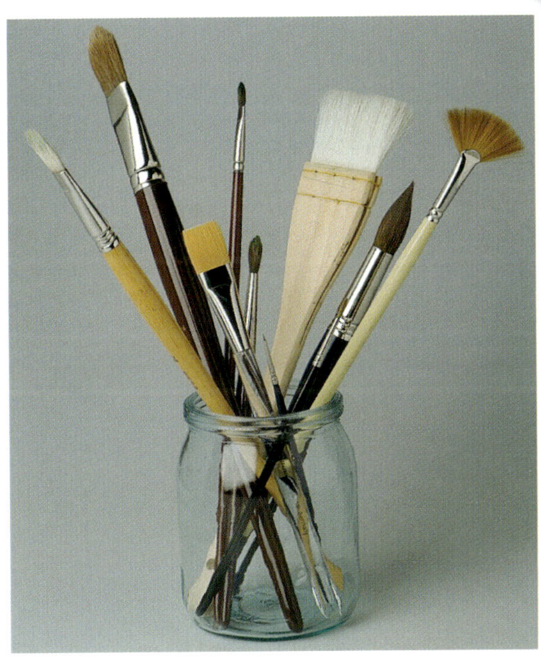

Brushes

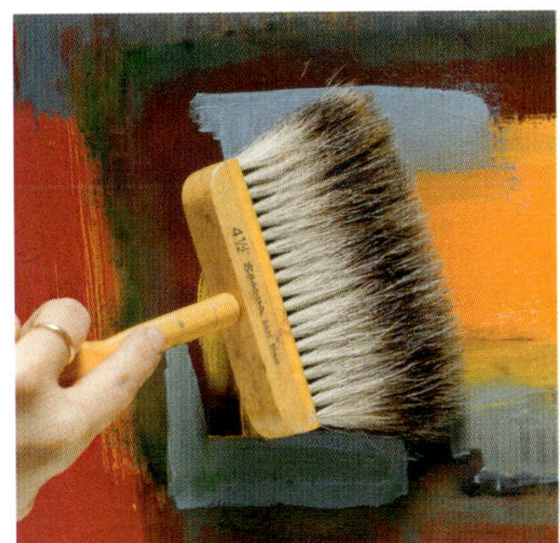

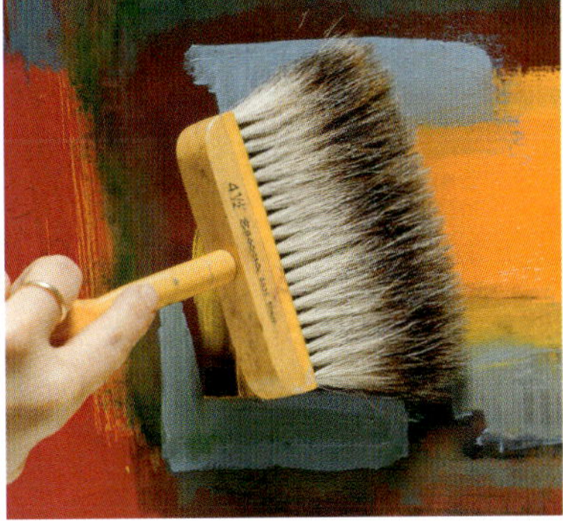

Badger-hair brush

Spatula

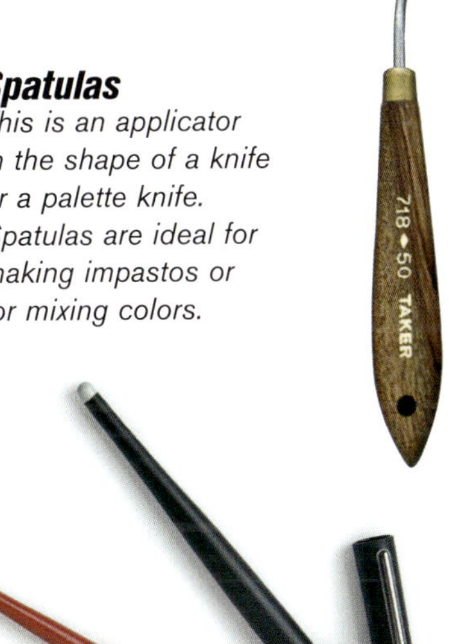

Spatulas

This is an applicator in the shape of a knife or a palette knife. Spatulas are ideal for making impastos or for mixing colors.

Nib pens

Nib pens

This type of pen consists of a plastic handle and interchangeable steel nibs. It is an inexpensive drawing tool. Each steel nib makes a wider or narrower line according to its shape. The lines are even since the nib always dispenses the same quantity of ink. They are ideal for making details and hatching.

Reed pen

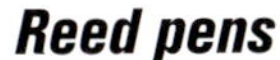

Reed pens

These pens are made of bamboo or reed and are very simple tools that can be made by the artist. Reed pens make irregular lines of varying width.

Sponges

Sponges are ideal for making washes and for glazing with water-based media. We can add or remove paint with a sponge, as well as wet paper before using it.

We recommend having small pieces of sponge that can be held in the hand to ensure more precision and control. Sponges can be hard or soft. The hard ones produce textured surfaces, the soft ones create smooth and even surfaces.

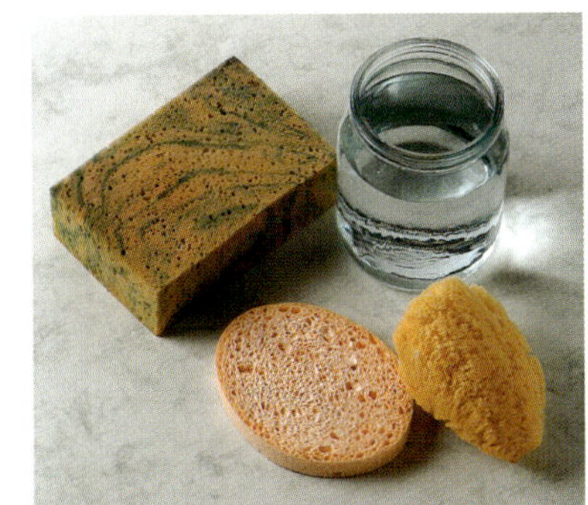

Sponges

Erasers

An eraser is not only used for removing pigment, it is also an excellent applicator. It cleans up colors, creates light and shadows, blends tones, and reinforces the lines made with wax crayons. We recommend soft rubber or plastic erasers for linear and heavy-duty work and kneaded erasers, which are softer and easy to control, for light and atmospheric results.

Techniques

A technique is the way a medium is utilized or a material is manipulated to achieve a specific plastic effect, although the term "technique" has commonly been used as a synonym for medium.

Hatching

Rubbing

Rubbing is the action of smoothing a color until its edges blend with the background or with another adjoining color, making sure that no traces of the applicator are left visible.

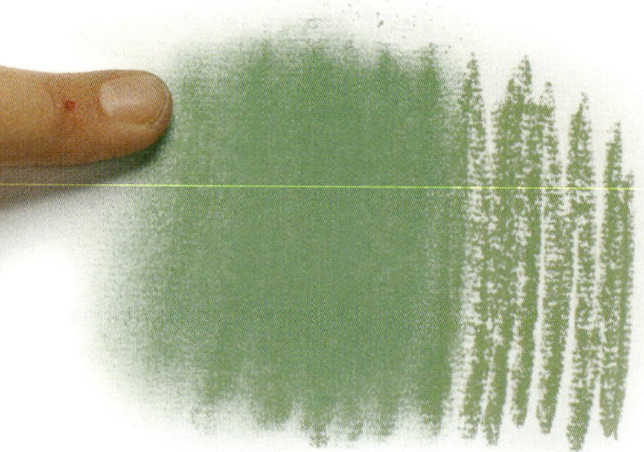

Rubbing

Blending

Blending is mixing paint directly on the support taking advantage of the fact that the paint is still wet.

Blending

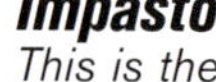

Impasto

This is the application of large amounts of thick paint with a spatula or a stiff brush, imparting a certain amount of relief to the surface of the paint.

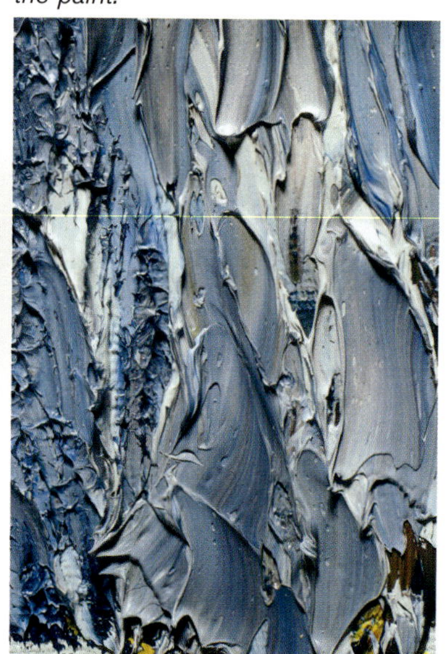

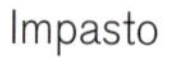

Impasto

Rinsing

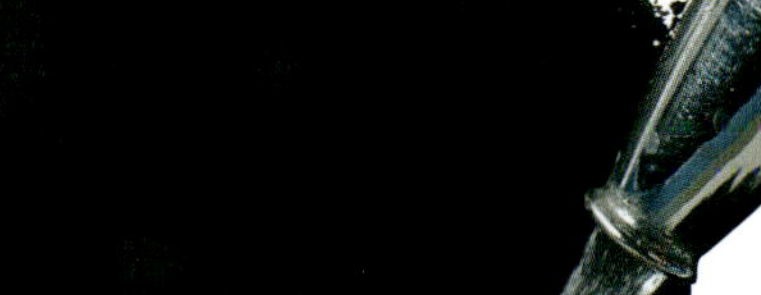

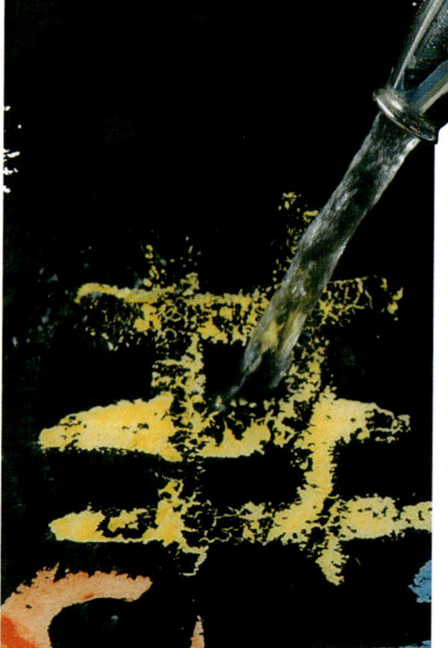

Hatching

This technique creates areas of color with parallel lines that can be overlaid to make fine grids. According to the distance between the lines and the amount of overlaid hatching, it is possible to make lighter or darker areas. If one color is hatched over another, they will combine optically and we will see the color of the mixture.

Rinsing

Rinsing is the technique of applying water to a painting to totally or partially eliminate a layer of paint and cause a worn effect in the image. It is only useful with water-based media (watercolor, gouache, ink, or acrylics). Water is applied directly to the paint or with a sponge or large brush. The amount of paint it removes will depend on the pressure and the amount of water, and whether the paint has dried.

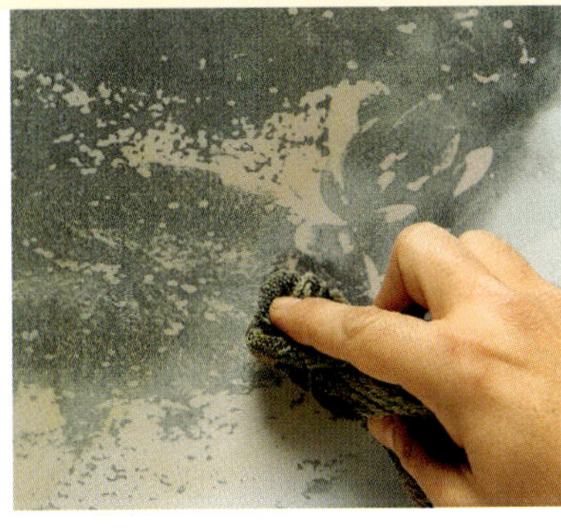

Transfer

Transfer

Transferring a printed image onto a support. The image we want to transfer is placed on the support face down and rubbed on its reverse with a cotton ball dampened with universal solvent. It is left to dry and the photocopied image is separated slowly, making sure that the image is reflected on the support.

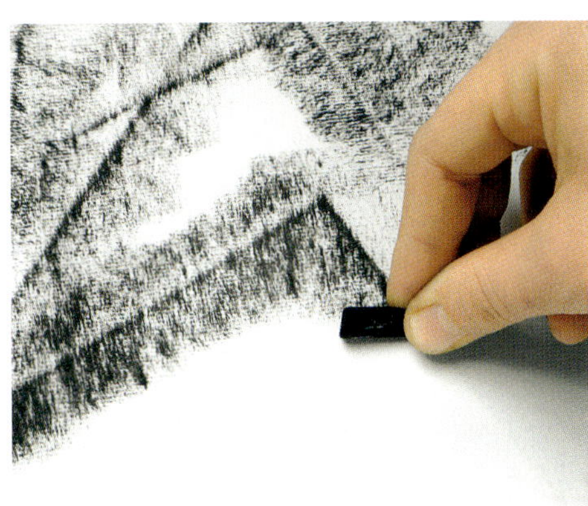

Frottage

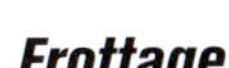

Frottage

This is a transfer technique for relief textures. It consists of placing the support—normally paper—over the object and rubbing with the medium until it makes a mark indicating the relief of the object. This technique is most commonly used with hard media such as wax crayon sticks, charcoal, or graphite.

Scraping

Scraping means partially eliminating a layer of paint using blades or needles to cause the background or a previous layer of color to emerge.

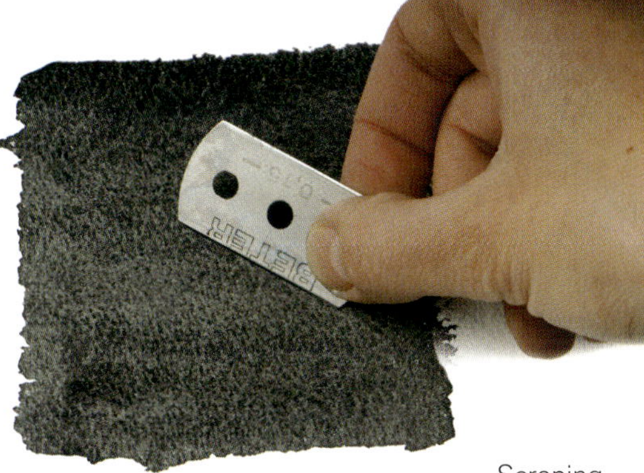

Scraping

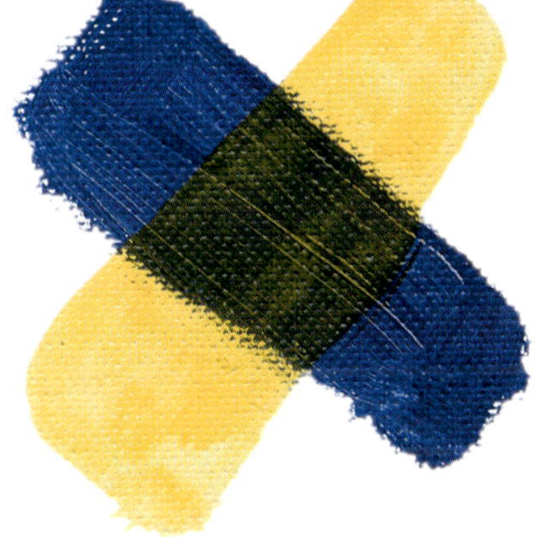

Glazing

Glazing

Totally or partially applying a transparent or semitransparent color over another color to vary its tone or value.

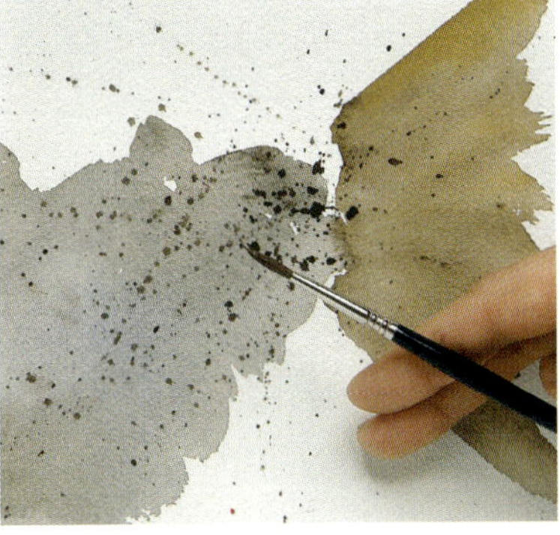

Dripping

Dripping

This is a painting effect produced by letting paint fall onto the support from a certain distance with more or less force and in small quantities, causing it to disperse in the form of drops.

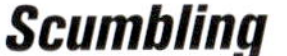

Scumbling

This effect is achieved by scrubbing paint that is still wet with a brush, rag, or other applicator, dragging and partially eliminating the paint, leaving part of the background visible.

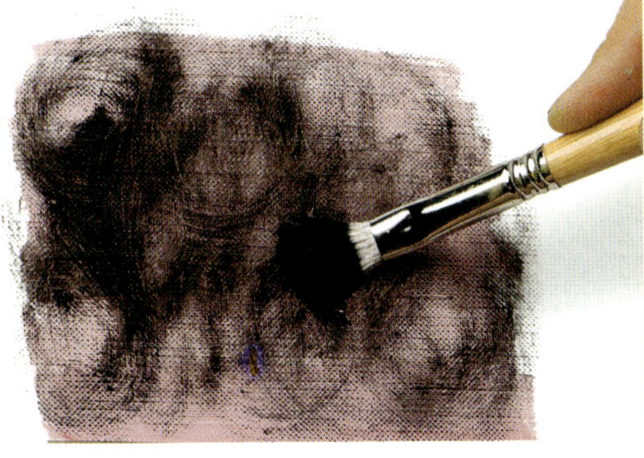

Scumbling

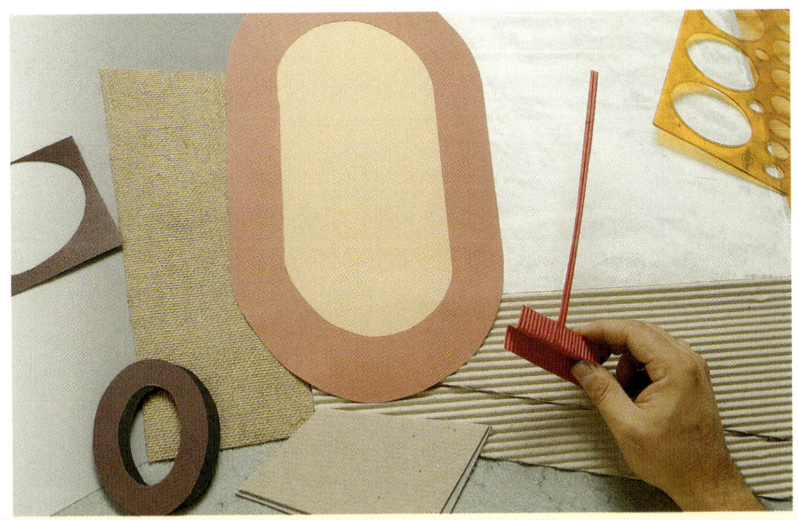

Collage

Collage

A collage is an image formed by gluing pieces of paper, fabric remnants, wood, sand, cardboard, or other materials to a support.

CREATIVE PAINTING

FORM COLOR SPACE LINE

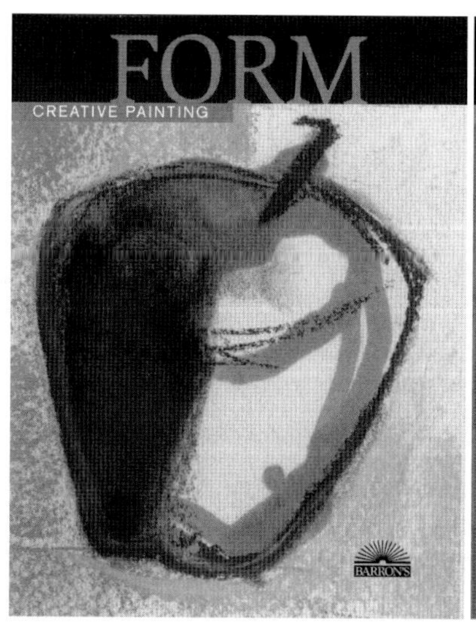

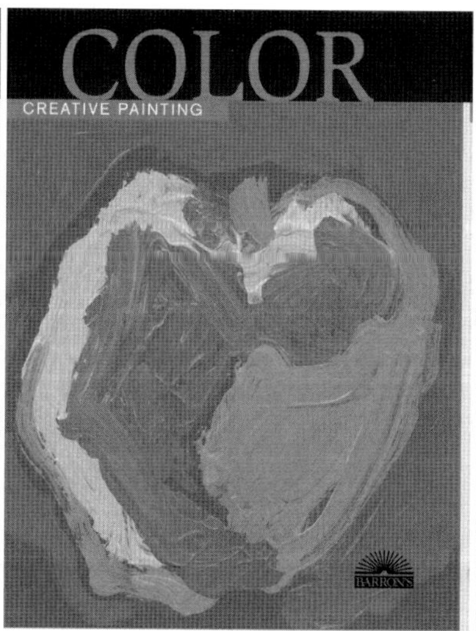

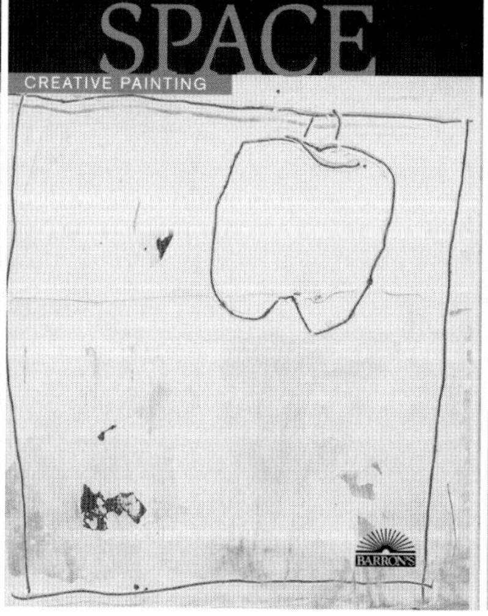

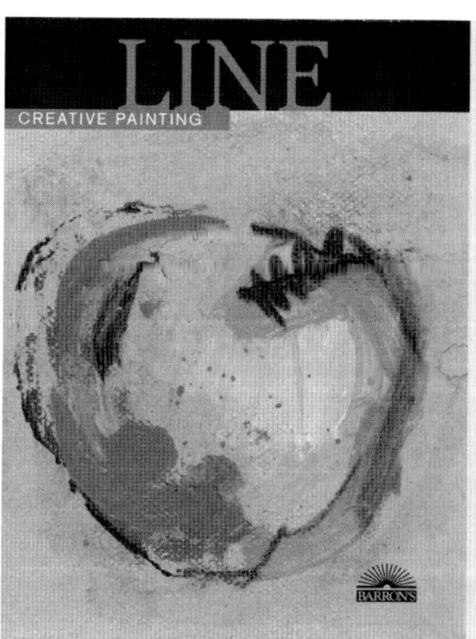

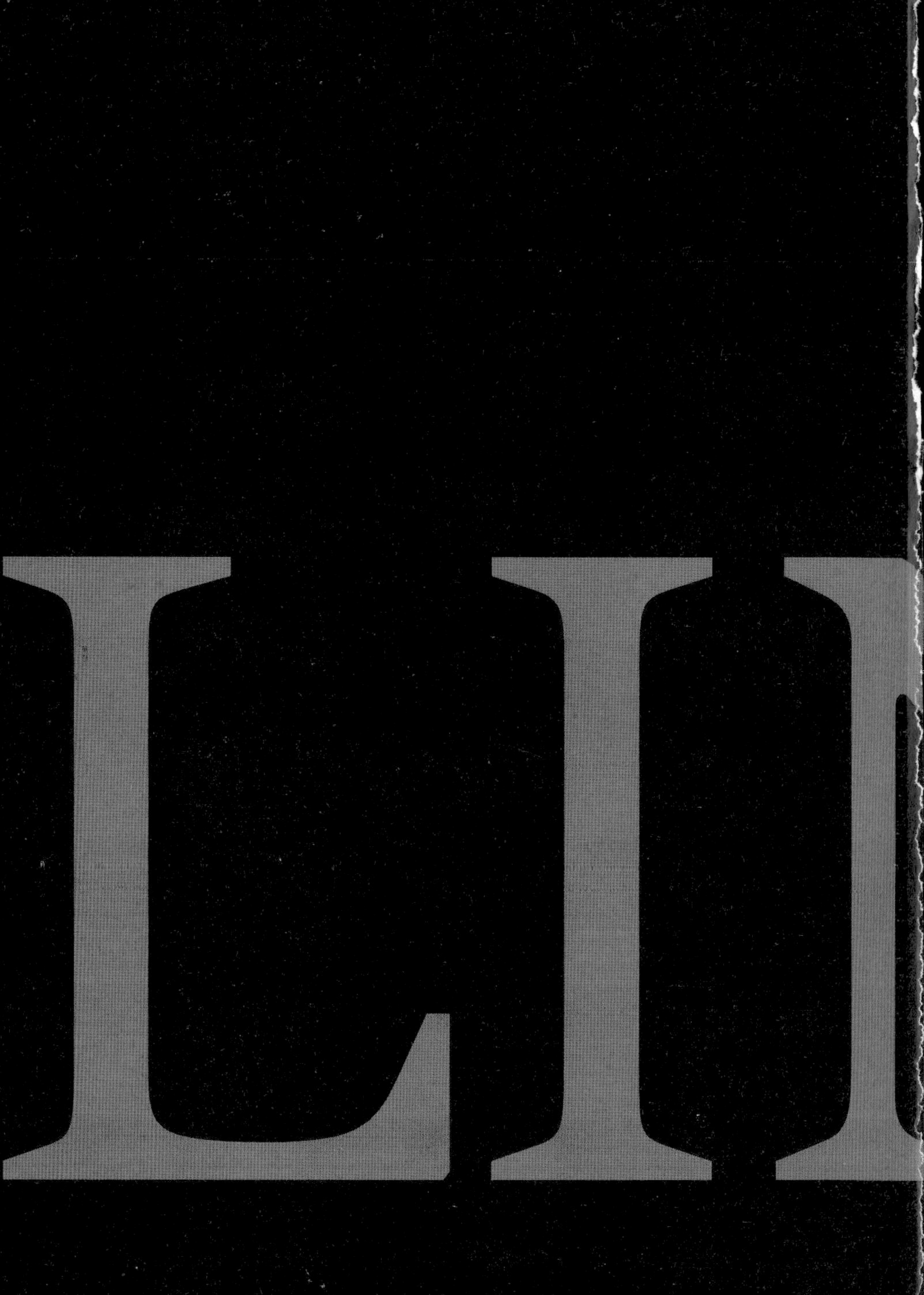